The Language of Organization

Mar
Tel

To be

The Language of Organization

Edited by
Robert Westwood and Stephen Linstead

SAGE Publications
London · Thousand Oaks · New Delhi

First published 2001

SAGE Publications Ltd
6 Bonhill Street
London EC2A 4PU

SAGE Publications Inc
2455 Teller Road
Thousand Oaks, California 91320

SAGE Publications India Pvt Ltd
32, M-Block Market
Greater Kailash – I
New Delhi 110 048

British Library Cataloguing in Publication data

A catalogue record for this book is available from the British Library
ISBN 978-0-7619-5335-0 C
ISBN 978-0-7619-5335-7 P

Library of Congress control number 2001 131872

Typeset by Annette Richards

Printed and bound in Great Britain by Athenaeum Press, Gateshead

Contents

Contributors

Rossana C. Alvarez is a visiting Assistant Professor at the Anderson School of Management, University of New Mexico. Her interests are organizational behaviour and diversity and action research in the areas of strategic planning and organizational design. Rossana's action research emphasis is on the development of social environments that are conducive to purposeful and ideal seeking behaviours.
Email: Alvarez@anderson.unm.edu

David M. Boje is a Professor of Management in the Management Department at New Mexico State University. His interests are in critical postmodern theory, storytelling and campaigning against sweatshops. He is division-chair of the Research Methods Division of the Academy of Management and a Board member of International Academy of Business Disciplines. David is editor of the *Journal of Organizational Change Management* and founding editor of *Tamara: The Journal of Critical Postmodern Organization Science* (http://www.zianet.com/boje/tamara/). His most recent book is *Narrative Research in Communication and Organization* (Sage).
Email: dboje@nmsu.edu

Jo Brewis is a Lecturer in Management at the University of Essex. Her current research interests centre around sex, sexuality, desire, passion and the body in organizations. Jo's main objective in these areas is to explore organizing as an activity as opposed to organization as a noun, to examine the construction and performance of the social reality of the workplace on a daily basis through, for example, the ways in which women prepare, dress, carry and use their bodies for and at work.
Email: jbrewis@essex.ac.uk

Robert Chia is Professor of Strategy and Organisation at the School of Business and Economics, University of Exeter. He is the author or editor of four books and a significant number of journal articles on Organisation Theory and Management and has presented numerous conference papers at the American Academy of Management, the British Academy of Management and other international conferences in Management and Organisation Studies. His main research interests revolve around the issues of world-views, modes of thought and their implications for strategic vision and foresight; complexity and

creativity; contrasting East-West metaphysical attitudes; critical cultural studies and postmodernism.
Email: r.chia@exeter.ac.uk

Dan Kärreman is a Lecturer at Lund University, Sweden. His research interests include knowledge work, organizational discourse, social identity and research methodology.
Email: Dan.Karreman@fek.lu.se

Ian King is currently a Senior Lecturer in the Department of Accounting, Finance and Management at the University of Essex. His research interests resonate around his interest in examining organizational life through a set of eclectic lenses informed from writings and practice in the theatre, language and Art.
Email: kingi@essex.ac.uk

Ian Lennie lives and works in Sydney and after a long career in management completed his PhD in Sociology at the University of New South Wales in 1997. He is the author of *Beyond Management* (Sage, 1999).

Simon Lilley is Director of MBA Programmes and Senior Lecturer in Management Information and Organisation in the Department of Management at Keele University where he is also an active member of the Centre for Social Theory and Technology. Research interests turn around the relationships between (human) agency, technology and performance, particularly the ways in which such relationships can be understood through post-structural approaches to organisation. He is currently pursuing these themes through investigation of the regulation and conduct of financial and commodity derivatives trading.
Email: s.lilley@mngt.keele.ac.uk

Stephen Linstead is currently Chair of Management at the University of Essex, UK, having previously been Associate Director (Research) at the University of Sunderland, UK and Chair of Management and Director of the PhD programme at the University of Wollongong, Australia. His other posts have included the Hong Kong University of Science and Technology and Lancaster University, UK. He has published seven books – including most recently *The Aesthetics of Organization* with Heather Höpfl (2000) and *Sex, Work and Sex Work* with Joanna Brewis (2000).
Email: linstead@essex.ac.uk

Rolland Munro is Professor of Organisation Theory and Director of the Centre for Social Theory and Technology at Keele University. He has co-edited two *Sociological Review* Monographs, *Ideas of Difference*, 1997 and *The Consumption of Mass*, 2001 and is currently at work on a book on identity and technology *The Demanding Relationship*.
Email: t.wood@keele.ac.uk

David Richards is currently Professor of International Business and Cross-cultural Management in the Sunderland Business School, University of Sunderland, UK. He was previously Associate Professor in International Management in the Graduate School of Business at Northern Territory University, Darwin, Australia and prior to that was Head of Business and Management at the Brunei Institute of Technology, Brunei, South East Asia. His research interests focus on language and culture particularly in the context of cross-cultural and expatriate management and behaviour. Conceptually his preference is for Interpretative Sociology and Ethnomethodology.
Email: david.richards@sunderland.ac.uk

Bruce Schooling is an Assistant Professor of Management in the Accountancy, Business and Economics Department at Point Loma Nazarene University. He received his PhD degree (1998) in management from New Mexico State University. His research focus is exploring and understanding the effect of the behaviours of leaders of non-profit organizations in changing situations. He has been active in non-profit governance for more than 18 years and has served as a board member, service volunteer and consultant to numerous non-profit organizations and health service organizations. Bruce is a member of the Academy of Management, an ordained elder in the Church of the Nazarene and an assistant basketball coach for Point Loma Nazarene University.
Email: BruceSchooling@ptloma.edu

Graham Sewell teaches organizational theory at the University of Melbourne, Australia. His research interests are wide ranging, although he is probably best known for his work on workplace surveillance. He has held visiting appointments at numerous institutions, including UC Santa Cruz, UC Berkeley and the University of South Florida. He is currently completing a book provisionally titled *The Truth About Management.*
Email: gsewell@unimelb.eud.au

Tojo Thatchenkery is an Associate Professor of Organizational Learning in the School of Public Policy and Director of the Masters in New Professional Studies program at George Mason University. His two distinct research interests are understanding knowledge work using hermeneutic perspectives, and career dynamics of Asian Americans as an ethnic group in U.S. organizations. Tojo is the program chair-elect of the Research Methods division of the Academy of Management and is on the editorial board of the *Journal of Applied Behavioral Sciences,* the *Journal of Applied Management Studies* and the *Journal of Organizational Change Management.*
Email: Joseph@gmu.edu

Bob Westwood is a faculty member of the Australian Graduate School of Management. He has worked and researched in the Asia-Pacific region for the last 17 years. Bob's research interests lie in the areas of cross-cultural/comparative management and organisation, gender and organisations,

the language-power-organisation nexus, the meaning and experience of work, and creativity and innovation processes.
Email: robertw@agsm.edu.au

1

Language/Organization: Introduction

Robert Westwood and Stephen Linstead

The importance of communication for organizations has, understandably, been an ongoing concern since management was first theorized. In this sense 'language' has always been on the agenda. However, communication was typically presented as a pragmatic problem related to the managerialist concerns of organizational effectiveness and management practice. The concern was with the problems of communication structures, patterns and practices and their impact on the efficacy of the managerial task and the effective operation of organizational systems. Language was viewed naively and simply as the medium of communication, its ontological status was not at issue, its epistemological role unexplored. Language *per se* was never subjected to theoretic problematization and investigation; it was taken for granted and used as an explanatory resource. It was not until relatively recently that language beyond its communicative function was recognized in organization studies. As recently as 1986 it was suggested that the investigation of language in organization studies was 'in its theoretical and methodological infancy' (Donellon, 1986), and a similar point is made by Aktouf (1986). This is despite the fact that the importance of language for organization and management was recognized some time earlier, for example in the work of Weick (1978) and Pondy and Mitroff (1979), the latter noting that the 'the chief feature of human organization is the use of language and symbolism'. Smircich (1983: 171), in discussing organizations as cultures suggested that language was an 'almost untapped area of investigation in the field of organization studies'. Even as late as 1998 it was suggested that organization studies had developed few models dealing with language–organization relationships (Cossette, 1998).

These statements are somewhat disingenuous since the language–organization relationship had in fact received attention in some quarters, albeit sometimes in a rather indirect way. For example, under the influence of Wittgensteinian concepts of language symbolic interactionist and ethnomethodological theorists explored the organization–language relationship in a fuller and more subtle way, connecting it to knowledge issues. However, this work tended to stay within the confines of sociology and did not directly attend to the full organizational implications. Nonetheless, there is a strong tradition here going back to Bittner, Goffman, Garfinkel and others. Of critical importance for organization studies in a more direct manner was the publication of Silverman's (1970) *The Theory of Organizations*, which positioned language more centrally in the organization theory project.

These early contributions, whilst siting language more pivotally, do not fully pursue the full implicate nature of the relationship of language and organization. As Cooper (1989: 494) has pointed out '"Routine" approaches to the study of organization rely unreflectively on a conception of writing that represents an already constituted object from which the "construction" function of writing is excluded.' It is only more latterly, with the advent of post-structuralist and post-modernist practices applied to organization studies that there has been a more radical challenge to the categories and concepts that were taken-for-granted and accorded an ontological status that would allow us to represent organizations in certain determined ways. This includes categories such as 'organization' and 'structure'. In this mode of critical thinking 'the very idea of organization itself becomes the problematic. How does it come to acquire its apparently concrete status? What primary organizing process allows it to take on the semblance of an "already constituted entity?"' (Chia, 1995: 583).

It is, then, really only since the 1980s that a more radical interest in the implicate relationship between language and organization has burgeoned. This has moved way beyond language seen in terms of mechanisms of communication and beyond simplistic representational perspectives in which language is conceptualized as the carrier of meaning and as means of representing organizational reality. There has been a progressive radicalization of the project of analyzing organization through the analysis of language. One of the aims of this book is to track that process, but not as a simple linear history or catalogue. We wanted to reflect on earlier contributions, for example from ethnomethodology and dramaturgy, but to situate those contributions and revisit them with respect to more recent considerations informed by postmodern discourse. Once an objectivist, representational view of language is left behind, a range of alternative conceptualizations of the relationship of language and organization open up. It was also our aim to provide a space for this diversity.

The diversity rests upon a varied foundational platform. One track of conceptual development has a trajectory through particular aspects of philosophy and social theory. This takes us through the phenomenological social constructionism of Schutz, Mead and others, the pragmatism of Peirce and Dewey, the hermeneutic philosophy of Dilthey, Heidegger and Gadamer and the linguistic philosophy of Wittgenstein. This enabled the emergence of symbolic interactionism, ethnomethodology and the dramaturgical perspective. Each of these positioned language more centrally in the constitution of social behaviour and social structures. They rejected correspondence, 'picture' theories of language and looked at language as elemental in the processes of the construction of social reality and identities. They reject an objectivist view in which language is seen as a fixed, external and abstract system in which meanings are predetermined *a priori* in the structure of the language independent of the occasions of language-in-use in social interaction (Winograd, 1980). Elements of this track are revisited and reconsidered in this volume.

Richards (Chapter 2) revisits ethnomethodology, but attempts to explore the commonalities and differences in relation to postmodernism. The dramaturgical position is explored by Kärreman (Chapter 5). His treatment examines the seminal contributions of Burke and Goffman, but draws on Baudrillard's notions of historicized orders of simulacra and suggests they can be read as representing different forms of human drama. The hermeneutic project is a pragmatic one in which the practice seeks to extract meaning from the ongoing dialectic of the relation of the particular to its infinite textual context. Meanings get 'fixed' in various textual inscriptions, such that whilst in process the meaning may be determined by context, the act of inscription creates a distanciation which makes the determination of meaning problematic. Thatchenkery (Chapter 6), drawing particularly on the work of Gadamer and Ricoeur, promotes the value of hermeneutic practice for organizational studies, which involves considering organizations as *texts* and submitting them to textual analysis. This involves a different practice from that involved in viewing organizations from a narratological perspective (Boje, Alvarez and Schooling, Chapter 7). The authors here maintain that narratology occupies a meta-position in which a number of ontological and epistemological paradigms can participate. Indeed, each philosophical/theoretical position is itself viewed as a narrative with different orientations towards organizational 'stories' and/or organizations-as-stories. Thus there are, among others, formalist narratologies, structuralist, post-structuralist, social constructionist, realist and postmodern varieties. Despite this polyphony, a narratological approach naturally situates language at the heart of understanding organization. Each of these chapters revisits positions constituted by the first philosophical track identified above, but interrogates them from positions informed by the second track.

The second track is somewhat different (although there are some parallels and overlaps) and proceeds from Nietzsche through Saussurean linguistics and structuralism to post-structuralism, deconstructionism and postmodernism. This discourse is constituted by contributions from across the humanities and social sciences – in historical theory, literary criticism, anthropology and philosophy. Positions in organization studies drawing on this track see the relationship between language and organization as having far greater intimacy. This has opened up a fertile radical perspective on organization represented in the work of Chia, 1998; Cooper, 1986, 1987, 1989, 1992, 1993; Gergen, 1992; Kallinikos, 1995; Law, 1994; Linstead, 1993a, 1993b, 1994, 1995, 1999, 2000; Westwood, 1999. The location of language is not just central to organization studies but is indivisibly enfolded in the conception of organization and the process of organization theorizing.

This is a conception in which the concern is with the mutually constituting nature of the relationship between language and organization. The specific nature of that relationship and the degree of its radical positioning varies. Interest has centered variously on: the significance of language in the structuring of organization; its place in the very constitution of organization; the use of language and other forms of signification in the very processes and activity of organization; the constitution of identities and subjectivities in the textual space of organization; and the conception of organization theories and theorizing as forms of language, as a *method* of language.

It is with the ontological interrogation of 'organization' that the 'turn' to language is at its most radical. Mainstream organization theory assumes and takes for granted the existence of organizations as material entities 'out there' in the world. But as Cooper (1989) suggests, the 'organization' that such approaches deal with is the product of an *a priori* theoretical model and what is being dealt with is not the model as a representation of the organization, but the organization as a representation of the model. As Degot (1982: 630) puts it 'The construction of the object results from the application of a theory to the real world; the constructed object exists (has sense) only in relation to this theory'. Cooper, Degot and others challenge the entitative, ontological status of organization and see organization as a text, or as constituted in discourse. This suggests that organization is language, but also that language is organization (Chia, 1996). This is a conflation that should not be unpacked. As Sewell (Chapter 8) notes there is a tendency in orthodox theorizing to unpack terms into binaries or discrete categories, to resolve the tension engendered by two terms/constructs occupying the same space. This is an outcome of Western Aristotelean logical traditions.[1] Sewell (Chapter 8) explores the historical tensions in agency/structure as a duality not a dualism and in the same manner the title to the present chapter has language/organization as a mutually constituting dualism. An analytic practice, rather than unpicking such dualisms and constructing linear or taxonomic explanatory structures should explore the tension in the relationship, partly because such mutuality, interpenetration and confusion is closer to our experience of the world than the world laid flat or laid out in tabular form.

An early expression of this viewpoint suggested that 'Organization exists in the text – there is no structure or boundary or bureaucratic manifestation that can meaningfully be represented as organization – these too would be discursive constructions' (Westwood, 1983: 604). Organization has no autonomous, stable or structural status outside of the text that constitutes it. The text of organization itself consists of a shifting network of signifiers in dynamic relations of difference. Text does not have entitative status either: it is a process, a process in which meanings are emergent, deferred and dispersed. The meaning of organization is located in the '"moving play of signifiers" ... that extends ... in a "seamless web", ever changing and in a constant process of coalescence and disintegration. Meaning consists of these shifting patterns of signifying relations. It is constantly in process, always emerging; not anchored to a permanent signified itself rooted in a stable, essential reality' (Westwood, 1987: 171). As such it cannot be captured, codified and represented in any static form – as an abstracted structure for example.

The notion of structure is illusory, representing only an ideological practice that pretends to stand in the place of the flux of shifting and seamless textual relationships. The achievement of structure is not really attended to in orthodox organization theory. The focus is on the determination of structure by external variables that are held to influence the particular configuration of structural elements – the elements themselves and their constitution are rather taken for granted.[2] Structure is a strategy of 'closure', a practice designed to impose an order and fixity on natural movement and flow. Structure is the freezing of meaning, an imposed constraint on the play of signifiers in the text of organization, a 'neutralization of meaning by form'. Organization is structure, but only when structure is recognized to be an effect of language, a tropological achievement. The analytic focus is not on the static structure of the organization (and its various assumed external determinants) but on the movement and productivity of the text. This means taking organization/text not as a product but as a productivity – the site of ongoing signifying work in a politicized arena of contestations over the signifying process.

This resonates with Cooper's view (1986) that organization actually depends on disorganization. Indeed, organization has to be carved out of disorganization. Or rather 'inscribed' out of disorder, since, in Cooper's (1989) view, organization is a process of writing in which order is inscribed on to the flow of events. The defining aspect of writing is not what it writes but rather with the structuring and organization of representations. Writing is a technology for interpolating the spacings, orderings, listings, groupings, relationships, differentiations and boundaries that structure and organize things. Lennie (Chapter 3) takes up this notion, that writing is organization, in his thoughtful consideration of lists and plans. As he makes clear, it is not only that writing organizes, it also creates the writer, it is implicate in the constitution and externalization of subjectivities. Writing (lists and plans) orders and externalizes, and in doing so provides possibilities for control.

There is a sense in which the notion that writing is organization and organization writing is direct in an immediate sense. Consider the process that we are engaged in here, this writing process. In front of us, in fact some 10,000 miles apart, we each have a list, a list of the writers and chapters. On the other side of the desk we have another list, of themes and issues. These have been past attempts to organize thoughts and ideas that this book is supposed to represent. The list of author and chapter headings is already a significant organizational accomplishment. It has sections and titles, groupings and differentiations that were not there earlier in the process. Indeed, they have gone through a number of mutations and rearrangements as the process has developed. At some point there was nothing, or rather there was a certain discursive moment which enabled certain things to be said, certain texts to be produced, which in turn enabled the possibility of this book being conceived of. The conception began in very vague terms and was largely formless. Indeed, it cannot be spoken of now since to speak of it in that form would create a structure that was not there at the time. There was no organization and there can be none without writing, but the writing cannot be accomplished because there was no organization. Whether the discourse and texts that came into our purview had coherence and structure prior to our intervention in assembling them in this form is a moot point. But clearly what this project does do is impose a structure, an organization on those things. We have extracted and worked up an order out of something that, for us at least, was formless before. We have called into being an order, we have constituted a sequence and a set of differentiations, we have introduced linearity, spacings, integrations – all the features of organizing and organization. And not just in the confines of this book, but also with respect to the wider discourse. There are distinctions, boundaries, relationships and integrations with other aspects of the wider discourse. There are connections we have made and others we have not. There are differentiations we have drawn and others that we have not. We are inscribing a space, we are interpolating an organization on something. This organization is emerging as we write. The version we are looking at now may not be the one that you engage with, it is an ongoing project at the moment and further transformations and re-configurations – fresh structurings – are likely.

The basic organization of the book has already been inscribed, but let's look more immediately at the process of us actually writing this. If you could see the state of this textual material at this point in time it would be quite legitimate to label it as disorganized, even formless or chaotic, but as we write (hopefully) order and organization will appear. As De Certeau (1984: 134) says (cited in Lennie, Chapter 3), the page creates a space in which 'the ambiguities of the world have been exorcised'. Here there is an even more direct relationship between writing and organization. It is a project greatly aided by the technology of writing (even more pronounced perhaps with keyboard technology). As we write the text is formed immediately into precise linear patterns of determined length ... look ... press a key and

We have a new paragraph, a new order. We cannot but organize. Not only is this process constructing an order out of an amorphous, and barely recognized assemblage of textual components, it is also constructing an order on this page/screen. Before we wrote (that) there was/is an empty space – it has no form, no organization (not quite true since it has a boundary and a border and a certain dimensionality). An order is inscribed, quite literally as we write, as the marks colonize the white space. These words provide an order, and in so doing they ignore other possibilities (they elide other potentialities) (they exclude another order that could be here). As soon as there are words here, the play of signifiers begins, the meaning potentialities are available. We cannot fix them despite the fact that certain words have been chosen and others not, despite the fact that we have done violence to the virginal potentiality of the empty space that was here. So two processes are at work. One is the colonization of a space, a reduction of potential, an inscription of a particular order. At the same time the writing offers a site of productivity in which other relationships and signifying possibilities are brought into being. As you interrogate this space, you can further that productivity with all manner of meanings that you can construct or locate. The organization remains incomplete, unfinished, always deferred and in potentiality. These are things – states and processes – that organizations are.

This brings us to another important aspect of organization – its assumed or claimed boundedness. All writing, all discourse works an inclusion–exclusion practice. What a writing presents is made meaningful, in part by what is not written. This is part of the paradigmatic properties of language. Every discourse appropriates an area of knowledge and in the move excludes others. Organization presupposes to instantiate a boundary – a frame that delineates it and separates it from its outside (however that outside is conceived). It is part of a claim to identity, this organization, not that one. It differentiates from its environment.

In mainstream organization theory much is made of the organization–environment relationship. The environment is often described as determining of organization. However, the environment is actually an outcome of the process of writing organization. Environment is that which is differentiated from organization by the constructed location of organization. In that sense 'environment' is defined by organization; how could it then determine what organization is? An aspect of the organization of writing is a boundary or frame. Materially, this writing has a boundary – for you it is framed by the page and by the margin.[3] The writing also creates a boundary by carving out a particular place in a discourse, by working its inclusion–exclusion practice. But, as Cooper (1986) points out a boundary is not just a separation, it is also a structure that joins together. It indicates differentiation and separateness, but also points to a connection, an idea of wholeness or unity. A boundary does not have clarity – it is not a finalizing break, but an indication of a relationship, a further site of potential and productivity. The question of what is inside and what is out always has an element of uncertainty about it. This notion has become fashionable in contemporary popular management discourse with talk of the boundaryless organization and of the dissolution of organizational boundaries. The practice of writing attempts to provide a fixity, a flow to the endless productivity of signifying relations, but it always fails. The meaning potentialities continue to reverberate through the text, the play of signifiers goes on. The boundary presumed by the writing takes on an undecidability and a fluidity. Cooper's point is that organization attempts to mark itself off from disorganization by constituting a boundary which is supposed to signal a difference. But the boundary actually draws attention to the relationship and the dependence of organization on disorganization. The boundary is permeable and malleable – organization can be invaded by or dissolve into disorganization. This has been expressed in a different context by Johnson (1981: 235): 'The "frame" thus becomes not the borderline between the inside and the outside, but precisely what subverts the applicability of the inside/outside polarity to the act of interpretation. It is the boundary that structures relationships and which shapes behaviour and talk within the spaces it frames'. Thus for Cooper (1990) the boundary is the site of organizational activity (and should therefore be the site of organizational analysis) since it is the practice of the very constitution of organization, a site that requires ongoing structuring work to inscribe a particular order out of disorder. Organization is the appropriation of order out of disorder, but organization is dependent on disorganization and remains in relationship with it.

The issue of boundary is critical to the notion of identity. Two chapters in this book have a concern with this issue: Westwood's (Chapter 11) on the language of the Other in comparative management discourse, and Brewis' (Chapter 12) on gender, language and organization theory. The boundary at stake is the self-other boundary held to be constitutive of identity. Westwood proposes that contemporary comparative management has echoes of the colonial project in that it continues to appropriate the Other and to represent the

Other in ways that are comprehensible to the West thus facilitating the more effective control of the Other. The Ego–Other boundary has always been critical to this type of project. It is particularly prevalent in those aspects of comparative management that rely upon a culturalist mode of explanation. Culture is a device that explicitly and definitionally trades in differentiation and boundary. The very concept depends upon the possibility of categorizing one group of people and insinuating a boundary of difference between them and other groups. But again, the boundary not only signals a separation, but implies a relationship. The postcolonial literature has frequently pointed out that the West's representations of its Others is actually an auto-representational practice, in gazing on the Other and representing the Other to self, one is actually mirroring Ego in the process. The representations of the Other are in the image of the self and the process is actually partly constitutive of Ego. This is particularly so when the Ego is actually rather ignorant of the Other and is in fact constructing a fictive representation of the Other which is really a projection of the desires, aspirations and expectations of Ego. In a similar vein the Other is not defined and pinned down by the writing practices of Ego. This does not unalterably fix what the Other is, the Others have the possibility to react to the framing, to reposition themselves, to re-write themselves. This is a central motif in postcolonial theory, most centrally marked by the Subaltern studies. There are possibilities for reversals, reappropriations and hybridities - which turn back on the Ego and reconstitute the Ego-Alter relationship.

Orientalist discourse constituted the Other in ways that typically denigrated the Other and valorized the Ego (Said, 1979). There is a motivated attempt to constitute the subject-position of the Other through discursive practice – supported by institutional apparatus. In the process the acts of signification made possible by those very discourses that construct difference and alterity also reflexively position the Ego that constructs the discourse, and reconfirm the differences. The same is true of the constructed relationships of gender. The discourse on gender creates subject positions and pretends to insinuate a relation of difference, a boundary of Otherness. Feminist organization theorists suggest that 'malestream' organizational theory and practice has created a discourse and a set of gendered subject-positions that have marginalized or occluded women. As Brewis (Chapter 12) points out, some writers on gender and organization (such as Kanter and Ferguson) conceive of the gendered nature of organizations as inherent to the nature of organizations and monolithic. There are held to be determined power structures that habitually exclude and marginalize women. Brewis, following Foucault, argues that the subject-position of women in organizations is not best viewed from this perspective of pre-constituted power discourses centralized and controlled by men, but rather through recognizing that subject-positions are constantly being constructed and re-constructed in the 'subjectifying micro-processes' which operate at all levels at all times, and in which women participate as much as men. Paying attention to the gendered nature of organizational discourse, and including women's voice, offers no greater prospect for the 'truth' of organizations than any other discourse, and, Brewis seems to imply, no greater liberatory opportunities. Giving voice to the previously marginalized does not make accounts more accurate or truthful, but it does point to the historically, localized, contingent and arbitrary nature of the dominant discourse that has created the marginalization.

In organizational analysis this type of analysis can be applied more generally. For example it is possible to consider the subject-position of 'manager' and the discursive practices and on-going 'subjectifying micro-processes' that constitute it. Foucault depicts subject-positions as being part of the discursive structures prevalent in society. It is these that allow for the construction of particular subject-positions and enable some to assume positions of dominance. They are reflections of the power-discourse relations circulating in the society. 'Manager' as a subject-position is enabled by certain dominant discourses such as economic rationalism and objective scientism that have a privileged position in the matrices of discourse in the society.

A challengingly different view of the positioning of persons is pursued by Munro (Chapter 9). He examines the discursive and institutional conditions that allow certain images and representations of 'information' to be promulgated and achieve centrality. The stated concern then is with a history of the language of information. He poses three important questions: what do we mean by 'information', what does the language of information mean for our conceptualization of organization, and lastly – and most pertinent to this point in our discussion – how does the language of information position us as persons? After pointing to the current obsession with information and its moral imperatives, he revisits classic information theory *a la* Shannon and Weaver (1949) and notes greater radical potentiality than has perhaps normally been recognized. However, it is his identification of two diverse points in contemporary discourse that really sets the path to his Lyotardian analysis of (post)modern language of information.

The first is the view that knowledge is not defined at its point of production but rather in its use. Citing Latour (1987), it is suggested 'that things do not hold because they are true, things are taken as true *because* they hold'. Knowledge circulates, but in circulating it must 'pass'. Passing involves two related things: information (as holding knowledge potential) must pass from person to person (or institution to institution) and to pass it must be seen to meet the knowledge need of the position it passes through – otherwise it will not pass on and circulation will cease. In the second, following Douglas and Isherwood (1980), knowledge is viewed as consumption. Knowledge is an exchange and it is in consumption, in the uses to which information is put that the status of knowledge is identified. In the postmodern context the new conditions of knowledge are determined by the technologies of information (Lyotard, 1984). This technology determines that knowledge be converted into 'bits' of information in order to travel through what Munro refers to as the 'cyber-pass'. Information circulates, but its circulation is now dependent on its ability to pass through the new 'cyber' technology, and to pass it must present in a certain form.

To 'pass' knowledge must be 'exteriorized', and this involves three sets of conditions – it must pass tests of a particular form of legitimacy, conferred on the basis of richness, utility and ease of decoding; it must partake in the process of commodification of knowledge under which 'the goal is exchange of information as goods'; and it must exhibit performativity with respect to those who are in the information network. In the information age, knowledge *per se* is not the issue, exchange is. People are positioned in information networks, as 'posts' through which certain types of information or messages pass. Persons are involved in a language game in which their role is to pass on (or not) information. However, they are judged by others in the network in terms of what and how they pass-on, and are subject to the criteria of legitimacy, commodification and performativity. Their subject position is dependent on their capacity to play the language game correctly and to participate in exchanging information that has value and utility, is transparent and has currency. Incompetence invokes a 'short circuit' and a devaluing of the post occupied by the person, threatening the person with being cut out, marginalized or eliminated. As Munro says 'Lyotard's key insight (is) to place persons and their wrapping of self in language games, *within* the cybernet'.

Cooper (1990), following Derrida, argues that the inscription of order out of disorder occurs in the context of power relations and that language is at the centre of that. For Derrida (1978) writing is an act of desire and is unthinkable without an accompanying act of repression. This is apparent because writing attempts a closure, to fix meaning, to carve out a specific set of meaning potentials, but in doing so rules out, elides or represses other possible meaning potentials. The same is true of discourse. Every discourse participates in a power/knowledge practice in that what is privileged by the discourse at the same time banishes alternatives. The discourse of contemporary rational science, for example, valorizes objectivity, reason, measurement and so on, it diminishes and delegitimizes metaphysical or mystical discourse and values such as subjectivity, the supra-natural, ideal forms, transcendence, intuition and so on. A discourse seeks to occupy space, to lay claim to an area of knowledge and to occupy it totally, pushing other ways of knowing out or to the margin. Discourse and power occupy the same space since to lay claim discursively to an area of knowledge is to engage in a practice of power, and to engage in a practice of power is to appropriate a discourse and an area of knowledge (Westwood, 1987). Language text and discourse are sites of productivity and potentiality in which the struggles for meaning and power are played out. Cooper (1990) also draws attention to the power effects of language. In this sense language and speech are not just the mechanisms by which conflict is expressed and power made manifest, but also the ground of power and that over which power contests are enacted. Language and discourse are, at the same time, the ground on which the struggle for power is waged, the object of strategies of domination, and the means by which the struggle is actually engaged and achieved.

Writing is an appropriation of the undecidable, an attempted closure on ambiguity and disorder. This is what power is; it is also what organization is – the inscription of order out of disorganization. In this sense power is a *diagramming* (Bersani, 1977), a particular ordering of knowledge within discursive frames that both appropriates a space claimed as truth, authority, authenticity, and in the same move excludes, rules out, banishes, represses and marginalizes alternatives. Cooper (1990) sees this as a violence, a violence that is masked by a meta-language of institutional authority in organizations that is itself a discursive practice constructed for this rationalizing purpose. Writing and discourse lay claim to a totalization, to be definitively authoritative. But they are fragile. Fragile because the boundary they set up already points to a relationship to what is excluded, to alternative possibilities. Fragile because the claim is an ideological accomplishment, not a necessary feature of the discourse. Fragile because the organization achieved is dependent on disorganization. Fragile finally because the attempted cessation of free play of signifiers that writing/discourse aspires to cannot be sustained. The constructed text remains a site of productivity in which new relations of signifiers are possible, in which new formations and meanings are immanent in the text. The claim to be knowledge, truth and authority rests on tropological practices which seek to present what is proffered as 'natural' as real and which mask the locally, historically and ideologically contingent nature of the claim. The will to power is cloaked in rhetorical practices, but this can be uncovered by a rigorous interrogation. Thus, in the same mode, organization is an attempted closure, a carving out of a particular discursive space, a suggested forgetting of the polysemous nature of language. Such closure can only be presented through a tropological practice that makes the situated notion of organization seen natural and innocent, rather than arbitrary, ideologically informed and an exercise of power.

Viewing things in this manner makes it difficult not to accept Foucault's view of power not as something possessed or centrally positioned, but as everywhere. Not everywhere because some monolithic source has enough of it to exercise it in all situations, but because 'it is produced at every instant, at every point to one another' (Foucault, 1976: 123). This point is made clear by Brewis (Chapter 12) in her analysis. Power is not inherent in some male dominated meta-structure but in serial acts of signifying-in-place. There is no fixed logos of power, it occurs in the surface practices, in every act of signification which invokes a discourse and a knowledge/power alignment. As Norris (1980: 59) puts it, 'Whatever is written partakes of textuality, and covers its rhetorical tracks only by an effort ... to efface its signature as writing and pretend to be a purely truth telling or communicative function'.

There is then, in every act of signification, an exercise of power. Each signifying act participates in a particular discourse and insinuates a particular set of meanings that are presented as authoritative, at the same time it excludes alternatives. It can be seen also as a political, ideological practice that invokes and reflexively supports hegemonic discursive positions and seeks a closure on the free play of language. Certain discourses, texts and supporting institutional apparatus attain a temporary position of dominance under which alternatives are delegitimized and resistance is weakened (Linstead, 1993a). This is true of the discourse on academic management, including comparative management as Westwood (Chapter 11) makes clear. But such power formation, such fixity is temporary and fragile, 'it must be reproduced and sustained, can be resisted and deconstructed, and is never *permanently* normalised' (Linstead, 1993a: 64).

The mundane accomplishment of order and closure was a central theme of the ethnomethodological enterprise. Garfinkel's (1967) 'etcetera clause', notions of indexicality and other aspects of everyday language practices are *methods* mundanely used to achieve such a temporary working order and closure on other possibilities. This is a pragmatic issue for the ethnomethodologists, required in order for routine interactions and other activities to be accomplished. In Chapter 2, David Richards reminds us of the ethnomethodological legacy and the continued value of its perspective on language and organized activity. Language has a pragmatic function; acts of signification perform, must do work and accomplish things. The free play of language may be a theoretical truth, but fixity – organization – is a pragmatic requirement. Interaction and the account people provide is in danger of running into an infinite regress since the possibility exists of an indefinite elaboration of meanings. The intensive focus on the mundane methods of speech and interaction by the ethnomethodologists reveals that closure and an achievement of order is a routine accomplishment of language-in-use. The pragmatic requirements for the production of authoritative accounts that hold the slide of meaning is constructed through such procedures or rules as 'let it pass', 'enough is enough' and the 'etcetera clause'. It is not necessary to view this as a matter of intentionality, but as the natural property of speech acts and indexical expressions.

Richards (Chapter 2) seeks to put ethnomethodological practice in relation to postmodern approaches and points to some adjacencies, but also some differences. Points of commonality include, according to Richards, the centrality of language in both projects, a shared reliance on notions of reflexivity and a shared debt to the hermeneutic-dialectical tradition. Ethnomethodology focuses more on the pragmatic of speech acts and interaction and shows little interest in the textuality that preoccupies the postmodernist. It must be noted, however, that although postmodern philosophy acknowledges the enabling conditions offered by hermeneutics and the dialectic, it rejects both – the first because it participates in the metaphysics of presence and logocentrism, and the latter because of its teleological implications. However, both positions recognize the ongoing productivity of language and the problematic nature of that. Richards suggests that Derrida sees undecidability as the pervasive quality of experienced reality and that this provides 'the human drive to organize, to order and structure the world' (Linstead and Grafton-Small, 1992: 341). However, not all postmodernists would accept this motivational perspective. For Derrida writing may be an ordering process, but he does not share the ethnomethodological concern for the pragmatics of human activity.

The hermeneutic tradition is explored more frontally by Thatchenkery (Chapter 6). He makes extensive use of Gadamer (1975) to explicate the hermeneutic project, but also draws on Ricoeur's (1971, 1981) 'paradigm of the text' and his view of the historicity of human experience and of the inevitable distanciation in communication which creates the hermeneutic problematic. Ricoeur shares the postmodern view that language is discourse and text, but the meaning he attributes to these display differences. For him the problem is the dialectic of speaking and writing, and of event and meaning. The dialectic constitutes the distanciation that makes the recoverability of meaning problematical. But, as Thatchenkery points out, Ricoeur holds on to the notion that discourse is referential, there are referents to the material world and to events, it is simply that the relationship is deeply problematized. What is shared with the postmodern purview is the view that writing irretrievably detaches authorial intention and meaning from text. Thatchenkery sees the hermeneutic tradition in several contemporary positions in organization theory. It can be discerned, he argues, in certain psychoanalytic treatments, exemplified by the work of Kets de Vries and Miller (1987). It is also present in versions of discourse analysis such as that summarized by Grant et al. (1998); in narratological perspectives (Barry and Elmes, 1997 – see also Boje, Alvarez and Schooling, Chapter 7).

It has been argued that organization is a writing that strives to achieve coherence, order and authority. To do so it must attempt a closure by engaging in a discursive and tropological practice that presents the version of reality on offer as truthful, complete, natural and innocent. It engages in an inclusion–exclusion practice that rules out alternatives and seeks to stop the free play of signifying relations that otherwise keeps the text 'open'. It has also been suggested that such ordering and organization is fragile and can only be sustained through continued 'work' – work with language and within routine interactions. Fragile too, because the free play of language cannot be halted, the signifying possibilities of language are always present and so alternatives, interrogations and resistances are at least immanent in language and in organization. In the same vein, as we have seen, power is an appropriation of a discursive space and an area of knowledge, it is a *diagramming*, a particular ordering/organizing of knowledge within a discursive frame. But language and discourse are irretrievably sites of productivity, a fluidity in which there exists, inherently, the possibility for a re-opening, a release of the free-play of signification, a reanimation of *difference* and undecidability. There is, as Foucault (1975) states, the possibility to adopt an interrogative, transgressive stance that challenges and 'provokes a mutation in the diagram'.

Since power is everywhere, and present in all signifying practices it cannot be seen as an external, homogeneous, centralized force. Power is a ceaseless, localized activity and is present in all relations of difference and all attempts to appropriate a discourse. Considered thus power is, as Bersani (1977) argues, in excess and 'leaks'. In excess because of the need to always say more, to offer accounts and justification which are not mere reiterations, but new sayings with new relations of difference and fresh meaning potentials. Leaky and excessive because of the polysemous, endless and ceaseless flow of signifying relations that have no finitude. Clegg (1989) also argues that resistance to the closure of meaning is an intrinsic to the nature of language. Chia (1995) suggests that the order, coherence and a sense of identity is a partial and temporary accomplishment. Social objects, such as 'organizations' and even 'individuals' are mere 'provisionally ordered networks of heterogeneous materials' whose resistances to ordering have been overcome, albeit temporarily.

The issue of resistance is important to the concerns of this book. In a sense each of them has something to say about resistance or at least they each deal with alternatives, with challenges to the orthodoxy. In various ways they each provide a critical analysis of orthodox language games in organization studies and their effects; this provides, at a minimum a space for an active interrogation of those positions. This is not always seen as liberatory, but at least opens up new conditions for being able to see and speak in an alternative language. For example, in Boje, Alvarez and Schooling (Chapter 7) there is the possibility of resistance through re-writing organizational stories, or reconstructing the narrative of our lives. By revealing the subject position through the information/knowledge conditions opens up the space where we might reflect on our interminable involvement in the 'ethical niceties' of particular language games and perceive the larger moral order. Whilst Sewell (Chapter 8) shows the complexities in the power/knowledge relationship in the language of power in organizational discourse, he offers the scope to avoid limiting attempts to de-conflate significant binaries. He may agree with Foucault that power is everywhere and inescapable, but he also agrees with Foucault (1979) that 'there can be no relations of power without a degree of freedom'. Westwood (Chapter 11) points to the hegemonic, dominating discourse of contemporary comparative management discourse; he also notes that there are points of resistance, through reversals, mirroring and hybridities.

Linstead (Chapter 10) looks specifically at the potential of rhetorical analysis to facilitate resistance to such hegemonies by identifying the linguistic technologies through which meaningful control is established and identifying lines of resistance. Such technologies, he argues in developing work by Gowler and Legge on the rhetoric of bureaucratic control, rest upon a range of rhetorics of control which characteristically collapse one or more epistemological dimensions into each other effectively to obscure their ontological status. Thus, just as Gowler and Legge observe in the rhetoric of bureaucratic control the implicational meanings of the moral-aesthetic order and the intentional meanings of the techno-social order being collapsed so that ideological imperatives become disguised as practical necessities, similar implosions occur elsewhere. In the rhetoric of social control, the common-sense assumptions of the natural order and the negotiated meanings of the politico-social order blend in order to normalize power inequities and power-broking strategies. Other rhetorics emerge to perform the practical functions of blending the demands of individual skills and abilities into the functional demands of organizational mechanics (the rhetoric of humanistic control); the demands of self-perfection with the demands for self-effacement in service (the rhetoric of altruistic control); reconciling the demands of developing self-identity with the alienating effects of deskilling technologies (the rhetoric of objectification); resolving the conflict between technological determinism and recalcitrant free will giving rise to the need for surveillance (the rhetoric of technological control); holding together the demands of creative self-gratification and disciplined self-denial (the rhetoric of self-control); and 'managing meaning' through linkages between artefacts and rituals and specific beliefs and values (the rhetoric of linguistic/symbolic control). Corresponding lines of critique are opened up by which the unacknowledged ideological dimensions of each rhetorical genre can be exposed in deconstructively revealing how they achieve their power/knowledge effects through their specific technologies – of language, image, story and symbol. Thus the rhetoric of bureaucratic control is transgressively reinscribed through the study and critique of its technologies of ideological power; the rhetoric of social control through the depiction of technologies of cultural power; the rhetoric of humanistic control through technologies of subjective power; the rhetoric of altruistic control through technologies of ethical power; the rhetoric of objectification through technologies of authoritarian power; the rhetoric of technological control through technologies of surveillance; the rhetoric of self-control through technologies of the self; and the rhetoric of linguistic/symbolic control through technologies of representational power. The linking of representational technologies to obscured ontological positions in rhetorical analysis thus has the potential to become a powerful critical tool – indeed this linguistic analytical scheme could be seen as synthesizing aspects of the work of Marx, Freud, Foucault, Weber, Durkheim, Derrida and even Baudrillard.

Relatedly, in earlier work Chia (1995) has argued that in orthodox organizational analysis the ontological status of organization is taken for granted and its actual status as a fragile accomplishment through various micro-practices which constitute what we label as organization is repressed or ignored. The micro-processes to which he refers are 'inscriptions' by which we mark out an order in our phenomenal world. In a similar, and summary way Law (1992) suggests that the proper project of organization studies is the investigation and critical exposure of the 'localized processes of patterning, social orchestration, ordering and resistance'. In this book Chia and King (Chapter 13) address the issue of the operation of language in the processes of theorizing about oganization: about the representational practices of organization theory. They note at the outset, and in agreement with what we have argued here, that representation *is* a mode of organization, indeed, is a 'quintessential organizing mode'.

Before we finish with a brief look at Chia and King's contribution we want to point out that among the various 'micro-practices' and 'heterogeneous materials' that inscribe the order that we call organization are 'plans', 'lists' and 'strategies'. These are dealt with in this book with a great deal of critical sophistication by Lennie (Chapter 3) and Lilley (Chapter 4). They both point to how the language of these things orders and organizes, but they go much further, particularly in pointing to how lists, plans and strategies are constitutive of subjectivities and identities. In Lilley's work there is a complex analysis of the 'conditions of possibility' for the current pervasive, all-embracing but often banal sayings of 'strategy'. He notes that this application of strategy to 'organizations' is a relatively recent phenomenon. He makes use of Deleuze's (1986) notions of mechanisms and regimes of systems of statements and visibility machines that are the historicized conditions for knowledge – that enable the two related but distinct forms of knowing, seeing and saying. In a particular era these allow what can be said and seen, and since all things that can be said (in an era), will be said, we see an endless proliferations of 'sayings' about 'strategy' – an excess that generates the banal, but which continues to problematize that which it seeks to resolve. Strategy (like Lennie's lists and plans) is an externalization of the subject; particularly, in Lilley's case, it is an exteriorization of intentionality – of what the subject sees as their aspired-to self in interaction with their outside, their proposed or desired move through their environment. The issue is what enunciations about strategy can circulate in the modern context, and with what effect, and whether we can find a way to extend what is sayable. The modern language of strategy is diverse and munificent – it talks militaristically, but more importantly it is a language of affect and intention. It is also gloriously, and emptily, totalizing by insinuating the notion that strategy is the plan of plans, or a policy of policies. Today strategy is applied to everything – and nothing. But Lilley is gloomy. He argues that the language of strategy problematizes identity. It does so because it pretends to materialize intentions and to position an interiority with respect to an exteriority, but the language of strategy is, in its nature, one which constantly makes the achievement of intentions an impossibility. It is a language of the future, as well as the present and the past, and trades in change. A strategized state remains in flux so that the formulated intention appears as an internalized act, but is in fact only a function of an exteriority, an exteriority that continues to change, to problematize the future and be elusive. Strategy must do this in order to have continuance, and the conditions of knowledge enable serial sayings which keep its project in motion. Under these conditions, 'intentional selves are both a cause and a consequence of strategy'. Strategy pretends to deal with the 'truth' of our intentions, and thus 'truths' about our identities and selves, but can never deliver this. The only escape is to give up notions of a foundational self and to find the 'fold' between outside and outside that is a more 'authentic' position – a place where there is an 'ever disappearing gap between intention and that to which it is directed' and where there is the prospect of different visibilities and articulations – albeit 'mad' ones!

Chia and King (Chapter 13) remind us that our theories of organization are, in effect, forms of language, and need to be analyzed in those terms. Language, as we have described earlier in this chapter, inherently inscribes order, and is an organization of the disorganized. The language of orthodox organization theory assumes a certain form and has certain determinate effects. It is a representational language which assumes the facticity of organization, something that none of the writers in this book accept at face value. It is also a language of rationality, reification, objectification and objectivism. Cooper and King reveal the aridity of this perspective, and also question the motives of power and control which it masks. The language of organization theory is a language of control, not least in the policing of its own discursive boundaries. As they say 'To construe organization as a 'thing like' entity … is already to overlook the meta-language of organization which deals with the ontologically-prior processes of fixing, forming, framing and bounding rather than with the content and outcomes of such processes'. For Chia and King, as with most of the contributors here, language *is* organization, and organization *is* language.

Notes

1 This is not a need that is as apparent in Eastern philosophical traditions where apparent 'dualities' are not dissolved or separated but remain entwined in productive confluence.
2 Structuration theory is an exception to this.
3 The margin is a retained virgin space. It frames the writing, but is also an unpenetrated space. Many people will use the margin to write their own interpretation – to add to the organization of the text. The margin may then become something like a supplement.

References

Aktouf, O. (1986) 'La parole dans la vie de l'entreprise: faits et mefaits', *Gestion: Revue Internationale de Gestion*, II (4): 31–7.

Barry, D. and Elmes, M. (1997) 'Strategy retold: toward a narrative view of strategic discourse', *Academy of Management Review*, 22 (2): 429–52.

Bersani, L. (1977) 'The subject of power', *Diacritics*, 7 (3): 2–21.

Chia, R. (1995) 'From modern to postmodern organizational analysis', *Organization Studies*, 16 (4): 579–604.

Chia, R. (1996) *Organizational Analysis: A Deconstructive Approach*. Berlin/NY: Walter de Gruyter.

Chia, R. (ed.) (1998) *In the Realm of Organization: Essays for Robert Cooper*. London: Routledge.

Clegg, S. (1989) 'Radical revisions: power, discipline and organizations', *Organization Studies*, 10 (4): 457–78.

Cooper, R. (1986) 'Organization/Disorganization', *Social Science Information*, 25 (2): 299–335.

Cooper, R. (1987) 'Information, communication and organization: a poststructural revision', *Journal of Mind and Behaviour*, 8 (3): 395–416.

Cooper, R. (1989) 'Modernism, postmodernism and organization analysis: the contribution of Jacques Derrida', *Organization Studies*, 10 (4): 479–502.

Cooper, R. (1990) 'Organization/Disorganization', in J. Hassard and D. Pym (eds), *The Theory and Philosophy of Organizations*. London: Routledge. pp. 167–97.

Cooper, R. (1992) 'Formal organization as representation', in M. Reed and M. Hughes (eds), *Rethinking Organization*. London: Sage. pp. 254–72.

Cooper, R. (1993) 'Technologies of representation', in P. Ahonen (ed.), *Tracing the Semiotic Boundaries of Politics*. Berlin: Mouton de Gruyter. pp. 279–312.

Cossette, P. (1998) 'The study of language in organizations: a symbolic interactionist stance', *Human Relations*, 51 (11): 1355–77.

De Certeau, M. (1984) *The Practice of Everyday Life*. Berkeley, CA: University of California Press.

Degot, V. (1982) 'Le modele de l'agent et le probleme de la construction de l'objet dans les theories des l'entreprise', *Social Science Information*, 21 (4–5): 627–64.

Deleuze, G. (1986) *Foucault*, trans. and ed. Sean Hand. Minneapolis: University of Minnesota Press.

Derrida, J. (1978) *Writing and Difference*, trans. A. Bass. London: Routledge and Kegan Paul.

Donellon, A. (1986) 'Language and communication in organizations: bridging cognition and behavior', in H.P Sims, Jr. and D.A. Gioia (eds), *The Thinking Organization:*

Dynamics of Organizational Social Cognition. San Francisco: Jossey-Bass. pp. 136–64.

Douglas, M. and Isherwood, B. (1980) *The World of Goods: Towards an Anthropology of Consumption.* Harmondsworth: Penguin.

Foucault, M. (1975) 'Ecrivain non: un nouveau cartographe', *Critique*, 373: 1222–34.

Foucault, M. (1976) *La Volonté de Savoir: Vol. 1 – Histoire de la Sexualité.* Paris: Gallimard.

Foucault, M. (1979) *The History of Sexuality: Vol. I – An Introduction*, trans. R. Hurley. Harmondsworth: Penguin.

Gadamer, H.G. (1975) *Truth and Method*, trans. D.E. Linge. Berkeley, CA: University of California Press.

Garfinkel, H. (1967) *Studies in Ethnomethodology.* Englewood Cliffs, NJ: Prentice Hall.

Gergen, K. (1992) 'Organization theory in the postmodern era', in M. Reed and M. Hughes (eds), *Rethinking Organization.* London: Sage. pp. 207–26.

Grant, D., Keenoy, T. and Oswick, C. (eds) (1998) *Discourse and Organization.* London: Sage.

Johnson, B. (1981) 'The frame of reference: Poe, Lacan, Derrida', in R. Young (ed.), *Untying the Text: A Post-Structuralist Reader.* Boston: Routledge and Kegan Paul. pp. 225–43.

Kallinikos, J. (1995) 'The archi-tecture of the invisible: technology is representation', *Organization*, 2 (1): 117–40.

Kets de Vries, M.F.R. and Miller, D. (1987) 'Interpreting organizational texts', *Journal of Management Studies*, 24 (3): 233–47.

Latour, B. (1987) *Science in Action: How to Follow Scientists and Engineers through Society.* Milton Keynes: Open University Press.

Law, J. (1992) 'Notes on the theory of the actor-network: ordering, strategy and heterogeneity', *Systems Practice*, 5: 379–93.

Law, J. (1994) *Organising Modernity.* London: Routledge.

Linstead, S. (1993a) 'Deconstruction in the study of organizations', in J. Hassard and M. Parker (eds), *Postmodernism and Organizations.* London: Sage. pp. 49–70.

Linstead, S. (1993b) 'From postmodern anthropology to deconstructive ethnography', *Human Relations*, 46 (1): 97–120.

Linstead, S.A. (1994) 'Objectivity, reflexivity and fiction: humanity. inhumanity and the science of the social', *Human Relations*, 47 (11): 1321–46.

Linstead, S.A. (1995) 'After the autumn harvest: rhetoric and representation in an Asian industrial dispute', *Studies in Cultures, Organizations and Societies*, 1 (2): 231–51.

Linstead, S.A. (1999) 'An introduction to the textuality of organizations', *Studies in Cultures, Organizations and Societies*, 5 (1): 1–10.

Linstead, S.A. (2000) 'Ashes and madness: the play of negativity and the poetics of organization', in S.A. Linstead and H.J. Höpfl (eds), *The Aesthetics of Organization.* London: Sage. pp. 61–93.

Linstead, S. and Grafton-Small, R. (1992) 'On reading organizational culture', *Organizational Studies*, 13 (3): 331–55.

Lyotard, J.-F. (1984) *The Postmodern Condition: A Report on Knowledge*, trans. G. Bennington and B. Massouri. Minneapolis: University of Minnesota Press.

Norris, C. (1980) 'Wrestling with deconstructors', *Critical Quarterly*, XXII: 57–62.

Pondy, L. and Mitroff, I. (1979) 'Beyond open system models of organization', *Research in Organization Behavior*, 1: 3–39.

Ricoeur, P. (1971) 'The model of the text: meaningful action considered as a text', *Social Research*, 38 (3): 529–62.

Ricoeur, P. (1981) 'The model of the text: meaningful action considered as a text', in J.B. Thompson (ed. and trans.), *Hermeneutics and the Human Sciences: Essays on*

Language, Action and Interpretation. Cambridge: Cambridge University Press. pp. 197–221.

Said, E.W. (1979) 'The text, the world, the critic', in Josue V. Harari (ed.), *Textual Strategies*. London: Methuen.

Shannon, C.E. and Weaver, W. (1949) *The Mathematical Theory of Communication*. Illinois: University of Illinois.

Silverman, D. (1970) *The Theory of Organizations*. London: Heinemann.

Smircich, L. (1983) 'Organizations as shared meanings', in L. Pondy, P. Frost, G. Morgan and T. Dandridge (eds), *Organizational Symbolism*. Greenwich, CT: JAI Press. pp. 55–68.

Weick, K. (1978) *The Social Psychology of Organizing*. Reading, MA: Addison-Wesley Publications.

Westwood, R.I. (1983) *Contests in Meaning: The Rhetoric of Participation*. Bath: University of Bath, unpublished PhD thesis.

Westwood, R.I. (1987) 'Social criticism: a social critical practice applied to a discourse on participation', in I.L. Mangham (ed.), *Organization Analysis and Development*. Chichester: John Wiley. pp. 167–205.

Westwood, R.I. (1999) 'A "sampled" account of organization: being a de-authored, reflexive parody of organization/writing', *Studies in Cultures, Organizations and Societies*, 5 (1): 195–233.

Winograd, T. (1980) 'What does it mean to understand language?', *Cognitive Science*, 4 (3) (July–Sept.): 209–42.

PART 1

LANGUAGE, ORGANIZATION AND ACTION

2

Talking Sense: Ethnomethodology, Postmodernism and Practical Action

David S. Richards

Introduction

This chapter examines two powerful and idiosyncratic views of language and social life and provides an account of their relationship with each other and with the natural world. Firstly, a sketch is given of the common interests of ethnomethodology and postmodernism in examining practices in the social world as taken-for-granted accomplishments. The ways in which both approaches address language as the realm of the said and the unsaid, the sayable and the unsayable, is linked to two strands in the development of linguistic analysis and philosophy that provide their conceptual underpinnings. We then go on to consider in more detail the ways in which the analytical concerns and practices of ethnomethodology and postmodernism intersect and diverge. It is argued that the tension *between* them is reflected *within* them, since they both represent a synthesis of Western intellectual traditions that are commonly considered mutually exclusive. The theme of difference and divergence continues with a detailed examination of the development of an empirical conversation analytic focus, an approach that, it can be argued, has moved ethnomethodology both farther from and nearer to postmodernism. The chapter then concludes with a resolution of some of the differences and an argument for the creative benefits of a new, or rediscovered, synthesis to examine sense-making and practical action in organizations.

The story

It is often thought that the social observer or organizational theorist must go 'beyond', 'beneath', or 'behind' surface appearances to the deeper unity of which these surfaces are the diffuse signs. He or she should attempt to fit details together to make a pattern, revealing some hidden secret, the buried truth which is the substance behind the dim signs with which they are surrounded. Consideration of the names, gestures and appearances of social actors, like those in a novel or drama, will provide indications of some hidden truth about them. Life can be seen as a document (or story or text) which the participant/observer must interpret, that is piece together, scrutinize and interrogate at every turn, in order, like the police detective, to understand 'what is going on'. Reading (or seeing) life as a story depends on some processes of an *allegorical* nature, indeed is itself such a phenomenon, in that one speaks of one thing (life), by speaking of another (story). Literary critics have argued that three closely aligned processes ('figures of speech') are required in order to read stories as stories (Miller, 1971):

1 *Synecdoche* – where a word stands for other words, a type for other types (a part is used to mean the whole, the whole to mean the part). In stories, characters, scenes or situations often have representative qualities and stand for other examples of a given type.
2 *Metonymy* – where the name of an attribute or a thing is used instead of the thing itself. In stories this allows disparate events and characters to be related.
3 *Metaphor* – which subsumes both, in that a word or phrase which denotes one kind of object or idea is used in place of another in order to suggest a likeness or analogy between them.

Story telling is only possible through these processes. For example, Miller argues that it is not possible in the absence of metonymy, since this 'presupposes a similarity or causality between things presented as contiguous', which allows connections to be made between events which initially appear unconnected (1971: 14).

Metaphor is, however, not merely a poetic device but an underlying mode of thought which 'implies *a way of thinking* and *a way of seeing* that pervade how we understand our world generally' (Morgan, 1986: 12). As Lakoff and Johnson say, metaphors are what we 'live by' (1980).

The story in (and of) this chapter is an account of the relationship between (with each other and with the natural world) two powerful but idiosyncratic metaphorical narratives concerning the nature of language and social life. Naturally our story cannot capture the complexity of these narratives, nor of their relationship, just as they in turn cannot capture the complexity of social life which they index and describe.

Ethnomethodology and postmodernism

At the time of ethnomethodology's inception and seminal early development, the term 'postmodernism' was not in use, but nevertheless, a considerable amount of the work that is now so characterized had already been done within traditions with different labels. Mehan and Wood, in their engaging 1975 review, make the convincing claim that ethnomethodology is the synthesis of two Western intellectual traditions that are commonly considered mutually exclusive – *scientism* and the *hermeneutic-dialectical* tradition:

> Scientism ... is the tradition that created Sociology in the nineteenth century ... (and) is known today as *logico-empiricism* ... The hermeneutic-dialectical tradition, logico-empiricism's antithesis, arose as a cry of alarm at first sight of science's face. (1975: 206–7)[1]

They further observe that ethnomethodology is

> a child of the two (traditions). It is an *activity* that transcends them. Ethnomethodology has borrowed its *methodology* from its logico-empiricist father. Ethnomethodology's *theory* has been derived from its hermeneutic-dialectic mother. Ethnomethodology does not choose sides in the war between its parents. As a result, both traditions find ethnomethodology anathema. (1975: 207)[2]

Postmodernism is linked to the roots, and to some extent to the branches, of the hermeneutic-dialectical tradition (although the precise articulation of this relationship is beyond the scope of us here), and it certainly shares a profound opposition to logo-centrism. Mehan and Wood agree that both the hermeneutic-dialectical tradition (and hence postmodernism) and ethnomethodology share an understanding that the observer is part of the scene that he or she observes, but argue that the difference is that ethnomethodology:

> is not primarily a talking discipline. It is a way of working. It is an activity that forces the practitioner to take risks. Although it adopts an empirical stance, empiricism itself is part of the phenomenon. This phenomenon is not to be found merely by writing about it. It must be experienced firsthand. (1975: 210)

Perhaps this is not an accurate distinction, since they go on to say, at the end of their book: 'Unlike social science and much earlier ethnomethodology, my ethnomethodology is a form of life. It is not a body of theory nor of method ... (it is) ... a collection of practices similar in purpose to the practices artists and craftsmen teach and use' (1975: 238). This seems very similar to what Czarniawska finds in the 'postmodern attitude', which 'denies formal logic any superior value, appreciates the power of speech, and heeds chance, random events and paradoxes – with bitterness or in a celebratory mood' (1999: 21).

The Text and The Talk

Ethnomethodology, following the empirical traditions of the Sociology of Language has concentrated on the centrality and nature of talk. The 'postmodern' writers – importantly Barthes, Baudrillard, Lyotard, Foucault and Derrida – seem to differ in that they provide a focus on the text, rather than the talk. The focus of postmodernists on The Text perhaps seems to come naturally from their background in French Philosophy, Structuralism, Sociology and literary analysis and criticism – or as they might put it, *theory*. Barthes' notion that The Text[3] is the fundamental building block of written discourse is shared by most writers in the postmodern vein. For Derrida consciousness is determined by writing (understood as an abstract ordering process), and therefore, paradoxically, the ordering and structuring practices of writing determine those of speech. Speech would not be possible without writing, and the ordering and structuring practices in speech are pre-conscious. This might appear to be a puzzling argument literally and historically, since speech preceded writing, but the argument can be illuminated by Derrida's notion of The Trace.

Human consciousness is the result of many traces left behind, or inscribed, much as they would be on a sheet of wax, the result of interaction with traces left by previous experiences. These many echoes and resonances provide a retrospective and prospective sense of structure and meaning for the person in society. Garfinkel and his fellow ethnomethodologists shape this notion of reverberations from that which has passed, into a different but related metaphor of the *retrospective-prospective sense of occurrence*. Common understandings take their own sense from a redefinition of both past and future as the 'present' unfolds and practical reasoning provides an accumulation of instructions to and by members of society as continual (reflexive) feedback through which members assign meaning to their environment. This has many similarities to Derrida's extension of the metaphor of The Trace, making use of the word's multiple meanings. The trace is both a harness which holds horses in a carriage and is also the evidence (on the ground) of the tracks taken by the horses (in the harness and attached to the carriage). Both ethnomethodology and postmodernism here paint similarly poignant pictures of social actors who are creative and yet bound by their own creations.

Postmodernists, particularly Barthes, Derrida and Foucault, can then, as Rogers argues 'offer ... grounds for understanding ethnomethodologists' goals and techniques' (1984: 167). Although a linear historical, logocentric relationship cannot be shown between the two, Rogers points to what we might, playfully, call 'a postmodern relationship'. With reference to Barthes, for example, she says that

> although he appears not to have directly influenced ethnomethodologists, one can trace a fundamental *resonance* between Barthes's and the ethnomethodologists' approaches to their objects of investigation. Barthes's treatment of The Text, in particular, illustrates that resonance. (Rogers, 1984: 167, emphasis added)

The Text is where language relations become transparent (Barthes, 1977: 164) which 'always involves a certain experience of limits ... rationality, readability, etc' (Barthes, 1977: 157). Although it profoundly limits discourse, that it does so, and the way in which it does so is usually hidden from participants. This is because experiencing the text derives from the activity of its creation, where routines 'speak' according to particular rules. The Text remains taken for granted until 'a discourser struggles with its constraints while trying to produce a particular text' (Rogers, 1984: 168).

Derrida sees texts as central to symbolic systems (Derrida, 1978). The nature of 'reality', Derrida said, is inherently undecidable and the stress of this 'existential ambiguity' results in 'the human drive to organize, to order and structure the world' (Linstead and Grafton-Small, 1992: 341). Derrida considers this ordering process as 'writing', and thus views all human conceptual products as 'texts'. Any social act, institution, organization or relationship is constructed, or 'written', by social actors, both those constituting the action and those observing it (Linstead and Grafton-Small, 1992: 341). A text, then, is a complex of language connections (within and without) which is the output of the productive activity of writing, the nature of authorship and the characteristics of the author.

It is important to realize, however, that the nature of the relationship between 'the text' and 'the author' is complex and is certainly neither unitary nor unidirectional. Barthes indeed famously observes that the author is as much a product of the text as the text is the product of an author (Barthes, 1981). Reading is not done by deciphering the original meaning 'intended' by the author but, rather, by the meaning of the text *emerging* through being created and recreated by the reader. This is the notion of *intertextuality*, used by Barthes and Derrida to show that meaning resides in between the author, the text, the reader and other texts and emerges from the process of interaction between them. It is a consequence of all previous interactions which author, reader (and text) have each had with all their others, including other texts. '(Meaning) is disentangled rather than deciphered' (Barthes, 1977: 159). 'The text has an intertextuality, a multiplicity of meaning which is inherent rather than a result of a variety of interpretations' (Linstead and Grafton-Small, 1992: 344).

Ethnomethodologists' attitudes towards practical action are similar. In the work of Garfinkel and the other 'situational ethnomethodologists',[4] there is a shared belief that the limits of everyday life and language can be revealed by exposing the taken-for-granted ground rules and background expectancies lying behind all social situations. They can be revealed in a variety of ways, which all permit the analysis of accounts of their features. These rules of common sense, unquestioned and unnoticed, allow social actors to demonstrate their competence as members (of society, of social groups, etc.). 'As the development of ethnomethodology implies, these competencies are essentially linguistic' (Rogers, 1984: 169).

The everyday life studied by ethnomethodologists can be understood as The Text of the postmodernists, an arena where meaning is sought and taken-for-granted rules are accounted for. 'Ethnomethodologists can be seen as facing a single Text (everyday life) whose features are accessible through any given text (mundane social situation) considered as a methodological field in need of a careful reading' (Rogers, 1984: 170).

A shared regard

From the foregoing analysis we can say that both ethnomethodology and postmodernism (at least as represented by Derrida and Foucault) address three shared concerns:[5]

1 The nature of social structure. Both see this emerging from and being created by the attribution of meaning in social interaction.
2 The centrality of speech, language and consciousness, together with an interest in the subject (and therefore in identity and subjectivity).
3 The importance of understanding the other (the object) and with examining the nature of objectivity (the 'ethno' of ethnomethodology) (see Linstead and Grafton-Small, 1992).

Garfinkel and ethnomethodology

Garfinkel's early projects with his students to breach taken-for-granted understandings usually involved the exposure of the background features and formal structures of everyday life through the manipulation of language and conversations (Garfinkel, 1967). This 'breaching' (or 'deconstruction') was an important part of the more experimental aspects of ethnomethodology (for evidence of this see the last chapter of Mehan and Wood, 1975). This, and the other investigative work of Garfinkel, and that of Erving Goffman (Goffman, 1963, 1972), into language and everyday conduct, in turn foreshadowed and was developed into the work of the Conversational Analysts, initiated and articulated by Harvey Sacks (Garfinkel and Sacks, 1970; Sacks, 1964–1972).

Ethnomethodology rejects the notions of conventional normative sociology that the meaning of situations and actions is determined by a pre-established shared symbol system. Instead it sees meaning as subject to reformulation, through and by language, on every new occasion. Cicourel provides a clear exposition of the relationship between language and the acquisition of social structure and argues that 'imputations of competence by members to each other and the recognition of the competence are integral elements of projected and "successful" social action' (Cicourel, 1971: 139). The critical issue for the sociologist then is 'what everyday speaker-hearers assume "everyone knows". Thus members' tacit knowledge about "what everyone knows" is integral to normal-form behaviour' (Cicourel, 1971: 139). The ethnomethodological concern with interpretive procedures is necessary, Cicourel argues, because these procedures are 'constitutive of the member's sense of social structure or organization' and provide the member with a basis for assigning meaning to his environment, (or a sense of social structure) which thus orients him to the relevance of 'surface rules' or norms (Cicourel, 1971: 139).

Sociologists dealing with natural speech (including their own) are concerned with the feature that the attribution of meaning in everyday settings relies upon 'what everyone knows'. This concern with the features of the background understandings of the world of everyday life is required because these background expectancies provide a socially standardized, seen but unnoticed, scheme for the interpretation of the world (Garfinkel, 1967). Utterances are generated under the assumption that their situated meanings are obvious, as 'the reliance on assumed common knowledge facilitates practical exchanges' (Cicourel, 1971: 140). Interpretive procedures are, additionally always operative within, or in reference to, social settings and this means 'that semantic issues are not independent of syntactic, phonological and ecological features, or of situated body movements or gestures' (Cicourel, 1971: 140) and are always tied to the occasions of their use. Norms in everyday life and scientific rules of procedure are treated within ethnomethodology as legal and extra-legal surface rules governing everyday conduct and scientific inquiry (Garfinkel, 1967). Ethnomethodology is

> the study of interpretive procedures and surface rules in everyday social practices and scientific activities. Hence a concern with everyday practical reasoning becomes a study in how members employ interpretive procedures to recognize the relevance of surface rules and convert them into practiced and enforced behaviour. (Cicourel, 1971: 145)

The nature of members' interpretive procedures requires the idea of a generative, praxiological or reflexive social structure, which attempts to show:

a How the acquisition of interpretive procedures and surface rules is necessary for understanding members' everyday activities; and
b How members (and researchers) assign structural descriptions to all forms of social organization. (Cicourel, 1971: 147)

The characteristics of interpretive procedures are the common-sense grounds of social-organizational life. All symbolic forms are incomplete and rely on contextual information to be understood. Competent actors 'reflexively' tie the features of organized settings to the descriptions of those features with language terms, non-verbal cues and behaviours that themselves constitute part of the setting. Utterances that require contextual information to be understood are called 'indexical expressions' (Bar-Hillel, 1954). Words themselves have an 'indexical' property; that is, they act as labels, whose meaning is situationally determined by virtue of their use within social settings. Schutz, Garfinkel, Cicourel and others have discussed the characteristics of the common-sense grounds of everyday life and their descriptions can be briefly summarized here.

1   *The reciprocity of perspectives.* Schutz (1953, 1955) describes this property as consisting of:
   a   The member's idealization of the interchangeability of standpoints whereby the speaker and hearer both take for granted that A assumes that B assumes things as A does, and that given a change in position, B would assume that A assumes things as B does; and
   b   That the speaker assumes the hearer will expect to emit utterances that are recognizable and intelligible and that the hearer will receive these as acceptable products, and will appear to 'understand' what is being discussed. Thus ordered interaction is possible.

2   *The et cetera assumption.* Conversational flow has an 'et cetera' quality. Garfinkel (1972: 28–9) suggests that understanding requires that a speaker and hearer 'fill in' or assume the existence of common understandings. This assumption allows things to 'pass' despite their ambiguity or vagueness. It relies on particular features of language itself. 'You know what I mean' is not only a conversational device, it is taken as being, literally, for the purpose at hand, true.

3   *Retrospective-prospective sense of occurrence.* Common understandings have the character of taking shape from the course of their own development. Things are seen as taking place within a context that orders both 'things to come' and things that have passed but takes its own sense from a redefinition of both past and future as the 'present' unfolds. A 'film of continuity' binds together conversationalists so that 'wait and see', 'I thought so' and 'you didn't mean that' can be employed to discount certain phrases and meanings while waiting for the 'real' meaning to 'come clear'. Events are taken as pointing to the norms in the situation. Yet non-members cannot unequivocally assign these same events that status. Sociologists trade on properties of practical reasoning as a means to 'make sense' of social action yet their use of these properties is derived from their own membership in society, not from 'expert' knowledge. Members use the properties of practical reasoning to 'clarify and make routine sense of their own environments, and sociologists must view such activities (and their

own work) as practical methods for constructing and maintaining social order' (Cicourel, 1971: 149). Garfinkel has suggested that the properties of practical reasoning be viewed as a collection of instructions to members by members and as a sort of continual (reflexive) feedback whereby members assign meaning to their environment.

4 *Normal forms of conversation are employed.* Thus if mistakes, misunderstandings, embarrassments and 'unclarities' emerge, efforts are made to normalize the presumed discrepancies through appropriate means for restoration (see Goffman, 1972). Garfinkel (1972: 12) suggests that 'competent members' (those who can claim to be capable of managing their everyday affairs without interference) recognize and employ normal forms in daily interaction under the assumptions that all communication is embedded within a body of common knowledge or 'what everyone knows'.

5 *Talk in settings is reflexive.* Talk is reflexive because it is seen as fundamental to normal scenes as both a feature of the setting and itself a description of the setting. Garfinkel observes that talk is a constituent feature of all settings because members count on its presence as an indication that 'all is well' and use it to produce a descriptive account of those same arrangements. 'Talk is continuously folded back upon itself so that the presence of "proper" talk and further talk provide a sense of "all is well" and a basis for members to describe the arrangement successfully to each other' (Cicourel, 1971: 150).

6 *Descriptive vocabularies are indexical expressions.* Garfinkel uses catalogues in libraries as an example of this reflexive feature of practical reasoning, in which the titles used to index the books are a part of the things described (books' titles). In the same way, vocabularies present in a setting are made up of links of actors' vocabularies. Vocabularies are an index of experiences and a constituent feature of the experiences described (actors' experiences). The significance of conversational or written indexical expressions requires some reference to the role of 'what everyone knows' in deciding the indexicality of the utterance or of some part of it.

> The significance of descriptive vocabularies as indexical expressions lies in their providing both members and researchers with 'instructions' for recovering or retrieving the 'full' relevance of an utterance; suggesting what anyone must presume or 'fill in' in order to capture the fidelity of a truncated or indexical expression whose sense requires a specification of common assumptions about context (the time or occasion of the expression, who the speaker was, where the utterance was made, and the like).
> (Cicourel, 1971: 151)

It can be suggested then that members are continually giving each other instructions such that members may be said to be programming each other's actions as the scene unfolds.

Common understandings, however, cannot possibly consist only of a measured amount of shared agreement among persons on certain topics. Garfinkel's well known colloquy, which he reports in *Studies in Ethnomethodology*, demonstrates this feature. Students were asked to report common conversations by writing on the left side of a sheet what the parties actually said and on the right side what they and their partners understood that they were talking about. Garfinkel gives the following example of a conversation between a husband and wife, with an interpretation of this text, which was written by the husband:

HUSBAND	*Dana succeeded in putting a penny in a parking meter today without being picked up.*	This afternoon as I was bringing Dana, our four-year-old son, home from the nursery school, he succeeded in reaching high enough to put a penny in a parking meter when we parked in a meter parking zone, whereas before he has always had to be picked up to reach that high.
WIFE	*Did you take him to the record store?*	Since he put a penny in a meter, that means that you stopped while he was with you. I know that you stopped at the record store either on the way to get him or on the way back. Was it on the way back, so that he was with you, or did you stop there on the way to get him and somewhere else on the way back?
HUSBAND	*No, to the shoe repair shop.*	No, I stopped at the record store on the way to get him and stopped at the shoe repair shop on the way home when he was with me.
WIFE	*What for?*	I know of one reason why you might have stopped at the shoe repair shop. Why did you in fact?
HUSBAND	*I got some new shoe laces for my shoes.*	As you will remember, I broke a shoelace on one of my brown oxfords the other day, so I stopped to get some new laces.
WIFE	*Your loafers need new heels badly.*	Something else you could have gotten that I was thinking of. You

> could have taken in your black
> loafers which need heels badly.
> You'd better get them taken care of
> pretty soon.

(Garfinkel, 1967: 25)

Garfinkel's analysis of this colloquy is that it reveals:

a   That there were many matters that the partners understood they were
    talking about that they did not mention.

b   Many matters that the partners understood were understood on the basis not
    only of what was actually said but what was left unspoken.

c   Many matters were understood through a process of attending to the
    temporal series of utterances as documentary evidence of a developing
    conversation rather than as a string of terms.

d   Matters that the two understood in common were understood only in and
    through a course of understanding work that consisted of treating an actual
    linguistic event as 'the document of', as 'pointing to', as standing on behalf
    of an underlying pattern of matters that each already supposed to be the
    matters that the person, by his speaking, could be telling the other about.
    The underlying pattern was not only derived from a course of individual
    documentary evidence but the documentary evidence was in turn
    interpreted on the basis of 'what was known' and anticipatorily knowable
    about the underlying patterns.[6]

e   In attending to the utterances as events-in-the-conversation, each party
    made reference to the biography and prospects of the present interaction
    that each used, and attributed to the other as a common scheme of
    interpretation and expression.

f   Each waited for something more to be said in order to hear what had
    previously been talked about, and each seemed willing to wait.

Thus the right-hand column in the colloquy could never, no matter how long it
was, convey all the background information as well as the way of speaking of
the left-hand column. What is missing (and what would always be missing) is
a description of the 'shared agreement' of the husband and wife about how
they will converse. Garfinkel goes on to observe that common understandings
would consist of a measured amount of shared agreement if they consisted of
events coordinated with events in standard time but his own example
demonstrates that this cannot be the case. Time, in the colloquy, is constitutive
of 'the matter talked about' as a developing and developed event, over the

course of action that produced it 'as both the process and product were known from within this development by both parties, each for himself as well as on behalf of the other' (Garfinkel, 1967: 26). All the information that conversationalists need in order to understand each other is not, then, located in the linguistic utterances exchanged between them. What the husband 'filled in' above is not all that he knows. Garfinkel set his students the additional task of filling in what the first filling in meant, and then the further task of filling in the circumstances of that filling in. 'The students despaired and gave up, and rightly so ... They had come to see that the incompleteness of symbols is irreparable. Every attempt at repair increases the number of symbols that needs to be repaired' (Mehan and Wood, 1975: 93). In everyday life we decide to 'let it pass' in the hope that we will understand it all later, or that it is not important or that no one will notice that we do not understand.

Garfinkel, Sacks and indexical expression

Ethnomethodology's central topic, as established by Garfinkel, is 'the rational accountability of practical actions as an ongoing, practical accomplishment' (1967: 4) and, as we have already indicated, the two notions central to this centrality are 'indexicality' and 'reflexivity'.

> Natural language serves persons doing sociology – whether they are laymen or professionals – as circumstances, as topics, and as resources of their inquiries (and this fact) furnishes to the technology of their inquiries and to their practical sociological reasoning *its* circumstances, *its* topics and its resources. That reflexivity is encountered by sociologists in the actual occasions of their inquiries as indexical properties of natural language. (Garfinkel and Sacks, 1970: 338)

Thus descriptions are a constituent feature of the circumstances they describe and therefore in indexing these features, they unavoidably and in endless ways, elaborate those circumstances and are elaborated by them. The task, as specified by Garfinkel, is 'the investigation of the rational properties of indexical expressions and other practical actions as contingent ongoing accomplishments of organized artful practices of everyday life' (1967: 11).

Indexical expressions are context bound, bound to the contexts in which they are employed and dependent upon these contexts for their rational accountability. They are 'tokens', characterizing their referent phenomena as specifically unique but they:

> name something not named by some replica of the word. Their denotation is relative to the speaker. Their use depends upon the relation of the user to the object with which the word is concerned ... Indexical expressions and statements concerning them are not freely repeatable; in a given discourse, not all their replicas therein are also translations of them. (Garfinkel, 1967: 4–5)

Garfinkel's treatment of indexical expressions owes much to the work of philosophers and linguists, as he makes clear, for example in the elegant paper which he wrote with Harvey Sacks 'On Formal Structures of Practical Actions' (Garfinkel and Sacks, 1970). Garfinkel and Sacks propose that all science is motivated by attempts to remedy indexical expressions because although indexical expressions are of enormous utility 'logicians and linguists encounter these expressions as obstinate nuisances' (1970: 349). The concern of any methodological study (lay or professional) comes from the concern to remedy indexical expressions and substitute objective expressions.

> In these programmatic studies of the formal properties of natural languages, and practical reasoning, the properties of indexicals, while furnishing investigators with motivating occasions for remedial actions, remain obstinately unavoidable and irremediable. (1970: 349)

The concern with such 'methods' is not of course limited to the sciences. Conversationalists are concerned with faults of natural language and with remedying shortcomings in the properties of indexical expression by referring them to their setting (the 'decisive relevance of context') and with establishing what was 'really meant'. The lay member is as concerned with 'reconstructed logic' as is the professional researcher, in other words, lay members' accounts of 'what really happened', for example after they have left the scene, are attempts to understand 'what really happened'. This 'reconstructed logic' is concerned with assigning meaning retrospectively and can be contrasted with the 'logic-in-use' which the member invokes during on-going interaction, in order both to assign meaning to the situation and therefore to act accordingly (for further discussion of this distinction see Kaplan, 1964). Reconstructed logic is as much the province of the lay conversationalist as of the professional sociologist.

Reconstructed logic, then, exhibits a concern to clarify talk in the interests of inquiry and such inquiries that make use of or are about members' talk, are not 'done' solely by 'professional' inquirers but by all conversationalists doing the inquiring that all conversation requires. The features of conversations that inquiry centres on are 'indexical expressions' (see Garfinkel and Sacks, 1970: 347). A list of such terms would start with 'here, now, this, that, it, I, he, you, there, then, soon, today, tomorrow' and such terms are regularly treated as occasions for reparative practices, for example by saying who 'I' am, where 'here' is, when 'today' is, by all persons concerned with doing research into talk, i.e. by 'everyone' (Garfinkel and Sacks, 1970: 347).

The sociologist finds the awkwardness of indexical expressions especially problematic, for the activities of sociologists involve the organization of social phenomena into types or classes and the positing of hypotheses about them in an attempt to account for the everyday social activities of members with objective expressions. However everyday activities are already accounted for 'in everyday ways and for all practical purposes (of members undertaking them), by members who use indexical expressions to do so' (Filmer, 1976:72).

It is in this sense that sociological accounts are second order constructs (see Schutz, 1962) of the constructs used by members (actors in the social scene). For Garfinkel argues that:

> The notion of member is the heart of the matter. We do not use the term to refer to a person. It refers instead to mastery of natural language, which we understand in the following way. We offer the observation that persons, because of the fact that they are heard to be speaking a natural language, somehow are heard to be engaged in the objective production and objective display of common-sense knowledge of everyday activities as observable and reportable phenomena. (Garfinkel and Sacks, 1970: 342)

Formal sociological discourse may be seen therefore as the accounting practices of professional sociologists in which they re-account for members' indexically expressed accounts so as to afford them common properties and deprive them of their specific uniqueness. 'These common properties are not intrinsic to the activities themselves, but are given to them as a necessary feature of their constitution as social phenomena (the 'natural' phenomena of the 'science' of society)' (Filmer, 1976: 73). The substitutability of members' indexical expressions with 'scientific' objective expressions is, Garfinkel argues, unsatisfied and programmatic, for two clear reasons. Firstly, that members' practical actions have no known objective character: '*wherever practical actions are topics of study* the promised distinction and substitutability of objective for indexical expressions remains programmatic in every *particular* case and in every *actual* occasion in which the distinction must be demonstrated' (1967: 6). Thus, unsatisfied and programmatic substitutability is an unavoidable feature of *all* accounts of practical social actions, whether lay or professional, and in accounting for their actions both lay and professional sociologists are constituting those activities as rational and reportable and are thus rendering social life as a coherent and comprehensible reality (which points to the constructed and accomplished character of all realities).

The second reason Garfinkel advances is that the substitutability of objective for indexical expressions may now be demonstrated as unnecessary, except as the self-contained and self-sustaining professional work of sociological inquirers. For if members' everyday accounts render practical actions observably rational and reportable for *all* practical purposes, including the purposes of formal sociological discourse, then considerations follow. Firstly members' accounts of practical actions would seem to demonstrate that they are already able to effect adequate substitutions of objective for indexical expressions. Secondly, 'indexical expressions have their own rational, ordering properties which are demonstrated on every occasion that members use them to collect, organize and account for apparently as-yet-unordered practical actions as coherent, ordered, comprehensive social realities' (Filmer, 1976: 74). And thus, thirdly, the professional work of sociological inquirers whose central task has usually been the repair of indexical expressions (which collections of practices Garfinkel characterizes as 'constructive analysis') can be contrasted with the ethnomethodological analyses, which now provide an alternative to those practices. Ethnomethodological studies have shown, Garfinkel argues, in demonstrable specifics

1 that the properties of indexical expressions are socially organized and accomplished properties, and
2 that they are ordered properties is an ongoing, practical accomplishment of every actual occasion of commonplace speech and conduct.

The alternative to the central task of constructive analysis is, then, to describe the accomplishments of members as practices of common-sense knowledge of social structures of everyday activities, practical circumstances, practical activities and practical sociological reasoning, through a description of members' mastery of natural language.

The notion that talk indexes more than that talk can ever say, no matter in how elaborate a manner it is constituted, that indexical expressions in natural language include the shared agreements or common understandings by and through which that talk is reproduced and which that talk reproduces, can be taken further by an examination of Garfinkel's use of 'gloss'. Garfinkel notes that, as accountable phenomena are practical accomplishments, they require 'work' to be done by members and this work consists of 'asscmblagcs of practices whereby speakers in the situated particulars of speech mean something different from what they can say in just so many words, that is, (of) "glossing practices"' (Garfinkel and Sacks, 1970: 342). These glossing practices exist in empirical multitude.

> In endless, but particular, analyzable ways glossing practices *are* methods for producing observable-reportable understanding, with, in and of natural language. As a multitude of ways for exhibiting-*in*-speaking and exhibiting-*for*-the-telling that and how speaking is understood, glossing practices *are* 'members', *are* 'mastery of natural language', *are* 'talking reasonably', *are* 'plain speech', *are* 'speaking English' (or French or whatever), *are* 'clear, consistent, cogent, rational speech'. (Garfinkel and Sacks, 1970: 343–4)

Additionally, glossing practices consist not only of the substantive sense or meaning of what is being said but also the means whereby that substance may be made available. For Garfinkel and Sacks understand

> mastery of natural language to consist in this. In the particulars of his speech, a speaker, in concert with others, is able to gloss those particulars and is thereby meaning something different than he can say in so many words; he is doing so over unknown contingencies in the actual occasions of interaction, and in so doing, the recognition *that* he is speaking and *how* he is speaking are specifically not matters for competent remarks. That is to say, the particulars of his speaking do not provide occasions for stories about his speaking that are

worth telling, nor do they elicit questions that are worth asking and so on. (1970: 344)

The idea of 'meaning differently than one can say in so many words' carries the implication, which Garfinkel and Sacks make explicit, that

> whatever (one) says provides the very materials to be used in *making out* what (one) says. However extensive or explicit what a speaker says may be, it does not by its extensiveness or explicitness pose a task of deciding the correspondence between what (one) says and what (one) means that is resolved by citing (one's) talk verbatim. (1970: 344)

The reflexivity of talk provides that a member's '*talk itself*', in that it becomes a part of the selfsame occasion of interaction, becomes another contingency of that interaction. It extends and elaborates indefinitely the circumstances it glosses and in this way contributes to its own accountably sensible character. 'The thing that is said assures to speaking's accountable sensible character its variable fortunes' (Garfinkel and Sacks, 1970: 344–5). Garfinkel and Sacks summarize their discussion of glossing by stating that 'the mastery of natural language is throughout and without relief an occasioned accomplishment' (1970: 345).

Ethnomethodologists examine the production of talk and not the objects reported by talk and in so doing they try to treat talk as a topic and not as a resource (Garfinkel, 1967: 1–4). Taking the ordinary language notion that activities are done in and by the talk that speakers and hearers use a stage further, ethnomethodologists argue that 'a *reality* is done in and by the use of social knowledge' (Mehan and Wood, 1975: 118, emphasis added).

The emphasis on 'naturally occurring talk' does not mean that only spontaneous conversations can be analysed. Talk does not vary in how far it creates a reality, although it may vary in how far it is constrained or in how far turns, or length of turns, in talking are 'pre-allocated' (Sacks et al., 1974: 729–31) or in many other complex ways. It is not that some situations are more 'natural' than others but that talk itself is a phenomenon for study, and that what people do with their language and how they do what they do with language is at the centre of analysis, that is important in the ethnomethodological emphasis on naturally occurring talk.

Sacks and conversation analysis

Conversational analysis was extensively developed and articulated by the lucid accomplishments of the remarkable Harvey Sacks. His work was, and still is, despite his death in a car crash in 1975, highly influential in shaping a field which has produced a substantial amount of impressive work (see Sacks, 1964–1972, 1972, 1975, 1992; Garfinkel and Sacks, 1970; Sacks, Schegloff and Jefferson, 1974; Schenkein, 1978; Atkinson and Heritage, 1984; Drew and

Heritage, 1992; Boden and Zimmerman, 1991; Boden, 1994; Schegloff, 1997; Silverman, 2000).

The research into naturally occurring social action and interaction from a conversation analytic perspective was initially conveyed in Sacks' privately circulated lectures (Sacks, 1964–1972) and then 'developed into a distinctive research literature in association with his collaborators, Emanuel Schegloff and Gail Jefferson' (Heritage and Atkinson, 1984: 1). Even in the manner of its dissemination the work of Sacks was remarkable. In an important volume collecting conversational analytic writing, the editors point out that: 'more than half the contributors learned about and became committed to conversational analysis at a distance of six thousand miles from the University of California campuses where Sacks and his colleagues were based' (Atkinson and Heritage, 1984: 411).[7]

Sacks did his graduate studies with Goffman and Garfinkel and so it was not surprising that he became concerned with studying naturally organized everyday activities. What was extraordinary was not just that he extended their work in elaborately detailed and technical ways but that he did so 'in such a way that it could be learned, applied, and expanded on by others' (Atkinson and Heritage, 1984: 412). Subsequent work has tended to become more detailed and more technical but without losing sight of the research tradition of conversational analysis, expressed so well in this extract from a transcribed lecture by Sacks:

> Whatever you may think about what it is to be an ordinary person in the world, an initial shift is not to think of 'an ordinary person' as some person, but as somebody having as one's job, as one's constant preoccupation, doing 'being ordinary'. It is not that somebody is ordinary; it is perhaps that is what one's business is, and it takes work, as any other business does. (1984: 414)

Ethnomethodology and conversation analysis can, Silverman observes, in an important recent evaluation, 'properly claim to be the major contemporary social science traditions oriented to ... the aesthetics of the mundane' (2000: 138). However, Silverman rightly points out, the impact of these traditions on organization theory has been disappointing: 'the dialogue has not been helped by Garfinkel's daunting prose or by misunderstandings of ethnomethodology by some writers on organizations' (2000: 141).[8]

The detailed work of conversational analysis offers the opportunity to renegotiate the relevance of ethnomethodological concerns with patterns of communicative behaviour for organization theory and practice. Boden (1994) shows that ethnomethodology shares with some organization theory and much contemporary organization practice, a focus on everyday skills and competencies.

In his standard text on Harold Garfinkel, which, often successfully, attempts to 'remedy' the problems of Garfinkel's prose, Heritage confirms this focus on skills and competencies: 'conversation analysis – like the other research streams of ethnomethodology – is concerned with the analysis of the *competencies* which underlie ordinary social activities' (1984: 241). He shows how conversation analysis offers a method for identifying such competencies (1984: 241–4). The approach involves three fundamental assumptions:

1 *Interaction is structurally organized.* Like all aspects of social action and interaction, talk exhibits stable, organized patterns, demonstrably oriented to by the participants. These patterns 'stand independently of the psychological or other characteristics of particular speakers' (Heritage, 1984: 241). Thus, it is 'difficult, if not impossible, to explain specific features of ... interaction by reference to social attributes (e.g. status, power, gender, ethnicity, etc.)' or psychological characteristics of particular speakers 'without a clear knowledge of what is characteristic of ordinary talk between peers' (Heritage, 1984: 240).

2 *Contributions to interaction are contextually and sequentially oriented.* In understanding the construction of social reality through language in action, it is always necessary to examine the local activities by which speakers assemble the 'here and now' meaning of their talk. So, whilst we rule out analysts' speculations about mental phenomena like 'minds', 'intentions' and 'motives', we are required to demonstrate an attention to how members attend to these and other matters. Talk is both '*context-shaped*' and '*context-renewing*'. Heritage observes that: 'a speaker's action is *context-shaped* in that its contribution to an on-going sequence of actions cannot adequately be understood except by reference to its context – including, especially, the immediately preceding configuration of actions – in which it participates' (Heritage, 1984: 242). A speaker's action is *context-renewing* because all conversational activity is context shaped. 'Since every "current" action will itself form the immediate context for some "next" action in a sequence, it will inevitably contribute to the framework in terms of which the next action will be understood' (Heritage, 1984: 242). So this context is addressed by conversational analysis largely in terms of the preceding sequence of talk: 'in this sense, the context of a next action is repeatedly renewed with every current action' (Heritage, 1984: 242).

3 *No order of detail can be dismissed and thus analysis must be empirically grounded.* These two properties can only be found in the details of interaction and therefore need to be identified in precise analyses of detailed transcripts. 'No order of detail can be dismissed *a priori*, as disorderly, accidental or irrelevant' (Heritage, 1984: 241). It is therefore necessary to: replace 'premature theory-construction' with 'a more strongly empirical approach to the study of social action'; and to avoid the idealization of research materials by focusing on the meaning which data has for the participants, rather than the meaning which the analyst imputes to it.

Heritage observes that the research objectives of conversational analysis, together with these assumptions, results in the following attitudes to analysis:

> Specifically, analysis is strongly 'data-driven' – developed from phenomena which are in various ways evidenced in the data of interaction. Correspondingly, there is a strong bias against *a priori* speculation about the orientations and motives of speakers and in favour of detailed examination of conversationalists' actual actions. Thus the empirical conduct of speakers is treated as the central resource out of which analysis may develop. (Heritage, 1984: 243)

Heritage adds that this means that it must be demonstrated that the regularities described 'are produced and oriented to by the participants as normatively oriented-to grounds for inference and action' (Heritage, 1984: 244). This requires the regular identification and analysis of deviant cases, in which such regularities are absent.

Conversation analysis and critical discourse

Ethnomethodology and conversational analysis demand and demonstrate cautious theorizing based upon participants' own theory work or practical reasoning, what Silverman calls 'a bottom-up approach' (2000: 139). In this respect they are similar to work which often identifies itself as being in the postmodernist vein (critical discourse and/or post-structuralist and/or social postmodernist analysis) but with a significant difference. As has already been indicated, conversation analysis requires scrupulous attention to the *data*, rather than the terms in which it is to be understood by the analyst. Schegloff (1997) carefully dissected, from a conversation analytic perspective, this aspect of the relationship between ethnomethodological/conversational analytical and critical discourse analysis approaches to *talk-in-interaction*. He argues for the conventional conversational analysis rubric that analysts should not impose their own categories (second order constructs) onto participants' discourse, but should focus only on the categories used by participants (first order constructs). He identified that for conversation analysis (what he called here, 'formal analysis'):

> [the] understandings *of the participants* [are crucial and are...] *internal* to the act of analysis itself. It is the product of the organization of practices of conversation itself, whose consequence is that contributors display their speaker's understandings of what has preceded. ... And if that is not what *critical* discourse analysis is to address itself to – discursive events in their import for their participants, then I'm not sure what it is about and what is to be hoped for from it. If it is what critical discourse analysis is to address itself to, then critical analysis and formal analysis are not competitors or alternatives. (Schegloff, 1997: 184)

That critical discourse analysis and conversation analysis are often alternatives can be seen in the contribution of Wetherell to this debate. In 1998 she took Schegloff's (1997) comments on critical discourse analysis and, coming from this tradition herself, unusually then presented what she termed 'post-structuralist' ('social postmodernist') interpretations of real data. She claims to 'develop a critique of both post-structuralist writers on discourse and (of) Schegloff's methodological prescriptions for analysts' (1998: 404). She agrees that conversation analysis provides a necessary useful discipline for critical discourse analysis but that, on its own, it is not sufficient. 'Conversation analysis alone does not offer an adequate answer to its own classic question about some piece of discourse – why this utterance here? Rather, a complete or scholarly analysis (as opposed to a technical analysis) must range further than the limits Schegloff proposes' (1998: 388). She summarizes her view of the difficulties with both positions:

> If the problem with post-structuralist analysts is that they rarely focus on actual social interaction, then the problem with conversational analysts is that they rarely raise their eyes from the next turn in the conversation ... (1998: 402)

Wetherell, in order to 'range further', wants to and does use further analytic categories than those used by the participants in her piece of talk. She finds, for example, 'interpretative repertoires' around 'male sexuality as performance and achievement, a repertoire around alcohol and disinhibition, and an ethics of sexuality as legitimated by relationships and reciprocity' (1998: 400).

Schegloff (1998), in his reply to Wetherell points out that these categories might or might not be of interest to conversation analysis, but only if they were 'observable features of the participants' talk and conduct' (Schegloff, 1998: 414). 'Why that now?' as a question first appeared in Schegloff and Sacks (1973) paper 'Opening up Closings' where it was of interest only if it was of interest to participants: 'The key point, however, is that the 'why that now?' question is in the first instance the *members*' question' (Schegloff, 1998: 414). Schegloff observes that the conversational analysis question is a second order question, but that it is 'prompted by, made relevant by, and grounded in the parties' conduct in each case' (1998: 414).

For Schegloff the data presented by Wetherell are an advantage because they allow her to exhibit the kinds of questions that are being asked of it, some of which are similar to those asked in conversation analysis. However, for him, the data have one serious flaw: they appear to be 'researcher-prompted'. An extract from Wetherell provides evidence for this:

> In Extract Eight, Nigel, *as interviewer* then attempts, in a complex discursive act, to repair a potential misreading of his earlier question in line 76: 'is that good?' His question leads to further formulations of Aaron's position:

Extract Eight

| 94 | Nigel: | =Yeah I mean I wasn't sort of saying is four in two days |
| 95 | | good I mean it's <u>impressive</u>   [you know] |

96	Aaron:	[hh[hhh] hh
97	Phil:	[hhhhh] hhhh
98	Nigel:	But I me::an like (.) it presumes that erm that's:: a
99		creditable thing (.) yeah? Is it?

(Wetherell, 1998: 397, emphasis added)[9]

Schegloff says that 'these are not just ordinary "conversations" among "members of the community"' but a series of interviews, with 'Nigel' the interviewer appearing in the text, apparently as a 'participant'. Who asks the questions, who answers them and what is understood by the asking and answering are central features of this, and of all similar, occasions. 'Yet what is most striking is the virtually total lack of attention to Nigel and his actions in this analysis ... he hardly appears in the analysis at all, and therefore does not enter into the analysis of the boys' talk' (Schegloff, 1998: 415).

Schegloff confirms what we have already demonstrated; that it is the attention paid to the *member's questions* rather than *analyst's questions* that distinguishes ethnomethodology and conversation analysis from this *soi-disant* postmodernist account of discourse.[10] Rather than begin with a concept such as 'gender ideologies' the analyst should begin by addressing what the participants understand themselves to be doing:

> For CA (conversation analysis), it is the member's world, the world of the particular members in a particular occasion, a world that is embodied and displayed in their conduct with one another, which is the grounds and object of the entire exercise, its *sine qua non*. (Schegloff, 1998: 416)

Ironically, as Linstead (1993) argues, it is the close reading of texts which gives Derrida's deconstruction its power. His oft-quoted argument that 'there is nothing outside the text' is subject to multiple readings, as one would expect, but one of those is that there is nothing that we understand that is not to some degree textual. If social life is to be treated as a text to be deconstructed, then the data generated by social investigation surely merit exactly the sort of close attention that Derrida gives to the literary and philosophical texts that he deconstructs – that is, they are deconstructed on and in their own terms. Thus styles of postmodernism and post-structuralism that are debased, such as what Linstead terms 'vulgar deconstruction', drift away both from ethnomethodology and the more rigorous varieties of the postmodernism whose name they appropriate.

Conclusion

Typically research into language and social processes relies on finding strategies which minimize the role of subjectivity by standardizing the interpretations which researchers attribute to data perceived by their senses – for example by devising 'systems' for coding behaviours observed in a classroom.[11] A coding scheme and framework for interpreting observed behaviours can be developed such that 'anyone' with some understanding of and training in the scheme will interpret the behaviours in approximately the 'same' way. This is seen as guaranteeing 'objectivity'.

Our argument here is that such 'objective' accounts are as much glosses over the context of talk, no more and no less, as any other accounts produced by members of society. In other words, sociological accounts are as much embedded or essentially reflexive accounts as are those of lay members, they are reconstructed logics, rather than logics-in-use. They provide a framework for interpreting and coding behaviour, which is based on an arbitrary selection of one meaning system rather than any of the many other meaning systems available. Social action is characterized by the evolution and development of meaning over the course of interaction through the sense of reality and order which language conveys to *all* members of society. The extent to which talk is still abstracted from the context in which it is placed by those investigating language use within society suggests that the interpretive structuring of the world as we experience it, could still be characterized as the 'neglected situation' (Goffman, 1972), at least in so far as the mass of research is concerned.

We have argued that the diversity of behaviour resists distillation into formulae or fixed meanings and categories, whether teachers, students or social researchers employ those categories. Ethnomethodological and postmodern views on social life emphasize notions of 'process' or 'becoming' as compared to notions of 'structure' or 'system'. Human behaviour is a social process and what is of interest are the things that happen 'in between' the categories which we use to describe the world. The idea of isolating language as a part of social life and classifying it further with categories based on the categories which social actors already use is in direct contradiction to the attempt to study social life in its natural setting. Language can only be understood, described and explained if the social situations within which speech takes place and which give it meaning are known and if this social context is preserved intact in the analysis.

Ethnomethodology and postmodernism share concerns with undermining the given, with deconstructing the taken-for-granted, in showing the pretence that lies behind notions that ideas can exist apart from language. Czarniawska says that 'it is an attitude of the observer who sees the paradoxicality of life and yet, as an actor, bravely engages in daily efforts to *deparadoxify* ... with not too many expectations of predictable results and lasting consequences, and the acceptance of the inevitability of unexpected consequences' (Czarniawska, 1999: 27). Mehan and Wood's vibrant ethnomethodological text in 1975 described, in a way which seems to anticipate the postmodernism of a decade later, the stratifying speech practices of alienated scholarly and scientific authors. 'Such authors distinguish their analysis from the analyses of those they speak about. They claim that their own speech is deauthored, and thus objective. Those they speak about are claimed to be subjective' (Mehan and Wood, 1975: 220). This ironic stance on social construction is complemented, however, by the ethnomethodological focus on the data which provides a special illumination sometimes lacking in so-called postmodernist or critical discourse analysis and which is of great value to the organization theorist. Here again, ethnomethodology is closer to the sources of postmodernism than their more popular applications.

David Silverman can provide us with a fitting way to conclude. He was one of the first organizational analysts to present a coherent view of the subjective approach to the analysis of organizations (Silverman, 1970), one of the first of the British ethnomethodologists (Filmer et al., 1972), and one of the first to explore what has now become recognized as a postmodern approach to organizations (Silverman and Torode, 1980). In an impressive recent chapter he argues for 'a clarity of expression and a focus on the aesthetics of the micro-order'. He goes on to 'show how the latter is found in ethnomethodology and conversation analysis and explain how these traditions link up with the focus of some organization theorists upon skills and practices' (Silverman, 2000: 131). He observes that:

> ... ethnomethodology shocks us by pointing to the logical impossibility and yet the routine achievement of a stable, ordered world. Somehow, through methods that await explication, the world-known-in-common is viewed anew as an amazing practical accomplishment. (Silverman, 2000: 131)

This concern with the impossibly magical yet intensely mundane practical construction of social reality through and by language, and therefore with the similarly astonishing practical achievements of social actors is surely ethnomethodology's lasting contribution to the investigation of everyday life. Of course the incompleteness of symbols is not repairable, and so there will remain a gap, the gap that Foucault described between *saying* and *seeing*: 'it is in vain that we say what we see; what we see never resides in what we say' (Foucault, 1970: 9).

Nevertheless, an ethnomethodology which has rediscovered irony, humility and self-reflection, under the influence of a rigorous yet playfully serious postmodernism, provides considerable richness for the organizational analyst concerned to identify locally organized phenomena as a basis for understanding the language, and therefore the social construction, of organizations.

Notes

1   By the mid 1970s the *hermeneutic-dialectical* tradition was represented by some phenomenologists and existentialists (see Manning, 1973), by the Frankfurt School (see Kellner, 1978), by philosophers such as Wittgenstein, and by radical and critical theorists such as Feyerabend, Merleau-Ponty and Habermas.

2   Mehan and Wood, in a footnote, admit that they are rather caricaturing both traditions, and by implication their reaction to ethnomethodology, but that they do

so, not to describe but 'to illuminate the very possibility of description' (1975: 224). We may think that this is a cop-out, but so it goes.

3   Barthes places *text* in capitals when referring to this fundamental form of written discourse, but does not when referring to any particular instance(s) of the form.

4   Douglas (1971: 33–4) compares *situational ethnomethodologists*, who focus on context, meaning and interaction, with *linguistic ethnomethodologists*, who focus on talk and conversation.

5   Likewise there are also three criticisms which are made of both ethnomethodology and postmodernism: that they are ahistorical, neglect power and are morally neutral. Our view is that these criticisms are mistaken, but that is as far as we shall go here.

6   Garfinkel takes the notion of the 'documentary method of interpretation' from Mannheim, 1952: 33–83.

7   There are many ironies in this of course. One of the most delicate is that most of Sacks' analytical work on talk was done by *talking*, and then communicated by dedicated students recording and transcribing what they believe *he actually said*, but without using the notation system that the same students had developed for transcribing conversational data.

8   Interestingly, Silverman correctly observes, even those sympathetic to ethnomethodology appear to misunderstand it. Hassard, for example (1993: 98) claims to have completed an 'ethnomethodological' analysis of Fire Service work, based on data obtained from open-ended interviews, rather than from naturally occurring talk. This, Silverman observes, 'is more appropriate to a romanticist project' (Silverman, 2000: 149).

Silverman points out that all the claims of investigators to be doing ethnomethodology need to be demonstrated. 'To demonstrate them, ethnomethodologists would argue that we need detailed studies of everyday interaction to give us a baseline and transcripts of talk in "organizational" settings to show us continuities and departures from this baseline' (see Schegloff, 1991, 1992). Thus the specific contribution of ethnomethodology is not to romantic versions of the actor but to the detailed study of organizational practices (Silverman, 2000: endnote). For some further implications of this see the discussion later in this chapter of the debate between Wetherell and Schegloff.

9   The extract continues until line 115, and the whole transcript, of 176 lines, is provided by Wetherell as an appendix. The transcription notation system is also provided by both Wetherell and Schegloff and in both cases, as in all conversation analysis, is based on the exemplary and dedicated work of Gail Jefferson.

10 This is partly because Wetherell adopts an approach within postmodernism which seems more influenced by socio-linguistics rather than anthropology. Hence she is less concerned with the ethnomethodology of the other, with the nature of otherness and with the writing of the other through language (see Linstead, 1993).

11 In contrast, for two important examples of ethnomethodological classroom analysis see Mehan, 1974, and McHoul, 1978, and for an important insight into the possibilities of such a view in schools see Mehan, 1978.

References

Atkinson, J.M. and Heritage, J. (eds) (1984) *Structures of Social Action: Studies in Conversational Analysis.* Cambridge: Cambridge University Press.

Bar-Hillel, Y. (1954) 'Indexical expressions', *Mind*, 63: 359–79.

Barthes, R. (1977) *Image-Music-Text*, trans. Stephen Heath. London: Fontana Collins.

Barthes, R. (1981) 'The theory of the text', in R. Young (ed.), *Untying the Text*. London: Routledge and Kegan Paul. pp. 31–47.

Boden, D. (1994) *The Business of Talk: Organizations in Action*. Cambridge: Polity Press.

Boden, D. and Zimmerman, D. (eds) (1991) *Talk and Social Structure: Studies in Ethnomethodology and Conversation Analysis*. Cambridge: Polity Press.

Cicourel, A.V. (1971) 'The acquisition of social structure: toward a developmental sociology of language and meaning', in J.D. Douglas (ed.), *Understanding Everyday Life*. London: Routledge. pp. 136–68.

Czarniawska, B. (1999) 'Management she wrote', *Studies in Cultures, Organizations and Societies*, 5 (1): 13–41.

Derrida, J. (1978) *Writing and Difference*. London: Routledge and Kegan Paul.

Douglas, J.D. (ed.) (1971) *Understanding Everyday Life*. London: Routledge.

Drew, P. and Heritage, J. (eds) (1992) *Talk at Work*. Cambridge: Cambridge University Press.

Filmer, P. (1976) 'Garfinkel's gloss', *Writing Sociology*, 1, October: 69–83.

Filmer, P., Phillipson, M., Roche, M., Sandywell, B. and Silverman, D. (1972) *New Directions in Sociological Theory*. London: Collier-Macmillan.

Foucault, M. (1970) *The Order of Things*. London: Tavistock.

Garfinkel, H. (1967) *Studies in Ethnomethodology*. Englewood-Cliffs, NJ: Prentice-Hall.

Garfinkel, H. (1972) 'Studies of the routine grounds of everyday activities', in D. Sudnow (ed.), *Studies in Social Interaction*. New York: Free Press. pp. 1–30.

Garfinkel, H. and Sacks, H. (1970) 'On formal structures of practical actions', in J. McKinney and H. Tiryakian, *Theoretical Sociology*. New York: Appleton-Century Crofts. pp. 337–566.

Goffman, E. (1963) *Behavior in Public Places*. New York: Free Press.

Goffman, E. (1972) 'The neglected situation', in P. Giglioli (ed.), *Language and Social Context*. Harmondsworth: Penguin. (Journal article, originally published in 1964).

Hassard, J. (1993) *Sociology and Organization Theory: Positivism, Paradigms and Postmodernity*. Cambridge: Cambridge University Press.

Heritage, J. (1984) *Garfinkel and Ethnomethodology*. Cambridge: Polity Press.

Heritage, J. and Atkinson, J.M. (1984) 'Introduction', in J.M. Atkinson and J. Heritage (eds), *Structures of Social Action: Studies in Conversation Analysis*. Cambridge: Cambridge University Press. pp. 1–20.

Kaplan, A. (1964) *The Conduct of Inquiry*. San Francisco: Chandler.

Kellner, H. (1978) 'On the cognitive significance of the system of language, in communication', in T. Luckmann (ed.), *Phenomenology and Sociology*. Harmondsworth: Penguin. pp. 324–542.

Lakoff, G. and Johnson, M. (1980) *Metaphors We Live By*. Chicago: University of Chicago Press.

Linstead, S. (1993) 'From postmodern anthropology to deconstructive ethnography', *Human Relations*, 46 (1): 97–120.

Linstead, S. and Grafton-Small, R. (1992) 'On reading organizational culture', *Organizational Studies*, 13 (3): 331–55.

McHoul, A. (1978) 'The organization of turns at formal talk in the classroom', *Language in Society*, 7: 183–213.

Mannheim, K. (1952) *Essays on the Sociology of Knowledge*. London: Routledge.

Manning, P.K. (1973) 'Existential Sociology', *Sociological Quarterly*, 12 (2): 200–25.

Mehan, H. (1974) 'Accomplishing classroom lessons', in A.V. Cicourel, K. Jennings, S. Jennings, K. Leiter, R. MacKay, H. Mehan and D. Roth, *Language Use and School Performance*. New York: Academic Press. pp. 76–142.

Mehan, H. (1978) 'Structuring school structure', *The Harvard Educational Review*, 48 (1), February: 311–38.

Mehan, H. and Wood, H. (1975) *The Reality of Ethnomethodology*. New York: Wiley.

Miller, J.H. (1971) 'Introduction' in Charles Dickens, *Bleak House*, ed. Norman Page. London: Penguin. pp. 11–34.

Morgan, G. (1986) *Images of Organization*. Beverly Hills, CA: Sage.

Rogers, M.F. (1984) 'Everyday life as text', in R. Collins (ed.), *Sociological Theory*. San Francisco: Jossey-Bass. pp. 165–86.

Sacks, H. (1964–1972) Unpublished transcribed lectures. University of California, Irvine. (Transcribed and indexed by G. Jefferson.) Part published as Sacks (1992), below.

Sacks, H. (1972) 'An initial investigation of the usability of conversational data for doing sociology', in D. Sudnow (ed.), *Studies in Social Interaction*. New York: Free Press. pp. 31–74.

Sacks, H. (1975) 'Everyone has to lie', in B. Blount and M. Sanches (eds), *Sociocultural Dimensions of Language Use*. New York: Academic Press.

Sacks, H. (1984) 'On doing being ordinary', in J.M. Atkinson and J. Heritage (eds), *Structures of Social Action: Studies in Conversational Analysis*. Cambridge: Cambridge University Press. pp. 413–29.

Sacks, H. (1992) *Lectures on Conversation*, ed. Gail Jefferson, with an Introduction by Emmanuel Schegloff. Oxford: Blackwell. 2 volumes.

Sacks, H., Schegloff, E. and Jefferson, G. (1974) 'A simplest systematics for the organization of turn-taking for conversation', *Language*, 50 (4): 696–755.

Schegloff, E.A. (1991) 'Reflections on talk and social structure', in D. Boden and D. Zimmerman (eds), *Talk and Social Structure: Studies in Ethnomethodology and Conversation Analysis*. Cambridge: Polity Press. pp. 44–70.

Schegloff, E.A. (1992) 'On talk and its institutional occasions', in P. Drew and J. Heritage (eds), *Talk at Work*. Cambridge: Cambridge University Press. pp. 101–36.

Schegloff, E.A. (1997) 'Whose text? Whose context?', *Discourse and Society*, 8 (2): 165–87.

Schegloff, E.A. (1998) 'Reply to Wetherell', *Discourse and Society*, 9 (3): 413–16.

Schegloff, E.A. and Sacks, H. (1973) 'Opening up closings', *Semiotica*, 8 (4): 289–327.

Schenkein, J.N. (1978) *Studies in the Organization of Conversational Interaction*. New York: Academic Press.

Schutz, A. (1953) 'Common-sense and scientific interpretation of human action', *Philosophy and Phenomenological Research*, 14 (1): 1–37.

Schutz, A. (1955) 'Symbol, reality and society', in L. Bryson, L. Finkelstein, H. Hoagland and R.M. MacIver (eds), *Symbols and Society*. New York: Harper. pp. 135–203.

Schutz, A. (1962) *Collected Papers, Volume 1*. The Hague: Nijhoff.

Silverman, D. (1970) *The Theory of Organizations*. London: Heinemann.

Silverman, D. (2000) 'Routine pleasures: the aesthetics of the mundane', in S. Linstead and H. Hopfl (eds), *The Aesthetics of Organization*. London: Sage. pp. 130–53.

Silverman, D. and Torode, B. (1980) *The Material World: Some Theories of Language and its Limits*. London: Routledge & Kegan Paul.

Wetherell, M. (1998) 'Positioning and interpretative repertoires: conversation analysis and post-structuralism in dialogue', *Discourse and Society*, 9 (3): 387–412.

3
Language that Organizes: Plans and Lists

Ian Lennie

Language, it might be agreed, is central to organization, but how exactly does language organize? For some postmodern accounts such as Chia (1996: 217, see also Chia and King in Chapter 13, this volume), language *is* organization. The organizational impulse, he claims, 'is traceable to the logical structuring of language and, more specifically, to a logic of "writing" understood as material marks punctuating space-time'. Chia, of course, is here following Derrida (1976) for whom the term 'writing' encompasses not only the more commonly used sense of the term, but that act of framing, spacing, cutting off and representing that is the very condition of language itself. Organization, for Chia, is a writing, and the failure of organization studies to understand this has constantly diverted attention 'away from the conditions of production of truth claims to the consequences of such claims' (Chia, 1996: 3). Chia calls for a shifting of organizational analysis 'upstream' to come to terms with the linguistic basis of its representations.

In some ways I would like to think of this chapter as responding to the challenge of Chia's book, the cogency and lucidity of whose arguments organization studies can only ignore at its peril. At the same time I think that posing 'writing' at this level of generality can blur the specific ways in which we actually experience and embody different writing, and become organized or disorganized in the process. I want to explore these differences in experience through that linguistic activity of organization par excellence – planning. To assist in this exploration I shall be using interview material from a study of 50 managers of community based health services, non-government agencies and academic departments in Australia and New Zealand, as well as reflection on my own practice.

Planning and ambivalence

'Planning' evokes a surprising range of responses from managers.[1] For manager EL, for instance, the mere mention of planning elicits vehement rejection:

> No. You can't. That's all shit. You spend all your energy serving the plan.

For this manager, a plan creates disorder: it is 'shit'. A plan draws away energy from freedom to manage as he sees fit.

Manager DM, on the other hand, finds planning essential:

> I do think you need a well documented (business plan) ... to say this is where you're going, because it gives people direction. It stops them feeling that they've got this sort of vacant, open void.

For DM, in a spatial metaphor that I shall be exploring further, a plan makes an otherwise formless void navigable. In doing so it stops people feeling that they are that void. A plan, in giving direction, confers shape and substance on the world, including those it directs.

A third manager, LR, is neither so enthusiastic as DM nor so dismissive as EL. She uses planning to get 'outside' the day-to-day flow of events:

> When I presented today that we achieved 70% of the actual plan, that's extra activities. It's not the day-to-day stuff, but things we want to change or are reviewing or are doing differently.

Here formal planning creates 'space' for independent movement at the margin of a day that would otherwise seem completely filled. However, LR also feels planning's potential to exclude her from a space of organization:

> I don't want to end up being a recluse in my office, being a planning or paper machine ... You need to have things on the pulse and be with people. That's my dilemma. I don't want to give up those that I've got organized because of those structures ...

LR thinks of planning as being in opposition to life, to being 'on the pulse', to being 'with people'. As she needs 'to have things on the pulse' in order to manage, planning can be disruptive, as she states, of what 'I've got *organized*' (my emphasis). Planning, for her, has potential to be actually disorganizing, as well as organizing.

That opposition between planning and life seems to be reflected by managers in their own lives. Very few of the managers I interviewed, even those enthusiastic about planning, actually planned to become managers. Typical of answers to the question 'How did you get into management?' are the following:

> I tumbled into it actually. (ST)

> Er, drifted I suppose is the best description. (PX)

> I think because it's what inevitably happens in this area if you want to get promoted. (CI)

> Probably by default. (BH)

I think I just evolved into it. (DM)

I suddenly realized about six weeks ago that I was managing thirty people. (GC)

You may tumble, drift or evolve into management, but you rarely, it seems, plan to be there. Perhaps such a feckless approach to life is an artefact of this particular group of managers, but here is a planning manager from New Zealand who, rather to her surprise, has failed to extend her planning skills to the rest of her life:

-So how did you come to live in Christchurch? (She came from the UK originally.)

I was sort of drifting around the world and I met someone and I've stayed ever since.

-Then you didn't plan to be living here?

It's funny, but I don't apply those principles to my life. (AC)

Why does the suggestion that formal planning be applied to life as a whole evoke such surprise?[2] How can planning be both helpful and inimical, essential and 'shit', organizing and disorganizing?

Making lists

To make sense of this ambivalence around planning, it is helpful to look at that simplest form of plan, the list. Writing lists is such a commonplace activity that it has escaped organizational attention, yet we can sometimes find the profound hiding itself in the obvious.

Managers are often writing lists and these lists evoke far less ambivalence than plans. GC, for instance, gets more satisfaction from lists than she thinks perhaps she should, so she jokes about it being an obsession:

-Do you make lists?

Yeah, yeah, because I'm a Capricorn. It's compulsive. Everyone tells me I'm really organized. I'm always making lists. I have computerised lists that go in my filofax of what I have to do. Then I have another system as part of the diary. At the end of one week, anything that hasn't been done will carry over to the next week. Then I have a master list to stream everything. I know I'm obsessive and I get teased about it a lot.

Lists are a sign of her management. They tell other people that she's 'really organized'. They help control time, creating continuity – 'anything that hasn't been done will carry over to the next week' – but also marking divisions, with the transfer of items 'at the end of one week'. Lists are also something personal that she makes for herself – 'I'm always making lists.' There is a craft satisfaction here in producing something. This production creates her as

organized. She speaks of '*my* filofax of what *I* have to do'. Writing lists makes
an ordered self.

This production of oneself as ordered is also evident in manager BH's
account:

-When in the day do you start managing?

When I'm thinking of lists in bed. The thing about this kind of job is there's so
many different things. I'd only have a sense of control from spinning out if I
have lists to be ticked off. There's too much to keep in one's head.

She starts being a manager in bed by making lists. Lists establish control of a
multiplicity that threatens order, 'spinning out' of control. Making lists
extends her body to a space that contains that multiplicity for which her head
alone feels insufficient. Her sense of control is reinforced as the lists are 'ticked
off', and her own control is made visible to herself. With the help of lists she
can deal with multiplicity. Writing lists has rendered her ordered.

Manager CI also talks similarly about the way lists order him:

-Do you make a lot of lists?

When I get really busy, yes. I'd always have lists going. I tend to update it when
I feel my mind's losing control; there's too much to keep hold of, and I'll sit
down and make a list.

Once again, lists are a way of taking control when things seem to be
multiplying out of control: 'when I feel my mind's losing control, there's too
much to keep hold of'. In that common managerial metaphor of handling, lists
allow this manager to keep 'hold of' what threatens to get beyond his reach,
outside the scope of his own body. Lists create a moment of stasis or fixity in a
world that threatens to endlessly move away. The very act of making lists stills
movement. CI sits down to make a list; BH makes lists in bed. This stasis
allows CI to 'organize priorities'. He dictates the order rather than being
controlled by the appearance of issues as they turn up in the flux of time.
Writing lists orders him within the flow of events. It works materially on his
body. We might say it re-embodies him as ordered.

Ordering the self

I want to now investigate further this process of writing lists as working on our
bodies. I am not talking here about physiological bodies, although
physiological processes will be involved, but of bodies as the locus of
relationship between ourselves and what we experience as outside us – what
Merleau-Ponty (1964: 162) refers to as 'the working, actual body – not the
body as chunk of space or a bundle of functions but that body that is an
intertwining of vision and movement'.

How, then, does writing items on a piece of paper, real or imagined,
embody us as ordered? When I worked as a manager I normally started the

week, and sometimes the day, with a list, and I want to look in detail at one of
my own lists here. But the list I am going to look at was made, as were many,
in the course of writing the chapter of my PhD thesis that formed the basis of
this article, because lists are a form of writing that can, amongst other things,
organize us to write (Figure 3.1).

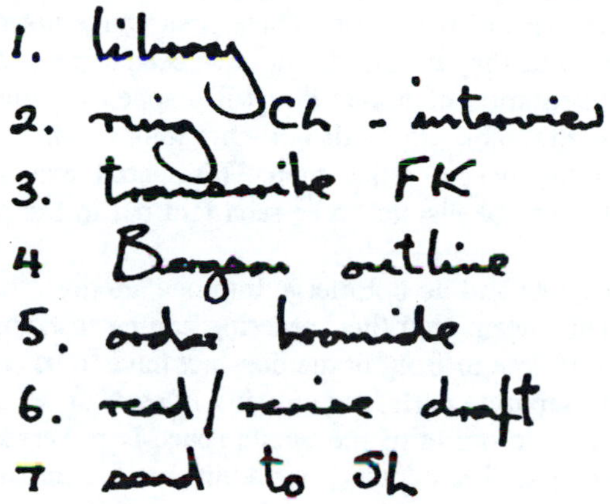

1. library
2. ring UCh - interview
3. transcribe FK
4 Bergson outline
5. order broomide
6. read/revise draft
7 send to Sh

Figure 3.1: My list

This list was made on a completely new page in a notebook, even though it
does not fill the page and there was plenty of space for it on the page before. It
was, then, a writing deliberately made on its own space: the blank page itself
marked a separation from an outside, and in doing so created everything else
as outside. The outside in this case was both my disorganized writing – the list
was not even made in the same notebook that I used for thinking about my
thesis – and the flux of thoughts around it. Setting myself up thus in front of a

blank page creates a Cartesian moment in which I as subject, abstracted from the flow of events, place myself in front of a space that separates its contents from the flow of events, making them into objects (De Certeau, 1984: 134).

On the space of this blank page I have represented in writing a number of tasks to be undertaken or, more accurately, I created events as tasks by representing them in this way. These events have been both made visible – externalized from my own memory – and have been put in focus – separated from each other and from the rest of the world. These items have not merely been transcribed from memory as they occurred, but have been subjected to an arrangement, a spatial representation of events that will happen in time. The separate items, one below the other, are also a chronology, one that is reinforced by the numbering that accompanies them. This spatial arrangement of time allows the flow of time to be visible, to be seen laid out in the present by a self that observes it.

Because the items are discrete and do not merge into one another, they can be attended to separately. This means that their ordering can be rearranged. It also means that the expanse of time in front of me does not have to be engaged all at once. It is divided into separate parts, the crossing of each of which will bring me to the next part, and so on, until the whole space is traversed. The multiplicity of actions is not just fragmentary, but additive, so I am not just 'spinning out', but going in a direction. Moreover, the parts taken separately seem to be within my grasp, even if the whole is not, just as we may feel sometimes that we can get through the next hour, but not through the whole day. The process of ticking off the list can show me that, if I have not yet grasped the whole, I am moving towards it.

But making the list is not just about making events into tasks. It is also about making me. One feature of this list is particularly revealing: it has never been ticked off. Actually, I think, once it had been made, it was never referred to again, suggesting it was the act of making the list itself that had already fulfilled a function. That function is revealed in the unusual neatness and uniformity of the writing when I compare it to other writing in the same notebook. Its order is reinforced by the numbering of each item, something I would normally never do. The numbers are in line, each carefully punctuated with a full stop. The spacing between the numbers and their items is very even. All this suggests an unusual care and deliberation, as if the very act of crafting this list was itself somehow ritually creating someone able to bring about the order that I was seeking. Acting out control in a space that I felt was manageable recreated me as more ordered.

Flow and space

Writing this list worked because it re-embodied me in a different relation to space and time, so that I experienced myself as more bounded and ordered in relation to a flux of events that seemed to be sweeping me away. Bergson's distinction between two sorts of time, for which he uses the terms 'time' and 'duration', is helpful in understanding this process. He defines the first type of time, what he calls 'duration' thus:

> Pure duration is the form which the succession of our conscious states assumes when our ego lets itself live, when it refrains from separating its present state from its former states. For this purpose ... it is enough that, in recalling those states it does not set them alongside its actual state as one point alongside another, but forms both the past and present states into an organic whole, as happens when we recall the notes of a tune, melting, so to speak, into one another. (1950: 100)

Duration, then, is a qualitative organization of conscious states, 'a continuous or qualitative multiplicity with', Bergson adds significantly, 'no resemblance to number' (1950: 105). Duration, then, is time as a flow of experience in which events merge into one another. It is not the sort of time that is created by lists. Bergson's second sort of time, for which he uses the term 'time' itself, is closely bound up with the concept of number. Number, he claims, implies an intuition of space:

> For though we reach a sum by taking into account the succession of different terms, yet it is necessary that each of these terms should remain when we pass to the following, and should wait, so to speak, to be added to the others ... where could it wait if we did not localise it in space? (1950: 79)

We could not count in duration, in which successive qualitative states merge into one another. To count, says Bergson, requires a homogeneous medium in which to hold objects simultaneously but separately. This medium is space. Introducing space into our experience of duration:

> we set out states of consciousness side by side in such a way as to perceive them simultaneously, no longer in one another, but alongside one another; in a word, we project time into space, we express duration in terms of extensity, and succession in terms of a continuous line or chain, the parts of which touch without penetrating one another. (1950: 101)

This suggests how making a list helps us create order. Instead of being swept along by a time in which one state merges into another, it allows us to experience events, like numbers, as a discrete multiplicity, side by side in space, each event waiting to be added to the next. A discrete multiplicity creates singularity. The flow of multiple events becomes separate items. These items can be dealt with one at a time, without worrying how one event merges into the next. They can also be dealt with in a different order, because their visible spatialization allows us to imagine different arrangements, just as we can rearrange a list of numbers.

The space Bergson is talking about is a homogeneous and continuous medium devoid of quality. It is space experienced as separated from duration – the space of Euclidean geometry – both empty, but given shape by geometric forms. The list, for example, relies on the concept of a line that gives the individual items direction and cohesion, and of points that fix locations along the line where the items can be placed separately. The points also divide the line so the completion of each individual point – ticking it off – can be imagined as adding up to the complete line. Transposing the flow of time to a finite list of points makes that flow finite, additive and so manageable.

The writing of control

Lists, by allowing the spatialization of duration, are a technology of control. For De Certeau (1984: 134–5) they would thus be an exemplary instance of writing in general, a writing that, for him establishes modernity as essentially 'Western'. De Certeau defines writing as 'the concrete activity that consists in constructing, on its own, blank space (*une espace propre*) – the page – a text that has power over the exteriority from which it has first been isolated'. He distinguishes three elements as decisive in this definition. Firstly, the blank page creates a space 'where the ambiguities of the world have been exorcised' (De Certeau, 1984: 134). This is Bergson's geometric space in which events no longer flow into and merge with one another. But such a space also creates, 'along with a place of writing, the mastery (and isolation) of a subject confronted by an object'. In front of the blank page 'every child is already put in the position of the industrialist, the urban planner, or the Cartesian philosopher – the position of having to manage a space that is his own and distinct from all others and in which he can exercise his will' (1984: 134). The space of writing, De Certeau thus contends, creates a relationship between a controlling self and a world waiting to be mastered. This mastery is effected by constructing on the space of the page a text, which is the production of a system that represents the reality of the world for the purpose of changing it.

We saw from the discussion of my list how representing the flow of events as spatialized items on a page allowed me to think the possibility of controlling and manipulating them. Cooper (1992), in fact, suggests that all organizational practices involve this sort of representation that reduces, condenses and concentrates the flow of events to allow control over the world. Organization itself, thus understood, is a writing, whether literally carried out on a page or not, because, as Chia (1996: 219) argues 'Writing, as the very condition for language, deals essentially with frames, boundaries, spacings and listings ...'

Organizing is, in this account, a process of writing the world. But writing does this by re-embodying in me a different relation between space and time. Is writing, even in its most generalized form as frames, boundaries and spacings – as the process of spatialization itself – always able to do this? If the answer is yes, we are left with some problems. How are we to understand both the ambivalence of managers to planning and the absence of ambivalence around lists? And why would I need a form of writing – a list – to organize my own writing? To explore these issues further I want to look at why lists are experienced differently to plans.

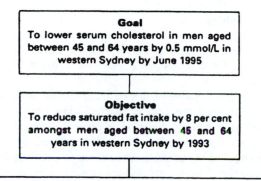

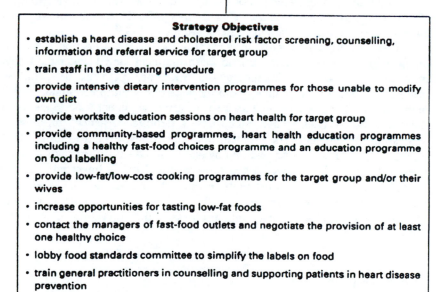

Figure 3.2: The plan of a Heart Health Programme (Hawe et al., 1990)

The geometry of plans

Plans, like lists, typically depict a development in time as a geometric layout in space. Figure 3.2, for example, is a plan for a heart health programme in western Sydney.

This plan is really a series of nested lists, so that one list 'adds up' to the next list and so on until the goal is reached. The goal is a specific point in future time, although actually depicted as present in space at the same time as everything else on the page. The future is mastered by showing it to be a logical development of the present, and therefore predictable. The plan allows the time between the 'future' goal and the present to be divided spatially into a series of 'steps' which, as they are completed, accumulate toward the goal. This depiction, moreover, allows for a division of labour, whereby people working on different 'steps' are contributing to the goal without having to concern themselves with the other steps.

A plan such as this allows a complex task to seem achievable. By depicting what has to be done in what order, it shows us, like the list, that the whole task does not need to be approached all at once. Small parts of the task may be experienced as doable, whereas the whole may seem overwhelming, stretching away beyond our grasp. It also makes people's activity visible to themselves and others, as ticks on a list indicate progress. 'You have to have it on paper to show people what you've done', was the way manager CI put it.

This additive or cumulative aspect of planning suggests why quantification is so important in management. For example, the objective of the Heart Health Plan is stated as: 'To reduce saturated fat intake by 8 per cent amongst men aged between 45 and 64 years in western Sydney by 1993'.

As we saw from Bergson's account, this sort of quantification is another application of spatialization. I am no mathematician, and I understand there may be other ways of imagining number other than as a spatialized multiplicity, but this latter understanding is certainly the predominant one in management. Time is imagined as a set of arbitrary, equal spaces, ending at the point called 1993.[3] This establishes a definite 'distance' to cross in addressing the problem. The problem does not stretch away to infinity. Over this space saturated fat is represented by one hundred equivalent points, and of these, eight must be removed when the space to 1993 is traversed. This not only gives a sense of the dimensions of the task, but also lets us know, each year, if the space is being traversed at the desired pace. Spatializing converts the unbounded flow of activity into progress – the traversing of a defined space.

Lists versus plans

So far plans seem to share many of the features of lists, so whence the managerial ambivalence? Returning to my own list, a key feature that differentiates it from the Heart Health Plan is that the whole picture is never stated. The list never quite turns into a plan. There is an implication that there is more to the picture than what is on the list, but what it adds up to is left to the imagination. The list does not even have complete sentences. Its connections are not made explicit. This particular list is not necessarily finished. There is the rest of the page, still waiting to be filled, giving this list an extemporized, ad hoc character that doesn't require a complete commitment. It can be changed at any time, or thrown away, or replaced by another list. While the list seems to organize an external world, it still connects to me and requires me to make it meaningful. It is very much *my* list. It is a space in relation to me, not something separate. Its setting as space is myself as flow. Hence, by writing it, I relate flow and space within myself. The Heart Health Plan, however, not only represents Bergson's duration as a series of objects in space, but itself moves closer to being an object. It sets itself apart from *my* particular experience. Unlike my list, the plan explicitly states the objective towards which the various items are accumulating. It is a self-contained presentation of space. The purpose of the plan is taken out of subjectivity: it is an objective. Moreover this purpose is represented as the objective, not of a person or persons, but of the plan itself. Its setting as space is the space of its goal. It comes to me already circumscribed.

Stating an objective at once creates the plan as more public.[4] Reconstructing events in the homogeneous space of the plan creates a common space. Any observer can see what the plan is adding up to. This common space is created, however, by imagining it as removed from subjectivity. Objects removed from their part in my qualitative experience are also removed from the qualitative experience of others. They are thus, in principle, observable by anyone, devoid as they are of any particular experience. However, this property of being observable can lead to the illusion that these objects or events somehow come that way, that this is their reality. In this object world, as Merleau-Ponty (1964: 162) has pointed out, my particular situation is then only a possible source of error. I am therefore forced to remove myself as far as possible in order to establish truth. Truth is not a part of that flow wherein I find myself embodied here and now.

But herein lies the source of ambivalence about planning. If I must constantly imagine myself as outside the order I produce so as to establish its truth, it will never work within me. I will be unable to embody it. I may think the plan represents order, but my body will not be ordered by it. I may, therefore, experience such a plan as irrelevant – I have no relation to it – or my attempts to conform to it may feel positively disorganizing as I attempt to relate things that my body experiences as unrelated or related differently. Through a triumph of the will I may still achieve the plan, but only with a continued residue of resistance, the resistance of the flow of myself that does not relate to the space of the plan.

The world, including ourselves, we may say is neither space nor flow, but the one in relation to the other. We live this relation in our bodies. Disorganization is that embodied experience of ourselves dissipating and flowing away from us. The language of planning can re-embody us as singular and ordered in relation to that flowing away. But such planning, to be effective, must embody us as closed and singular within a fluid openness of possibility, or it leaves us stranded in a disembodiment at odds with the order of duration that we continue to experience around it. Planning, to work, must embody us as spatialized within the flow of time. Then we experience it as organizing. Treating spatialization as somehow fundamental, effectively alienates us from our own order. Order becomes a space that traps us and cuts us off from living. Lists are less likely to be alienating in this way because their ad hoc and personal character gives them an inbuilt relation to the differently embodied subjectivity that developed them.[5]

Writing, then, as manifested in plans or lists, cannot just be understood as an activity of marking and spacing that produces our sense of organization, because that is to leave its experienced effect on ourselves out of the picture. Writing that organizes is a re-embodiment of ourselves in space and time. That re-embodiment must come about for organization to happen. Writing that works in this way is not so much a technique of order as a material reinscription of ourselves.

Fixity in movement

The capacity of planning to embody fixity within movement, to order us within the flow of time, is critical to the experience of planning as organizing or disorganizing. The following two accounts differ radically about the value of formal planning, but the difference really revolves around that capacity. The first account, from manager TG, begins with a common distinction in management between 'policy/planning' and 'operations', to the detriment of the former:

> When I was working in the Health Department I was working in a classic policy/planning role, and I realize how ineffectual as far as achieving a result is concerned a planning and policy role is in the balance between policy and operations – that operations, if effectively managed, is where the control and decision lies ... When you write papers or guidelines or frameworks or whatever, they never get translated into what you thought it would be.

As opposed to a process that foreshadows and controls operations, TG experiences the planning process as quite removed from action, and therefore from organization, because of its very nature as writing. That 'paper', he complains, never gets 'translated' into 'what you thought it would be.' That translation fails, he goes on to say, because management is characterized by rapid movement:

> I think the successful operational manager is the rapidly assessing and analysing, and rapidly making judgements.

Planning, on the other hand, creates a different mind in a different body:

> It's a different mind and different skill to the capacity to sit down and spend long periods of time writing, analysing. A completely different skill to an

operational manager's skill, and rarely do the two come together in the one person.'

Planning creates a fixed, not a moving body. The two bodies are incompatible, so much so that contact with what he calls 'the realities' – operations – actually paralyses what little movement there is in policy:

> Basically you can't write policy if you know much about operations ... If you know a lot about the realities you become completely paralyzed in a policy sense.

Rapidity and stasis: there is no flow between them. Even where the two bodies are contained in one body, they do not combine; there can only be a difficult switching from one to the other:

> And doing them both at the same time, it's extremely difficult to flip from one role to the other.

Planning does not embody the operational manager as organized. Fixity, for TG, removes him from reality, which is movement.

If TG moved out of planning in order to manage, ML thinks that managing in her area of work is impossible without it:

> You have a strategic plan and business plans and annual reports. And every program should have a plan. I'm just completely into that. All that architecture and planning, that's just what I bring with me as a style of working.

TG thinks of planning as outside of himself as a manager; for ML it forms her as a manager. It is an 'architecture' that she is 'just completely into', so much so that it gives her manner of acting in management, her 'style'. The 'architecture' of planning works to embody her as organized. Its space creates her as ordered in relation to the multiplicity of possibilities outside it.

Planning, in TG's account, immobilizes, whereas for ML, it make movement possible. To explain this she uses another metaphor of spatiality, the map:

> One of the strategic plans we've made is a nutrition plan, and it sort of maps out the way that we thought ahead that we'd cover. And WP (the nutritionist) works her way through that. What exactly she works on in any one year is opportunistic. Like we might put something on hold until next year, but the plan maps it out. It's a reference point, and she uses it really well. But that doesn't mean it controls you, or you can't change things. I think it's a really good plan. I get involved in that. I like how she uses it. It's incredibly helpful.

Planning here is a map that represents as present in space 'the way we thought ahead' in time. 'WP works her way through that' – it sets her moving, translating space back into time again. Mapping in this way allows movement around time. Something can be put 'on hold' this year, and will still be there next year. Events this way can be grasped, held. By providing a 'reference point', movement in time becomes a journey rather than just wandering. But because it is a journey, not a stasis, the plan does not feel like a trap. Rather than serving the plan, ML feels it re-creates her bodily as organized: it creates an 'I' that can 'get involved' rather than remain at a distance. The plan moves her pleasurably: she likes how WP uses it. So it can be 'incredibly helpful'. Planning here is a writing that does not leave its users outside their own organization. It creates an embodied organization, not a body at odds with its organization. In the case of TG, writing the plan is actually disorganizing; for ML it is organizing.

Duration or time?

Because spatialization – Bergson's 'time' – has been so traditionally enmeshed in thinking about management and organization there has been, in recent postmodern writing, a tendency to privilege metaphors of flow and change over those of space and stasis.[6] Change has become a mantra for management gurus like Peters (1992: 378) – 'Everything is in flux. Everything is flux' – while more sophisticated arguments like those of Chia (1996: 117) have essentially the same emphasis:

> The postmodern style of thinking is one which privileges an ontology of movement, ... emergence and becoming whereby the transient and ephemeral nature of what is 'real' is accentuated.

By adopting, in contrast, an ontology of stasis, organization studies, and indeed, Western thought in general, Chia argues, attempts to control this flow by representing it as fixity, seducing us 'into thinking about organizations as free-standing entities rather than as effects produced through precariously balanced figurational patterns of actions and interactions' (Chia, 1996: 143). He sees this human impulse to organize as deriving from the logical structuring of language itself (Chia, 1996: 217).

This postmodern tendency is, in fact, prefigured in Bergson himself. His concern to rescue duration from time, often gives the impression of rescuing life from death: '(S)ensations and tastes seem to me to be *objects* as soon as I isolate and name them, and in the human soul there are only processes' (1950/1910: 131). Language – the process of naming – turns things into objects and so places them outside the soul, which only lives in duration. For Bergson in this vein, spatialization defeats process, and hence life, by turning duration into time.[7]

Elsewhere, however, Bergson is less dualistic about his time/duration distinction in a way that is, I think, more helpful for our argument. Multiplicity itself, he states, whether in its discrete form as time or its merged form as duration, only exists for consciousness. It is not some primary form of being, because our experience of being is never primary. It is a product of interaction between ourselves and the world:

> Each of the so-called successive states of the external world exists alone: their multiplicity is real only for a consciousness that can first retain them and then

set them side by side by externalizing them in relation to one another. (1950: 120)

Each of the two states of time, then, is a product of consciousness as it either retains, or sets side by side, successive states of the external world. Time and duration can in fact be seen as mutually dependent, the one always creating the other for us as the undefined background from which it differentiates itself.[8] We can see this mutual dependence more clearly in revisiting Bergson's definition of 'duration' given earlier:

> Pure duration is the form which the succession of our conscious states assumes when our ego lets itself *live*, when it refrains from separating its present state from its former states. For this purpose it need not be entirely absorbed in the passing sensation or idea; for then, on the contrary, it would no longer *endure*. Nor need it forget its former states: it is enough that, in recalling those states it does not set them alongside its actual state as one point alongside another, but forms both the past and present states into an organic whole, as happens when we recall the notes of a tune, melting, so to speak, into one another. (1950: 100)

As he points out, if we were entirely absorbed in passing sensations or ideas, they would not *endure* – there would be no duration. But how could we conceive ourselves as not absorbed in the flow of events unless we could somehow project ourselves as *outside* them – as a consciousness that 'refrains from separating its present state from its former states', but allow them to melt into an organic whole? But the very movement of getting *outside* the flow requires a relation between space and flow. A sense of 'duration' creates our sense of 'time', and vice versa, because our bodies – Bergson would say consciousness – can only experience relationally.[9] To simply substitute flow for stasis, 'duration' for 'time', creates an unchanging change that, as Game (1997) has pointed out, itself feels curiously static.

The ability to externalize events from one another by writing lists and plans, to imagine their 'radical distinctness', to have them waiting in space where we left them while we examine different events, to imagine ourselves as somehow outside this space, all these ordering activities create a sense of organization and control. From a duration that seems to be 'spinning out', dissipating us with it, to imagine events as spatialized re-embodies us as organized. It can only do this however, if there is an embodied relation between space and flow. Otherwise space and flow produce incompatible embodiments, as in TG's experience, and our ordering disorganizes us.

However, if flow and space depend on one another, it follows that the embodiment of ourselves as organized might require a movement in either direction. This possibility is implicit in the paradoxical attitude to planning that we reviewed at the beginning of the chapter. Experiencing the world as a discrete multiplicity may leave us disconnected, fragmented, lifeless. Re-embodying a sense of organization will not be achieved by a further movement into spatialized time, but will more likely require a movement back towards the continuous multiplicity of duration. This latter sense of organization is beautifully expressed by Wallace Stevens, whose combination of the careers of poet and manager should remind us that there are other sorts of writing than plans and lists, and that this other writing can also organize us, but quite differently. In a letter to his wife, Stevens wrote:

> Sometimes 1 am terribly jangled, full of clashing things. But always the first harmony comes from something I cannot just say to you at the moment – the touch of you organizing me again. (Quoted in Richardson, 1986: 332)

I can immediately respond to this, but am also constantly surprised by that juxtaposition of touch and organization. The surprise comes, I think, because our sense of organization is so formed by the order of spatialization, with its dependence on vision, on seeing things as an arrangement in space. Touch, as evoked here, seems the very antithesis of this. In Stevens' expression, it reconnects a you and a me. He experiences himself, not as disconnected and separate, but relationally, to another person who takes him beyond his isolated self and reconnects him to his own organization.

Language as a door

I should like to end with a rather different image of the language of organization than that of a violence done to the flow of experience. Georg Simmel (1994), a sociologist with a remarkable capacity to discover the fundamentals of human life in quite ordinary things, offers a palpable image of such a language in his account of the door:

> The human being who first erected a hut ... revealed the specifically human capacity over against nature, insofar as he or she cut a portion out of the continuity and infinity of space and arranged this into a particular unity in accordance with a single meaning. A piece of space was thereby brought together and separated from the whole remaining world. By virtue of the fact that the door forms, as it were a linkage between the space of human beings and everything that remains outside it, it transcends the separation between inner and outer. (Simmel, 1994: 7)

People, Simmel is saying, organize the infinitude of space by creating a space which is securely theirs, in which they can become themselves. But they are also part of that from which they are separated, and the separation only remains meaningful if there is still a connection. Hence 'the door becomes the image of the boundary point at which human beings actually always stand or can stand' (Simmel, 1994: 7). Opening the door to the flux of infinity can create a sense of freedom that revitalizes the order and enclosure of the hut, or closing the door and turning inward to the singularity of the hut allows us to meet the chaos and infinity of space from a sense of order and security, so that the world outside is a flow of experience and not just a vacant, open void. Without the possibility of movement, the claims of infinite demand and the enclosure of the prison actually feel the same (cf. Bachelard, 1969: 215).

The image of the door lets us think of organizing beyond the imposition of spatialization on the flow of events. Spatialized time and duration are no longer in opposition, but are always experienced as potentially or actually in relation. There is a door between them that opens and shuts. Planning may momentarily shut the door on a flow of events that seems bewildering and disorienting, in which we feel ourselves dissipating. It then re-embodies us as whole and ordered in relation to that flow, allowing us to re-enter it meaningfully. Planning in this case works to organize us. But if it is a locking of the door, we will feel cut off from that possibility that our body still dimly experiences. Like TG, we will feel that planning has somehow put us in the wrong body – still, when we feel moving; or, like LR, we will no longer feel 'on the pulse', but instead forced 'to give up those (things) that (we've) got organized'. Our organization will disorganize us. Organization, then, is not something we can achieve absolutely, but neither is it something we can abandon.

Language organizes because it makes us articulate, but what is the nature of that articulation? It is, Simmel's image suggests, a relation of infinity and singularity, of possibility and closure, of flux and stasis, of time and duration, and the possibility of movement between them. Our body is the locus of experience of that articulation because it houses us in a singularity made out of the infinity of nature. Through embodiment 'the human being is', in Simmel's (1994: 10) words, 'the bordering creature who has no border', and language organizes us, whether as plans, lists or poetry, when it lets us experience that bordering creature, making a door between the different possibilities of ourselves.

Notes

1 A range of responses also reflected in other research (Marshall and Stewart, 1981).
2 As a manager I frequently received promotional material for seminars and publications encouraging me to do just that – to plan my entire life. Here, for example, are the 'Tactics for Winning' identified by one such course:

- identify appropriate goals and formulate them
- develop a plan to effect these goals
- create a system for monitoring your own progress
- identify personality and character flaws that might impede your goal achievement
- design a self development program to overcome the above impediments
- do effective daily, weekly, and long term time management planning. (*The Learning Lab*, June 1996)

3 In the same way, of course, men, who are living in duration, are imagined as crossing a series of equal, arbitrary points, and the ones between point 45 and point 64 are selected from all the others as the object of the programme.
4 This public and impersonal character is implicit in the spatialization of time itself, as Durkheim (1965: 23) makes clear in terms akin to Bergson's:

(Time) is an abstract and impersonal frame which surrounds not only our individual existence, but that of all humanity. It is like an endless chart, where all duration is spread out before the mind, and upon which all possible events can be located in relation to fixed and determined guidelines. It is not my time that is thus arranged; it is time in general such as it is objectively thought of by everybody in a single civilisation.

5 Arnold Lobel's (1992) story, 'A List', however, gives a delightful account of being trapped in the space of the list. One morning in bed Toad decides to make a list to organize his day. It contains items such as 'Wake Up', 'Get Dressed', 'Take a Walk with Frog', and so on, which he can cross off as they are completed. On the walk with Frog, however, the list blows away. Toad can't run and catch it because that wasn't an item on his list. He and Frog are forced to sit and do nothing until it gets dark, when Toad remembers the last item on his list: 'Go to Sleep'. He writes this on the ground with a stick, crosses it out and they both fall asleep.

6 While characterizing the tendency as 'postmodern' it can also be seen as developing from the reaction to the role of rational control in organization brought about by empirical studies in the 1970s, findings summarized thus by Stewart (1983: 96–7):

> The picture that emerges from studies of what managers do is of someone who lives in a whirl of activity, in which attention must be switched every few minutes from one subject, problem and person to another; of an uncertain world where relevant information includes gossip and speculation about how other people are thinking and what they are likely to do ... In short, it is a much more human activity than that commonly suggested in management textbooks.

7 Gurvitch (1990) notes that both Bachelard and Piaget expressed surprise at Bergson's contention that he 'had nothing to learn from Einstein, given the latter's profound interest in the relation of space and time. Gurvitch himself concludes that Bergson 'lacked the dialectical frame of mind' (Gurvitch, 1990: 39).

8 Metzner (1994) points out that historically there have been two main metaphors for consciousness, one spatial or topographical, and the other temporal or biographical.

9 Loy (1988: 217) expresses the antithesis thus:

> Consider a solitary rock out of an ocean current, protruding above the surface. Whether one is on the rock or floating past it, it is the relation between the two that makes both movement and rest possible.

References

Bachelard, G. (1969) *The Poetics of Space*, trans. M. Jolas. Boston: Beacon Press.

Bergson, H. (1950/1910) *Time and Free Will*, trans. F.L. Pogson. London: George Allen and Unwin.

Chia, R. (1996) *Organizational Analysis: a Deconstructive Approach*. Berlin, NY: Walter de Gruyter.

Cooper, R. (1992) 'Formal organization and representation: remote control, displacement, abbreviation', in M. Reed and M. Hughes, *Rethinking Organization*. London: Sage.

De Certeau, M. (1984) *The Practice of Everyday Life*, trans. S. Rendall. Berkeley: University of California Press.

Derrida, J. (1976) *Of Grammatology*, trans. G.C. Spivak. Baltimore and London: The John Hopkins University Press.

Durkheim, E. (1965/1915) *The Elementary Forms of Religious Life*, trans. J. Swain. New York: The Free Press.

Game, A. (1997) 'Time unhinged', *Time and Society*, 6(2/3): 115–29.

Gurvitch, G. (1990) 'The problem of time', in J. Hassard (ed.), *The Sociology of Time*. New York: St Martins Press.

Hawe, P., Degling, D. and Hall, J. (1990) *Evaluating Health Promotion: A Health Worker's Guide*. Sydney: MacLennan and Petty.

Lobel, A. (1992) *Frog and Toad Together*. London: Mammoth.

Loy, D. (1988) *Nonduality*. Newhaven and London: Yale University Press.

Marshall, J. and Stewart, R. (1981) 'Managers job perceptions, II', *Journal of Management Studies*, 18(3): 263–75.

Merleau-Ponty, M. (1964) *The Primacy of Perception*, ed. J.M. Edie. Evanston: Northwestern University Press.

Metzner, R. (1994) 'Addiction and transcendence as altered states of consciousness', *Journal of Transpersonal Psychology*, 26(1): 1–17.

Peters, T. (1992) *Liberation Management*. London: Macmillan.

Richardson, J. (1986) *Wallace Stevens: The Early Years 1879–1923*. New York: Beech Tree Books, William Monow.

Simmel, G. (1994) 'Bridge and door', *Theory, Culture and Society*, 11(I): 5–10.

Stewart, R. (1983) 'Managerial behaviour: how research has changed the picture', in M.J. Earl (ed.), *Perspectives on Management*. Oxford: Oxford University Press.

4

The Language of Strategy

Simon Lilley

Positioning

Strategy is up there. Right up there. At the top. And, above all, the language that it mobilizes, and is mobilized by it, is what puts it there. In a critical text on the language of organizations a chapter dealing with the language of strategy must address a number of key questions. Primary amongst these is that of the 'conditions of possibility' of the strategy language game. Which is to say, how is it that *we* find ourselves able to talk about strategies of organizations, when those who came before us (and who have long been confronted by both organizations and strategies) did not? In other words, we must understand how the practices, visibilities and articulations of strategy are able to reside within and around that rather odd set of entities that we term 'organizations'. For they have not always lived there. Strategy, as a material form of words, is possessed of a long lineage. But it is only in the last century that we witness significant incursions by this (concomitantly transformed) discourse into those forms of commercial and administrative orderings that we now call 'organizations'.

My own interest in this subject comes from two rather disparate sources. Firstly, I have always been intrigued by those accounts that justify organization in terms of a whole that exceeds the sum of its parts. Accounts that express an, albeit often implicit, affinity with functionalism. For I find such accounts both plausible and unconvincing at one and the same time. Strategic discourse, it seems to me, exemplifies this orientation towards organization (Pearson, 1990, makes a similar point from a perspective very different from that adopted in the rest of this chapter) and this alone makes it worthy of a little more attention. Secondly, and more prosaically, I have recently been required to teach business strategy to both undergraduate and MBA students. And it is perhaps this experience that constitutes the central drive behind the argument I present here. What struck me most immediately when re-reading the business strategy literature in preparation for these undertakings was its curious ability to fluctuate between the seemingly sublime and the seemingly ridiculous, often within the same argument. This does not seem to be a facet of the literature only available to those who have previously immersed themselves in other discursive streams, as recent personal experience in a third year undergraduate tutorial in business strategy made clear to me. The tutorial had been spent considering the circumstances facing the *SKIL Corporation*, as rendered by a Harvard Business School video, in the light of Michael Porter's theories of competitive strategy (Porter, 1980) and sustainable competitive advantage (Porter, 1985). As the students were leaving the room I overheard one of them, an individual who was certainly not the brightest in the class, say to his friend that in his three years of considering such cases he was yet to encounter one which was not amenable to solution through the application of knowledge gleaned during a prior secondary school level course in business studies. My initial reaction on hearing this was to laugh, but this laugh started to stick a little as I began to consider its cause. For on one level at least, it is very difficult to disagree with his assertion. Much of the strategy literature, once one has acquired the ability to translate its jargon, *does* appear to say little that extends that form of knowledge that we normally term 'common sense'. To parody somewhat, the strategy literature enjoins us to buy low and sell high, to add value, to co-ordinate our activities, to remain focused, to make sure that the world we serve has not changed without us noticing, and to serve that world 'better' than our competitors. And yet, there are thousands and thousands of worthy titles devoted to an understanding of this seemingly simple set of practices. It is to the discovery of why this might be so that the following argument is devoted.

Contemporary interweavings of the languages of strategy and organizations may be seen to constitute part of a knowledge regime defined by a specific combination of 'visible and articulable' (Deleuze, 1986: 51) elements that are unique to the age or epoch of which we are part. Which, somewhat more simply means, that we can only identify 'strategy' when we see it, and speak of it when we seek to create or transform it, because we can draw upon specific sets of techniques that allow us to turn the concept of strategy into a 'thing' that we can represent in words and/or pictures. This is true not only of strategy, but of all the other 'things' that make up our contemporary world.

This 'knowledge' of our world is seen by Deleuze (1986: 51, my emphasis) as 'a *practical* assemblage, a "mechanism" of statements and visibilities' that provides us with an ability to talk about, and to see, strategies of organizations (among other 'things'), as parts of our world. And it is crucial to note here that the notion of *knowledge* being mobilized by Deleuze is not (only) that associated with dry and disinterested erudition. Rather, as the term *practical* makes clear, Deleuze's notion is much better captured by the images conjured up by terms such as *know-how*, and indeed, *technology*, in its broadest sense (Cooper, 1993; Heidegger, 1977; Lilley, 1998). Knowledge in this rendering is a pre-condition of our ability to act, an ever present facet of our existence, not some arcane practice limited to only those places, like universities, that we sometimes associate with 'knowledge production'. The terms 'regime' and 'mechanism' which Deleuze chooses to use, serve to emphasize this encompassing notion of 'knowledge' which is central to our concerns here.

According to Deleuze, the forms of words that we use to describe, prescribe and proscribe things are related to the ways in which we can picture things, the non-verbal techniques through which we apprehend our world. This relation is, however, far from simple. Deleuze sees these two distinct techniques of practical knowledge, seeing and saying, as related through something that he terms, following Foucault (1977: 205), a 'diagram'. This diagram is not directly amenable to our senses, just as things 'in themselves' are not available to us directly – we can only grasp things if we can see them and/or say them. The diagram, like things in themselves, is creative of a 'gap' into which it virtually disappears, a gap that resides between what we can say and what we can see. The diagram becomes immanent to both the system of statements (our techniques of saying) and the visibility machine (our techniques of seeing) that it brings forth, leaving a 'non-place' (Deleuze, 1986: 38; Foucault, 1981), or virtual marshalling yard, between them. We thus see and can speak of the effects of the 'diagram' but we can never sensibly speak of it, or see it, directly.

This rather confusing notion needs a little further unpacking and is perhaps best exemplified through Foucault's (1981) extended commentary upon Rene Magritte's famous work: *Ceci n'est pas une pipe* (in English, 'This is not a pipe'). The work in question is made up of a conventional, iconic representation of a pipe along with a literal copy of its title, the words *Ceci n'est pas une pipe* appearing in italic script beneath the pipe icon. According to Foucault (1981), the work shows us the impossibility of direct translation between words and pictures, between what we say and what we see, for it invites the viewer/reader to take multiple images/messages from the work which remain incommensurable. Words and pictures stay steadfastly separate, despite their coincidence in the work. For example, the words, *Ceci n'est pas une pipe,* are literally 'true' when read as words, for they are words, not a pipe. And when read as a label, they are also 'true', for they label a picture of a pipe and not a pipe 'itself'. But the fact remains that in our common discourse we say 'this is a pipe' when we point to a picture of a pipe. And it is just this sort of unpicking of common sense that is required to further the aims we have set ourselves in this chapter.

So, we can say that the 'diagram', although unidentifiable in itself, is that which brings forth the system of statements upon which articulation depends as well as the machine upon which consonant visibilities depend. The distinction between a *system* of statements and a visibility *machine* seeks to further emphasize the lack of homology, or direct correspondence between these two distinct forms of knowledge. According to the Concise Oxford Dictionary (6th edition, 1977) a *machine* is, among other things, 'an apparatus for applying ... power, having several parts, each with definite function' or an 'instrument that transmits force or directs its application'. A *system* is, on the one hand, similar to a machine, being described by the same dictionary as a 'complex whole', a 'set of connected things or parts', and an 'organized body of material or immaterial things'. But it is also, on the other hand, a 'method' or 'organization, considered principles of procedure [or] classification'; a 'body of theory or practice' as it pertains to a particular domain. Thus we see that, in this rendering at least, a machine is deeply material whilst a system *may* be immaterial. Moreover, we can also see that this materiality of machine renders it as a device or instrument, whilst the potential immateriality of system allows alternative notions of method and technique. And we may distil the distinction between these seemingly similar terms according to this latter difference of emphasis. A machine is a material *device* whilst a system is a (potentially) immaterial *method*. For example, if we take this distinction at perhaps its simplest level we may see both telescopes and microscopes as examples of visibility machines whilst we would see both grammatical conventions and rules of conversational turn taking as parts of the method of a system of articulations.

So where are we now? What has this detour enabled? Firstly it has shown us that although what we see and what we say are linked, this linkage is far from simple and is only amenable to interrogation indirectly. We have seen that there is an inevitable gap between these two ways of knowing our world, a gap through and across which visual and verbal elements of our unique historical situation prod each other into action as our epoch establishes and transforms itself. And this last point also alerts us to the status of each of the three things we have considered. Neither machines, systems nor diagrams are pre-given, each results from the unprogrammed interaction of the other two, and thus each of these bases of knowledge are seen to be immanent to the current body of knowledge they support. Which, put another way, means that diagrams, systems and machines are all historically determined. We cannot consider any of them in isolation, or even, indeed, all of them in isolation from the contexts of their production and use. So how then do we apprehend these 'things'? And what, if we can apprehend them, can they tell us about both strategy's literary proliferation and its frequently banal content?

Reading systems

A system of statements does not lie 'hidden' beneath the surface forms of words and phrases that inscribe the field(s) in which it operates. Rather, just as the 'diagram' is *immanent* to the system that *it* brings into being, the system of statements is *immanent* (Eagleton, 1981)[1] in the 'sayable and readable' whose possibility *it* conditions. The system of statements resides within and across the statements of an age, forcing sayings into being, as it is itself transformed by what is said. Systems of statements live in the forms of words of the age in which they are dispersed and disseminated. They connect the unities of language, the subjects and objects of statements, as they simultaneously determine the 'systems, places, occasions and interlocutors' (Deleuze, 1986: 53) of the ways of saying that, in part at least, constitute their age. But although not hidden, statements are not 'directly readable or even sayable' (Deleuze, 1986: 53). They only become so when they are approached 'in relation to the conditions that make them so' (Deleuze, 1986: 53), the *contexts* of their production.

According to Deleuze, everything that *can* be said in an age *is* always said in that age, including the most cynical and raw elements pertaining to the linguistic unities produced. The most cynical and raw elements or aspects of an entity are often also the most banal things we can say about it and thus we can begin to see the virtue of Deleuze's reading of Foucault for our project here. To take just one example, consider the following seemingly dismissive comment on the recent managerial panacea of multiskilling, which comes from a Financial Controller in British manufacturing industry (cited in Ezzamel et al., 1994):

> We've introduced multiskilling which is, it seems to me from a cynical point of view, more training people who are trained as electricians, or whatever, to learn how to paint.

What is interesting about this quote is not whether we agree or disagree with the 'cynical' tone in which it is avowedly delivered. Indeed, in some senses it is hard to see the sense in the seeming surprise which conditions this 'cynical' display. What is it that the speaker saw 'multiskilling' as meaning before the scales were lifted from his eyes on witnessing its 'cynical' application? Surely the literal meaning of the term is the existence of multiple skills in the same body along with the practices associated with bringing about such a state of affairs. Surely one of the key purposes of such dis- and re-embodying techniques is precisely to increase the flexibility of labouring bodies in order that they may be 'better' deployed in the service of capital? Why then would teaching electricians to paint be seen as a particularly 'cynical' form of the beast? The answers, of course, lie in a delineation of the context in which this commentary was offered. What we do seek to highlight however, for it is of central importance to our purposes here, is the simultaneity of this sense of cynicism, and that of banality. This cynicism seems to be primarily associated with a sense of surprise at the seemingly literal expression of the term 'multiskilling' in working and training practices, the triteness or commonplaceness of the term's referent. This coincidence between banality and cynicism is, it would seem, no *mere coincidence*, for it is a common feature of that mode of expression that we often glorify as 'straight talking'. And as we have already intimated, strategic discourse, when stripped of its jargon, would certainly seem to qualify as another example of this literary form. To take this line of argument a little further, if all that can be said is said, in all its cynical and raw aspects, it is through the naked proliferation of sayings that the system of statements underlying those sayings may itself be apprehended. That is, if we approach a specific and finite body of texts, such as those associated with the strategy of organizations, along with the contexts to which they pertain, we may hope to isolate and elucidate the unique 'enunciative regularities' (Deleuze, 1986: 56) that are partially constitutive of the age in which those texts are produced and read. And, by so doing, we may hope that we can begin to produce a system in which other things may be said. A system in which a language of strategy does not assume centre stage. In short, a different way of (talking about) organizing.

Seeing machines

The machine of visibilities, presupposed by the statement system, may be seen to carry out a similar function in the realm of the 'seeable'[2] to that carried out by the system of statements in the realm of the 'sayable'[3]. Indeed, everything already said about the system of articulations also applies to the visibility machine. This *context* of the sayable is, as we have already intimated, largely captured by the notion of the 'seeable'. But neither is reducible *to* the other nor directly deducible *from* the other. Each of these two forms of knowledge has its own inviolable specificity, as our reflections on Magritte's work made clear.

In this sense then, the visibility machine does not so much provide a network of lines of sight to the 'things' which we can verbally describe. Rather it provides a 'system of light' (Deleuze, 1986: 57), the combine of 'a visual assemblage and a luminous environment' (Deleuze, 1986: 32) in which only certain things are able to 'shimmer', to come to our attention. This system of light allows us to see only certain things, those which are both illuminatable *and* illuminated by the source(s) of illumination. Again, to give but one example, manufacturing's oft mentioned infatuation with the monitoring and allocation of man-hours, and the overheads supposedly associated with them – a practice seemingly inappropriate for current 'realities' (see, for example, Johnson and Kaplan, 1987) – could only be overcome once this 'inappropriateness' itself could be seen via an appropriately transformed visibility machine (see, for example, Ezzamel and Willmott, 1995). As a British Manufacturing Director described this recent shift (cited in Ezzamel et al., forthcoming):

> ... in the past people have been predominated with looking at man hours and the cost of payrolls. I couldn't give a monkey's. What I am interested in is the things that drive the big numbers and the big numbers in this context is, look out of the window. They're all around us [– the components in stock]. They're on what I describe as the dust test.

In this example, the accounting tables that used to allocate costs to products on the basis of man hours applied are seen to be blind in the face of present exigencies. Rather, the more immediate visual impression of components on site and new 'Gantt' charts, representing the associated costs of time, are seen as key. The rather simple point being made here is merely that only certain things are seen at certain times (see also Polanyi, 1957). A rather more complex question is that of how and why this should be the case, a set of questions that can again only be answered through reference to the context of visibilities, to the backgrounds against which things are seen.

Visibilities, like statements, are themselves also 'invisible' if 'we consider only objects, things or perceptible qualities, and not the conditions which open them up' (Deleuze, 1986: 57). If we seek to understand them, we are enjoined to pay attention to those distributions of 'light and dark, ... seen and non-seen' (Deleuze, 1986: 57), opacity and transparency, that condition the *particularities* of visibility in a given age or situation. Deleuze (1986) draws upon Foucault's (1970) description of Velasquez's *Las Meninas* in order to exemplify this form of apprehension. *Las Meninas* is a painting in which the painter is himself represented, looking out at the position in which we, as viewers of the painting, are standing. The front of the canvas on which the painter is painting is invisible to us, but we may perhaps assume that it is us, standing in front of the picture as we now view it, who (will) appear in the painting which we cannot see. On the wall behind the painter are other pictures, one of which shines brightly, attracting our attention to it. We recognize this element of the picture as a mirror, for it seems to shimmer in a way that the other pictures do not. The painter cannot see this mirror for it is behind him and neither can the other characters appearing in the picture for they too face either towards us in our viewing position or towards the sides of the work as we see it. This, however, is a strange mirror, for it does not reflect what is before us in the picture (and neither does it reflect 'us', perhaps because we were not present at the time when the picture was painted). Instead it reflects a couple, represented nowhere else in the picture, a couple that we assume to have stood in the place in which we now stand as viewers, at the time that the picture was created. We can, according to Foucault (1970), give names to the characters we see in this work: standing around the painter, who we may recognize as Velasquez himself, we see small people, some recognizable as the children of the royal court, others as dwarves. We see some larger people too: courtiers, maids of honour etc. And we can also recognize the couple, painted as images reflected in the mirror at the back of work, they are King Philip IV and his wife, Mariana. Foucault's (1970) description of this scene, his articulation of the visibilities it exemplifies, describes precisely the mechanism of seeing and non-seeing, and the distribution of light, that characterizes and partially constitutes classical representation. In this *order of things*, certain objects and qualities exhibit and inhabit the luminescence upon which the sovereign eye depends, whilst this eye, in itself, can only be inferred (see also Rotman, 1987).[4] The seeing eye of the sovereign is not directly visible, we see only its reflection. And this is not the only sovereign eye inferred. For we as viewers stand in the place it once occupied. Such that we, as viewers, have a sovereign eye too, the scene being enacted again for *us*, as *we* look at it for *our* own reasons. These two sets of sovereign eyes (or sovereign 'I's), those of the Royal parents as well as those of current and future viewers, are invisible elements of the visibility machine. Invisible that is, until we attend to their necessity, and thus to conditions of possibility of the visibilities with which they are associated.[5]

Visibilities and articulations are, then, 'two forms of exteriority within which dispersion and dissemination take place' (Deleuze, 1986: 59). They provide the materials and rules for our ongoing extension from our bodies, our ongoing making of the world. Which means that our task here, if we seek to track the ways in which the language of strategy is implicated in these moves, is 'to speak and to show in a simultaneous motion' that 'prodigious ... interweaving' (Foucault, 1963: 147–8, cited in Deleuze, 1986: 67) of statements and visibilities in which the power/knowledge of a modern strategy of organizations consists.

Planning

So why strategy? Why the strategy of organizations? What makes this field an appropriate site for the pursuit of a system of statements and a visibility machine? We have already noted the presence of a curious mixture of banality and cynicism in the field of strategic discourse, something which our detour into the work of Deleuze and Foucault offers some promise of explaining. But it is perhaps the other side of the notion of 'everything being said that can be said' that should attract us to the strategic arena. For the strategies of organizations are ripe for such a survey by virtue of their *proliferation*. Just as the Victorians 'dedicated themselves to speaking of [sex] *ad infinitum*, while explaining it as *the* secret' (Foucault, 1984: 35, original emphasis), so we are enamoured of strategy, seeking to extend its purview and promises to entities of all kinds in an effort to uncover the secret of their and our 'natures'.

According to my reading of Liddell and Scott (1855), the word 'strategy' carries with it notions of the leadership, *agein*, of an army, *stratos*, and particularly those aspects of leadership associated with an expedition or campaign, *strateia*.[6] Strategy here then seeks to centre an origin of *intention* as it disperses and disseminates its effects (see also Arendt, 1958 and Kallinikos, 1994). And this point remains valid regardless of the choice we make between the different renderings of strategy that we find in the literature. Distinctions and interrelations between strategy 'as plan, ploy, pattern, position and perspective' (Mintzberg, 1991) may move intention around, but the notion of intention remains key and it is to this notion that strategy stands as an obligatory point of passage (Callon, 1986) in our contemporary world. The centering of intention in terms of strategy provides something of a marshalling yard, a (virtual) site that can receive affects and unleash effects as it strives to embody a relationship between the internal characteristics of organization and that which is outside (Knights and Morgan, 1991: 257). The notion of 'affect' is not chosen here merely for the symmetry it provides with the notion of 'effect', for the emotional connotations of the term are key to the understanding we seek to develop here. Emotional overtones have increasingly been emerging in the strategy literature in the face of the culturalization of organizational life brought about by the work of such eminent theorists as Tom Peters. It is precisely these aspects of the drive to achieve through organization that Mintzberg seeks to capture in broadening conceptions of strategy from the limitations associated with notions of mere 'planning'. And it is just such an understanding that is mobilized when we read in the *Harvard Business Review* about the importance of 'insight' to matters strategic (Campbell and Alexander, 1997). Such techniques do not abandon 'planning': 'Trying to develop a strategy without insights is dangerous: it leads to unrealistic plans' (Campbell and Alexander, 1997: 50), but they do seek to extend the purview of strategy beyond any notion of rationality that is limited to simple and direct calculation. The affective domain is, according to such a view, positively ripe for conquest.

Others differ slightly in their emphasis, particularly in their willingness to move beyond notions of rational plan. For Shaw (1990: 467), for example, strategy constitutes a 'large ... , co-ordinated campaign', a definitional form entirely consonant with his desire to pursue connections between military and 'general social usage' (Shaw, 1990: 465) of the term.[7] This form of words emphasizes and illuminates strategy's links with battle, competition and capture. As Knights and Morgan (1991) note, strategy as it is represented in the modern organization also draws a great deal of legitimation from its use of the terms of marketing, a way of speaking about organizations that seems to have usurped, or at least diminished, the pre-eminent position previously held by economics and its derivatives. But the 'also' in the sentence above is something of a dissimulation for although marketing may provide the most proximal source from which the language of strategy is taken when it is applied to commercial organization, this source is itself deeply indebted to militaristic origins. Thus marketeers speak of 'target' markets which they seek to 'penetrate' with their coordinated 'campaigns'. And all this occurs in a context in which competition and its consequences provide the ultimate grounds for action. Strategic discourse may have moved through several intermediaries, but it seems difficult to argue with the assertion that its primary source is militaristic.

The hierarchical elevation of strategy (see also Knights and Morgan, 1990, 1991, 1995) that is achieved through restricting the term's application to only the grandest of plans and the most distilled of reflections reaches its apotheosis in Alfred P. Sloan's rendering of the notion. For here, (Sloan, 1967: 202) 'strategy' is seen to constitute nothing less than the policy 'of policy itself'. What we seek to understand are the implications of this conceptual ladder. For there are risks associated with any technique that moves too far from the grounded realities of organizational life as authors such as Herman Hesse (1969) and Kurt Vonnegut (1971) have made abundantly clear. Risks that may help us to understand better how banality may result from somewhat groundless and cynical processes of over conceptualization.

Culture

It is in Sloan's terms that we witness most clearly strategy's linguistic demand for the position of top dog. And it is also perhaps here, in a line of thought purportedly articulated in 1933 (Sloan, 1967: 202), that we can begin to grasp the enormity, indeed the infinity, of the modern strategy language game. For in this reflexive turn, in this subjection of policy to policy, of the crafting of conduct to the crafting of conduct, we initiate an infinite recursive, self-referential spiral of division and reflection. A spiral that may go some way towards explaining our extraordinary fascination with matters strategic. Particularly when we note that the *self* at the centre of this spiral is precisely that which is most problematized by the proliferation of matters strategic.

This claimed proliferation seems to me at least, to need little detailed empirical validation. For the language of strategy is undoubtedly everywhere. Its primary statement takes the following form: '_____ strategy'.[8] And it seems as though anything can fill the space to the left of our quarry. We talk of corporate strategy, organizational strategy, divisional strategy, IT strategy, human resource strategy, career strategy, technology strategy, marketing strategy, military strategy, financial strategy, fund raising strategy, public relations strategy, etc. This would certainly seem to be the realm of the *ad infinitum* that we intimated earlier. And it is an imperial realm, a realm that sits at the centre of all things seemingly without touching any of them *directly*.[9] It is a realm in which the grail is itself a quest, a realm of interminable reflexion. A place in which to engage in a *Glass Bead Game* (Hesse, 1969) of ever more esoteric erudition.

Here is a place in which there is nothing. Nothing but an ability to influence *everything*. And everything is precisely what we mean here, for the most strategic of strategies seem to be, rhetorically at least, those which can claim the greatest purview or scope (Summa, 1992). Strategy influences by inciting this, promoting that, curtailing this, and constricting the other. Yet in the absence of *anything* upon which to act directly, the sphere of strategy, empowered by the forces it mediates, is powerless in the absence of a visibility machine which allows it to see and a system of statements which allows it to say. Strategy requires ways of perceiving and articulating what is appropriate in order to be *realized*.

The notion of 'realized strategy' being mobilized here should not be confused with that intended by Mintzberg's use of the words. For Mintzberg (1991), realized strategies are those that actually occur. They are seen as a combine of deliberate plans and those patterns that emerge through ongoing interaction with an (ever-changing) environment. There are obviously certain similarities with our usage above, but also a key difference. In our rendering intention is explicitly addressed as 'the problem' of strategy whilst for Mintzberg the problem of intention is avoided through distribution. We have, in Mintzberg, explicit intentions in plans, and implicit intentions 'given' to us through something akin to an evolutionary process of natural selection. But this distribution can, in the final analysis, be nothing more than a partial avoidance of the problem of intention since realized strategies can only be seen as both intended intentions (plans that are actualized) and unintended intentions (patterns that emerge). We grasp intention only to see it disappear.

Strategy and the powers associated with it are nowhere and everywhere, for they exist only in relations. Intention, as Hannah Arendt demonstrates (1958), incites and is imbued in all action, inseparable, yet always apart, from action. It can only be stabilized and apprehended when we impoverish action, when we reduce action – that which goes on between people – to *making* (Arendt, 1958: 175–88; see also Summa, 1992) – that which occurs between people and things. This is because action, being inherently political, is unpredictable, for the intentions it embodies are labile, context dependent and wont to change in the light of shifting contingencies introduced by the intentions of others. Making, on the other hand is much more able to support predictability through its stabilization of intention. This stabilization is achieved through substituting contact between humans and devices or methods, for contact between humans and humans. The predictability that results undoubtedly provides advantage for large scale organization, enabling action to be modularized as making, and thus allowing the construction of extensive coordinated networks from pre-made modules (see Kallinikos, 1994; see also Fisher, 1978). But it also rather neatly depoliticizes human activity (Arendt, 1958; Kallinikos, 1994; Lilley, 1995; Summa, 1992). Means become subordinated to pre-given ends, as idealized future states reach back to dominate the activities of the present.

When we conceive of strategy as formalized intention, the roles of visibility machines and systems of statement become clear to us. To survive and proliferate formalized strategy requires the lines opened up by the system of statements and the visibility machine that both entice and seek to marshal it. In the context of strategic discourse, the products of systems of statements are forms of words that enable the separation of entities and the differential attribution of status to them. Thus we are able to speak of subjects *and* objects, actors *and* resources, organizations *and* environments, strategists *and* strategies, and, indeed, organizations *and* strategies. The system of statements provides us with rules, a method, for dividing up our world into sites where intentions are formed and arenas where intentions are realized through the articulation of made objects into coordinated networks of action. The visibility machine provides us with devices for seeing both the things that we have thus created and the status we should currently attach to them. We can view through the pentads, matrices and diamonds of Porter (1980, 1985 and 1990, respectively). Or we can visit the beloved menagerie of the Boston Consulting Group (Henderson, 1989), with the beasts again being penned in a two by two formation. We may even examine pictorial and diagrammatic representations of the statuses of various aspects of those virtual empires that constitute the main part of the plethora of computerized 'strategy' games, *Civilization, Civilization II, SimCity, Theme Park*, that are probably, and increasingly, more influential in defining the notion of strategy in the mind of the man (sic.) on the Clapham omnibus than any number of academic texts on the subject (see Grey and Lilley, forthcoming). All these devices enable us to see 'things', and to comment on their worth, but only in certain ways. Ways that construct the world, and this is the crucial point, *from the horizon of own intentions* as they themselves are constructed by the language of strategy. We see what may be of use in meeting our ends. If we want to see anything else, then we must look in another way, enabled by another machine.

The picture we have constructed above is, superficially at least, amenable to criticism on the grounds of its stasis, its inability to capture change. But the game of strategy never stands still. Witness the emphasis placed on the notion of *sustainable* competitive advantage that pervades current literature on the subject. Strategy, and the intentions it seeks to stabilize, forever exceed the devices and rules of their construction and deployment, inciting these devices and rules into extensions, until everything that can be seen is seen and everything that can be said is said.

Strategy is articulated in this context and can never be complete. As it differentiates and constructs intentions that are consumed and deconstructed by the visibility machine, it creates and inhabits a multisensorial surveillance society (see Foucault, 1979; Dandeker, 1990). A place where everybody looks and everybody speaks, but where no-one quite believes what they see or hear. For strategy and its interpretation are inextricably bound up with the construction and deconstruction of *artifice* (Skeat, 1946; see also, Virilio, 1988 and Guillet de Monthoux, 1996). And this uncertainty surrounding the intentions of others reflects and reinvigorates an uncertainty of self. Such uncertainty has, on occasions, driven proponents of the strategy literature out of their comfortable but congenitally failing search for the optimum rules of strategy construction and implementation. For example, Westley and Mintzberg (1989) pursue strategy through the terrain of the visible and visualizable in their account of the relations between 'visionary' leadership and strategic management. However, as Guillet de Monthoux (1996) makes clear, just at the moment when this move could become interesting, when one could start to consider the ontological status and consequences for action of those quasi-objects (Serres, 1987) of which 'visions' are an example, Westley and Mintzberg back away, resorting to exhortations for further research that would delineate the role played by those 'real' bodies of the leader and her assistants in practices of 'visionary' leadership. They want to know what types of people, in the rather banal psychological sense, and what manner of communicative techniques are required to make such a style of strategic management work. Rather than problematizing the notions of 'people' and the 'things' with which they work, these somewhat dubious representational products are merely reified as the authors remain 'caught in the dualistic labyrinth of subject and object' (Guillet de Monthoux, 1996: 158). The uncertainty of artifice does nothing more here than provide grounds for the perpetuation and extension of the practices that themselves served to create the uncertainty to which we are supposedly trying to respond.

Consistency

Strategy, as we have noted, problematizes identity, or better, it disperses, disseminates and so problematizes identity. And it does so in order to persist, to move, to re-actualize. A language of strategy is conducive of a language of future, of the here and now extending into the there and then (Kallinikos, 1994, 1995; Lilley, 1995). Indeed, as we noted, idealizations of the there and then are frequently constructed as reasons or justifications for that which we seek to achieve in the here and now. Talk of strategy elongates organization, providing future space as a new place for commodity exchange (Levitt, 1960). When we purchase life insurance, for example, it is the visibilities and articulations of strategy, 'set' before us on the 'screen' (Weber, 1996a), laid out before us in pictures and words, that in part constitute a future for the organization who receives our payment and thus a possible realization of the product we have purchased.[10] But these articulations and visibilities do much more. By continually re-invoking[11] the spectre of competing, but inferior, alternatives for our allegiance, for us to identify with, they distribute potential sources of identity widely. They exaggerate and problematize boundaries, agitating the existential unease of an interminably uncertain question of 'us' and 'them'.

This unsettling and inciting side of the language of a strategy of organized entities is, according to a Foucauldian schema, more closely associated with the 'power' side of the power/knowledge imbroglio.[12] Power relations excite and destabilize the integrations of 'knowledge' upon which they depend for their extension, providing ongoing grounds for re-integrations through both re-articulations and refinements of visibilities (or re-visions). This is why strategy is so concerned with movement. It seeks to keep up with a changing world, to enable its host to stay ahead of competitors, to bring about sustainable advantage. But it attempts to do all this through stabilization, through setting objectives, goals and visionary ends to which current activities can turn themselves, as means to ends. In so doing it forever, inevitably, exceeds itself, providing again and again the grounds for its own perpetuation.

The drive or desire behind strategy, the emotive force of its power does not itself speak and see. It, as we noted above, can tell us nothing directly. It is blind. Rather, 'precisely because it does not itself speak and see, it makes us see and speak' (Deleuze, 1986: 82). Power here is the 'spontaneity' to which knowledge and its devices and methods stand as 'receptivity'. Together power/knowledge constitutes a shifting multiplicity of 'informal' relations between, respectively, the 'affective' and the 'formal', the forces and techniques of action. Power, in this rendering, is more than force, 'not only because it passes in itself through categories that express the *relation* between two forces' (emphasis added) 'but also because, in relation to knowledge, it produces truth in so far as it makes us see and speak' (Deleuze, 1986: 83). Power marshals forces, playing them off against each other to enable stability, adding them together to initiate change. The things, the agents, that we become as a result of this process, are both cause and effect of power, just as intentional selves are both cause and consequence of strategy (see also Hoskin, 1996). As a result of our construction by, and enrolment in, power, we are forced to speak and see, for it is only through such practices that we can wield power and it can wield us. And the things that the power associated with the language of strategy allows and impels us to see and to say are interminable questions and answers about the 'truth' of our intentions.

Deleuze suggests that: 'If knowledge consists of linking the visible and the articulable, power is its presupposed cause' (1986: 39). This statement of the relation between our techniques of knowledge and the power that imbues them with the potential for transformative action expands upon one of the most cited quotations from the Foucauldian *oeuvre*: 'There is no power relation without the correlative constitution of a field of knowledge that does not presuppose and constitute at the same time power relations' (Deleuze, 1986: 39; Foucault, 1979: 27). This power proceeds, re-actualizing and destabilizing techniques of knowing, precisely because '*it produces truth as a problem*' (Deleuze, 1986: 83). And the problem of truth for matters strategic, is the problem of divining and expressing 'true' intentions. Intentions which themselves come to be taken as signs of the truth of our (human) nature.

Coherence?

Strategy presents us with a problem of truth around identity. In its invocation of competing positions for our allegiance it poses interminable questions whose answers truth demands. Questions like: Who are we? Who are we for? and, perhaps most explicitly, Who are we against? In more managerialist texts such questions present themselves in a suitably scientistic progressive garb. The triptych outlined above would perhaps expand to represent itself as: What is our 'corporate culture' and how does it relate to our 'core competencies'? Who are our customers and what are their interests? How can we add to the 'value' they receive from consuming our products? Through what strategic alliances can we best serve them? How can we achieve and sustain a competitive advantage against our competitors who are seeking to 'add value' to our prospective customers by meeting their 'needs' in similar ways?

As we have already intimated, the multiplicity of appropriate sites for our possible allegiance and inappropriate sites for us to stand against ensures that our answers to these questions are inevitably only tentative and temporary. Any potentially enduring site is always and immediately exceeded as irradiating webs of microstrategies emanating from other sites of identity coalesce and disintegrate. Identity appears here as an essentially contingent and fragile assemblage, a temporary marshalling yard of power/knowledge that endeavours to endure in a congenitally failing battle with a bewildering array of multifarious potential allies and assailants (Lilley, 1995). To take just one example, does the manager at an oil refinery ally herself with the technological imperatives of the systems she operates, the commercial demands of the circuits of capital into which she is inserted, the parochial demands of her department or the personal and idiosyncratic whims of desire which emerge from her extra-organizational activities? The questions of who we are for and who we are against are never ultimately answered. And, as a result, the question of who we *are* remains forever moot.

Identity, or self (consciousness)[13], is a crucial 'third element' in Foucault's work (particularly, 1979; and the unfinished investigations into sexuality that appear from 1984). 'Knowledge', 'power' and 'self' constitute three irreducible, historical dimensions for Foucault, three 'ontologies' (Deleuze, 1986: 114) or modes of being. They are 'historical' in that their (relative) value is derived from their historical status, from relations with and between *particular* systems of statements and visibility machines; from relations with and between *particular* forces; and from the *particular* ways in which subjectivization is achieved within 'humans' by the 'folding' of the exteriorities of power/knowledge, the making of *particular* interiorities in which we reside, by the convolutions of a *particular* historical 'outside'. We return to consider this 'fold' in more detail later in our account for as it is rendered by Foucault, it is a place which 'surpasses intentionality', where 'there is no intentionality' and no possibility of 'refounding' it (Deleuze, 1986: 111 and 109 respectively). But this is to put the cart before the horse. We must investigate the limits of intentionality before we exceed or 'surpass' them. And an appropriate strategy for doing so is perhaps one which continues our pursuit of the problematization of intentionality and identity through the language of a strategy of organizations.

Process

Organizations, as their very name suggests, consist of, exaggerate and extend *organs* – lines of sight, auditory channels, arbitrations of taste, specified 'wings' and 'arms' – sensors and effectors of all sorts. *Strategic* organizations do this in order to explore and attempt to see all that the vision machine, the arch-itecture (Kallinikos, 1995), and its associated luminescence allow. And in so doing their articulations 'stabilize' the 'shimmerings' of this luminescence differentially. Particularly important here are those articulations that recur or can otherwise be enlisted to ramify the network of sensors and effectors that search for ever increasing correspondence with the shifting results of the luminescent aura of the vision machine. But this, as Heidegger (1977) has shown us, is a 'gigantic' process that begins to feed off itself as its ramifications extend (see also Lilley, 1998). It is Baudrillard's (1984) world of *simulacra* in which everything radiates from and around temporary centres of nothing (see Rotman, 1987, for an application of such a notion to our contemporary finance community).

In this process, as we have already noted, the world is increasingly laid out not from the horizon of man that Heidegger points to, nor from the 'disinterested' horizon of God much favoured by Panglossian functionalism. Rather the horizons on which the world is seen and said become increasingly, and indeed self consciously, motile: shifting horizons that reflect an endless process of organization/disorganization in which temporary stabilities of identity slip in and out of being, as they are enticed by the language of strategy into assertions and denials of identity. Identities that seek to define and defend the boundaries shown to them, but forever exceeded by, the visibility machine. This process is ongoing precisely because the moves that progressively stabilize and evolve identities into being, themselves destabilize and dissolve identities, creating a world in which, as Marx and Engels inform us, all that is solid melts into air (see also Eagleton, 1987).

This process of organization is not one, as should be clear by now, to which we stand on the outside, as immutable agents. As sources of intention, invigorating the world into action, we do not remain inviolable. Rather our boundaries are forever breached and remade in the light of our shifting activities. In such circumstances the notion of 'organization' is insufficient to comprehend what is happening, for it presupposes a relatively stable distinction between that which is to be organized and that which does the organizing. The notion of cyborganization is much better suited to our purposes here (see for example, Gray, 1995; Haraway, 1991) for it seeks to emphasize the intimate relations between our current sensorial boundaries and the affects we are able to receive and the effects we are able to unleash. If we 'see' an object in the distance, for example, only through appending the artefact of a telescope to our eyes, then the 'we' that sees this object necessarily includes the telescope as part of its being. The telescope is integral to the seer for without it distant objects remain unseen. The key trope utilized for explicating this rather odd form of understanding is that of *prosthesis* (Wills, 1995), a term that describes the way in which the body is augmented by the addition of parts which extend its powers by rectifying its deficiencies. These deficiencies are, of course, to be seen as dependent upon the task or practice at hand. And they are remedied through re-presentation (Cooper, 1993; Scarry, 1985). The deficiencies of the body, such as its inability to see beyond certain limits are re-presented, inverted and materialized in a device that can be attached to the body to overcome that deficiency. This understanding enables us to see different bodies, doing different things, differences that depend upon the particular array of prosthetics through which a particular body, or group of bodies, and its powers are extended. Indeed, these different bodies may be seen to inhabit different worlds. The body with the telescope for example, lives in the realm of the far away, the body with microscope in the realm of small. Such an understanding is deeply materialistic, allowing us to ground understanding of what we do and what we are through reference to the artefacts that allow us to do what and of which we are consequently partially made. And as we have already discovered, these materials are not to be seen as limited to mechanical devices. Systems, those methods and rules that allow us to read and to speak, also extend us, for they allow words to travel from us to others and from others to us. Words too may be seen as prosthetics.

These extensions of the body are precisely the resources we need to understand intentions since intentions are, in part, 'given' by them. Aspects of our intentions are amenable to us through consideration of the extensions through which they are realized. The body and its capabilities thus appear as no more fixed than the motile intentions with which we have been dealing up to now.[14] This is precisely why those relatively progressive aspects of the strategy literature that seek to expand upon understandings of strategy as either a grand plan or as the more modest rationality of logical incrementalism (Quinn, 1980) are inadequate. The cultural turn introduced by authors such as Johnson (1988, 1992; Johnson and Scholes, 1988) appears to exceed the understanding of the rationalists but only through a rather neat sleight of hand. 'Action' is split into two parts: 'substantive' action which occurs when we manipulate 'real' things, and 'symbolic action' which is seen to occur in a somewhat separate cultural realm. This distinction is deeply problematic, as our preceding discussion makes clear, if not completely untenable (Feldman, 1996). It merely replicates the problem it seeks to solve at another level (Strathern, 1991).

Identity and Organization; Intention and Materialization; Strategy and Implementation: each latter partner promises to deliver the former but in doing so can do nothing more than exceed it, robbing it of ontology, of 'being in itself', as the promise of that ontology comes into view. Or, to put it the other way around, each latter partner seeks to persist as its shifting former partner renders it obsolescent. All of which inscribes for us an inevitable paradox at the centre of the strategy language game, a paradox of identity which we have skirted already. We can either have stable organizations with shifting strategies, or shifting organizations that bend to reflect our stable strategies. But we cannot have both. Which is perhaps the same as saying that we have to have both and thus no possibility of (stable) identity. It is this latter formulation that seems to offer the most fruitful avenue to pursue and thus we explore it in order to conclude our account of the (im)possibility of strategic intention.

Flexibility and the attractions of the gap

The root to the (dis)solution of the paradox outlined above is only to be found in flexibility. Not the limited flexibility much loved by pseudo-academic managerial prescriptions. But rather a generalized flexibility of form and content that demands a willingness to live without foundations and a consequent ability to think.

According to Deleuze's (1986) rendering of Foucault's own 'strategy' as it is exemplified in his work, thinking is at its most profound[15] (and thus at its most profane) when it itself operates in the 'gap', in the 'non-place', between seeing and speaking. For then and only then is common sense exceeded through the revelation that it only *makes* sense *because* it is common.

> Seeing is thinking, and speaking is thinking, but thinking [also] occurs in the interstice or disjunction between seeing and speaking. (Deleuze, 1986: 87)

This thinking may produce subjection through subjectification, through the dominance of an insistent identity, for it is precisely the result of a folding in of the forces of the 'outside'. Such a form of thinking is most likely when seeing and speaking as they currently occur are taken as natural, unquestionable and immutable. When the outside folds in in this way the inside is made predictable for it is given solely by the outside. In such circumstances

> ... thinking is not the innate exercise of a faculty, but must *become* thought. Thinking does not depend on a beautiful interiority that would reunite the visible and the articulable elements, but is carried under the intrusion of an outside that eats into the interval and forces or dismembers the internal. (Deleuze, 1986: 87, my emphasis)

Thinking thus occurs only when we are able to disrupt the taken for granted as it is given to us by the internalization of our modes of extension. When we presume foundations and depth to our being and behaviour, and accept them as the basis upon which we can seek to actualize our intentions and realize our strategies, we are trapped in a place that seems our own but that is given to us by the outside. A place, to be sure, to assuage our existential dread, but one that is governed by a choice that is made for us by contingencies that remain largely outside of our influence. Such a choice is chimerical but it is one with which we have to comply if we wish to retain our so-called strategic ability to choose. If, however, we are able to recognize the inside as *nothing* but the fold of the outside, as nothing but a 'gap' or a non-place, as nothing but nothing, then at last we may find that we have a place to be. For

> 'When the outside collapses and attracts interiority', the interior presupposes a beginning and an end, an origin and a destination that can coincide and incorporate 'everything'. But when there are only environments and whatever lies between them, when works and things are opened up by the environment without ever coinciding, there is a liberation of forces which come from the outside and exist only in a mixed-up state of agitation, modification and mutation. (Deleuze, 1986: 87)

Which is to say that when we give up on notions of an interior space that is ours and ours alone, a space from which we can create and unleash our idiosyncratic desires free from the control of outside forces, we may actually gain a space to think after all. Such an empty space exists precisely at that point on which the outside turns in, at the fulcrum of the fold that is the boundary between outside and inside. Such a boundary is always shifting, as we have noted, as we are extended in different ways through different arrays of prosthetic artefacts. And it is only in such a place,[16] in the ever-disappearing gap between intention and that to which it is directed, in which (strategic) thinking can occur. It is a place in which we may hope to experience '*life within the folds*. [A] central chamber, which one need no longer fear is empty since one fills it with oneself' (Deleuze, 1986: 123, original italics), with ones unique and ever-changing movements through the prosthetics of extension.

Selfless strategies will certainly be the result of a move to such a place, strategies that may seem 'mad', for these strategies will not be the products of either the rational self direction of autonomous humans or those given to us by the divinities of the outside. Rather, they will be the result of the happenstance of our movement and the serendipity of our experiences. Unpredictable to be sure, and ill suited for large scale coordination, at least those forms of large scale coordination which form the litany of success stories that make up the majority of accounts of management. But when we are everywhere confronted by the violence of current, supposedly sane, strategies which seek to do their 'good' in the name of either self interest or seemingly immutable ideals which appear to us to be beyond the scope of reasonable argument, it would seem that such a mad alternative is certainly worth thinking. Madness, according to Foucault (1995), 'cancels itself out in becoming manifest' (Brown, 1997) for it is at just this moment that it becomes nothing more than another aspect of our usual *work*, our ongoing attempts to put things in their place (Weber, 1996b). Great works, according to Foucault, are those that maintain their ability to allow the madness of *displacement* to unfold within them, at the self-same time as they hold that madness in place. Brown (1997, following Foucault) gives us the example of 'Borge's "impossible" encyclopaedia which changes its entire index and contents every time it is opened' (see the Preface of Foucault, 1970, for an account of this wondrous book). Such works provide equal support for processes of ordering and disordering.[17] They are just the sorts of products which our strategies should strive to create.

Notes

1   It is maybe worth noting here that for Eagleton the immanence of critique is taken as a welcome sign of its modern, quasi-Marxian status. Such forms of critique are valorized in his work and made to shine all the more brightly through being shown against the foil of a suitably charicatured, and thus politically quietist, 'postmodernism'.

2   Or otherwise 'perceptible'.

3   And inscribable.

4   It is important to re-emphasize here that talk of visibilities is not intended to emphasize an optical aspect of the machine at the expense of other sensorial modalities. 'A machine does not have to be optical' (Deleuze, 1986: 58). For

'visibilities are not defined by sight', rather they 'are complexes of actions and passions, actions and reactions, multisensorial complexes, which emerge into the light of day' (Deleuze, 1986: 59).

5   Foucault (1970) offers one final reading of the subject of *Las Meninas*, that of representation itself. In this view, the absence of a directly constructed image of the subject being represented by the painter who we see is key. This absence frees the act of representation from a direct relation to pre-existing things and thus shows, in something of an alchemic moment, the absurdity of a view of representation that is centred on mere copying. The absence of a reflection of the painter, the representer, in the mirror which is behind him, further exemplifies the point. The work of representation is (partially) occluded in this impossible representation of representation. (Editors' note: in a topical layering of irony upon irony, Annie Leibovicz has recently quoted *Las Meninas* in a photographic portrait of Victoria ('Posh Spice') and David Beckham.)

6   I am grateful to Bob Cooper for the helpful suggestions upon which many of these etymological forays are based.

7   Shaw sees broader usage as a 'dilution' which is ideally to be avoided, for such usage probably involves 'substantial shifts in the meaning of strategy' (1990: 467).

8   It can of course also work very well in the reversed form: '**strategic** _____ '. A prime effect of this move is a signalling of the importance of the type of second term activity that is to be engaged in.

9   In this sense strategy may be said to exemplify *power*. It concerns the relations between forces. Its being is purely *relational*. It purports to orchestrate 'action upon an action, on existing actions or on those which might arise in the present or future'; it is 'a set of actions upon other actions' (Foucault, 1982: 220; Deleuze, 1986: 70 *et seq.*).

10 This chain too is recursive. Claims against insurance are offset by collections of premiums into managed funds, stocks and shares whose values depend upon the strategic articulations and visibilities of, and around, other organizations.

11 But infrequently naming, at least in the UK.

12 As the '/' makes clear, any total association with one side or other of the divide would be a mistake that misses the virtue and value of this particular Foucauldian combine. It also alerts us to the marshalling yard, the 'gap', of connections and disconnections, unities and divisions, through which the combine works (see Barthes, 1974; Munro, 1997).

13 Self knowledge?

14 This understanding can also be grasped in simple terms as a radical extension to other modes of consumption of the dictum, 'you are what you eat'.

15 Literally, *before depth* (J.B. Sykes (ed.) (1979) *Concise Oxford Dictionary of Current English* (6th edition). Oxford: Oxford University Press).

16 The place of the 'non-place'.

17 Magritte's *Ceci n'est pas une pipe* is another obvious example here.

References

Arendt, H. (1958) *The Human Condition*. Chicago: University of Chicago Press.
Barthes, R. (1974) *S/Z*. New York: Hill and Wang.
Baudrillard, J. (1984) *Simulations*. New York: Semiotext(e).

Brown, S. (1997) 'To have done with the judgement of God', paper presented at the Uncertainty, Knowledge and Skill Conference, Limburg University, September.

Callon, M. (1986) 'Some elements of a sociology of translation: domestication of the scallops and the fishermen of St Brieuc Bay', in J. Law (ed.), *Power, Action and Belief: A New Sociology of Knowledge?* Sociological Review Monograph 32, London: Routledge. pp. 196–233.

Campbell, A. and Alexander, M. (1997) 'What's wrong with strategy?', *Harvard Business Review*, Nov–Dec.: 42–3.

Cooper, R. (1993) 'Technologies of representation', in P. Ahonen (ed.), *The Semiotic Boundaries of Politics*. Berlin: de Gruyter.

Dandeker, C. (1990) *Surveillance, Power and Modernity: Bureaucracy and Discipline from 1700 to the Present Day*. Cambridge: Polity.

Deleuze, G. (1986) *Foucault*, ed. and trans. Sean Hand. Minneapolis: University of Minnesota Press.

Eagleton, T. (1981) *Walter Benjamin: Or Towards a Revolutionary Criticism*. London: Verso.

Eagleton, T. (1987) 'Awakening from modernity', *Times Literary Supplement*, 20 February.

Ezzamel, M. and Willmott, H. (1995) 'Using accounts to blast changes through: from particularism to holism in cost and quality control', paper presented at the 12th EGOS Colloquium, University of Istanbul.

Ezzamel, M., Lilley, S. and Willmott, H. (1994) 'The "new organization" and the "new managerial work"', *European Management Journal*, 12 (4): 454–61.

Ezzamel, M., Lilley, S. and Willmott, H. (forthcoming) 'Accounting representation and the road to commercial salvation', *Accounting, Organizations and Society*.

Feldman, S. (1996) 'Management in context: culture and organizational change', in S. Linstead, R. Grafton Small and P. Jeffcutt (eds), *Understanding Management*. London: Sage.

Fisher, P. (1978) 'The recovery of the body', *Humanities and Society*, 1: 133–46.

Foucault, M. (1963) *Raymond Roussel*. Paris: Gallimard.

Foucault, M. (1970) *The Order of Things*, trans. A. Sheridan. London: Tavistock.

Foucault, M. (1977) *Language, Counter-Memory, Practice*, ed. D. Bouchard. Oxford: Blackwell.

Foucault, M. (1979) *Discipline and Punish. Birth of the Prison*, trans. A. Sheridan. Harmondsworth: Peregrine.

Foucault, M. (1981) *This is Not a Pipe*, trans. J. Harkness. Berkeley: University of California Press.

Foucault, M. (1982) 'The subject and power', in H. Dreyfus and P. Rabinow, *Michel Foucault: Beyond Structuralism and Hermeneutics*. Brighton: Harvester.

Foucault, M. (1984) *The History of Sexuality, Volume 1: An Introduction*. Harmondsworth: Penguin.

Foucault, M. (1995) cited in S. Brown (1997) 'To have done with the judgement of God', paper presented at the Uncertainty, Knowledge and Skill Conference, Limburg University, September.

Gray, C.H. (ed.) (1995) *The Cyborg Handbook*. London: Routledge.

Grey, C. and Lilley, S. (forthcoming) 'Civilization as we know it: organizing the world', Working Paper, University of Keele.

Guillet de Monthoux, P. (1996) 'The theatre of war: art, organization and the aesthetics of strategy', *Studies in Cultures, Organizations and Societies*, 2 (1): 147–60.

Haraway, D. (1991) *Simians, Cyborgs, and Women: The Reinvention of Nature*. New York: Routledge.

Heidegger, M. (1977) *The Question Concerning Technology and Other Essays*. New York: Harper and Row.

Henderson, B.D. (1989) 'The origin of strategy', *Harvard Business Review*, November-December: 139–43.

Hesse, H. (1969) *The Glass Bead Game*. London: Holt, Rinehart and Winston.

Hoskin, K. (1996) 'The "awful idea of accountability": inscribing people into the measurement of objects', in R. Munro and J. Mouritsen (eds), *Accountability: Power, Ethos and the Technologies of Managing*. London: International Thomson Business Press.

Johnson, G. (1988) 'Re-thinking incrementalism', *Strategic Management Journal*, 9: 75–91.

Johnson, G. (1992) 'Managing strategic change – strategy, culture and action', *Long Range Planning*, 25 (1): 28–36.

Johnson, G. and Scholes, K. (1988) *Exploring Corporate Strategy* (2nd edition). London: Prentice Hall.

Johnson, H. and Kaplan, R. (1987) *Relevance Lost: The Rise and Fall of Management Accounting*. Boston: Harvard Business School Press.

Kallinikos, J. (1994) 'On writing and rationality and organization', paper presented at the EIASM Workshop on Writing, Rationality and Organization, Brussels, March.

Kallinikos, J. (1995) 'The arch-itecture of the invisible', *Organization*, 2 (1): 117–40.

Knights, D. and Morgan, G. (1990) 'The concept of strategy in sociology: a note of dissent', *Sociology*, 24 (3): 475–83.

Knights, D. and Morgan, G. (1991) 'Corporate strategy, organizations, and subjectivity: a critique', *Organization Studies*, 12 (2): 251–73.

Knights, D. and Morgan, G. (1995) 'Strategy under the microscope: strategic management and IT in financial services', *Journal of Management Studies*, 32 (2): 191–214.

Levitt, T. (1960) 'Marketing myopia', *Harvard Business Review*, July/August: 45–56.

Liddell, H.G. and Scott, R. (1855) *A Greek-English Lexicon* (4th edition). Oxford: Oxford University Press.

Lilley, S. (1995) 'Disintegrating chronology', *Studies in Cultures, Organizations and Societies*, 2 (1): 1–33.

Lilley, S. (1998) 'Regarding screens for surveillance of the system', *Accounting, Management and Information Technologies*, 8: 63–105.

Mintzberg, H. (1991) 'Five Ps for strategy', in H. Mintzberg and J.B. Quinn (eds), *The Strategy Process: Concepts, Contexts, Cases* (2nd edition). Englewood Cliffs, NJ: Prentice-Hall.

Munro, R. (1997) 'Connection/disconnection: theory and practice in organization control', *British Journal of Management*, 8, Special Issue: 43–63.

Pearson, G. (1990) *Strategic Thinking*. London: Prentice Hall.

Polanyi, K. (1957) *The Great Transformation: The Political and Economic Origins of Our Time*. Boston: Harvard University Press.

Porter, M.E. (1980) *Competitive Strategy: Techniques for Analyzing Industries and Competitors*. New York: Free Press.

Porter, M.E. (1985) *Competitive Advantage: Creating and Sustaining Superior Performance*. New York: Free Press.

Porter, M.E. (1990) *The Competitive Advantage of Nations*. New York: Free Press.

Quinn, J.B. (1980) *Strategies for Change: Logical Incrementalism*. Homewood, IL: Irwin.

Rotman, B. (1987) *Signifying Nothing: The Semiotics of Zero*. Basingstoke: Macmillan.

Scarry, E. (1985) *The Body in Pain: The Making and Unmaking of the World*. New York: Oxford University Press.

Serres, M. (1987) *Statues*. Paris: Francois Bourin.

Shaw, M. (1990) 'Strategy and social process: military context and sociological analysis', *Sociology*, 24 (3): 465–73.

Skeat, W.W. (1946) *An Etymological Dictionary of the English Language*. Oxford: Clarendon Press.

Sloan, A.P. Jr. (1967) *My Years With General Motors*. London: Pan.

Strathern, M. (1991) *Partial Connections*. ASAO Special Publication 3, Savage, Maryland: Rowman and Littlefield.

Summa, H. (1992) 'The rhetoric of efficiency: applied social science as depoliticization', in R.H. Brown (ed.), *Writing the Social Text: Poetics and Politics in Social Science Discourse*. New York: Aldine de Gruyter.

Virilio, P. (1988) *La machine de vision*. Paris: Editions Galilee.

Vonnegut, K. Jr. (1971) *Cat's Cradle*. London: Victor Gollancz Ltd.

Weber, S. (1996a) 'Television: set and screen', in *Mass Mediauras: Form, Technics, Media*. Stanford: Stanford University Press.

Weber, S. (1996b) 'Upsetting the setup: remarks on Heidegger's "Questing after technics"', in *Mass Mediauras: Form, Technics, Media*. Stanford: Stanford University Press.

Westley, F. and Mintzberg, H. (1989) 'Visionary leadership and strategic management', *Strategic Management Journal*, 10: 17–32.

Wills, D. (1995) *Prosthesis*. Stanford: Stanford University Press.

PART 2

METAPHORS OF ORGANIZATION

5

The Scripted Organization: Dramaturgy from Burke to Baudrillard

Dan Kärreman

The sociologically informed, Peter Berger says in his *Invitation to Sociology* (1969), has but two ways available to understand society: either as a prison or as a play. If we accept Berger's distinction, suggested only half in jest, it is quite clear that organizations, undeniably both part of and a kind of society, have for a long time mainly been studied and understood from a prison's point of view – as behavioural, psychic and/or cultural prisons. As such, they have particularly been studied from 'the governor's' perspective, with the occasional study from the 'inmates' point of view; prison, of course, being a metaphor that exaggerates the carceral, confined and disciplinary character of organizations (but perhaps not by much, as Foucault [1977] indicates).

However, there are fewer examples of research that take seriously the possibility to view organization as a play. True, dramaturgical concepts such as role, actor, and – to a lesser degree – script are not alien to the vocabularies of organizational theory. But in most studies the potential in dramaturgical concepts is not fully utilized. They are typically used to describe static relationships and not the dynamic and perpetual ongoing in organizational settings – the acts carried out, the roles performed and the scripts executed. As Trujillo (1983) points out, in discussing Mintzberg's (1973) manager roles:

> Although Mintzberg observed the communicative actions of different managers, he offers a somewhat static list of roles without really telling us how those roles came to be enacted in the particular organizations he studied. His

emphasis is on context-free nouns – such as 'leader' and 'spokesman' – not verbs in context. (Trujillo, 1983: 76)

Insofar as researchers have been sensitive to the 'dramatic' aspects of organizational life, it is pretty much a sensitivity that ascribes a surprising amount of significance to the motionless aspects of the play: to scenography and to the props. Consequently, play and actual performance – and their dramaturgical underpinnings – are poorly understood aspects of the everyday drama of organized action, at least from the perspective of organizational analysis.

There are some exceptions to this general rule worth noting. Rosen's (1985, 1987) penetrating analyses, for example, demonstrate convincingly how dramaturgy and dominance – and particularly the dramaturgy of dominance – shape organizational life in an advertising agency. Mangham (1988) shows, in another example on what seemingly is a regular business meeting, the fruitfulness of analyzing the dynamics in dramaturgical terms. Moreover, Mangham and Overington (1987) and Czarniawska-Joerges (1997) illustrate how useful tools and devices developed for the analysis of literature and drama can be, when applied on organizational realities.

This chapter is indebted to the work of Rosen, Mangham, Mangham and Overington, and Czarniawska-Joerges insofar as they have shown the value and usefulness of a dramaturgical perspective on organizational activities. However, previous interpretations of organizational activity from a dramaturgical perspective will play a secondary role in this chapter. Instead, it will mainly focus on the dramaturgical perspectives themselves.

In particular, the chapter aims to explore key elements in two perspectives: *dramatism*, as most prominently described and elaborated by Burke (1969, 1989) and *dramaturgical sociology*, here represented by the work of Goffman (1959, 1967); and to point out their relevance to the field of organizational analysis. Dramatism and dramaturgical sociology, of course, does not exhaust the list of dramaturgical perspectives available. Such a list would be long, and would probably start with Aristotle's *Poetics*. The two perspectives are chosen because both provide rich and fairly consistent frameworks, and both are specifically developed to produce insights on social phenomena, such as organizations.

The chapter will also explore and discuss a set of concepts, developed by Baudrillard (1988, 1993) that, although hardly constituting a perspective, offer a thought-provoking way of analyzing the various ways organizational activity is scripted. While both Burke's and Goffman's frameworks explicitly connect to and use dramaturgical concepts, the work of Baudrillard does not, at least not in a systematic fashion. However, I will claim that Baudrillard's ideas of *simulation* and *orders of simulacra* have dramaturgical significance, and provide a helpful tool in analyzing the various ways scripting occurs in organizations.

Ultimately, this chapter aims to cast light on ways of analyzing the scripted and dramaturgical aspects of organizational activity. It does not aspire to make an exhaustive account of the contributions made by Burke, Goffman and

Baudrillard. Rather, it seeks to uncover useful and illuminating ideas provided by them; ideas that can help organizational analysts to understand and interpret the scripted and dramaturgical aspects of organization and organizing.

The chapter will proceed with an exploration of the dramaturgical perspective offered by the work of Goffman. The section will focus on the key elements in Goffman's framework. It will also attempt to show how one of his concepts, unfocused interaction, can be helpful in understanding the professional bureaucracy. The chapter will then shift to explore Burkean dramatism in general. It also will attempt to briefly illustrate the usefulness of a dramatistic approach in organizational analysis through a dramatistic analysis of organizational hierarchy. The exploratory parts of the chapter will end in a discussion of Baudrillard's idea of simulacrum, and how this particular idea can help us to understand better the various ways organizational realities are scripted. Finally, the chapter will bring the perspectives together in a concluding discussion that attempts to highlight differences and similarities between the approaches, and also their strengths and weaknesses as tools for analyzing organizational realities.

Social interaction as performance – the dramaturgy of the social according to Goffman

When talking about dramaturgical perspectives on social realities one cannot avoid mentioning the work of Erving Goffman. In fact, for many social researchers Goffman's work and the dramaturgical perspective are the same thing. Goffman summarizes his own perspective as follows:

> The perspective employed in this report is that of the theatrical performance; the principles derived are dramaturgical ones. I shall consider the ways in which individuals in ordinary work situations present himself and his activity to others, the ways in which he guides and controls the impression they form of him, and the kinds of things he may or may not do while sustaining his performance before them. (Goffman, 1959: xi)

Goffman's approach to dramaturgy has two major characteristics. First of all, he uses drama as a metaphor for human interaction. Human interaction is not identical with drama, but rather something that is, from an analytical viewpoint, usefully viewed *as if* it was dramatic and theatrical. Second, Goffman's dramaturgical perspective locates performances in the foreground and puts much more emphasis on this than other potential aspects of drama. He is primarily interested in the structural arrangements of the performance: the principles that drive and regulate the performances, both those who are engaged in the fulfillment of successful performances, and those activated in failed ones. Hence, it should always be kept in mind when adopting Goffman's framework that one enters a system of concepts that is developed for – and better suited for – analyzing the mechanics of human interaction rather than interpreting its meaning. Goffman's true contribution is, perhaps, that he demonstrates how much mileage there is in such an approach.

Goffman is probably most famous for his concept of *impression management* – that people continuously attempt to manage and control the impressions they create among others. Performances are, put simply, situations where impression management occurs. Impression management is a suggestive concept, but it is also somewhat misleading. The 'management' part may lead one to think that this is purely a conscious activity in the complete control of the performer. Also, it may imply that performers can choose to *not* manage their impressions. But Goffman's use of impression management and performance clearly indicate that he thinks that the terms are also applicable to situations where people rather behave habitually than purposefully. For example, when discussing a particular instance of performances, face-to-face interactions, he states that, although the field is marked by unclear analytical boundaries, the subject matter can be identified:

> It is that class of events which occurs during co-presence and by virtue of co-presence. The ultimate behavioral materials are the glances, gestures, positionings, and verbal statements that people continuously feed into the situation, whether intended or not. These are the external signs of orientation and involvement – states of mind and body not ordinarily examined with respect to their social organization. (Goffman, 1967: 1)

In the final analysis, impression management is not a mechanism that we can turn on or off, after our own choosing. Rather, impression management is something we all necessarily engage in when meeting other people. It is not optional, and can not be used to distinguish 'faked' behavior from 'authentic', since it is a necessary condition of being social. Thus, even 'authentic' expressions are mediated through the logic of impression management.

An anatomy of performances

Performances often, Goffman notes, include different regions where different types of activity take place. Typically, one can find a region that is directed towards a wider audience – the front stage, in Goffman's vocabulary – and a region where access is more restricted – the backstage. Performances occurring front stage are generally public performances, laden with scrutiny and evaluation and thus exposing performers to pressures to conform to public codes of conduct – for example, to be polite, to show good manners, and so on. Backstage events, on the other hand, are generally more intimate in character. It is backstage we typically express ourselves in relaxed and informal ways. However, back regions are not only breathing spaces. They are also the places where front stage performances are put together; where rehearsals are made, deals are struck and compositions are worked out. It is here casting take place, auditions performed and routines trained.

Although the events that take place backstage may strike the observer as places where people remove their masks and stop acting, it is important to remember that Goffman's perspective offers no space for any thinking of that kind. The performance may be different backstage, but it is still a performance, and the performer still performs. Rather than looking for places where people stop performing – because, in his framework, there are no such places – Goffman advises us to take a particular interest in passages *between* regions:

> One of the most interesting times to observe impression management is the moment when a performer leaves the back region and enters the place where the audience is to be found, or when he returns therefrom, for at these moments one can detect a wonderful putting on and taking off of character. (Goffman, 1959: 123)

The performances never stop. They are enacted in public places generally, brought to successful completion, Goffman seems to claim, by the omnipresent fear – shared by both performers and the audience – of the embarrassments that a failure would produce. They are produced backstage – by friends, family and acquaintances – perhaps less codified and generally performed with greater ease, with less pain at stake, displaying broader repertoires of conduct considered legitimate. And they can be observed in the passage between the regions, in people's preparations for entering either the front stage or the backstage regions – performances without audiences, save the accidental by-stander and the curious social scientist.

However, it must be stressed that Goffman does not offer a framework for the study of performances. He uses the term for analytical purposes. Performance might be a, if not *the*, key concept in his perspective, but it is not (really) what he is studying. Rather, Goffman's concern is *social organization*.

> A sociology of occasions is here advocated. Social organization is the central theme, but what is organized is the co-mingling of persons and the temporary interactional enterprises that can arise therefrom. A normative stabilized structure is at issue, a 'social gathering', but this is a shifting entity, necessarily evanescent, created by arrivals and killed by departures. (Goffman, 1967: 2)

Thus, performances are the molecules rather than the atoms in Goffman's framework. Performances are, in essence, sequences and sets of *interaction*. Goffman distinguishes between three basic modes of interaction, what he calls 'interaction units': *the social occasion, the gathering* and *the social situation* (Goffman, 1967: 144).

The social occasion is an event that is temporally and spatially situated in such a way that it forms into a unit that can be looked forward to and back upon, by participants and others that are informed by the event. It can, for example, be a dinner, a meeting, a soccer game or a party. Social occasions are to some extent self-contained events, that itself 'sets the tone for what happens during and within it' (144).

Gatherings refer to 'any set of two or more individuals whose members include all and only those who are at the moment in one another's immediate presence' (144). A gathering is, thus, a mode of interaction that is both more general and more specific than the social occasion. A party can, for example, include several gatherings and consequently be specified through an enumeration of its various gatherings. But gatherings do not need social occasions to occur. They occur everywhere people meet and intermingle – for example, in office spaces, street corners, at beaches and in restaurants.

The social situation refers to the full spatial environment that embraces interacting people. A social situation is created as soon as people engage in interaction, when 'mutual monitoring occurs' (Goffman, 1967: 144) and is brought to an end when the next to the last person departs. If gathering is a term that helps us to focus on the interactants in an interaction, the social situation instructs us to take notice of the spatial surroundings of the interaction and the impact it may have.

Furthermore, Goffman distinguishes between *focused* and *unfocused* interaction:

> Focused interaction is the kind that goes on in a state of talk; unfocused interaction is the kind that goes on, say, when two persons size each other up while waiting for a bus, but have not extended to each the status of co-participants in an open state of talk. (145)

Social science, Goffman argues, has spent much more effort in understanding focused interaction – what he calls *encounters* or *engagements* – than in understanding unfocused interaction. It is high-intensity drama that has occupied social scientists, rather than low-intensity ones. Organizational analysis is not an exception to this rule. For example, studies that have taken an explicit interest in patterns of interaction in organizations typically support their claims with empirical evidence from events where participants engage in focused interaction (Alvesson, 1996; Forester, 1992; Kunda, 1992; Rosen, 1985, 1987).

Low-intensity performances and normative control

There are, of course, good reasons for organizational analysts to concentrate on focused interaction in organizations. Much of what happens in organizations is achieved through focused interactions. It can also be argued that this is what organizations, to a considerable degree, are about. Work in organizations is focused activities and made possible through focused interactions.

However, there are both empirical and conceptual reasons why organizational analysts should take an interest in the low-intensity dramas of unfocused interactions. It is an empirical fact that many interactions in organizations are unfocused, especially in large corporations. The mere frequency of unfocused interaction in organization does not, of course, automatically make it important. But it makes it something worth checking out.

In some types of organizations – lawyer partnerships, financial organizations, computer consultancy firms and so on – unfocused interaction may even be the main mode of interaction among its members (Morrill, 1995).

In such organizations – labelled *atomistic organizations* by Morrill, but perhaps more generally known as *professional bureaucracies* (Mintzberg, 1983), or, in more recent terminology, as *knowledge-intensive firms* (Alvesson, 1993; Blackler, 1993; Starbuck, 1993) – focused interaction between its members is sparse and, in general, of little relevance for the ways work is carried out in the organization. Although the members of the organization share some things, such as office spaces and other common resources, they generally interact more, and in a more focused way, with clients than with co-workers.

To understand this type of organization – to understand, for example, how they are controlled and coordinated – an attention only on focused interaction seems insufficient. Unfocused interaction seems to be the main mode of interaction in this type of organization. Thus, it is likely to significantly affect control and coordination in this type of organization.

Goffman points out that there is more in unfocused interactions than we usually think:

> When persons come into one another's immediate physical presence, they become accessible to each other in unique ways. There arise the possibility of physical and sexual assault, of accosting and being dragged into unwanted states of talk, of offending and importuning through the use of words, of transgressing certain territories of the self or the other, of showing disregard and disrespect for the gathering present and the social occasion under whose auspices the gathering is held. The rules of face-to-face conduct obtaining in a given community establish the form that face-to-face co-mingling is to take, and there results a kind of King's Peace, guaranteeing that persons will respect one another through the available idiom of respect, keep their social place and their interpersonal commitments, allow and not exploit a traffic flow of words and bodies and show regard for the social occasion. (Goffman, 1967: 147)

Studies in organizational culture (cf. Kunda, 1992; Martin, 1992) have shown that if we want to understand the nature of control in organizations – what it targets and how it is exercised – it would be foolish of us to overlook the possible existence of normative control: 'the attempt to elicit and direct the required efforts of members by controlling the underlying experiences, thoughts, and feelings that guide their action' (Kunda, 1992: 11). Normative control is, Kunda claims, not only a way of maintaining the normative order but also a way of trying to shape it in a preferred direction. To study this type of normative order is to focus on and reveal its ideological underpinnings. Normative control, the kind Kunda elaborates, is generally exercised through focused interactions. This is revealed in Kunda's analysis: he analyzes the transformation of ideology into action in the organization he studied as executed through three different modes of *talk*: the ceremonial voice of hierarchical authority (talking down), the ritualized discussions in work groups (talking around), and the intermittent but highly stylized conversations between members of different work groups and organizational departments (talking across).

Still, as Goffman suggested, unfocused interaction also presumes, supports and reproduces normative order. But its scripts and modes of execution differ from the ideologically soaked normative order Kunda analyzed. It is a normative order regulated by the rules of tactful conduct rather than the rules and statements of an ideology: a centre-less, dispersed and almost anonymous authority, presumably operating in all organizations and presumably of particular importance in those Morrill (1995) labels 'atomistic'. Goffman shows a way to analyze such interaction. It is the task of organizational researchers to follow him.

It is easy to understand the relative popularity of Goffman's dramaturgical perspective. After all, it is accessible and offers concepts that are immediately useful. Kenneth Burke, on the other hand, provides a perspective that, perhaps, is richer and more far-reaching, but also more enigmatic and difficult to put to work. Nevertheless, in the next section I will seek to demonstrate that Burke's perspective may yield productive results when used in organizational research. At first allow me to briefly introduce the man and his ideas.

Staging the play – Burkean dramatism and the pentad

Unimpressed by the traditional division of labour in academia, Kenneth Burke has contributed to sociological, theological, philosophical and literary thought (Simons, 1989). He is also a poet and an author. While perhaps best known as a literary critic, Burke has throughout his long career – Burke was born 1897 – put forward ideas that have transgressed the demarcation between the humanities and social science. Much of his work is difficult to classify: whether it is literary critique, treatises in sociology, philosophy and/or social psychology, none of above, or all. This is, perhaps, one reason why organizational analysis – itself an eclectic discipline – should pay special attention to him and his ideas.

This section attempts to follow some of Burke's pursuits. It will, of course, not claim to do this exhaustively. Rather, it aims to point out some of Burke's central ideas and their relevance for organizational analysis. Hence, it will focus on a) his particular approach, which he labeled *dramatism*, and on b) his theory on the relations between the elements included in his dramatistic understanding of the social – what Burke call *dramatistic ratios*.

Unfolding dramatism

Humans are, according to Burke, 'symbol-using animals', separated from their natural condition by instruments of their own making (Burke, 1989: 16). It is the human capacity to communicate through symbolic means, that humans possess languages, that ultimately makes humans what they are. However, in contrast to what might be called the mainstream, representationalist view on language, Burke viewed language use as a mode of action, rather than a medium for propagating information.

> Human action is distinguished from animal motion by virtue of its symbolic
> character. For Burke, language is very much more than a means of pointing to
> referents. How we talk about things, how we name them, how we think about
> them and about ourselves, and how we tell others what we think are all shaped
> by language and by our own actions as symbol-using animals. (Gusfield, 1989:
> 32)

Burke's conviction that humans act rather than move, and use language as
their primary mode of action, leads him to adopt a dramatistic stance when
interpreting human conduct. In developing the dramatistic approach Burke
focuses his discussion on human motives. Dramatism, which surfaces as a full-
blown analytical framework in *A Grammar of Motives* (Burke, 1969, first
published in 1945), is Burke's answer to the question of what is involved when
we say what people are doing and why they are doing it. It is worth noting that
Burke concentrates on what we *say* that people are doing and why, in *our ways
of saying* what people do and why. In Burke's analysis, what distinguishes
humans is not that we are capable of having motives for our action – that we
are capable of behaving purposefully – it is that we can say something about
our own and other's motives. Consequently, what we say about motives is of
the highest significance if we want to understand the human condition.

What, then, is going on when we say what people are doing and why?
What is going on when we give statements about motives – our own and other
people's? According to Burke, the following is going on:

> In a rounded statement about motives, you must have some word that names
> the act (names what took place, in thought or deed), and another that names the
> scene (the background of the act, the situation in which it occurred); also you
> must indicate what kind of person (agent) performed the act, what means or
> instrument he used (agency), and the purpose. (Burke, 1969: xvii)

Furthermore:

> ... any complete statement about motives will offer some kind of answer to
> these five questions: what was done (act), when or where it was done (scene),
> who did it (agent), how he did it (agency), and the purpose. (xvii)

Act, scene, agent, agency and *purpose*. These are the elements of Burkean
dramatism – the pentad. It is not entirely clear what Burke means by 'complete
statements about motives' in the quotation above. One interpretation is the
obvious one: that statements about motives are incomplete if one of the
elements in the pentad is omitted. A statement about motives that, for
example, does not include naming of the act or the scene is incomplete in this
sense. But Burke to some extent, invalidates this interpretation in his claim
that *every* statement about motives implicates *all* elements in the pentad. One
cannot mention one of the elements (for example the scene), he argues,
without touching on or implicating the others.

Another interpretation is that Burke's emphasis on complete statements, on
completion, highlights and emphasizes the anti-reductionist character of the
pentad (Asplund, 1980; Gusfield, 1989). Thus, we should read this as a critical

remark aimed towards various scientific vocabularies regarding human motivation. As we all know, most scientific – or scientistic – attempts to explain human motivation adopt various reductionist strategies. For example, psychologists locate motivation in the human psyche (the agent), while sociologists tend to find motivation in the conditions that surround the human subject (the scene).

> The *Grammar* goes beyond the pentad to a general analysis of how our prefigured systems of thought emphasize some things at the expense of others. Academic disciplines, pushing their concepts to the ultimate, end by 'oversociologizing', 'overpsychologizing' and 'overeconomizing' the human subject. Psychology can be seen as a language which emphasizes the agent; sociology as a language of scenes. (Gusfield, 1989: 38)

Such vocabularies, Burke suggests, provide an incomplete and one-dimensional understanding of the subject matter. Thus, the pentad is not only a way of ensuring complete statements of motives, nor is it just an interpretation of the social world, it is also a tool for critical analysis of the way a perspective, be it psychological, sociological or economical, bends and biases the subject matter. The pentad is thus also useful as a *metaperspective*.

Although all elements in the pentad are involved, according to Burke, whenever social action occurs, different types of action – different types of drama – put different emphasis on the elements. In some accounts, the scene dominates, as it does in sociological accounts. In other accounts the agent is firmly established in the foreground, as he or she is in psychological accounts. And in yet other accounts, acts –the action – become the focal point, as they are in accounts of crime and in moral storytelling in general.

The literature on organizational analysis, for example, provides several examples that illustrate this point. *Contingency approaches* are clearly a way of writing on organizations – a way of stating what 'motivates' organizations – that emphasizes the scene. Contingency approaches state that organizational structure and behaviour are contingent upon the actual *situation* of the organization – especially the situation in its environment (cf. Lawrence and Lorsch, 1967, 1969). If the situation changes, so will (or must, there is some confusion on this particular point) the organization.

As a contrast, the *strategic choice* perspective (cf. Child, 1972; see also Sandelands and Drazin, 1989) puts as much emphasis on *agents* as contingency perspectives do on the scene. From this point of view, some people in the organization, the decisional elite, have sufficient degrees of freedom to make strategic choices that have an impact on how organizations work and operate. This is a reversal of the explanatory model offered by contingency theorists. From the strategic choice perspective, agents determine the scene – management (agents) can choose what conditions the organization (the scene) will operate in – while the contingency approach suggests that situational conditions (the scene) determine the structure of the organization (anthropomorphized to agent).

To complete the symmetry, we can also mention constructionist approaches – on the surge in contemporary organizational analysis – that tend to focus on *acts*, rather than agents and scenes (cf Czarniawska-Joerges, 1992). From this point of view, the various acts of construction, production and reproduction of, for example, organizational boundaries, power relations, products and memberships that take place in organizations is also what organizations are about. Hence, acts – especially acts of organizing – become not only what is important to study but also, in a sense, what is possible to study when studying organizations.

The multiple logics in dramatistic ratios

Burkean dramatism also includes a theory on how the elements relate to each other. The elements are not arbitrarily related, Burke claims. However, the relationships between the elements do not comply to a logic that is mechanically fixed and casually locked. The relationship between the elements, the way they implicate each other, is *dramatistically* bound:

> Burke expresses this as the ratios of propriety, suitability, or compulsion that prevail among the elements. There exists, in other words, a mutual round of requiredness among them ... They are, as Burke says, 'principles of determination' (Burke, 1962: 15). An act can require a particular scene insofar as that scene is appropriate to that specific act. (Signorile, 1989: 81)

Each relation – the relation between scene and agent, agent and act, scene and act, agent and agency, act and agency, and so forth – put up specific *dramatistic ratios* that restrict the ways particular specifications of the elements, from a dramaturgical point of view, can be combined. Bureaucracies, for example, make a scene that requires specific agents – bureaucrats – who perform specific acts, codified in rules and regulations. If we substitute 'bureaucracies' with 'hospitals' the statement above seems to lose something important. Bureaucrats and formalized rule-governed acts are not required in the scene that hospitals evoke. To picture hospitals as scenes that contain bureaucrats performing bureaucratic acts may be a picture with some empirical validity, but this picture also seems to miss the whole point with hospitals and what makes hospitals specific.

The notion of hospitals implicates other agents than bureaucrats and other acts than the formalized, rule-governed behaviour of the bureaucracy. Although hospitals, in their empirical manifestations, typically are rather bureaucratic institutions, hospitals are scenes that require their own particular agents – patients, doctors, nurses – and their own particular acts, such as medical treatments and surgical operations, in order to be hospitals. In this sense, dramatistic ratios both express the restricted nature of the relationship between the elements and, at the same time, essential aspects of the elements. They point out the mutually inclusive nature inherent in the elements of the pentad and, thus, the requirements of consistency between them (Asplund, 1980).

The consistency between the elements can take on different forms. It can be *causal* (cf. Burke, 1969: 227–9 where he elaborates at length on different forms of causes and their relationship to the elements in the pentad; see also Signorile, 1989; Asplund, 1980). For example, acts can cause changes in the scene – a very popular thought in the genre of organizational change, which thrives on the idea that specific acts can cause changes. Causal consistency can, of course, appear along all the ratios between the elements; scenes can cause acts, agents can cause acts, purposes can cause acts and so on. Obviously, some causal ratios are more likely to occur, or are at least somewhat easier to imagine, than others.

However, consistencies between the elements do not exclusively build on causality. Consistencies between the elements can be *coincidental* rather than casual. Burke illustrates this with Joseph Conrad's novel *Victory* where the plot reaches its dramatic peak simultaneously as a volcano erupts (Burke, 1969: 443ff.; see also Asplund, 1980: 149). Although the volcanic eruption provides more drama to the scene, consistent with what is going on plot-wise, Burke notes that the volcanic eruption cannot be said to cause the eruption in the story, and vice versa.

Furthermore, the principle of consistency expressed in dramatistic ratios between the elements in the pentad need not be causal or coincidental. It can also operate as a *principle of selection*, where it states that specific scenes *privilege* specific agents (and specific acts), rather than causing or coinciding with them. Hospitals are, for example, scenes that privilege nurses, doctors or patients. They do not cause them – at least not in any simple, clear-cut way – and the presence of nurses, doctors and patients at hospitals is, of course, not coincidental.

Combining dramatism and organizational analysis – some hints and suggestions

Expressions of hierarchy and hierarchical relations in organizations provide an opportunity to demonstrate the analytical usefulness in Burkean dramatism and its specific relevance for organizational analysis. Hierarchy is generally recognized as a powerful and popular tool for managing social relations. Few, if any, organizations lack hierarchical arrangements of some sort. It might mean different things in different organizations, but it is to some extent always present.

From a common sensical point of view, hierarchy and hierarchical position is something that mainly, if not exclusively, involves people – agents in Burkean vocabulary – since it is people that are hierarchically positioned in organizations. But since hierarchy is an abstract and intangible notion, saying something of how relations *between* people are expected to be managed, people themselves are poor indicators of hierarchical position. One cannot run a DNA-test to figure out whether a person is a superior or a subordinate.

People in organizations, thus, face the practical and pedagogical problem of converting the abstract and intangible character of their hierarchical position to concrete expression, to make it manifest. The ways and means available for this transformation are mainly dramaturgical in character. Office spaces, quarters, dress-codes, codes of conduct and so on, are more or less carefully orchestrated to fit to the accurate expression of hierarchical position.

Following Burke, we can say that expressions of hierarchy make use of the dramatistic ratio between scene, agent and act. Powerful agents (CEOs, Presidents), for example, are equipped or equip themselves with scenes that communicate their powerfulness: with staff of lesser important people that take care of problems of lesser importance (thus with other people operating as part of the scene), with rooms, office floors and even buildings devoted to the powerful, and with special means of transportation (limousines, corporate jets) at his or her disposal. The scene is often further elaborated: access is limited, time is scarce, the powerful is almost always on the move and in a hurry. This, taken together and in sum, underscores the importance of the agent and of his or her acts, and also communicates his or her potent capacity to deal with them.

In some organizations, a point is made of not marking hierarchical relations in too obtrusive terms. Fewer distinctions are made between those with different hierarchical positions. All employees, for example, may eat in the same restaurant, have roughly the same office space and so on. Sometimes reversals are made, where upper management is placed in the ground floor of the building rather than the top floor, often with the intention to reflect and communicate the emphasis that is made on egalitarian values in the organization (cf. Martin, 1992). However, this does not mean, from a dramatistic point of view, that they break the rule of dramatistic consistency. Or rather, they break it alright, but in breaking – or challenging – the literal rule of dramatistic consistency they accomplish the paradoxical result of obeying its spirit. This is so because the break, and the effects this produces, is intentional. It is an ironic gesture, so to speak, that acknowledges the usual rules of the game in breaking them. Thus it underscores rather than undermines the rule of dramatistic consistency, since the break is pointless without it.

If we are to believe Burke, almost all activity within organizations is dramatistic: where humans act, drama emerges. The scripting of hierarchy is but one of the everyday dramas taking place in organizations. The scripting of leadership – or followership – is another obvious candidate, scripts of conflict and cooperation are others. The pentad provides a way of thinking of such scripts, of becoming sensitive to them in all their aspects, and to analyzing and interpreting them, their inner relations and their connections to other scripts.

Drama in hyper reality – Baudrillard and the order of simulacra

Until now, this chapter has focused on perspectives that explicitly draw from dramaturgical ideas and concepts. In this section I will, for a brief moment, steer away from the explicitly dramaturgical. Instead, I will explore ways of scripting organizational realities through a discussion of Baudrillard's (1988, 1993) idea of simulations and, more specifically, on orders of simulacra. However, as the concept of scripting suggests, this section should not be interpreted as a departure from the dramaturgical, at least in the broad sense of the term. It is, in a sense, rather a matter of addressing a specific issue – the issue of scripting – that is central in any dramaturgical perspective.

The term simulacra refers to a world of reproduction, to a world constituted through systems of signs. It 'specifies the presence of human values and identities, particular practices and various accounts of reality' (Deetz, 1994: 210). According to Baudrillard simulacra arise with the modern epoch, with the decline of feudalism and with the novel idea that the sign expressed something other than the natural order (Baudrillard, 1983, 1993). In the feudal epoch, social position could be read from signs such as dress, where the sign and the signified were fixed in an absolute and unbreakable relationship.

> There is no fashion in caste society, nor in a society based on rank, since assignation is absolute and there is no class mobility. Signs are protected by a prohibition which ensures their total clarity and confers an unequivocal status on each. (Baudrillard, 1993: 50)

The modern epoch presents a break with this naturalistic conception, introducing the idea that signs *represent* social position, thus giving new meaning to the real and to counterfeit. The counterfeit in the feudal period was not only fake, it was also unnatural – a break against the natural order. The modern epoch introduced an element of arbitrariness between the sign and the signified. This gave birth to symbolism and the idea that the world can – must – be *represented*.

The idea of simulacra thus suggests a view of the world as socially constructed – a performance, so to speak. In that sense, it accommodates both to the dramaturgical perspectives discussed elsewhere in this paper, and to an understanding of social reality that is on the surge in contemporary social science. But, as Deetz (1994) points out, simulacra do not only suggest the social construction of reality, they also suggest its main mode of construction: through the rule of the sign.

Baudrillard identifies three orders of simulacra: *counterfeit, production* and *simulation*. The counterfeit schema builds on the idea that although the sign is representational, it is capable of representing the essence of the signified: its natural and intrinsic value. In a sense, first order simulacra is a representational practice that is nostalgic in character, since it claims to restore what it once destroyed: the unity between the sign and the signified:

> The modern sign dreams of its predecessor, and would dearly love to discover an *obligation* in its reference to the real. It finds only a *reason*, a referential reason, a real and a 'natural' on which it will feed. (Baudrillard, 1993: 51, emphasis in original)

Thus, first-order simulacra are representational practices that build on the idea of *imitation*, of counterfeiting, of creating perfect copies of real, or, perhaps more to the point, *natural* objects. As a sign system, it finds its value as a simulacrum of a 'nature' (cf. Baudrillard, 1993: 51).

Second-order simulacra – or production – arose, Baudrillard claims, with the Industrial Revolution. Rather than imitation and counterfeit, it builds on the idea of large-scale serial reproduction.

> A new generation of signs and objects arises with the Industrial Revolution – signs with no caste tradition that will never have known restrictions on their status, and which will never have to be counterfeits, since from the outset they will be products on a gigantic scale. The problem of their specificity and their origin is no longer posed: technics is their origin, they have meaning only within the dimension of the industrial simulacrum. (Baudrillard, 1993: 55)

In second-order simulacra, the natural (traditional) is replaced with the rational. Nature and 'natural' is no longer an ideal to be counterfeited, but rather something to objectify and instrumentally act upon, thus made possible to transform into objects, to commodify and exchange on markets. Value is consequently no longer intrinsic but extrinsic, based on the calculated effort to produce the object in question, and ultimately on its exchange value on a market.

Simulation, or third-order simulacra, is based on the idea of the *model* of the real – of the not yet-real, but yet better-than-real. The model, or the simulation, works in what Baudrillard called the 'hyper-real' world, whose construction is exemplified with the way media creates public opinion:

> By a circular operation of experimental modifications and incessant interference, like nervous, tactile and retractile impulses, probing an object by means of short perceptual sequences until it has been localized and controlled, the media localize and structure not real, autonomous groups, but samples, modeled socially and mentally by a barrage of messages. 'Public opinion' is evidently the finest of these samples – not an unreal but a hyperreal political substance, the fantastic hyperreality which survives only by editing and manipulation of the test. (Baudrillard, 1993: 64)

Thus, third-order simulacra is not only the idea of the model but also the idea that the model becomes more important than what is modelled. The arbitrariness between the sign and signified introduced in first-order simulacra is both further increased and, in a way, losing in importance, since the signified is overtaken – overruled – by the sign:

> People buy the model house which is needed only since it exists to be needed, rather than a home. The comfort of a home itself is a model rather than a feeling. The model job, the model career, the model home, each are needed not to fulfill aspirations and meet needs, but define what a better person than I in a better world would have as real aspirations. They define what a model 'I' would be. (Deetz, 1994: 210)

Ultimately, in simulation the border between the model and what is modelled – the sign and the signified – breaks down. And so do vital distinctions: the distinction between real and imaginary, between true and false, and between authentic and fake. The difference between feigning an illness and simulating it captures the point:

feigning or dissimulating leaves the reality principle intact: the difference is always clear, it is only masked; whereas simulation threatens the difference between 'true' and 'false,' between 'real' and 'imaginary'. Since the simulator produces 'true' symptoms, is he or she ill or not? (Baudrillard, 1988: 168)

Baudrillard claims that the different orders of simulacra have dominated in different periods in history. Counterfeiting was the dominant order of simulacra during the classical epoch – between the Renaissance and the Industrial Revolution. Production dominated during the industrial epoch, and present time in history is dominated, simulacra-wise, by simulation. The idea that there is a historical pattern in the way orders of simulacra evolves is perhaps Baudrillard's most imaginative claim. It is certainly his most provocative and – as many critics have pointed out (see, for example, Norris, 1992 for a particularly forceful critique) – least defensible claim.

However, as Deetz (1994) points out, although Baudrillard claims that this is the epoch of the hyper-real, his framework allows – in fact, presupposes – the potential simultaneous co-existence of different orders of simulacra. The orders of simulacra also, Deetz argues, roughly correspond to dominant conceptions of organizations: first-order simulacra being the representational. practice in use when scripting the organization in *cultural/traditional* terms; second-order is called for when scripting organization in *rational* terms; and third-order is evoked when scripting organization in *chaotic/postmodern* terms. Thus, Deetz claims, we must resist the temptation to view the orders of simulacra as belonging to successive phases of history, at least in the context of the modern corporation:

> Like with the three orders of simulacra, when organizational descriptions like traditional, rational and chaos are applied, it is very easy to think in terms of historical succession of types partly because dominance is more easily seen at different points in time. But organizations as constructed in our world today are composed in all three principal representational forms and dominance by a form is only momentarily held. The organization is a mixed site of the traditional/early modernity, rational/late modernity and chaotic/post-modernity. The various representational practices intersect, overlap and compete. (Deetz, 1994: 232)

Baudrillard's framework allows us to build an understanding, not only of the how of scripting in organizations, but also how, and to what extent, various modes of scripting – orders of simulacra in Baudrillard's vocabulary, representational practices in Deetz's vocabulary – interact. The way this occurs in empirical cases is in itself a significant and important issue. His framework also points at the possibilities of changing the play: of transforming the subject matter by changing mode of simulacrum. As Deetz notes:

> a discussion of worker rights can only be had in the context of competing rights of management, capital providers and general society. But when one advocates worker rights, and the reply is in the terms of economic costs or the open giving away of such rights in signing the work contract, the notion of 'rights' in

traditional discourse has already been transposed into the rational one. Rights is suddenly like other personal desires like owning a second car. (1994: 231)

The notion of orders of simulacra provides a tool that brings some light on these issues. Although it might not automatically be helpful in resolving conflicts over definitional authority, such as that one described in the quotation above, it helps us understand its scripted nature, the nature of the scripts that create them and the representational practices used in creating them.

Dramaturgical sociology, dramatism, simulacra and organizational analysis

Goffmanesque performances, Burkean dramatism and Baudrillardian orders of simulacra provide similar but yet different ways to address, interpret and analyze organizational realities. They are obviously similar in their productive use of drama to understand social processes. This is explicit in Goffman's and Burke's frameworks. Baudrillard draws less on dramaturgical notions, at least explicitly. However, it is quite clear that the realization and reproduction of simulacra involves their execution. Thus, they have to be performed and enacted. As Travers suggests, Baudrillard's idea of simulation can thus be interpreted as specific forms of performances, and, for example, be helpful in extending Goffman's perspective (Travers, 1990: 271–2).

The role and nature of language is another theme where there are significant similarities between Goffmanesque performances, Burkean dramatism and Baudrillardian orders of simulacra. They view language as an active and constructive force that shapes social reality, rather than as a medium that merely represents social reality. In this sense, they are proponents and parts of the linguistic turn that currently is making its mark on social science (Alvesson and Kärreman, 2000), and that currently inspires numerous researchers to rethink their subjects, methods and fields of inquiry, as demonstrated, for example, by the contributors to this book. Burkean dramatism and Baudrillardian orders of simulacra are, as demonstrated above, clear and explicit in theorizing language as a productive force, rather than as a mirroring media. Goffman's framework is, it might be argued, less outspoken about the role of language. Nevertheless, it is quite clear that Goffman adopts a constitutive view on language. This is particularly obvious in his analysis of verbal interaction, where Goffman views language use in conversations as connecting devices that take part in the creation of the social situation, rather than a medium for the exchange of meanings.

The differences between the frameworks, especially between Burke's and Goffman's approaches, are in a sense more interesting and revealing than the similarities. Since Goffman undoubtedly found much inspiration in Burke's writing it is no surprise that they share many assumptions and points of view. However, although Goffman explicitly refers to Burke in his writing, the dramaturgical perspective he advocates and develops breaks with Burkean dramatism in crucial ways that lead him to a distinctive framework of his own. Perhaps the most significant difference between their frameworks lies in the fact that Burke does not use drama as a metaphor for social action. On the contrary, he *literally* means that social action is necessarily dramatic.

> 'Drama' for him [Burke] is not a metaphor to be used in certain areas of social life but a fixed term that helps us discover what the implications of the terms 'act' and 'person' really are. In interpreting and depicting character the dramatist faces the same problem as does the sociologist. This is because human action is necessarily dramatic. Conflict, purpose and choice are inherent in action as distinct from motion. These characteristics follow from the fact that humans use and respond to symbols in creating meanings for themselves and their situations. (Gusfield, 1989: 36)

The 'hard' or 'strong' interpretation of the dramatic nature of human conduct advocated by Burke thus focuses on the meaning of meaning in human life. Burkean dramatism ultimately understands human conduct as an enterprise in meaning creation – as relentless production, enactment and distribution of meaning. Goffman, on the other hand, offers a 'softer' or 'weaker' interpretation of the dramatic character of human life that focuses more on the technical aspects of drama, rather than its meaning and consequence. From Goffman's point of view, the meaning of the performances is of lesser importance, or, at least, of lesser consideration:

> In Goffman's usage the stage is a metaphor drawn on to understand and analyze interaction. The play is not the thing, the way it is played is the focal point. There is much continuity with Burke in the conception of meaning as a creation of the human being and of the audience-oriented nature of interaction. But there are also significant differences which flow from Goffman's emphasis on the stage actor and Burke's on the play itself. Goffman's emphasis is on performances and performers; Burke's is on language and interpretation. (Gusfield, 1989: 37)

Strictly speaking, Goffman's focus is firmly on performances. Performers are certainly important for Goffman, but not in their own right. They are important because they are necessary conditions for performances to occur. In fact, Goffman works hard to *minimalize* the performer, or at least its possibilities to exercise ways of conduct not already specified by the performance itself:

> What minimal model of the actor is needed if we are to wind him up, stick him amongst his fellows and have an orderly traffic of behavior emerge? What minimal model is required if the student is to anticipate the lines along which an individual, qua interactant, can be effective or break down? ... A psychology is necessarily involved, but one stripped and cramped to suit the sociological study of conversation, track meets, banquets and street loitering. Not, then, men and their moments. Rather moments and their men. (Goffman, 1967: 3)

This leads us to another major difference between Burke's and Goffman's frameworks. Goffman's approach is, in the final analysis, an exercise in sociological reductionism. He aims for a minimal model of the actor, an actor that ultimately can be explained and understood through the social processes that trigger his or her responses. Burke, on the other hand, aims for a maximal model of the actor, a model that neither is stripped from its social context nor from its capacity to produce imaginative responses. The problem is not, from Burke's point of view, whether to choose between 'men and their moments' or 'moments and their men'. It is rather to adopt a perspective that is capable of handling 'man and their moments' *and* 'moments and their men'.

Baudrillard offers, through his idea of the orders of simulacra, yet another take on the dramaturgical character of human conduct. If Burke claims that human conduct is literally drama, and Goffman opts for a metaphorical perspective, Baudrillard invites us to view the dramaturgical character of human conduct as a historical process. The orders of simulacra point to different types of drama that, according to Baudrillard, dominate different historical epochal periods. Baudrillard may overstate his point in claiming that a new and higher order of simulacra completely replaces its predecessor, but offers, nevertheless, a provocative view on the matter.

Goffman's principal interest might be the mechanics of human interaction but there is nothing mechanical – in the sense of being flat and charmless – about the observations he makes and the vocabulary he employs to dissect and communicate his observations. In fact, one of the most attractive features of Goffman's work is, as Asplund (1980: 101) points out, its charm. A good part of the charm lies in the imaginative ways Goffman acquires empirical support for his claims; empirical sources including books on etiquette, odd newspaper paragraphs, casual observation of everyday life in homes and in the streets, casino behaviour and in-depth study of asylums.

Another part of the charm of his framework, and a great deal of its persuasive power, comes from his choice of terminology. Goffman's vocabulary consists almost exclusively of words anchored in everyday language use. These words are made into concepts through precise definitions and systematic application. For this reason alone, his work is instructive and worthwhile to read. Goffman's use of everyday concepts is a genuine advantage, not only because it makes his thinking accessible, but particularly because it makes it easier to connect his vocabulary to organizational realities.

The major weakness with Goffman's version of the dramaturgical perspective is that in many ways it isn't particularly dramaturgical at all. As Mangham (1988: 57) put it:

> It is odd that he [Goffman] should have become the champion of the dramaturgical school when one considers that he makes little use of the analogy and that little is ill-informed. In Goffman's theatrical frame, social actors perform, for the most part, within well-understood, well-rehearsed scripts which they have little or no part in creating.

While Goffman's use of dramaturgical concepts may be underwhelming, the opposite is true for Burkean dramatism. The upside of Burke's perspective is that it offers a rich, imaginative and generative way of looking at organizational phenomena that truly invites the analyst to take full advantage of the potential in dramaturgical concepts. Burke makes a compelling case for the usefulness of a dramatistic understanding of human conduct. He also provides a complete framework for analyzing human conduct in dramaturgical terms, a framework so complete that it almost takes the form of a philosophical system.

However, this is also a major difficulty with Burke's framework. There is an 'all-or-nothing' quality in it, in the sense that it is very difficult to make use of a few concepts, rather than the whole framework. Since the framework is vast, complex and covers areas that are unfamiliar and uncharted for most kinds of organizational analysis, it is all too easy to end up as a student of Burkean thought, rather than as a student of organizational activity through Burkean thought. Burke's framework is intriguing, original and insightful. It is also demanding, somewhat enigmatic and difficult to master.

Conclusion

Morgan (1986) may, in his seminal book, have proved Berger (1969) wrong in demonstrating that viewing organizations, and society, as prisons or plays does not exhaust the possibilities. Curiously, Morgan found no use for a dramaturgical understanding of organizations. Hopefully, this chapter has proved Morgan wrong. Dramaturgical perspectives on organizations are clearly useful in a number of ways. Particularly, they are helpful and productive in precisely those areas where mainstream organization theory performs poorly. Below, I will point to some of the more obvious useful aspects of dramaturgical perspectives:

They highlight interaction. Contrary to most organization theory, dramaturgical perspectives allow for an informed and rich understanding of conduct and human action in organizations. They provide vocabularies for the analysis of both routine and improvised interaction, and thus allow for humans to be both creative and repetitive.

They are sensitive to context. Most organization theory lacks ways of accounting for contextual features in a systematic way. Dramaturgical perspectives, particularly Burkean dramatism, provide a framework where context is accounted for, in both theoretical and empirical terms. Thus, dramaturgical perspectives make it possible to explicate and analyze contextual impact, rather than ignore or suppress it.

They are helpful for analyzing everyday situations. Most organization theory addresses human life within organizations in an abstract and reified manner. Processes of selection, for example, are difficult to translate to everyday situations, regardless of whether population ecologists, strategic choice theorists or contingency theorists describe them. Dramaturgical perspectives, on the other hand, provide vocabularies that translate rather easily into everyday experiences of organizational members. Goffman, in particular, shows how everyday concepts can be used for analysis from a dramaturgical perspective, if applied in a systematic and consistent fashion and also how productive such an analysis can be.

They emphasize the active and constructive role of language. The model of language in dramaturgical perspectives, as described in this chapter, stresses that language is in itself active and constructive, used for a variety of functions. They claim that language does not contain meaning in any simple sense but rather is used to construct or achieve meaning. Meaning is assigned by users to distinguish certain experiences from one another. The distinction between language and external realities is, from this point of view, a red herring. Language is external and real. The positivist dream of a pure observational language is not only pointless and misguided but also contradicts everyday use of language, a point elegantly made by Burke, in particular. Thus the study of social phenomenon inevitably includes the study of language and linguistic acts, an insight perhaps stretched beyond its limits by Baudrillard, but nevertheless worth emphasizing.

This chapter has attempted to explore some influential dramaturgical perspectives and show their relevance for organizational analysis. Hopefully, it will inspire others to take on dramaturgical perspectives on organizations. I have hinted at some of the areas where dramaturgical perspectives seem obviously helpful. I have also attempted to illustrate how dramaturgical perspectives allow us to reframe old concepts, such as hierarchy, and also to discover new areas of inquiry, as in the case of unfocused interaction.

Although there is some continuity, especially between Burke and Goffman, it should be clear the perspectives provided by Burke, Goffman and Baudrillard do not build on each other in any simple sense. Rather, they highlight different issues and provide different approaches to understanding the dramaturgy of organizing. Burke provides a framework that includes a set of fundamental elements, the pentad, useful – necessary in Burke's opinion – for understanding how social realities are constructed, and also an overarching idea – the idea of dramatistic ratios – of how the elements relate to each other. Goffman offers a penetrating and insightful vocabulary on the requisites of performances and also an argument of the fruitfulness of dramaturgical perspectives on social realities. And Baudrillard demonstrates the importance of understanding how representational practices are engaged in building drama and performances, and a framework that helps us analyze its modes of operations. Although none of the perspectives and sets of concepts discussed in this chapter are unproblematic, organizational analysis would be a richer and more insightful enterprise if it took advantage of them. They tell us important and useful things. We had better pay attention.

References

Alvesson, M. (1993) 'Organization as rhetoric. Knowledge intensive firms and the struggle with ambiguity', *Journal of Management Studies*, 30 (6): 997–1015.

Alvesson, M. (1996) *Communication, Power and Organization*. Berlin/New York: de Gruyter.

Alvesson, M. and Kärreman, D. (2000) 'Taking the linguistic turn in organizational analysis: challenges, responses, consequences', *Journal of Applied Behavioral Science*, 36 (2): 136–158.

Asplund, J. (1980) *Socialpsykologiska Studier*. Göteborg: Korpen.

Baudrillard, J. (1988) *Selected Writings*. Cambridge: Polity.

Baudrillard, J. (1993) *Symbolic Exchange and Death*. London: Sage.

Berger, P. (1969) *Invitation till Sociologi*. Lund: Rabén Prisma.

Blackler, F. (1993) 'Knowledge and the theory of organizations: organizations as activity systems and the reframing of management', *Journal of Management Studies*, 30 (6): 863–84.

Burke, K. (1969) *A Grammar of Motives*. Englewood Cliffs, NJ: Prentice-Hall.

Burke, K. (1989) *On Symbols and Society*. Chicago: University of Chicago Press.

Child, J. (1972) 'Organisation structure, environment and performance: the role of strategic choice', *Sociology*, 6: 1–21.

Czarniawska-Joerges, B. (1992) *Exploring Complex Organization*. Newbury Park: Sage.

Czarniawska-Joerges, B. (1997) *Narrating the Organization: Dramas of Institutional Identities*. Chicago: University of Chicago Press.

Deetz, S. (1994) 'Representative practices and the political analysis of corporations: building a communication perspective in organization studies', in B. Kovacic (ed.), *Organizational Communication: New Perspectives*. Albany, NY: State University of New York Press.

Forester, J. (1992) 'Critical ethnography: on fieldwork in a Habermasian way', in M. Alvesson and H. Wilmott (eds), *Critical Management Studies*. London: Sage. pp. 46–65.

Foucault, M. (1977) *Discipline and Punish: the Birth of the Prison*. London: Allen Lane.

Goffman, E. (1959) *The Presentation of Self in Everyday Life*. New York: Doubleday.

Goffman, E. (1967) *Interaction Ritual: Essays on Face-to-face Behavior*. Chicago: Aldine.

Gusfield, J.R. (1989) 'The bridge over separated lands: Kenneth Burke's Significance for the study of social action', in H. Simons and T. Melia (eds), *The Legacy of Kenneth Burke*. Madison, WS: The University of Wisconsin Press. pp.28–54.

Kunda, G. (1992) *Engineering Culture. Control and Commitment in a High-Tech Corporation*. Philadelphia: Temple University Press.

Lawrence, P.R. and Lorsch, J.W. (1967) 'Differentiation and integration in complex organizations', *Administrative Science Quarterly*, 12 (1): 1–47.

Lawrence, P.R. and Lorsch, J.W. (1969) *Organization and Environment*. Homewood, IL: Richard D. Irwin.

Mangham, I. (1988) *Power and Performance in Organizations: an Exploration of Executive Process*. Oxford: Blackwell.

Mangham, I. and Overington, M. (1987) *Organizations as Theatre*. Chichester: Wiley.

Martin, J. (1992) *Culture in Organizations: Three Perspectives*. Oxford: Oxford University Press.

Mintzberg, H. (1973) *The Nature of Managerial Work*. New York: Harper & Row.

Morgan, G. (1986) *Images of Organization*. Beverly Hills, CA: Sage.

Morrill, C. (1995) *The Executive Way: Conflict Management in the Corporation.* Chicago: Chicago University Press.

Norris, C. (1992) *Uncritical Theory: Postmodernism, Intellectuals and the Gulf War.* London: Lawrence & Wishart.

Rosen, M. (1985) 'Breakfast at Spiro's. Dramaturgy and dominance', *Journal of Management*, 11 (2): 31–48.

Rosen, M. (1987) 'Producer cooperatives, education and the dialectic logic of organization', *Praxis International*, 7 (1): 111–24.

Sandelands, L. and Drazin, R. (1989) 'On the language of organization theory', *Organization Studies*, 10: 457–78.

Signorile, V. (1989) 'Ratios and causes: the pentad as an etiological scheme in sociological explanation', in H. Simons and T. Melia (eds), *The Legacy of Kenneth Burke*. Madison, WS: The University of Wisconsin Press. pp. 74–98.

Simons, H. (1989) 'Introduction: Kenneth Burke and the rhetoric of the human sciences', in H. Simons and T. Melia (eds), *The Legacy of Kenneth Burke*. Madison, WS: The University of Wisconsin Press. pp. 3–27.

Starbuck, W. (1993) 'Keeping a butterfly and an elephant in a house of cards: the elements of exceptional success', *Journal of Management Studies*, 30 (6): 885–921.

Travers, A. (1990) 'Seeing through: symbolic life and organization research in a postmodern frame', in B. Turner (ed.), *Organizational Symbolism*. Berlin: de Gruyter. pp. 271–289.

Trujillo, N. (1983) 'Performing Mintzberg's roles', in L. Putnam and M. Pacanowsky, *Communication and Organization*. Beverly Hills, CA: Sage. pp. 73–97.

6

Mining for Meaning: Reading Organizations using Hermeneutic Philosophy

Tojo Joseph Thatchenkery

The mere observing of a thing is no use whatsoever. Observing turns into beholding, beholding into thinking, thinking into establishing connection, so that one may say that every attentive glance we cast on the world is an act of theorizing.

Goethe (1930)

In 'Stories of the storytelling organization' Boje (1995) describes his experience of watching one of Los Angeles' longest running plays, *Tamara*[1]. In this interactive, multi-dimensional play, a dozen characters unfold their stories before a walking (sometimes running) audience. During the play, the audience splits into small groups that chase characters from room to room, and from floor to floor in order to co-create the stories that interest them the most. Assuming a dozen stages and a dozen characters, the number of story lines an audience could trace chasing the wandering discourses of *Tamara* is significant (726 to be exact). For example, Boje (1995) followed the chauffeur from the kitchen to the maid's bedroom; there she meets the butler who has just entered from the drawing room. Later, they each move on to different rooms, leaving Boje and the audience to choose whom to follow. As the audience decides to follow different characters through different spaces, each of them experiences a different story. No one in the audience can follow all the stories since the action is *simultaneous*, involving different characters in different rooms and chambers on different floors. As a result, *Tamara* cannot be understood in one visit, even if a group of friends split off into six different directions and share their stories later. 'One can even be in one room with one's best friend and if they both came to this room by way of different rooms and character sequence, each friend can walk away from the same conversation event with entirely different stories' (Boje, 1995: 4). Thus, though the audience can trace a multitude of evolving discourses in the play, they cannot find one story to hold it all together, because each member of the audience experiences a different story depending on his/her choices of character/stage.

The *Tamara* play is a good metaphor for introducing the concept of organizations as texts. Depending on where one is coming from, the readers of organizations (such as customers, employees, managers and other stakeholders) experience the same organization differently. Dilthey said the same about life in general several decades ago:

> Our understanding of life is only a constant approximation; that life reveals quite different sides to us according to the point of view from which we consider its course in time is due to the nature of both understanding and life. (1976: 109)

In the same vein, our understanding of organizations too is only a constant approximation, they reveal quite different sides to us according to the point of view from which we study them. For example, Morgan (1996) has shown that organizations can be analyzed as 'machines', 'organisms', 'brains', 'cultures', 'psychic prisons', 'political systems', 'instruments of domination' or as 'flux or transformation'.

The intent of this chapter is to explore a notion of organizations as texts using hermeneutics as the underlying philosophical foundation. The notion that organizations can be read as texts has been suggested by only a few writers before (e.g. Barry and Elmes, 1997; Czarniawska, 1997; Grant et al., 1998; Kets de Vries and Miller, 1987; O'Connor, 1995; Thachankary, 1992; Woodilla, 1998). Using narrative theory, Barry and Elmes (1997) explored strategic management as a form of fiction. They aptly started their analysis by quoting narrativist Wallace Martin who said,

> By changing the definition of what is being studied, we change what we see; and when different definitions are used to chart the same territory, the results will differ, as do topographical, political, and demographic maps, each revealing one aspect of reality by virtue of disregarding all others. (1986: 15)

Similarly, Kets de Vries and Miller (1987) have discussed the roots and modes of the analysis of text as it can be found in the fields of cultural anthropology, psychoanalysis and hermeneutics. They saw methodological similarities despite the clear differences among the three traditions. For example, in anthropology, Geertz (1973) looked for deep underlying structures while remaining firmly in touch with the observable reality. In doing so, Geertz made his now well-known distinction between 'thin' and 'thick' descriptions. While the former focuses on the narrow observable and the simple relating of facts, the latter is interpretive. As in literary criticism, thick description involves an iterative process of analysis that seeks out the underlying significance of events. In other words, this is a study of 'text', an analysis of a 'multiplicity of complex structures, many of them superimposed or knotted into one another, which are at once, strange, irregular, and inexplicit, and which we must continue somehow first to grasp and then to render' (Geertz, 1973: 10). Within that context, texts may be viewed as groupings of interrelated elements, all types of data that contain messages and themes that can be analyzed. According to Kets de Vries and Miller (1987), in decoding texts, significance is extracted from interrelated factual, cognitive and affective units that make them up and are themselves constructed out of similar units representing experiences. 'The observer in his or her search for meaning becomes like a translator and cryptographer, transforming different levels of understanding' (Kets de Vries and Miller, 1987: 235).

Psychoanalysis as an interpretive science is a good example of a hermeneutics where the hermeneutic analysis tries to recreate or re-experience the thoughts of the creator of the text (Kets de Vries and Miller, 1987). The text deepens as we re-experience it. In the same vein, Zaleznik and Kets de Vries (1984) argued that in studying organizations one could interpret their texts through an analysis of managerial statements, writing and observable behaviour. For doing so, one needs to be alert to themes, meaning behind metaphors, reasons for the selection of certain words and the implication of certain activities (Barley, 1983; Riley, 1983).

Grant et al. (1998) devoted an entire book to compiling works that look at organizational discourse, a concept closely aligned with the text metaphor. This, combined with their earlier work on *Metaphors and Organizations* (Grant and Oswick, 1996) and Linstead's (1999) edited special issue of the journal *Studies in Cultures, Organizations and Societies* on the textuality of organization, makes a strong case for seeing organizations as texts.

Before further discussion of organizations as texts is embarked upon, it is necessary to briefly outline the philosophic and epistemological context that supports such a textual analysis. It is commonly referred to as the *linguistic turn,* after Charles Taylor (1985).

The 'linguistic turn' in the study of organizations

One of the distinguishing features of the current era is the linguistic turn that has prompted social scientists to recognize the force with which language shapes the course and meaning of human affairs. Post-Wittgensteinian philosophers have seen language as the basic vehicle by which we construct the reality of our shared world (for example linguist and sociologists Whorf, Schutz and Garfinkel). Sociologists Berger and Luckman's (1966) treatise on the social construction of reality brought about a minor revolution within the sociology of knowledge discourse. Since then scholars in legal studies, cultural studies, political science, psychology, history, communication, management and anthropology have framed human interaction as occurring within a socially constructed, linguistically created world (Gergen, 1999; McCloskey, 1985; Taylor, 1981). In addition, postmodern thinkers such as Foucault and Derrida regard language and discourse as the force through which humans create the historical and cultural traditions that in turn create a self-referential (Lyotard, 1984) reality for them. As Stanley Fish notes, 'we live in a rhetorical world.' Our world is framed by language and has meaning because of linguistically created social structures. In fact, a variety of vocabularies have developed to represent this linguistic turn. Grant and colleagues (1998) cite a number of examples: language games, discourses, narratives and stories, conversation, sense making, drama, theatre and texts.

To a large extent, the linguistic turn in the social sciences is about treating the world as a text. The social actor is immersed in an incredibly complex and vast semiotic field of mixed messages, conflicting meanings and inconsistent impulses. As Bourdieu (1990) points out, language is part of our worldview – as water is to fish. Lyotard has remarked that all individuals are located through language and that language games are a 'minimum relation required for society to exist.' Language affects what we see and even the logic we use to structure our thought (Gergen and Thatchenkery, 1996: Graumann and Gergen, 1996). Therefore, 'being-in-the-world' (Heidegger, 1962) itself is an experience of being with language. In *Truth and Method* Gadamer (1975) argues that language is a medium within which we move and understand ourselves and the world from various perspectives. It is an inter-subjective fabric of semantic relations that both makes possible and limits understanding. In his own words 'being that can be understood is language' (Gadamer, 1975: 432) and 'in language the reality beyond every individual consciousness becomes visible' (1975: 437).

As Weick (1979) points out, organizing is rooted in *linguistic* agreements regarding what is real and illusory, a grounding that is called '*consensual validation*'. In other words,

> organizing is like a grammar in the sense that it is a systematic account of rules and conventions by which sets of interlocked behaviors are assembled to form social processes that are intelligible to actors. It is also a grammar in the sense that it consists of rules for forming variables and causal linkages into meaningful structures (called cause maps) that summarize the experiences of the people who are organized. (Weick, 1979: 3–4)

One of the key pillars of the linguistic turn is hermeneutic philosophy, a brief description of which follows.

What is hermeneutics?

The term 'hermeneutics' comes from the classical Greek verb Hermeneuein, *to interpret*. In ancient Greece the priest at the Delphi oracle was called Hermeneios. The Greek god Hermes, the messenger of Zeus, was credited with 'transmitting what was beyond human understanding into a form that human intelligence can grasp' (Palmer, 1969: 13). During the seventeenth century, hermeneutic study emerged as a discipline devoted to establishing guidelines for the proper interpretation of Biblical scripture (the Protestant Reformation created a need to interpret the scriptures without church authority). Since then, hermeneutic study has evolved into a form of inquiry primarily concerned with the processes by which human beings interpret or discover the meaning of human action in general and linguistic expression in particular (Bleicher, 1980; Gergen et al., 1986). In other words, hermeneutics deals with the understanding of understanding. In Palmer's words, 'whenever rules and systems of explaining, understanding or deciphering texts arise, there is hermeneutics' (Palmer, 1981: 458). Thus, hermeneutics is defined as the study of the methodological principles of interpretation and explanation of any kind of text or action (Ricoeur, 1971). It involves two different and interacting foci of attention: (1) the event of understanding a text, and (2) the more encompassing question of what understanding and interpretation, as such, are (Palmer, 1969).

The scope of hermeneutics expanded in the nineteenth century thanks to the work of Schleiermacher and Dilthey who moved the focus of hermeneutic inquiry from texts to all human productions – verbal and nonverbal. Dilthey (1988) was keen on securing an independent status for humanistic disciplines separate from the physical sciences and the way to do so, for him, was to model the social and cultural sciences on the interpretation of texts. Dilthey (1988) saw the differences between the natural and human sciences as one between 'explanation' and 'understanding'. Explanation in the natural sciences comprehends its object through causal connections whereas understanding 'knows' its object (in this case human production) from the inside. In the twentieth century Heidegger and his pupil Gadamer expanded the scope of hermeneutics considerably. In his well known work *Being and Time* (1962), Heidegger gave an ontological dimension to hermeneutics by describing understanding and interpretation as essential features of being. Gadamer refined this notion further by emphasizing the notion of historicity (explained later in the chapter).

To summarize, according to hermeneutical philosophy, language is the medium of all human experience. 'Language allows humans to dwell in the house of being ... Language is the fundamental mode of operation of our being-in-the-world and an all embracing form of the constitution of the world' (Gadamer, 1976: 3). We are able to understand the world only through the use of words. Yet, the human world is *linguistically preconstituted*. We inherit language in the '*social uterus*'. In other words, language precedes us in the world.

Historicity and contexuality

Historicity is a key element of hermeneutics. Hermeneutical thinkers resist the notion of a wordless and a timeless source of insight. Human understanding always takes place within an emerging linguistic framework evolved over time in terms of historically conditioned concerns and practices. Gadamer (1975) maintained that to have a method is to already have an interpretation. As pointed out by Phillips (1996) in his interpretation of Gadamer,

> the interpreter does not interpret and understand from an Archimedean point but is always immersed in his or her own historicity. Hermeneutics is an encounter between the researcher of the present, aware of his or her historically conditioned categories of understanding, and a past that presents itself for interpretation. From this perspective the very notion of a historical object separate from myself as the interpreter, does not make sense. (Phillips, 1996: 2)

In Gadamer's words, 'a text is understood only if it is understood in a different way each time' (1975: 275–6). In summary, language and history are always both *conditions* and *limits* of our understanding.

The thesis of historicity is central to the understanding of organizations because historicity colours our ability to make sense of what is happening in organizations. Our knowledge of organizations is intertwined with the historical situation of both its creators and users. In other words, there is no knowledge or truth in organizations independent of a historical context. They can only be true in a pragmatic sense of being the best solution at that time to a problem that has been generated out of a set of historically mediated understandings, interests and practices. For example, scientific management was the dominant paradigm to explain efficiency during the period between the 1930s and 1950s. Later, the human relations school became highly influential followed by the contingency approaches. Such simultaneous privileging of certain discourses and deprivileging of others can also be seen in organizations if one looks at them historically (Thatchenkery and Upadhyaya, 1996).

Applying historicity to individuals, Sampson (1989) has argued that psychology's current theories of the person were developed during the era of modernism in a world dominated by industrialization, technology, secularism, individualism and democracy, and a world in which the self-contained individual emerged from embeddedness in various collectivities to become the free-standing, central unit of the new social order. Premodern western society, on the other hand, understood persons as defined by their particular social contexts. Persons were fundamentally citizens of the *polis,* members of their religious communities, family members, soldiers and so forth, not merely individuals as such. Unlike our current understanding, which distinguishes between real persons and the roles they must play, in premodern society roles were the elements that constituted the person as such (Sampson, 1989).

Another construct in hermeneutics that is closely related to historicity is 'contextuality'. Understanding a particular activity is not possible without understanding the context within which it occurs. Heidegger called this the *referential totality*. The same action or event will have different meaning in different contexts. For example, consider an organizational intervention to introduce team-based management within a context of mistrust and suspicion. It may be perceived as an attempt on the part of the management to remove employees they don't like, a public relations ploy, etc. On the contrary, in a context where openness and trust exist, the same intervention may be received enthusiastically.

Most hermeneutic inquiry begins by articulating the historical and contextual dimensions of the variable or questions under study. This is typically accomplished by a process called the hermeneutic circle.

The hermeneutic circle

The process of hermeneutic inquiry is an iterative one in which the examination moves between the whole, the parts and back again. The process of understanding is a dialectical one between the parts and the whole and comprehension and explanation. This is so because every understanding must be based on some pre-understanding of the concepts used to express meanings. This is called the '*hermeneutic circle*' where '… the anticipation of the global meaning of a text gets articulated through a process in which the meaning of the parts is determined by the whole and also determines the global meaning of the text, etc., as a whole' (Radnitzky, 1968: 23).

It was Frederich Schleiermacher who gave the first description of the hermeneutic circle (Palmer, 1969). Understanding inevitably involves reference to that which is already known; it operates in a circular, dialectical fashion. For example, consider the meaning of a sentence. The sentence derives its meaning from the individual words it comprises, but our interpretation of word meanings within a sentence is also governed by their relation within the sentence and the meaning of the sentence as a whole. Thus, interpretation always occurs in a circle in which the parts are always interpreted within some understanding of the whole, which in turn is understood by coming to understand constituent parts.

The hermeneutic circle, in the final analysis, describes the contextual nature of knowledge mentioned above. A fact does not stand on its own independent from its context or its interpreter, but rather is partially constituted by them. A fact can be evaluated only in relation to the larger structure of theory or argument of which it is a part. At the same time, this larger structure is dependent on its individual parts, as well as on other related information. In explicating the circle of understanding, we move back and forth between part and whole. Geertz described this as a 'continuous dialectical tacking between the most local of local detail and the most global of global structure in such a way to bring both into view simultaneously' (1973: 239).

Theoretically, the hermeneutic circle is indefinite. As one probes further, still deeper layers of meaning begin to emerge. However, hermeneutics is a pragmatic endeavour and 'suspends' the engagement with hermeneutic circle iterations as soon as a coherent interpretation that is free of apparent contradictions has been obtained. This is also called the point of saturation in hermeneutic inquiry.

The above introduction to hermeneutics is very elementary and over-simplified. Yet, it is time to make a transition and ask the questions: How can one apply the hermeneutic paradigm for understanding the role of language in organizations? What are the benefits of using hermeneutic philosophy in studying organizations? The *paradigm of the text* is introduced below as a potential answer to these questions.

The paradigm of the text

Textuality is not easy to define. In *Textualities: Between Hermeneutics and Deconstruction*, Silverman (1994) sees it as being a 'meaning-structure' opened up in a text but not necessarily contiguous with it. According to him, 'the text is what is read, but its textuality or textualities is how it is read' (Silverman, 1994:

81). For example, if we read a text as an autobiography, we have embedded ourselves in a 'autobiographical' textuality. Sometimes a text might be incorporated in a number of textualities, such as reading the autobiographical text of Nietzsche's *Ecce Homo* as a philosophical text. Thus, we may not simply assign the text to a single genre as if this assignment defined the limits of the text's meaning.

A text refers to any structure that contains a network of interrelated meaning. According to Gadamer (1975), the meaning of a text is decided not by the subjective intention of its author, but by the horizon of meaning provided by the cultural setting in which the author writes. A horizon is the 'range of vision that includes everything that can be seen from a particular vantage point' (Gadamer, 1975: 269). By 'horizons' Gadamer captures the situatedness of all interpretations occurring as they do within a tradition of discourse. Horizons move as those looking at them move (Fay, 1996).

Gadamer rejected both the epistemological primacy of the knowing subject and positivist's injunction to ignore the actor's meaning. Understanding is a dialectical process involving both the interpreter and the interpreted. It is the fusion of these two horizons that constitutes interpretation. That is, to read the organizational text, the actor's (author's) horizon of meaning should be merged with the reader's (researchers' or stakeholders'). Yet, there is no one correct fusion or interpretation of the text, rather, they are subject to revision because the horizon of the interpreter can vary both historically and ideologically (Gadamer, 1975). In other words, depending on the conceptual schemes (models) or theoretical predilections of the researcher or practitioner, there will be different analyses of the organization though the organizational text remains the same. Explication of this overlooked notion is perhaps the most valuable contribution of Gadamerian hermeneutics to the study of organizations.

By fusion, Gadamer hopes to capture the process in which a past or foreign object speaks to specific interpreters situated in their own cultural milieu. It is important to note that fusion might suggest that the two horizons become one and that differences between them are eliminated. But that is not what *fusion* means. In interpretation a tension is maintained between a past or foreign act or object situated within its own conceptual context and the interpreters situated within their own conceptual contexts. However, Gadamer is not claiming that a text is whatever an interpreter says it is. He does not suggest that interpreters simply read themselves into past events and objects so that interpretations become a form of mere self-reflection.

> The interaction of the interpreter with the interpreted elicits from the interpreted various dimensions of meaning which become evident as it is placed in a new historical setting. Interpretation involved tapping new reservoirs of (potential) meaning hidden from those in other historical moments, including those who lived at the time of its production. In new contexts different aspects of meaning emerge; that which is interpreted speaks in new ways. (Fay, 1996: 144)

Finally, the fusion of horizons is framed in terms of what Gadamer calls the logic of question and answer.

> The text, as a response to an implicit question, challenges us to address the same implicit question that it has confronted. Hermeneutic understanding of the past is then not a simple reconstruction of the context in which the historical text emerged; it is rather a conversation with the tradition in which the issues that exercised the particular epoch continue to exercise us. (Phillips, 1996: 2)

To explicate the notion of the *fusion of horizons*, Gadamer also defined a concept called 'prejudice'. Prejudice refers to the inevitable existence of prejudgements and preconceptions regarding any subject of inquiry. It is this pre-understanding that is the necessary condition of all human understanding. For Gadamer prejudice is not a barrier to truth, but a 'positive possibility' of interpretation. For example, consider the concept of hierarchy in organizations. Most conceptions of organizations are so deeply engraved in structure that one of the first things a researcher wants to see before starting an inquiry is the organizational structure (organizational chart). In other words, the prejudice of some form of hierarchy is a given and often unexamined precondition in our understanding of organizations. A reflective practitioner or researcher could see this as an opportunity and bring others' attention to it by facilitating a dialogue about hierarchy in organizations. For doing so, it is not necessary or even advisable to start with the assumption that hierarchy is undesirable or 'bad'. As the text of hierarchy is read (for example, through the facilitated dialogue), it will reveal its many facets to its readers, eventually enlightening them about the paradoxical nature of hierarchy. The end result will be a new understanding of organizational hierarchy and its complexity. And as a byproduct, the process would have generated concrete action steps to reconcile with the new understanding (for example, interventions).

Thus, as in the above example, by reflexively examining this prejudice of hierarchy in organizations, actors may recognize the fragility of their understanding. Or, hopefully, with a different 'prejudice' they may see a different reality. For example, most approaches to understanding organizations are embedded in a 'problem-solving' paradigm. It is assumed that organizations are full of problems that need to be solved and that research/consulting equals problem solving. To do good research is to solve 'real' problems. Similarly, the notion of organizational 'diagnosis' implies the existence of a basic clinical condition that characterizes organizations. This deficiency model of organizational research calls for researchers and consultants to develop techniques to accurately identify and diagnose problems. Even the familiar case method in social sciences originates from a medical model where the history of the pathology is thought to provide insights into what actions to take.

In contrast to this clinical or problem-solving focus, another approach known as *appreciative inquiry* (Cooperrider and Srivastva, 1987) focuses on what is working in an organization or group. By exploring events when employees are at their best, appreciative inquiry identifies the core values that people cherish and attempts to find ways to channel their fundamental desire to contribute. The inquiry begins with a process of affirmation of the basic 'goodness' that exists in the group and tries to create a climate of collaboration and true inquiry within the unit. Per Gadamer's logic, appreciative inquiry must be a different conceptual framework or prejudice because it questions the hierarchical structures in organizations in the hope of replacing them with egalitarian ones (for a concrete example, see Srivastva and Coopperrider, 1987).

Though Gadamer has discussed the notion of texts, it is the French philosopher Paul Ricoeur (1971, 1981) who has provided the most comprehensive account of the 'paradigm of the text' so far. For Ricoeur, the text displays a fundamental characteristic of the very historicity of human experience, namely that it is 'communication in and through distance' also called distanciation in communication (Ricoeur, 1981: 131). Further, Ricoeur argues, it is the dialectic of speaking and writing that creates the hermeneutic problem of distanciation.

According to Ricoeur (1981), a text is a *work* of *discourse* (fixed by writing). It is a work because it is a structured whole that cannot be reduced to its individual components (like a sentence). A text as a work also reveals a unique style and is produced according to a series of rules that define its literary genre (cited in Honey, 1987). As a discourse, the text preserves the properties of the sentence, but preserves them in a new constellation which calls for its own type of interpretation (Thompson, 1981). Taken together the categories of composition, genre and style are the 'categories of production and labour' (Ricoeur, 1981: 136) justifying his definition of text as work.

Though both speaking and writing are legitimate modes of discourse, the realization of discourse in writing involves a series of attributes that effectively distance the text from the conditions of the spoken discourse. Ricoeur insists that it is this dialectic of speaking and writing that creates the hermeneutic problem of writing and distanciation. However, this dialectic of speaking and writing is built upon a more primitive form of distanciation evident in oral discourse itself, namely the relationship between event and meaning (cited in Honey, 1987). Distanciation may be seen as the process by which the intended meanings of the speech or act are separated (distanced) from the acting, speaking or writing of a text.

Ricoeur discusses several criteria of textuality the most important of which is the realization of language as discourse.

The realization of language as discourse

The central theme here is the dialectic of *event* and *meaning*. Discourse (speaking) is given as an event; it is realized temporally and in the present, whereas a system of language is virtual and outside. The dialectic of event and meaning implies that if all discourse is realized as an event, all discourse is understood as meaning. What needs to be understood is not the fleeting event, but the meaning that endures. 'Just as language, by being actualized in discourse, surpasses itself as system and realizes itself as event, so too discourse, by entering the process of understanding, surpasses itself as event, and becomes meaning' (Ricoeur, 1981: 134).

The important point to consider here is that it is the meaning that gets inscribed in writing. This is achieved, according to Ricoeur, by the 'intentional exteriorization' of the speech-act. To outline this relationship, Ricoeur underscores the importance of seeing language as discourse. He makes a case for seeing spoken discourse as an event by identifying four instances:

1   Discourse has a temporal dimension that refers to the here and now of the speaker.
2   Discourse has a self-referential component whereby a person expresses himself or herself in speech.
3   Discourse is always about something. Discourse refers to a world, which it attempts to describe, express or represent.
4   Discourse is always addressed to another source, i.e. discourse is always a dialogue or exchange among people.

Integrating these four notions, one may state that in speech or conversation meaning exists among participants and that meaning is located in the event of discourse itself. So far as a conversation is going on in the here-and-now and the actors in the dialogue communicate their intent to each other, the object of the conversation is apparent. However, as soon as the spoken word is 'fixed' by writing, a hermeneutic problem of understanding what was actually said emerges. In other words, at this stage, the relationship between events and their meaning is altered. This transformation occurs in all the four instances mentioned above and is further explicated below.

1   In speech, the temporal dimension appears and disappears. That is, speech happens in real time and then it is over. In writing, on the other hand, the discourse is 'fixed' because writing involves a translation, a fixing of the 'saying' in the 'said'. Therefore, what is inscribed in the writing is not the event as an event, but the *meaning* of the event. In order to identify the meaning in what is said, Ricoeur turns to speech act theory (Austin, 1962; Searle, 1969). The act of speaking, according to Austin and Searle, is constituted by a hierarchy of subordinate acts which are distributed at three levels:
    a) the level of the locutionary propositional act, i.e., the act *of* saying;
    b) the level of the illocutionary act or force, that which we do *in* saying; and
    c) the level of the perlocutionary act, that which we do *by* saying.

To demonstrate, let us look at the following event: A vice president summons one of her managers to her office and says, 'sit down, we need to talk'. A detailed description of what is observed in this event will be the locutionary level: the manager walking in, the VP saying we need to talk etc. The second, the illocutionary level, is concerned with what is conveyed in the situation: the VP might have conveyed to the manager that she was concerned about his performance. The third, perlocutionary level, is the performative part of the speech act. This is the impact the statement had on the manager. The perlocutionary aspect of the speech act is the social situated achievement of the utterance. In many situations, this is self-evident. The classic example is that of the priest saying 'I now pronounce you man and wife'. However, in other situations, it is not. As a result, this is the most problematic part of the textual analysis; the manager might have become angry or fearful. Yet he might have nodded and agreed to everything that was said to him while struggling hard to contain his anger or fear.

To summarize, distanciation is achieved here by the surpassing of the event of saying by the meaning of what is said. Of the above three, the perlocutionary act is the least inscribable aspect of discourse. Illocutionary acts, because they rely on the author's intent, fall next in line, whereas locutionary acts can be culled from the predicative structures of the sentence itself. These three components, taken together, reveal the first instance where meaning surpasses discourse as event.

2 The second dimension of discourse as event 'self-referential nature of speech' refers to the relationship between subjectivity and the speaker, i.e.

> The subjective intention of the speaking subject and the meaning of the discourse overlap each other in such a way that it is the same thing to understand what the speaker means and what his discourse means. (Ricoeur, 1971: 78)

This is not the case with written discourse. The intent of the author and the meaning of the text no longer coincide. In speech-acts the meaning is present with the event, whereas in a text there is a separation of event and meaning temporally. Simply put, a piece of text records something but the meaning is not disclosed until the act of reading – a further distanciation. Ricoeur explains this in detail:

> This dissociation of the verbal meaning of the text and the mental intention is what is really at stake in the inscription of discourse. Not that we can conceive of a text without an author; the tie between the speaker and the discourse is not abolished, but distended and complicated ... The text's career escapes the finite horizon lived by its author. What the text says now matters more than what the author meant to say ... Using Plato's expression again, written discourse cannot be 'rescued' by all the processes by which spoken discourse supports itself in order to be understood – intonation, delivery, mimicry, gestures ... Only the meaning 'rescues' the meaning (in discourse), without the contribution of the physical and psychological presence of the author. But to say that the meaning rescues meaning is to say that only interpretation is the 'remedy' for the weakness of discourse which its author can no longer save. (1971: 78)

In other words, according to Ricoeur, the text outlives the life of its author and is opened up to an infinite number of readings. So what must be interpreted is what the text says, not what the author intended. The meaning of the text surpasses the meaning and intentions of the author. A similar observation is made by Barthes (1980) who eloquently describes what he calls the 'death of the author.'

As an example, consider the case of the president of a company who says she wants to empower employees and create a team-based structure. This may be interpreted in many ways such as the following:

a) She truly believes in empowering everyone and is committed to team-based governance.

b) She read an article in the *Harvard Business Review* about teams and empowerment and wants to try it out.

c) Team-based structure means decentralization and that means lay-off which in turn may mean increase in market valuation of the company.

d) This is an opportunity for the President to get rid of people she doesn't want or like.

e) The competition has done 'teams' so the President is trying to catch-up.

f) The President wants to be seen as an innovator and industry leader by trying something new.

The author of the text, in this case, the President, has only limited control on how others will make sense of her utterance. In all probability, employees will interpret the plan in a manner that would make personal sense to them, thereby creating a wide variety of meanings.

3   Let us now consider the third instance where the event is surpassed by the meaning. Discourse refers to the world, to a *world of the text*. The notion of the world of text denotes to *reference* or *denotation* of discourse. Following Frege, Ricoeur distinguished between the *sense* and *reference* of any proposition:

> The sense is the ideal object which the proposition intends, and hence is purely immanent in discourse. The reference is the truth-value of the proposition, its claim to reach reality. Reference thus distinguishes discourse from language. (1981: 140)

To give an example, in 1998, AT&T, the global telecommunications giant announced a mega-merger with the giant cable company, Tele-Communications, Inc. For the top management and board of directors of both companies, the deal made perfect sense. Other consolidations in the telecommunications sector, such as the $37 billion merger of MCI Communications Corp and WorldCom Inc. were taking place. The merged company will be a strategic big player in telecommunications and cable. Yet, as soon as the merger was announced, the market reacted in a manner totally unexpected by the two companies. AT&T shares lost 25 per cent of their value in the next few weeks. The 'sense' of this announcement was very clear: a strategic partnership in the context of similar alliances taking place all across the industry. The deal should add shareholder value by enhancing the presence of the company in a very dynamic market. Consensus on the 'reference' or truth-value of the proposition, however, was harder to reach. After watching how the market reacted, Wall Street analysts came up with conflicting estimations on the soundness of the merger though they were all 'reading' from the same text (database). In the final analysis the 'reference' of this event was extremely 'plurivocal' (Packer, 1985), signifying its potential for multiple interpretations.

The question for someone interested in organizational analysis at this point should be: what happens to reference when discourse becomes a text?

In oral discourse, reference is ostensive. When one watches a World Cup soccer game, one's understanding of the event is influenced by what one sees on the field and by the statements of the commentator. In contrast, written discourse does not have any ostensive reference such that when we read about the game next day in the newspaper we may be constructing a different interpretation of what happened. Ricoeur considers this lack of ostensiveness a blessing. He calls it the 'spirituality' of the text. 'In the same manner that the text frees its meaning from the tutelage of the mental intention, it frees its reference from the limits of ostensive reference' (1971: 79). According to him reference 'opens up the text' and thereby the world for us. The text is thus 'freeing us from the visibility and limitations of situations by opening up a world for us' (1971: 79).

Ricoeur took this Heideggerian notion of 'the projection of our own most possibilities' and applied it to the theory of text. Only writing, according to Ricoeur, frees itself from its author and the narrowness of the dialogical situation, and thereby reveals this destination of discourse as projecting in a world. In other words, to interpret is to explicate the type of being-in-the-world unfolded in front of the text. What is open for interpretation in a text is a *proposed world* of possibilities.

Sometimes, however, such possibilities create panic and turmoil. For example, during the months of July, August and September of 1998, the global financial markets experienced volatility of unprecedented levels. In this context of unpredictability, the words of one man, American Federal Reserve Bank Chairman Alan Greenspan would move global financial markets in either direction. He is master of opaque economic jargons which are known as 'Fedspeak' and 'Greenspeak'. During his 11-year tenure at the helm of the Fed, he has coined countless catchphrases that reverberate in the lexicon of world markets for months or even years. Though he is famed for his convoluted sentences which defy diagramming, when Greenspan mumbles, markets often tremble.

Typically, it has been noted that immediately after he says something about the monetary situation, the markets would react in one direction, but once his statements are fixed in writing (text), they acquire different meaning, mostly moving the markets in the opposite direction. This is clearly the distanciation of event and meaning that Ricoeur outlined above. For example, in a speech in September 1998, Greenspan made a few statements such as pledging to 'consider carefully ... ongoing developments' and that he didn't think it was 'credible that the United States can remain an oasis of prosperity unaffected by a world that is experiencing greatly increased stress'. Greenspan did not say what the Federal Reserve Board would do, or when. But traders concluded that an interest rate cut was imminent, sparking explosive rallies in Asia and Europe and a record 381-

point gain in the Dow Jones Industrial Average. However, during the next two days, the market gave up most of the gains once the speech was fixed in writing. According to a *Business Week* story (Foust, 21 September 1998), this was an example of how the chief banker uses his opaque public utterances to carry out a virtual monetary policy, also humorously called 'open mouth policy'. Here is one more example of Greenspan's words, quoted by Achenbach (1999: C01):

> Probability distributions estimated largely, or exclusively, over cycles that do not include periods of panic will underestimate the likelihood of extreme price movements because they fail to capture a secondary peak at the extreme negative tail that reflects the probability of occurrence of a panic.

Throughout the last six years Greenspan's carefully timed words have sent stock and bond prices soaring or plummeting. The act of reading the Greenspan text created a multitude of possibilities that were not evident as the market was listening to the spoken words of Greenspan in real time. According to economist Paul Kasriel, Greenspan likes to use the language to its fullest effect: 'there is a bit of an artist in him ... He prides himself on wordsmithing. He can't say exactly what he means. He has to use analogies and allusions'.

Moving from markets to the organizational context, this distinction between event and meaning implies that once an event takes place, it acquires an indefinite potential for interpretation for as long as language exists. The intent of the author of the event is no longer relevant. For example, consider the countless times people have narrated humour with good intentions but only to hurt the sentiments of a few people in the audience. The statement 'that's not what I meant' is only too common. Organizational life is populated with hundreds of such instances of distanciations where the text decontextualizes itself producing new meanings.

In many cases, the event may soon get 'fixed' into writings. Consider the two separate cases of the Mitsubishi and Texaco Corporations' landmark sexual harassment settlements with the Equal Opportunity Employment Commission in the United States. The series of high profile events that preceded the settlement and the settlement itself will soon be fixed into writing in fields of corporate law, business ethics, government and business, public administration, public policy, journalism and personnel management. The text of the case will be interpreted in a multitude of ways in times to come. As the social and cultural contexts evolve, the meaning and significance of the text too will change. Looking back, what is considered sexual harassment has undergone significant changes in Western society during the last decade. Looking prospectively, ten years from now, what constitutes sexual harassment will be different from what it is now. Again, another example of the same text creating different meanings and the role of historicity and contextuality in understanding.

To summarize, in the third form of distanciation the text 'decontextualizes' itself from its social and historical conditions of production, opening itself to unlimited series of readings. Scholars of organizational science will therefore benefit by developing a greater sensitivity to the potential of an event (for example, an intervention) to acquire a wide variety of interpretations independent of its original intent.

4   The fourth form of distanciation emancipates the text from the limits of narrow reference. In speech discourse the audience is known whereas in written discourse, the audience is potentially unknown. In writing

> the narrowness of the dialogical relation explodes. Instead of being addressed just to you, the second person, what is written is addressed to the audience that creates itself ... In escaping the momentary character of the event, the bounds lived by the author, and the narrowness of ostensive reference, discourse escapes the limits of being face to face. It no longer has a visible auditor. An unknown, invisible reader has become the unprivileged addressee of the discourse. (Ricoeur, 1971: 80)

In other words, the audience to whom the text addresses itself both defines and creates itself over time.

To come back to the previous example of global financial markets, the comments by Greenspan may not have been aimed at the public either, according to the *Business Week* story and other market analysts. His comments might have been intended for other members on the Federal Reserve Board who, at that time, were pressing for a rate hike to ward off inflation. The Berkeley speech suggested Greenspan was 'publicly lobbying the hawks to think about the possibility of a rate cut', says David D. Hale, an economist at Zurich Kemper Investments Inc (quoted in the *Business Week*). Thus, in this instance, the text has been emancipated from the limits of ostensive reference as well. The audience to whom Greenspan's comments were addressed defines and creates itself over time.

Returning to our description of the text, the above four criteria together constitute what Ricoeur called the 'paradigm of the text'. In effect, as we can see, it addresses the issue of 'distanciation in communication' because in each of these instances the meaning surpasses event. Throughout his writings, Ricoeur maintains that text is the medium through which human beings understand themselves. 'To understand is *to understand oneself in front of the text*. It is not a question of imposing upon the text our finite capacity of understanding, but of exposing ourselves to the text and receiving from it an enlarged self' (Ricoeur, 1981: 143). In this perspective, the goal of organizational science researchers and practitioners should not be to impose their models or frameworks upon the organizational text, but to be open and fully appreciate what the text is trying to reveal. In a typical organizational research work or change effort, the researcher or practitioner collects data at the locutionary level, analyzes it using an existing model and feeds the interpretations back to the client. The 'distanciation' of the event into multiple meanings does not usually engage the attention of the change agent or the researcher. Over a period of time and with experience, researchers or practitioners develop what is called a routine of practice or procedures, which prevent reflexivity on their part. Such use of a preconceived model or framework in organizational analysis is antagonistic to the possibility of letting the text reveal its meanings.

In summary, it is not hard to see how the model of the text can be easily applied to actions and events in organizations. Actions and events in organizations get fixed just as in writing and therefore they are subject to all the qualities of writing. In other words, organizational 'speech' (i.e. events in organizations) is transformed into 'writing', which in turn generates plurivocity (potential for multiple meaning). By applying the principles of textual analysis one can unpack the different layers of meaning about action in organizations.

Implications for organizational change and development

Hermeneutic inquiry opens up immense possibilities for the practically minded consultant or researcher. The model of the text is a less threatening framework to people in organizations than traditional ones for various reasons. By defining the data collected as a text, the researcher or the practitioner is conveying an idea that research/consulting work is something like a series of readings. The notion of plurivocity, that there are multiple meanings in the story, is very empowering, because it gives organizational stakeholders some flexibility to participate in the meaning making process. This is particularly significant when we realize that one of the most basic reasons for 'resistance to change' in organization change efforts is the affected parties' belief that interpretations arrived at by the researcher or the practitioner do not appear credible, or that they were imposed upon. From a hermeneutical point of view this is not surprising since such interpretations are necessarily unilateral having achieved no *fusion of horizons*. A textual analysis that involves both the reader and the read appears to elicit more commitment from people who are key to helping implement changes.

The process of capturing the distanciation of event into meaning is normally an enriching experience. Recognizing the potential of events or actions in organizations to acquire meaning far beyond what their creator had anticipated is normally an eye-opener to people in organizations. It also provides a framework to explain the innumerable 'miscommunications' that typically exist in organizations. Actors begin to realize that they were all looking at different 'texts' or reading the same text differently. Such an awareness normally prompts dissenting parties to co-create a 'consensus reading' of the text so that their efforts and energies are directed more or less to a shared organizational outcome.

The hermeneutic approach is gradually getting accepted in organization theory. Arbnor and Bjerke (1997) in their widely read *Methodology for Creating Business Knowledge* provide extensive treatment of the hermeneutic approach. They have categorized knowledge creation and theory building process in organization science into three approaches – the analytical, systems and actors approaches. Under the actors theme, they provide an insightful use of hermeneutics using concepts such as preunderstanding, understanding and everyday reality. Their explication is useful because it not only recognizes the potential of hermeneutic tradition in organization theory but also shows that the approach is practical and applied.

Most recent organization theory textbooks refer to interpretive approaches (for example Hatch, 1997; Morgan, 1996). While many of them do not use the term hermeneutics, key themes in hermeneutics such as meaning making, historicity, contextuality and multiple interpretation of events are used. Writers in social constructionist approaches too make good use of hermeneutics (Boje, 1995; Gergen, 1999; Gergen and Thatchenkery, 1996). Looking at the trend it is more likely that the core holdings of hermeneutic philosophy will find increasing use and acceptance in mainstream organization theory while the use of the term itself might not be popular.

Note

1 *Tamara* is a production of Tamara International, 2035 N. Highland Avenue, Los Angeles, CA 90068.

References

Achenbach, J. (1999) 'Ready, set, panic! The day after Greenspan hiccuped', *The Washington Post*, 16 October: C01.

Arbnor, I. and Bjerke, B. (1997) *Methodology for Creating Business Knowledge*. Thousand Oaks, CA: Sage.

Austin, J.L. (1962) *How to do Things with Words*. Cambridge, MA: Harvard University Press.

Barley, S.R. (1983) 'Semiotics and the study of occupational and organizational cultures', *Administrative Science Quarterly*, 28: 393–413.

Barry, D. and Elmes, M. (1997) 'Strategy retold: toward a narrative view of strategic discourse', *Academy of Management Review*, 22 (2): 429–52.

Barthes, R. (1980) *The Pleasure of the Text*. New York: Noonday Press.

Berger, P. and Luckman, T. (1966) *The Social Construction of Reality*. New York: Anchor.

Bleicher, J. (1980) *Contemporary Hermeneutics*. London: Routledge & Kegan Paul.

Boje, D. (1995) 'Stories of the storytelling organization: a postmodern analysis of Disney as "Tamara-land"', *Academy of Management Journal*, 38 (4): 997–1035.

Bourdieu, P. (1990) *The Logic of Practice*, trans. R. Nice. Stanford, CA: Stanford University Press.

Business Week (1998) 'Greenspeak: when rhetoric creates reality', commentary by Dean Foust. 21 September.

Cooperrider, D.L. and Srivastva, S. (1987) 'Appreciative inquiry in organizational life', *Research in Organizational Change and Development*, 1: 129–69.

Czarniawska, B. (1997) *A Narrative Approach to Organization Studies*. Qualitative Research Methods, 43. Thousand Oaks, CA: Sage.

Dilthey, W. (1976) *Selected writings*, ed. and trans. H.P. Rickman. Cambridge: Cambridge University Press.

Dilthey, W. (1988) *Introduction to the Human Sciences: an Attempt to Lay a Foundation for the Study of Society and History*, trans. Ramon J. Betanzos. Detroit: Wayne State University Press.

Fay, B. (1996) *Contemporary Philosophy of Social Science*. Cambridge: Blackwell.

Gadamer, H.G. (1975) *Truth and Method*, trans. D.E. Linge. Berkeley: University of California Press.

Gadamer, H.G. (1976) *Philosophical Hermeneutics*. Berkeley: University of California Press.

Geertz, C. (1973) *The Interpretation of Cultures*. New York: Basic Books.

Gergen, K. (1999) *An Invitation to Social Construction*. Thousand Oaks: Sage.

Gergen, K. and Thatchenkery, T. (1996) 'Organization science as social construction: postmodern potentials', *Journal of Applied Behavioral Science*, 32 (4): 356–77. (Special issue on *Science and Service in Organizational Scholarship*.)

Gergen, K.J., Hepburn, A. and Fisher, D.C. (1986) 'Hermeneutics of personality description', *Journal of Personality and Social Psychology*, 50: 1261–70.

Goethe, J.W. von (1930) *Faust*, trans. B. Taylor. New York: The Modern Library.

Grant, D. and Oswick, C. (eds) (1996) *Metaphors and Organizations*. Thousand Oaks: Sage.

Grant, D., Keenoy, T. and Oswick, C. (eds) (1998) *Discourse and Organization*. Thousand Oaks: Sage.

Graumann, C. and Gergen, K. (eds) (1996) *Historical Dimensions of Psychological Discourse*. Cambridge: Cambridge University Press.

Hatch, Mary Jo (1997) *Organization Theory: Modern, Symbolic and Postmodern Perspectives*. New York: Oxford University Press.

Heidegger, M. (1962) *Being and Time*, trans. J. Macquarrie and E. Robinson. New York: Harper & Row. (Original work published in 1927.)

Honey, M.A. (1987) 'The interview as text: hermeneutics considered as a model for analyzing the clinically informed research interview', *Human Development*, 30: 69–82.

Kets de Vries, M.F.R. and Miller, D. (1987) 'Interpreting organizational texts', *Journal of Management Studies*, 24: 233–47.

Linstead, S.A. (1999) 'An introduction to the textuality of organisations', *Studies in Cultures, Organisations and Societies*, 5 (1): 1-10.

Lyotard, J. (1984) *The Postmodern Condition: A Report on Knowledge*. Minneapolis: University of Minnesota Press.

Martin, W. (1986) *Recent Theories of Narrative*. Ithaca, NY: Cornell University Press.

McCloskey, D.N. (1985) *The Rhetoric of Economics*. Madison: University of Wisconsin Press.

Morgan, G. (1996) *Images of Organization*. Beverly Hills, CA: Sage.

O'Connor, E. (1995) 'Paradoxes of participation: textual analysis and organizational change', *Organization Studies*, 16: 769–803.

Packer, M.J. (1985) 'Hermeneutic inquiry in the study of human conduct', *American Psychologist*, 40: 1081–93.

Palmer, R. (1969) *Hermeneutics: Interpretation theory in Schleiermacher, Dilthey, Heidegger and Gadamer*. Evanston, IL: Northwestern University Press.

Palmer, R. (1981) 'Hermeneutics', in G. Floisad (ed.), *Contemporary Philosophy, a New Survey*, Vol. 2. Boston: Martinus Nijhoff.

Phillips, J. (1996) 'Key concepts: hermeneutics', *Philosophy, Psychiatry, & Psychology*, 3 (1): 61–9.

Radnitzky, G. (1968) *Contemporary Schools of Metascience*. Goteborg: Akademiforlaget.

Ricoeur, P. (1971) 'The model of the text: meaningful action considered as a text', *Social Research*, 38 (3): 529–62.

Ricoeur, P. (1981) 'Hermeneutics and the social sciences', in J.B. Thompson (ed. and trans.), *Hermeneutics and the Human Sciences: Essays on Language, Action, and Interpretation*. Cambridge: Cambridge University Press.

Riley, P. (1983) 'A structurationist account of political culture', *Administrative Science Quarterly*, 28: 414–37.

Sampson, E.E. (1989) 'The challenges of social change for psychology: globalization and psychology's theory of the person', *American Psychologist*, 44: 914–21.

Searle, J.R. (1969) *Speech Acts: An Essay in the Philosophy of Language*. London: Cambridge.

Silverman, H. (1994) *Textualities: Between Hermeneutics and Deconstruction*. New York: Routledge.

Srivastva, S. and Cooperrider, D.L. (1987) 'The egalitarian organization', *Human Relations*, 39: 683–724.

Taylor, C. (1981) 'Interpretation and the sciences of man', *Review of Metaphysics*. Cambridge: Harvard University Press.

Taylor, C. (ed.) (1985) 'Human agency and language', *Philosophical Papers*, Vol. 1. Cambridge: Cambridge University Press.

Thachankary, T. (1992) 'Organizations as "texts": hermeneutics as a model for understanding organizational change', *Research in Organization Development and Change*, 6: 197–233.

Thatchenkery, T. and Upadhyaya, P. (1996) 'Organizations as a play of multiple and dynamic discourses: an example from a global social change organization' in D. Boje, R. Gephart and T. Thatchenkery (eds), *Postmodern Management and Organization Theory*. Newbury Park, CA: Sage.

Thompson, J.B. (1981) 'Editor's introduction', in J.B. Thompson (ed. and trans.), *Hermeneutics and the Human Sciences: Essays on Language, Action and Interpretation*. Cambridge: Cambridge University Press.

Weick, K.E. (1979) *The Social Psychology of Organizing*. New York: Random House.

Woodilla, J. (1998) 'Workplace conversations: the text of organizing', in D. Grant, T. Keenoy and C. Oswick (eds), *Discourse and Organization*. Thousand Oaks: Sage. pp. 31–50.

Zaleznik, A. and Kets de Vries, M.F.R. (1984) 'Leadership as a text: an essay on interpretation'. Boston: Harvard Business School, Division of Research working paper.

7

Reclaiming Story in Organization: Narratologies and Action Sciences

*David M. Boje, Rossana C. Alvarez and
Bruce Schooling*

According to TwoTrees (1997), stories have three properties: time, place and mind. We believe that many narratologies currently being applied in the field of organizational analysis and the social sciences more broadly marginalize these three properties. In effect, narratology marginalizes *story*. In what follows, we will critically review common narratologies and suggest some ways in which the idea of story can be returned to analysis.

Stories, TwoTrees suggests, have:

1 A *time*: 'You tell stories at a certain time of the year, a season, or time of the day. There are Fall and Spring stories.'
2 A *place*: 'You recount stories at this place, and places have their own story.'
3 A *mind*: 'Every creation, even a story, has a life of its own. We create a story and it has a life. The stories have origins. You must tell a story with permission.'

For TwoTrees, stories must be re-contextualized back to their time, place and mind. The stories live and there are penalties for getting a story wrong or telling it without permission. 'What is the Lakota penalty for changing a story, telling a story wrong or without permission?' David Boje asked at a presentation by TwoTrees. 'It is death', she replied (TwoTrees, 1997). Why death? 'Because, the story in an oral culture is the entire living history of the community' (TwoTrees, 1997). Stories live, unless we kill them. Watch as each of the narratologies we will discuss kills off story. She also told Boje to watch it when he used the word 'we'. This brings us to consider what 'we' are doing.

Toelken (1996), a folklorist who questions the style of Eurocentric folklore narrative scholarship that fits stories into neat typologies and collections, said:

A couple of years ago at the American Folklore Society Annual Meetings I gave a paper in which I detailed why I no longer felt I could discuss Navajo coyote stories in depth; a singer – a medicine man – told me that either I or a member of my family would pay for it with our lives. (Toelken, 1996: 52)

His academic colleagues had two reactions. One was agreeing with the decision. Another was to tell him 'it was anti-intellectual to quit and that it was [his] duty to the folklore profession to go as deep into the field as [he] could and share the results'. He 'was surprised by how many in both of these camps soon began inviting [him] to their campuses to talk about Navajo stories some more' (Toelken, 1996: 53). For the Navajo, stories are living embodiments of reality, living dramas, a language that creates reality, not the reverse (Toelken, 1996: 53). Telling 'Native stories for non-Natives out of context may be dangerous to our mental health: for we know there will always be a discrepancy between what the story *is* – as a living articulation – and what you and I think it *means* as an example of something-or-other' (Toelken, 1996: 56). We think, however, that stories *live* in both modern and postmodern culture, not just in indigenous culture.

In this chapter, we explore three concerns about reclaiming story from narratologies that do not possess an epistemology or ontology of the living story. First is Culler's (1981: 169) observation of a hierarchy and indeterminacy between narratology and storytelling that can be deconstructed. Second is the duality of narrative and story as exhibited in the structuralist traditions of the Russian Formalists, American structuralism and French Structuralists. Hereafter, we refer to this as the formalistic approach to narrative.[1] Third is Culler's (1981: 169) observation that if any of 'these theorists agree on anything it is this: that the theory of narrative requires a distinction between what I shall call "story" – a sequence of actions or events, conceived as independent of their manifestation in discourse – and what I shall call "discourse", the discursive presentation or narration of events'. We think the work of Clair (1993, 1994, 1996 and 1997) on narrative and story in organizations and nations allows us to resituate the narrative/story duality. We will raise three issues in our resituation.

First is the issue of how to reclaim story from the varied narratologies in organization theory (OT). Narratologies are boundless and wonderfully varying. Our short list of narratologies, in contrast to living story, ranges from realist to formalistic, social constructionist, post-structuralist, critical theory and postmodern narratologies. (See Table 7.1 for contrast of methods, epistemology and ontology.) Narratologies are the characters in the story we are about to tell you. It becomes the work of the realist narratology to tell true stories; of structuralist narratology to sort out good and bad stories by their form; social constructionist narratology to look retrospectively for sense making of stories; post-structuralist narratology to erase the differences between story and materiality (those who think that they mean 'it's all text' will disagree); critical theory to put story back into its material condition, and postmodern narratology to shatter Grand narrative into many fragments called *petit histoires*, or just local stories.

Second, in Part II of this chapter we explore the application side of storytelling theory, and how various approaches to practice are rooted in the various narratologies. We review four cases in which storytelling is applied to consultation. We contend that 'restorying' the lived stories (White and Epston,

1990) is a different action science from Cooperrider and Srivastva's (1987) 'appreciative inquiry', Hopewell's (1987) approach to re-narrating congregation narratives and F. Emery (1993, 1997) and M. Emery's (1997, 1998) 'Search Conference' environmental scan and history sessions. We think each use of storytelling relies upon quite different epistemologies and ontologies of narratology.

Restorying, for example, is rooted in deconstruction, approaching action with a post-structuralist narratology, while appreciative inquiry acknowledges its action roots in social constructionist narratology (Gergen's 1991, 1994 and Weick's 1979, 1995 work). Search Conference and re-narrating congregations are both more in line with the pragmatist epistemology of Peirce (1940) and Pepper's (1942) contextualism. The Emerys explicitly situate their environmental scan and history session in contextualism (Pepper, 1942) and pragmatism (Peirce, 1940), while Hopewell (1987) focuses on the formalist aspects of Pepper's model. We try to avoid pronouncing one better than another: they simply combine different epistemological and ontological assumptions in their narratologies.

Third, in Part III of the chapter we have something to say about interdisciplinary approaches that, to us, span three or more narratological positions. We will contrast four narrative studies of organization. First, Czarniawska's (1997a) *Narrating the Organization* (spanning pragmatism, formalistic scene-act ratio typologies and the dramaturgy of social construction). Second is the *Storytelling Organization Theory* of Boje (1991a, 1995b; Boje et al., 1999), Boyce (1995) and Kaye (1996) that spans post-structuralist, folkloric, social constructionist and postmodern positions. Third, is the *narrative-organization equivalency* work of James Taylor and his colleagues where communicating, including narrating, is equivalent to acts of organizing. Finally we look at Clair's (1993, 1994, 1996, 1997) work which embeds *multiple nested narrative genres* (i.e. historical narratives, ancestral narratives, personal narratives and contemporary narratives). The three interdisciplinary approaches in Part III of the chapter differ in complex and significant ways from the Part II single discipline approaches. In order to explore these differences (and similarities) we must first review our short list of narratologies and the associated applied work. This we do in Part I.

We will briefly summarize the claims of each narratology against the other to show their different extensions into applied story theories in organizational consultation. We intend this as a self-reflexive inquiry – whilst somewhat ironically telling you a narrative and laying out a chronology, as if we as narrator-authors had nothing to do with selecting and ordering the various narratologies (Czarniawska, 1997b; Hatch, 1996; Weick, 1995). We explicitly caution the reader, then, that the narratives we are about to tell are fictions. We have made up and invented a narrative of narratological history, with our own reading of plots and characterizations. Our narrating continues as we map four action science approaches (Appreciative Inquiry, Restorying, Narrating Congregations and Search Conferences) and four highly eclectic interdisciplinary approaches (Narrating Organizations, Storytelling Organization Theory, Equivalency and Nested Narratives) to narrating/storying organization among the various narratologies. We begin with Part I, a typology of narratologies.

Part I: Contrasting alternative narratologies in organization studies

Realist narratology: In realist narratology people and organizational stories are treated as dead objects without exploring lived context. Realist narratology mimics the positivistic and Cartesian scientistic rhetoric of operationalization, and causality, to collect stories as though they were so many mirrors of reality (Rorty, 1980). Events are strung together into chronologies to vibrate with realness. Story becomes the in-place-metering device to measure culture or some other construct. Story becomes a transparent mirror of an objective realism with little or no empirical attention to the behavioural performance context in which stories were socially enacted or to their embedded situation within situated political and economic discourses. Realism stories mimic naturalism by supplying rich narrative details, scientific facts and figures, references and chronology to authenticate their performance as non-dead and non-fiction. The focus is on interpreting the story as an organizational artifact, an object-text in laboratory, biography and interview studies.

In laboratory research, the experimenter varies the content of the object-story to assess outcomes such as memory and believability (Martin and Powers, 1979; Martin et al., 1979, 1980). For example, Martin and Meyerson (1988) reify stories-as-objects when they identified stories as mere 'its'. To reify means to ignore or forget the socially constructed context of the story and then to apprehend it as an object. It is as if stories are both mere cultural artifacts and cultural measuring devices without exploring stories performed in place and time. An example of the text-as-object paradigm for story research would also be the early work by Martin et al. (1983). Their study contrasted how markedly similar story texts, abstracted from organizational histories and CEO biographies manifested themselves in different types of organizations without examining how the stories were used or whose voice was privileged in their telling. Mumby's (1987) power and politics analysis of Martin et al.'s (1983) IBM story was a re-reading from a more critical narratology. Clark's (1972) accounts of organizational uniqueness were also texts without *in situ* story-behaviours, but with rich historical context. Lombardo's (1986), and McCall et al.'s (1989) interviews with 86 executives as they recalled and retold stories provided interesting life-history work, but did not afford a behavioural analysis of *in situ* performance or historical context. In this early work, Wilkins (1979) asked storytellers to recount their stories while raters scored the re-enacted story on a set of response scales. Siehl and Martin's (1982) survey of sales trainee knowledge of four stories measured recall, but once again, not performance. Finally, McConkie and Boss (1986) report how one story, the 'Firing of Elayne', was mentioned by 85 per cent of their interviewees. While these analyses are astute, rigorous and provocative, we do not learn much about the natural behaviour context in which stories are performed, or the organizational implications of such performances.

Most of these object-story researchers have moved on to less realist narratologies. Martin's (1990) more recent work, for example, deconstructs the story of a pregnancy in economic, gender and racial contexts. (See also Martin and Knopoff's (1997) deconstruction of gender). Wilkins and Thompson (1991) have also moved to a more situated and polyvocal (many-voiced) storytelling inquiry.

National and organization narratives reduce many stories to a totalized, universalized and unitary realism narrative. In Nazi Germany, Bosnia, and now Albania, 'positivist histories were marshaled to the causes of ethnic cleansing and genocide' (Currie, 1998: 92). Hitler commissioned totalized histories, as did the Serbs. But so did the US commission histories of Columbus, which were full of narrative exclusion of the indigenous, imposing strange linear plots of manifest destiny to tell its story of slavery and the American Holocaust. Bhabha (1989: 297) puts it this way: 'The scraps, patches and rags of daily life must be repeatedly turned into the signs of a national culture, while the very act of narrative performance interpolates a growing circle of national subjects'. Indeed most historians until recently have done this, but with the post-colonial and postmodern challenges to unitary and linear histories, more minority voices are being included. Also building upon the pragmatist traditions of Peirce (abduction, for example), the Italian microstorians (for example Muir (1991); Ginzburg (1980); Levi (1992) and others writing in the *Quaderni Storici* journal) also call into question Grand narratives of macrohistory, particularly elite Great-man histories by collecting 'little people' microstories (Boje, 2001 in press). Great-man and Great company histories are popular in basic texts of organization theory and management in the US. Microstoria includes both quantitative and qualitative focus upon systematic archival analysis from property registries, notary records, ecclesiastical archives, trial proceedings, pamphlets, etc. Microstorians insist that they are dealing with real subject matter that can be analyzed pragmatically and empirically to ascertain a 'right meaning' (Boje, 2001).

Finally, consultant stories are oftentimes realist tales, taken out of their *in situ* context with other stories in a series of interviews, or whistle stop story-collection tours, to be summed and aggregated together and used in another context (a book or tape), as if stories in this new context meant the same thing. The microstorians object to aggregating stories since it presents an overly harmonious and integrated understanding of context. Aggregating stories strips them of their (performance and historical) context, a common practice in guru texts written for managerial consumption (e.g. Hammer and Champy, 1993; Peters and Waterman, 1982) or made into a realist tale with all the supportive charts, letters and tables of a Harvard case. Textbooks import hundreds of realist tales to authenticate the practicality of OT and management theory. Harvard and other case reports rely upon second and third-hand accounts of stories, typically told from management's or social science points of view (as in the ones we assemble now).

In sum, we, along with Fineman and Gabriel (1994) and Kaye (1996) argue that organizational behaviour (OB) textbooks, with their recipe of palatable and incontestable definitions of organizational concepts and stylized case reports, are treated as 'real', while stories from the working folks are treated as 'unreliable', 'unscientific', 'unreal' and in the final analysis, 'mythical'. We obviously think myth making is an essential part of organization change (Boje et al., 1982). Other narratologies we shall explore, such as postmodern, post-structuralist and microstoria (pragmatist) seek to see through the synthesizing, aggregated, utopian-progress, allegory of objective, Cartesian-reality, or what Tyler (1986: 132) refers to as moving beyond the 'totalized story of stories'.

Formalist narratologies: Formalist traditions for Culler (1981) include Russian Formalists, American structuralism and French Structuralists. Formalists did a narrative turn away from realism narratology but replaced it with an appreciation for forms that were more real than the narratives. Fisher's (1984, 1987) narrative paradigm theory, Burke's (1945) dramatistic method, sociolinguistics, semiotics and other formalisms we have no space to mention, are colonizing story work in OT. As we said at the outset, narrating is the death of storytelling; narrative dominates story; narrative is plot and coherence, while story is a mere element in narrative plot theory (e.g. Burkean narrative theory).

For Saussure story is a signifier (a system of signs) that is disconnected from what it represents or signifies. In this narratology, time, place and mind do not matter, only form counts. Saussure argued 'that the ability of narrative to refer to something other than itself was an illusion' (Currie, 1998: 35). Formalist narratology rests on three radical claims: (1) that the sign (story) and the signified (context) have separated in some arbitrary ways; (2) a deductive analysis transparently reveals the *form* of narrative *is* its content; and (3) the narrator uses framing devices to make narratives appear real but they are just signs.

Fisher's (1984, 1987) narrative paradigm theory seems to argue that humans as 'storytelling animals' construct 'good reasons' for believing and acting upon some stories, while rejecting others. The reasons for accepting or rejecting a story come from logical and value-based reasoning (Fisher, 1984). Key concepts in narrative paradigm theory are a narrative's 'probability' and 'fidelity' (Fisher, 1987: 5). Narrative probability is the observer's evaluation of a story's coherence; 'does it hang together?' Narrative probability addresses a story's credibility by analyzing internal consistency, missing elements and the consistency of character behaviour given what the observers know of the storyteller or character in similar stories. Probability is what juror's assess given the accompanying testimony of the defendant and those who know the defendant. Fidelity analyzes the truthfulness of a story – 'does it ring true to other stories of the same type?' – 'Does it pass the jury's tests of rational and value laden reasons?'

Burke (1945) has various topological models to describe basic narrative structures, such as agent, purpose, scene, agency and act in his formalistic theory of 'scene-act ratios'. Czarniawska (1977a: 32) applies Burke's 'dramatistic' model to Swedish public administration. For example she argues that 'according to Burke's dramatistic method, people assume a dialectical stand in face of paradoxes, in order to achieve the dissolution of the paradox-

Table 7.1: Metaphysics of Selected Alternative Narratologies

Narratology	Organization studies	Ontology	Epistemology	Methodology
Living story	TwoTrees (1997) Toelken (1996) Clair (1993, 1997)	Stories live and possess time, place and mind.	Knowledge is the story performed in time, place and has a life of its own (mind). Story can not be dualized from context without imbalance and other consequences.	Restory the relation between dominant narrative and authors' preferred story.
Realist Peters and Waterman (1982) Hammer and Champy (1993) Harvard cases	Early Martin lab. and uniqueness studies Wilkins (1979) Lombardo (1986) McCall et al. (1989)	'Real' reality mirrored more or less imperfectly in narrative or case. Narrative is a cultural artifact and object. Social facts.	Dualist: real is real, narrative is subjective interpretative knowledge; story is an object to know other objects (culture, etc.); managerialist; strategic.	Experimental manipulation; interview with narrative as measures; narrate with rating scales; biography of narrative uniqueness.
Formalist Barthes (early) Ricoeur Levi-Strauss Propp Shklovsky Fisher; Frye de Saussure H. White	Czarniawska (1997 in use of Burke's scene–act ratio); Ford and Ford (1995 in use of speech act theory).	'Real' is unknowable, but some forms are pragmatic or possess fidelity and probability, or scenes, plots, act, agency, purpose.	Narrative is sign system separated from knowledge of the signified. Narrative is rhetorical device. Contextualist epistemology of historical event unfolding in the present.	Collect and contrast forms of narrative and coherence of narrative elements.
Pragmatist Peirce and Pepper; Microstoria work e.g. Ginzburg, Muir, Levi.	Emery's Search Conference; Hopewell's congregation studies.	Assertion of the reality of general terms or laws. Meaning is oriented toward the future.	Ideas not mere abstractions; they are essences – things are what they are. Names are intended to show the nature of things. 'Any sort of fact is easily real for a contextualist' (Pepper, 1942: 143).	History session by the actors. Learning from the past in view of future action.
Social con-structionist Berger and Luckmann Geertz Blumer/Mead Denzin Weick Gergen	Boyce (1995) Czarniawska (1997 applying Blumer and Weick). Cooperrider and Srivastva (1987)	Individual and socially constructed realities.	Narrative is subjective account reified as objective knowledge. Narratives are acts of sensemaking.	Explore relative differences in narrative social construction.

Table 7.1 (cont.)

Post-structuralist Derrida DeMan Culler Fairclough Foucault (archaeology) White and Epston	Mumby (1987) Martin (1990) Kilduff (1993) Boje (1995a) Martin and Knopoff (1997)	There is no 'outside' to the 'inside' of the text to warrant meaning; duality or originary narrative.	Narratives are intertextual to knowledge of other narratives; narratives are ideological with political consequence.	Deconstructive reading of narratives.
Critical theorist Marx Marcuse Horkheimer Adorno Debord (in situationist movement)	Alvesson and Willmott (1996); Mills and Simmons (1996); Fulop and Linstead (1999)	Historical materialism (even dialectical teleology) shaped by class, ethnicity, gender and socio-economic values.	Grand narratives dominate local knowledge. But there can be local resistance to grand knowledge narratives.	Hegemonic reading of narratives; ideology readings of narratives.
Postmodernist Best and Kellner (on Debord) Baudrillard Lyotard Jameson Deleuze and Guattari	Burrell (1988); Clegg (1990); Hassard and Parker (1993); Boje (1995a) Harju (1999); Boje et al. (1996); Bergquist (1993); Hatch (1996); Burrell (1997)	Virtual and cultural hyper-real, sceptic critiques of late capitalism, to affirmation of spiritual world.	Knowledge and power are narratively fragmented; to affirmative knowledge living cosmos.	Polyphonic and juxtaposed readings and writing of a chorus of narratives.

induced drama' (Czarniawska, 1997a: 167). The function of dramatistic approaches to narrative is to look at rhetorical devices by which the author controls the position of the listener in relation to the narrative forms (i.e. agent, purpose, scene, agency and act). We will expand on this below.

Austin (1962) proposes the performative of speech acts, such as naming an act (i.e. 'I declare you man and wife') or promising to act ('I will marry you') as utterances that can change conditions. Ford and Ford (1995) examined how speech act performative is related to organizational change. Managers who can distinguish four types of conversation: initiative, understanding, performance and closure are thought to be more effective. 'Change is created, sustained and managed in and by communications' (Ford and Ford, 1995: 560). When someone speaks a story, for example, he or she is taking an action by asserting claims from experience, expressing preferences for the future and initiating changes. The effectiveness of these 'deeds of change' depends upon what was said, how it was said, when it was said and the impact it had (Ford and Ford, 1995: 545, 561). In short, many narrative approaches put form ahead of living story.

Pragmatist narratology: Pragmatism analyzes narrative in context to ascertain principles for meaningful communication. 'Pragmatics highlights the discrepancies between what is said and what is meant, and examines how people work out what is meant' (Fairhurst and Putnam, 1999: 4). The semiotic theory of Peirce (1940) is different from the formalist paradigms of speech-act, scene-act, narrative fidelity, etc. We mention in Table 7.1 the Italian Microstoria School that applies Peirce's abduction theory to trace stories and people in their embedded social networks. Logical deduction seeks to verify *a priori* formal theory (e.g. Fisher's narrative paradigm theory), while induction or grounded theory focuses on generating theory from *in situ* observations (e.g. speech-acts in ethnographic studies or Geertz's thick description of Balinese Cock Fighting). Microstorians such as Ginzburg (1980), Muir (1991) and Levi (1992) are quite adamant in applying Peirce's abduction theory that they are not interested in deconstruction, formalistic or postmodern narratologies. The hazard in both deduction and induction is 'exampling' stories by just collecting grounded stories to confirm and fit into the analyst's logically deduced theory (Glaser and Strauss, 1967: 5). The middle ground that Glaser and Strauss (1967) call 'constant comparative analysis' is similar but not identical to what Peirce terms 'abduction.'

Microstorians focus on the recovering of forgotten and marginalized history through both quantitative and qualitative study. The analysis focuses upon identifying names of places and people in ways that allow microstories to be told. Microstoria is sensitive to the micropolitics of power, the middle ground between local and Grand narrative, and treats historical material as real. At the same time the interpretative inquiry is based in abduction to interrogate the gap, contradictions and disjuncture between what was said and what was recorded, and between the preconceptions of elites and exotic characters.

Two applications we will explore in Part II are the impact of Peirce, through Pepper's (1942) work, on the storytelling work of Fred and Merrelyn Emery in storied aspects of their Search Conference approach and in Hopewell's (1987) narrative studies of church congregations.

Both Ricoeur (1984: 165) and White (1973: 13–21, 353) have wrestled with Pepper's world hypotheses (see Table 7.2) because of the puzzle that it presents to their narrative theses. White (1973: 13–21) in *Metahistory* has borrowed Pepper's typology to classify leading historians of the nineteenth century stating 'history is not a science or is at best a protoscience with specifically determinable nonscientific elements in its constitution.' We have also listed the historians identified by White in Table 7.2 along with exemplars listed by Pepper. Indeed, argues Ricoeur (1984: 165), historians narrate in so many ways, White's call for a typology of narrative forms seems reasonable.

Pepper's (1942) *World Hypotheses* introduces a typology in an attempt to organize all facts about knowledge within coherent systems, world hypotheses. According to Pepper, a world hypothesis is distinct from the restricted hypothesis characteristic of the special sciences in the sense that, if adequate, it shows the connection of theory with common sense. Pepper's major concern is to reconcile or to find a 'common root' between the perceptual (sense) and the conceptual (thought) poles of knowledge. In doing so, he addresses the 'tension between common sense and expert knowledge ... the interior dynamics of the knowledge situation' (1942: 44). Pepper identifies a limited set of 'root metaphor theories' or 'world hypotheses' that are robust enough (as adequate in precision and scope) to provide a relatively adequate interpretation of the full scope of the world's facts. These world hypotheses are formism, mechanism, contextualism and organicism. Each has a root metaphor. For example, the root metaphor of mechanism is the machine and emphasizes the discovery of empirical facts and their part to whole relationships in closed systems. Organicism develops the root metaphor of an organism emphasizing its developmental processes. Formism is the root metaphor of similarity that allows the correspondence of forms in ideal type contrasts. Contextualism, our main focus here, employs the root metaphor of the historical event in the present.

Table 7.2: Four world hypotheses of Stephen Pepper

Dimensions	Analytical Theories		Synthetic Theories	
Dispersive theories	Formism		Contextualism	
	1	Root Metaphor: Similarity	1	Root Metaphor: Historic event in the present.
	2	Explanation: Order and function are real; disorder and dysfunction unreal or exceptions.	2	Explanation: Only horizontal theory; focus on change and novelty in the unfolding immediate event.
	3	Exemplars: Plato, Aristotle	3	Exemplars: Pragmatists like Peirce, James, Bergson, Dewey and Mead
	4	Categories: • Immanent Formism – Theories of ideal types and classifications • Transcendent Formism – Blueprint growth models; ideal plans.	4	Categories: • Quality (spread, change and fusion) • Texture (strands, contexts, referents).
	5	Truth Theory: Correspondence – mirror theory from metaphor to reality.	5	Truth Theory: Operationalism – verifiable hypotheses and working theories.
Integrative theories	Mechanism		Organicism	
	1	Root Metaphor: Machine	1	Root Metaphor: Integration
	2	Explanation: Elements are parts in a mechanistic, spacio-temporal framework.	2	Explanation: Historic events are steps in organic process toward ideal progress (thesis-antithesis-synthesis of Hegel).
	3	Exemplars: Descartes, Galileo, Hobbes, Locke, Hume, Berkeley and Reichonbach.	3	Exemplars: Hegel, Schelling, Green, Bradley, Bosanquet and Royce.
	4	Categories: • Configuration of parts. • Lawfully ordered.	4	Categories: Fragments result in nexuses, leading to contradictions, and an organic whole
	5	Truth Theory: Causal adjustment – abstract general terms and formulae.	5	Truth Theory: Coherence – each level of integration resolves contradictions of the levels below.

Pepper's (1942) typology excludes 'explanation by ideology' that White (1973) according to Ricoeur (1984: 165) 'puts in the fifth rank of narrative structures' by including 'an ethical stance inherent in a particular manner of writing history.' White, says Ricoeur, reintroduces a post-Marxist, Frankfurt School concept of ideology, and Habermas and Gramsci and Althusser, to make the case of 'history's tie to action in the world of the present', since 'history orders events and processes in narrative' (Ricoeur, 1984: 165, fn. 58).

White (1973) turns to Frederick Nietzsche to extend Pepper's typology. In writing about legal systems and punishment, Nietzsche (1956/1887: 209) argues:

Yet the criterion of purpose is the last that should ever be applied to a study of legal evolution. There is no set of maxims more important for an historian than this: that the actual causes of a thing's origin and its eventual uses, the manner of its incorporation into a system of purposes, are worlds apart; that everything that exists, no matter what its origin, is periodically reinterpreted by those in power in terms of fresh intentions; that all processes in the organic world are processes of outstripping and overcoming, and that, in turn, all outstripping and overcoming means reinterpretation, rearrangement, in the course of which the earlier meaning and purpose are necessarily either obscured or lost.

In these few sentences, according to White (1973: 363), Nietzsche rejects 'the Mechanistic, Organicist and Contextualist conceptions of historical explanation, at one and the same time'. But note that White has excluded the formalist world hypothesis. White is seeking to include ideology. White, says Ricoeur (1984: 165) 'submits ideology to the same rule of discussion that applies to the mode of explanation by formal arguments'. Ricoeur (1984: 164) notes that White thereby sets up a hierarchy (duality) of narrative structure (plot types) and formal argumentation over ideology. Ricoeur (1984:167) charges that White constructs typologies of plot, argument-style, ideology and world hypotheses to classify historiographical style. In the end White forms a complex, three-dimensional formalist typology of ideologies, plot types and Pepper's typology.

Boje and Luhman (1999) argue that each of these world hypotheses have provided a way to narrate organizations with metaphoric 'images of organizations' since the mechanical apparatus of Hobbes' Leviathan and Newton's mechanistic science in the seventeenth century. The world, society, human body and mind were seen as machines within machines that could be controlled and scripted by human knowledge. Machine metaphors have been popular in OT since the industrial revolution. Each technology becomes a discourse to read and fashion organizations, from Frederick Taylor's scientific management to more recent machine models of TQM and reengineering. Formalist (ideal type typologies centred on bureaucracy) images of organization have been the icons of formal Weberian readings of organization theory. Fayol (1916: 70) based his fourteen commandment-principles of management and his five basic managerial functions on an organic metaphor of the firm (the living tree). Contingency theory sought to appropriate mechanistic and organic into yet another formalism.

Native stories, we believe, need not be considered animistic. But for Pepper's (1942: 120–1) project, native stories of the life of stories, animals, the living planet and cosmos are not considered to be adequate for science. 'Animism, as a metaphysical hypothesis, is the theory that takes common-sense man, the human being, the person, as its primitive root metaphor' (1942: 120). 'It is characteristic of animism that we can never precisely capture spirit in conceptual terms and list a set of categories that will stand firm' (Pepper, 1942: 121). Pepper (1942: 122) uses the example of lightning:

It is a Great Spirit clanging his arms. It is the roar of the lightning bolts hurled by a Great Spirit. It may even be a spirit itself roaring in pursuit of some other spirit to devour. These interpretations are all consonant with the categories of spirit, and there is nothing but the limitations of poetic fancy to put a stop to such interpretations.

Pepper objects to the metaphysics and dogmatism of spiritualism and animism. Contextualism has two applications to organization studies and intervention work. In Part II of this chapter, we will offer two examples of how Pepper's work is applied to organization studies.

Pragmatism has other applications to other narratologies. For example, Zanetti (1998: 279) argues that 'critical theory' is 'infused with American pragmatism and linguistic philosophy' and 'has become increasingly domesticated and utopian at the same time'. Of the critical theorists, Habermas, in particular (see below), envisions a utopian speech community brought about by following specific speech procedures.

Social constructionist narratology ranges from interpretativist, constructionist and social constructionist paradigms with many different theories within each (Schwandt, 1994). To Weick (1995), and most of the storytelling work in organization studies, storytelling is an act of sensemaking without any presumption of a material condition. People tell stories and make sense of their reality. For Berger and Luckmann (1967) reality is socially constructed as subjectivities become treated as if they are objectifications, and people reify the conversion forgetting that the objectifications were actually constructed in and through social interaction. Schwandt (1994) does an excellent review of the variegated terrain of social construction theory; we narrate only briefly and superficially. Interpretivist schools vary from Geertz's (1973) interpretative Anthropology, Blumer's (1968) Symbolic Interactionism, and Denzin's (1992) Reformed Interpretative Interactionism. Constructivists range from work by Nelson Goodman (1984), Von Glaserfeld (1989) (radical constructionism), Kenneth (and Mary) Gergen's social construction work and Guba and Lincoln's constructivist paradigm. Our point is that different narrative studies can say they are doing 'social construction' but be doing very different traditions. Since we do not intend to linger here, we will direct you to Schwandt's (1994) work and summarize the challenges to social construction that apply to narratology.

We will contrast approaches that apply social construction differently in the next two sections. Here, we will mention that Mary Boyce's (1995) work on storytelling organization theory is based on Gergen's approach to social construction, as is part of Czarniawska's (1997a) Narrating Organization approach.

Post-structuralist narratology: Post-structuralist narratologists saw the form-fixation of formalistics as an unnecessary reduction to complexity, heterogeneity and slippage of narrative meaning. Post-structuralists problematize the 'mimetic transparency' of realism narratology by denying any defensible difference between fiction and the real (Currie, 1998: 63–4). For example, DeMan posed problems for Saussurean structuralism by distinguishing between the referential beyond a text, and the autotelic within a text (Currie, 1988: 44). Along similar lines, Derrida in *Of Grammatology* also challenges Saussure about the supposition of the inside and outside of text.

Only particular social construction narratologies look reflexively at the privileging of status, gender, race and other cultural baggage in the narrative construction and reading process (Stanfield, 1994: 180–1). Others do not address power. Few structuralist linguists put the sign into the historical context of a given utterance's social production. In the formalistic approaches we reviewed, the historical dimension of synchronic structures (or processes) was generally just disregarded, so that spatial relations or differences in ideal types could be highlighted.

Derrida's (1978, 1981, 1985) deconstruction is not a method with steps and procedures, it is more of an inductive epistemological practice. Derrida's (1978) concept of *différance* put temporal meaning back into the analysis of structural relations. In terms of story, the story (form) elements are always in motion. Derrida's non-metaphysical theory of time resisted both 'history in general and the general concept of history' (Currie, 1998: 79). Resisting history in general resists, for example, Marx's preference for a Hegelian dialectic model of linear history, by arguing that this is no one single history, but many differentiated histories (Derrida, 1981: 58).

We can also question the common idea of a 'founding story' in organization studies. Derrida calls into question an 'origin' or any 'first moment in an historical sequence' of stories (Currie, 1998: 82). This would include the mythical first moment when the demand to recite a story that has yet to be articulated is met with a story performance. An alternative view is that there are multiple stories told from many views.

There is also a point of confusion about inside/outside text, we wish to briefly comment on. 'Il n'y a pas de-hors-texte' is Derrida's most misinterpreted slogan. 'The slogan' says Currie (1998: 45) 'does not mean there is nothing outside the text as most commentators have taken it. It is closer to "There is no outside-text"'. We assume then, from this narratology, if narrative is a text, then there is no outside narrative because outside of a text is more text. Language, says Currie (1998: 90) '*is* a material practice not only in the sense that it is to be understood in isolation from the mind as the material marks of writing but also in the sense that textual and linguistic constructs are (to use a word that Derrida avoids) *reified* or transformed into material things and practices in the world'. Standing 'outside' the organizational text to read it is impossible (Currie, 1998: 47). It is impossible for two reasons: (1) intertextuality, and (2) outside-text is another text. Intertextuality 'posits a model of referentiality which cannot distinguish between reference to the world and reference to another text, since textuality is woven into all' (Currie, 1998: 70). For narratives, it means narratives refer to other narratives, and we can not distinguish the world from just another narrative. As we shall explore various narratologies vehemently reject these assumptions of no origin and no outside of text.

There is some middle ground. Our reading is that Derrida deconstructs the duality of mind and things by resituating text in its material forms, including its technical, political and ideological practices as well as bombs, factories, wars and revolutions (Currie, 1998: 90). This does not mean those factories, wars and revolutions are mere texts or just narratives. Derrida's problematic is a refusal to dichotomize between material and narrative.

In search of a middle ground, therefore, we assume organization is a material and a discursive formation. Its materiality comes into being through discourse, established in a multiplicity of stories and transformed by more stories. Stories are meaningful in their embeddedness in the webs of stories. Others may deconstruct and then resituate the mind/materiality duality differently. In deconstruction, it is up to each practitioner to script their own moves, and this we have done. There are other viable readings, such as a feminist deconstruction of story (Martin, 1990) or a rereading of March and Simon's or Weber's classic works (Kilduff, 1993; Martin and Knopoff, 1997) and deconstructive readings of organization research (Kilduff and Mehra, 1997). Martin's (1990) study for example approaches deconstructionist readings of a CEO story from multiple positions, constructing new storylines by changing the gender of the main character.

Discourses can be deconstructed to reveal masked pluralities, hegemonic rhetoric and inconsistencies. By discourse, we mean the expressed knowledge/power nexus that promulgates a cohesive social practice.[2] Discourse is also the infinite play of differences in meaning mediated through socially constructed hegemonic practices (Boje, 1995a: 998). The discursive metaphors (play, text, conversation) can be empowering as Thatchenkery (1992: 231) argues because they provide 'organizational participants considerable flexibility to create their own interpretation of what is going on.' At the same time, even discursive metaphors, selected for their polyvocal flexibility, can still be sites for panoptic discipline (Foucault, 1979: 217).

Critical theory narratology: Critical theory like pragmatist narratology is less willing to bracket the material condition from acts of narration than is social construction or realist narratology. Yet unlike pragmatists, critical theorists favour macrohistorical narratives of class struggle and technological development. Karl Marx narrated with critical attention to the material conditions of labour practice and at one point foresaw the overthrow of the bourgeoisie by the proletariat, although in his later writings he saw that the revolution was not to be. Horkheimer, Adorno, Marcuse and the Frankfurt School in particular revised his work in the mid-twentieth century.

Marx called the factory the 'House of Terror' (1867/1967, *Capital*, Volume 1, hereafter C1: 277). His narratives are rich with metaphor. 'The capitalized blood of children' and women feeds global political economy to this very day (C1: 757). As Marx puts it 'the vampire will not lose its hold [on him] so long as there is a muscle, a nerve, a drop of blood to be exploited' (C1: 302). In industrial capitalism, 'the small and nimble fingers of little children' and young ladies are in constant demand to feed 'the "vampire" of global capitalism' (C1: 757–8). Marx's narrative of the labour process described skilled industrial workers as once attending lectures on trigonometry, engineering and physics to learn more knowledge about their craft. Were they not the ideal knowledge workers? Yet work them till they drop and work them again until they die of exhaustion seemed to be the governing principle of their managers.

The objective here is to maximize the level of exertion that is put forth in production and service, to deny any sunlight or leisure, to exhaust labour to death:

> It usurps the time for growth, development and healthy maintenance of the body. It steals the time required for the consumption of fresh air and sunlight. It higgles over a meal-time, incorporating it where possible with the process of production itself, so that food is given to the labourer as to a mere means of production, as coal is supplied to the boiler, grease and oil to the machinery. It reduces the sound sleep needed for the restoration, reparation, refreshment of the bodily powers to just so many hours of torpor as the revival of an organism, absolutely exhausted, renders essential. (C1: 265)

> Mary Anne Walkley had died from long hours of work in an over-crowded workroom, and a too small and badly-ventilated bedroom. (C1: 255)

Capital, says Marx, 'cares nothing for the length of life of labour-power' (C1: 265). Once a peasant is removed from land tenure or entrepreneurial ventures (e.g. cottage industry, small shop ownership) the labour power must be sold. 'It quenches only in a slight degree the vampire thirst for the living blood of labour. To appropriate labour during all the 24 hours of the day is, therefore, the inherent tendency of capitalist production' (C1: 256–7).

Determinist theories read history through a retrospective lens of capitalist concepts. This is done in order to make the case that markets, technology and even history evolves and unfolds the teleology of the capitalist project. History is seen as unfolding in stages, as various civilizations get more advanced and progressive in their application of markets, technology and the natural evolution of the survival of the rich over the poor. The critical position is that there is no teleology, a political economy can evolve or it can devolve depending upon the situation.

For example Horkheimer turned from the revolutionary potential for the working class to an appeal to 'critical intellectuals' (Zanetti, 1998: 282). What we mean by a critical theory narratology ranges from Marx's macrohistorical narratives, Marcuse's call to move beyond one-dimensional narratives of systemic modernism (i.e. Taylorism, social engineering and what we now call managerialist control), to Habermas' preference for speech communities that can exhibit consensus based upon agreed language rules.

Habermas has given his own reading to critical theory, influenced by the pragmatics of speech communities and his hope for reasoned consensus (Zanetti, 1997, 1998). 'Habermas shifts the focus of critical theory from *agents* of change to *procedures* of change' (Zanetti, 1998: 279). Those working more in the Frankfurt School tradition, still see the potential for agents of change. Alvesson and Willmott (1996) and Fulop and Linstead (1999) have written critical readings of management, and Mills and Simmons (1995) have a critical reading of OT. Each gives much support to Braverman's neo-Marxist (1974) book, *Labor and Monopoly Capital* and calls into question managerialist narratives in the hope that emancipation from the hierarchy of managerialist and social engineering control is possible. 'Integral to the emancipatory intent of Critical Theory is a vision of a qualitatively different form of management: one that is more democratically accountable to those whose lives are affected in so many ways by management decisions' (Alvesson and Willmott, 1996: 40). It is hoped that alternative forms of work will allow communications that 'are progressively less distorted' than those of 'socially oppressive, asymmetrical relations of power' (Alvesson and Willmott, 1996: 18). They also (1996: 12, 13) question the ideology of individualism in managerialist writing, challenging empowerment writing as yet another discourse of control, and critique the relentless expansion of globalizing capitalism without attending also to its more destructive social and ecological aspects. Critical theorists contend that cooperatives and collective-self-determination systems pose more democratic options to hierarchical firms. Mills and Simmons (1995) look at Braverman's deskilling but deviating from a strictly class-based approach, ask why the managerialist discourse of OT excludes race and gender from its pages. They also see managerialist narrative as apologetics for greater control of work by management (1995: 68–9). Fulop and Linstead (1999: 63), for example, point out that Braverman can be used to show that Mayo and Taylor are linked in various ways. Each of these texts deconstructs managerialist narratives and substitutes neo-Marxist narratives of liberation. The potential of critical narratology is to analyze people's microstories in relationship to grand, macro-story contexts: a worker after a downsizing episode, the plight of temporary workers, or the toxic conditions of new sweatshops accumulating in Asia – in contrast to the mechanistic myth of ultimate perfectibility or global progress.

A critical narratology perspective is being applied to studies of Nike's spin on its claims in codes of conduct (Boje, 1998a, 1998b, 1998c, 1999). I want to include the critical narratology work (my term) of O'Connor (1996, 1999a, 1999b, 2001 in press). O'Connor has been doing a resituation of Taylor, Mayo, Follett and other foundational management and organization authorities by researching the political, economic, social and autobiographical narratives. Her work traces Mayo's relationship with the Harvard Business School, putting it in political and economic context. This work combines narrative and organization study, as will as rehistoricizing these personalities.

Postmodern narratology: (Francese, 1997; Lyotard, 1997; Currie, 1998; Dixon, 1998) resituates structuralist, social constructionist and critical theory narratology. Like critical theory and post-structuralist narratology, postmodern narrative theories situate power and politics in narrative, but this time within the cultural milieu of late capitalism (Dixon, 1998).

Postmodernism is a contested discourse. Some posit a break with modernity, while others focus on an epistemological critique of culture. Francese (1997) sees the postmodern condition as something to withdraw from with the help of several late modern narrative writers. There are also quite radical positions such as Baudrillard's hyper-reality (it's all simulacra), and Lyotard's death wish to Grand narratives, and critical postmodern positions such as Jameson (postmodern culture situated in late capitalism) and Debord's Marxist critique of the consumption and production spectacle (Best and Kellner, 1997).

In search of a middle ground, we will argue that Grand narratives are not dead and have not been replaced by fragmented local stories. Rather the two are intertwined and contesting in ways that have important organization implications we explore in Part III. There is also a middle ground between sceptical and affirmative positions.

In postmodern management and organization writing the more sceptical positions have been reviewed with an eye to exclude any affirmative postmodernists. At the other extreme some affirmative writing ignores the dark side of the postmodern condition, which ends up creating another progress myth or replacing one totalizing account with another. The sceptics are sensitive to this danger. Sceptics include Alvesson and Deetz, 1996; Hassard and Parker, 1993; Kilduff and Mehra, 1997; Parker, 1997; Schwartz, 1994; Thompson, 1993. Sceptics argue that postmodernism is nihilistic and that the postmodern condition has decidedly negative effects on identity, community and ecology. Affirmatives posit a paradigm shift from modern to postmodern. Affirmatives would include Bergquist, 1993; Boje and Dennehy, 1993, Boje et al., 1996; Clegg, 1990 and Hatch, 1997. Some affirmatives consider management and organization from a postmodern epistemological perspective such as in the writings of Burrell and Cooper in *Organization Studies* beginning in 1988, as well as the work of Linstead and others. Other affirmatives look at postmodern organizational forms (e.g. Bergquist, 1993) that exhibit chaos and complexity patterns or are post-Fordist (e.g. Boje and Dennehy, 1993; Clegg, 1990) or are potentially more ecological (Boje et al., 1996; Hatch, 1997). Many sceptics call into question the very idea of a postmodern organization or a cultural epoch that is postmodern or see postmodern organization as a new cultural artifact. So-called 'postmodern organization' 'affirmative' and 'episodic' writing is given dismissive replies:

1 'Nonsense' (Thompson, 1993: 188)
2 'A distraction from rigorous analysis' (Parker, 1993: 212)
3 Unreflective 'in regard to cultural elitism and modern conditions of power' if it does not include critical theory (Parker, 1993: 211)
4 'Little is to be gained by ... talking about postmodern organizations' (Alvesson and Deetz, 1996: 192)
5 Merely 'relabeling' so-called organic, adhocratic or post-Fordist organizations as postmodern (Alvesson and Deetz, 1996: 192)
6 'McPostmodern' (Parker, 1997)
7 The work of 'self-declared organizational postmodernists' (Kilduff and Mehra, 1997: 454, footnote 1)

The point we are making that relates to narrative is that there are narratives of a postmodern organization and postmodern condition, just as there are quite sceptical narratives of nihilism and exploitation. We think the point is to look at their interrelationship in organization studies. Hassard (1993), for example, calls for middle range theories between epoch and epistemological positions, pointing to Ken Gergen's work as a primary example. In a recent review, Alvesson and Deetz (1996) called for critical theory and postmodern theory to work together in ways that could combine what we here are calling sceptical and affirmative analyses.

A critical/postmodern narratology would, for example, question the stories told to us in the media (Boje, 1999). And it is in the media that stories of managing so called 'postmodern organizations' under conditions on the edge of chaos, the new Biotech Century and the knowledge worker Virtual corporation continue to proliferate. Dixon (1998: 182), for example, argues that we get socialized by the spectacle of Hollywood cinema, with its 'translucence of coalescing narrative structure, signification systems exhausted through ceaseless recycling, and a star system which cannibalizes all who participate in it.' There is a blurring of the line between martial and storied condition. In the midst of televised baseball, football and soccer games, digitized images not only scroll across the screen, but the game becomes digitized replays, and there are digitized commercial decompositions of the screen to superimpose this or that corporate logo onto the field of play. 'Our connection to the world has become one of images rather than contacts, of surfaces rather than interior motivations' (Dixon, 1998: 185). This way the same commercial sporting space and time can be sold over and over again. 'Thus, viewers of a baseball game in New York might see an advertisement for Miller Beer behind the batter's box; the same viewer in France might see the Citroen corporate logo in the exact same location' (Dixon, 1998: 184). Coke logos just appear on the field of play, and it can be done with such finesse the spectator does not distinguish it from 'real.' The next step here is to digitize and airbrush the rough edging off the dream plays and star players, from archives of instant replay; to hype up the spectacle of continuous consumption (Dixon, 1998: 184).

Finally, we include Currie (1998) who calls for a socio-narratology. He advocates first a critique of synchronic narration by tracing stories of time told in linear sequence. As such, he is striking a middle ground between postmodern and pragmatic narrative. This is embedding the fragmented present in traces of its historical context. And the recognition that there is not one, but many histories (1998: 79). It is a questioning of teleological narratives to trace the differences that have been excluded. Second is Currie's narrative exclusion. Metaphors and models exclude by a tyranny of sameness. Traces of context reveal absences of political importance, of agents bent to ideology. The focus on pure presence is an exclusion of past and future. A fall from natural existence implies that ecology has some metaphysical priority against which the history of capitalism can be seen as a process of progress or deterioration (1998: 83). Best and Kellner (1997) for example look at production and consumption within the ecological limits of Earth's resources. In Part II we explore more middle ground by looking at different applied approaches to narrative, and continue this theme in Part III where more decidedly interdisciplinary approaches are compared and contrasted.

Part II: Applied approaches to narrating organization

In this section we contrast four applied approaches:
1 appreciative inquiry and
2 restorying
and two approaches rooted in pragmatism
3 Emery's Search Conference method for strategic planning and
4 Hopewell's congregation narrative work.

Appreciative inquiry is rooted in social constructionism, restorying is rooted in post-structuralism, Emery's method in Peirce's pragmatic philosophy and Hopewell and Emery in the contextualism as interpreted by Pepper (1942). We will begin with appreciative inquiry and, as we proceed, point out middle ground.

1. Appreciative inquiry is a very different social construction narratology that has an expanding following. It is less eclectic and more applied. For Ludema et al. (1996), Srivastva and Cooperrider (1999) and Cooperrider and Srivastva (1987) appreciative inquiry is thought to achieve positive transformation outcomes by side-stepping negative inquiry and the negative influence of problem stories. Appreciative inquiry puts negative stories aside and moves directly to constructing a new and more positive array of stories through guided acts of participation and inquiry. This is done by asking members to only recall positive stories and move beyond any negative context analysis. They are asked to dream and invent the narrative they want to live. According to the editorial position of *Global Social Innovations* (Wilmot, 1996: 7), a journal of Case Western Reserve's OD programme professors and PhD candidates,

> ... appreciative inquiry is premised on the logic that organizations move in the direction of what [people] study. For example, when groups study human problems and conflicts, they often find both the number and severity of complex and problematic issues has grown. In the same manner, when groups study high human ideals and achievements, such as teamwork, quality or peak experiences, these phenomena, too, tend to flourish in human systems. [Additions ours]

One assumption of the Case Western OD programme is that all forms of negative inquiry are not breathing positive life into organization. This privileges being positive over being critical of narratives within for example a critical theory reading of the political economy. For example, in the GSI publication (Wilmot, 1996: 7), readers are told that GEM consultants work with top management teams in 'appreciative interviews' with each other about their original attractions to the organization, peak experiences, core values and wishes for the organization's future.

At the 1997 Academy of Management meeting, I chaired a session in which the deconstructionists (Boyce, Luhman, Dennehy, Rosile and Barry) debated the appreciative inquiry people (Ludema, Sorensen and Yaeger). Then our discussant, Joanne Martin, challenged us to learn to get along because we have much in common, and pointed out our premise for the session, a debate, was a duality in need of deconstruction. Why not remove the duality? This would mean looking at some of the narrative deconstruction practices in the following section along with the appreciative storytelling.

2. Restorying narratives originate in narrative family therapy practices in Australia and New Zealand (and now around the world) in which the deconstruction approach of White (1989, 1991) and Epston (1989) is prominent. Narrative therapy (White and Epston, 1990) is increasingly being applied to organizational studies (Barry, 1997; Barry and Elmes, 1997). Barry (1997) for example is applying narrative family therapy practices to organizational consulting. His application from family to organization might look at how stories are typically 'problem-saturated' in dysfunctional organizations as they are in dysfunctional families. Narrative therapy assumes that people's lives are strongly influenced by their story sensemaking and that poor relations are embedded in the structure of these stories (Barry, 1997).

Narrative therapy assumes each story is ideological and each representation of reality is ideological (White, 1989: 148). Stories are not individually authored – there is always the individual and someone else – within the context of a family, organization or broader society. And within these embedded contexts of family structures, organizations and societies there is much in life that is inconsistent, discrepant, incoherent, disharmonious, muddled and irrational (this parallels the assumptions of the microstoria approach discussed earlier). In narrative therapy it is the excluded material from the more oppressive and debilitating narratives that can be restoried, after deconstructive exploration (again White and Epston have their own interpretation of Derrida's practices). The idea is to recall and rehearse microstories of resistance to the dominant storyline. Deconstruction plays a role in loosening the grip of a dominant story.

> In Western culture there is a dominant story about what it means to be a person of moral worth. This story emphasizes self-possession, self-containment, self-actualization and so on. It stresses individuality at the expense of community and independence at the expense of connection. These are culturally specific values which are presented as universal, 'human' attributes to be striven for. The attempt to live up to these dominant prescriptions can have profoundly negative consequences for people's lives. (Aboriginal Health Council (hereafter AHC), 1995: 19)

Deconstruction allows the dominant stories to be named and externalized (e.g. 'put down stories', 'injustice stories'), their hierarchical effects to be explored (e.g. loss of self-esteem): 'Many Aboriginal people have had put on them negative stories about who they are' (AHC, 1995: 20). Narrative therapy reverses the claims (claiming strengths in face of domination), and the story to be restoried and resituated in preferred stories of being (reclaiming Aboriginal ontologies).

Characterizations in dominant stories (for example the role of women in the workplace, rights of managers over workers) do not tell the complete story and distort people's sense of self in debilitating ways. Narrative therapy addresses questions such as, 'What has been silent in the organization's account of you?' 'Can an alternative characterization of the self be told?'

An example may help illustrate the application. The Aboriginal Health Council put out a newsletter (1995) titled 'Reclaiming Our Stories, Reclaiming Our Lives'. The government was investigating the pain and suffering of relatives of Aboriginal people who had died in custody. The idea was to reclaim Aboriginal knowledges about ways to respond to grief and pain, to honour Aboriginal healing knowledge. Narrative therapy was 'identified by Aboriginal health workers in different parts of Australia as more appropriate to

Aboriginal culture than the more conventional Western mental health approaches' (AHC, 1995: 3). Aboriginal and non-Aboriginal counsellors trained in narrative therapy gathered with family groups to hear their stories and recommendations. For five days family groups (26 adults) told their stories of deaths in custody, effects on the family, the healing knowledge of those experiences in Aboriginal culture and the context most appropriate to further discussion, including recommendations for future counselling services to Aboriginal people. Narrative therapists acted as facilitators for the small group discussions.

There is a relationship between narrative therapy and seeing the story as living with place, time and mind (TwoTrees, 1997). One example:

> The history of genocide, loss of land, removal of children from their parents and families, and the forcible destruction of community and family traditions lives on in an immediate way in the lives of the Aboriginal people participating in this project. ... Injustices experienced by past generations are carried actively in the form of shame and sadness by the present generation, and have real effects on their lives. (AHC, 1995)

This describes the sense of living story in a community. Aboriginal children are 'regularly stopped and questioned for no particular reason other than their race' and there were stories of 'adolescent girls being strip-searched by male police without anybody else being present' (AHC, 1995: 7). One more story:

> One woman reported asking the police if she could see the cell in which her brother had died, because she needed to do this in order to be able to put his spirit to rest. When this was refused, she committed an offense so that she would be arrested. She was then able to personally experience what her brother had been through – having her pockets emptied, her belongings taken away, and she was actually put in the cell where her brother had died. She felt that, by doing this, she was able to get a much better sense of what may have happened to her brother, and to release his spirit so that it was a peace. (AHC, 1995: 8)

Storytelling is part of how Aboriginal, and other people, share and care about their feelings of pain, hurt and injustice over the last 200 years. As part of the group process, 'listening teams' formed to reclaim the strengths of Aboriginal culture. These included humour, self-pride, determination and hope, turning negatives into positives, pride in Aboriginal identity, family connections, 'seeing myself in my family's eyes', 'being strong for my family', the old people, reconnecting at this camp, spirituality, Aboriginal organizations, naming injustice, caring and sharing, remembering Aboriginal ways and knowledges and sharing stories.

Reclaiming stories was said to be 'the ability to share their own stories and hear other people's stories' and was identified as a major theme of the five day event (AHC, 1995: 16). Stories and storytelling are an essential part of Aboriginal culture. Present deaths are connected to past and present injustices, such that storytelling and hearing allows memories to be sifted to reclaim self-esteem. 'Within the context of the camp, people felt freer to start remembering those things they wanted to remember about the people they had lost, rather than only remembering the loss and the injustice' (AHC, 1995: 16). 'Narrative therapy places a great deal of importance on finding ways in which an audience can be invited to play a part in authenticating and strengthening the preferred stories that are emerging in therapy' (AHC, 1995: 19). This includes finding people to contact who experience us in ways that manifest our preferred stories.

To bring this back to organizations and OT, the Aboriginal restorying examples point to how people are affected by state organizations and to examples of how just appreciating a new story does not in and of itself change the political and economic context. Restorying allows for resistance to the dominant context.

In this next section, we will contrast two self-defined pragmatist approaches that are both rooted in Pepper's (1942) work (refer to Table 7.2). Contextualism (Pepper, 1942) has been applied to organizations by F. Emery (1977, 1997) and M. Emery (1993, 1997, 1998) and by Hopewell (1987).

3. Emery's Search Conference. For the Emerys, contextualism is one of the open systems theory concepts that serve as a foundation of the Search Conference method for organizational strategic planning. The method was specifically developed to operationalize organizational action in turbulent environments (Type IV). Within the Search Conference, there are calls for narration such as relating the history of the system. The Emerys' work is rooted in pragmatism narratology. For example, to the Emerys, contextualism is the most adequate world hypothesis because, as Pepper (1942: 243) points out:

> Change goes on continuously and never stops. Change is a categorical feature of all events; and, since on this world theory all the world is events, all the world is continuously changing in this manner. Absolute permanence or immutability in any sense is, on this theory, a fiction.

F. Emery (in M. Emery, 1993: 37) asserts that contextualism had to be the paradigm because it's 'the only one that's appropriate to what is happening culturally and in action research. ... It's the only paradigm, which has ever taken change as the reality from which we start, the others have all started from static substances as the real world'.

As a method grounded in contextualism the Search Conference is a model of the evolving environmental features that fundamentally determine the conditions required for active adaptation and development of a human system. The Emerys' method for strategic planning is a wholehearted and consistent commitment to, and demonstration and learning of, contextualism and thereby pragmatism.

Pepper (1942: 107) asserts that 'Peirce and James intuited the pragmatic, or contextualistic, root metaphor'. In fact, 'contextualism is commonly called "pragmatism"' (141) which, in the form of contextualism, 'has thickened into ... a world theory' (268). The Emerys are contextualist systems thinkers who, like Peirce's pragmatic-realism, anchor their premises in the objective world of matter. Peirce offered a number of definitions for pragmatism. In examination of his work Feibleman (1946: 295, 296) lists seven. Out of the seven definitions, Feibleman asserts that the following is 'the clearest of all':

[Pragmatism is a] maxim for obtaining clearness of apprehension: … In order to ascertain the meaning of an intellectual conception one should consider what practical consequences might conceivably result by necessity from the truth of that conception; and the sum of these consequences will constitute the entire meaning of the conception. (1946: 295)

According to Feibleman, under this maxim, pragmatism 'is a method of reflection having for its purpose to render ideas clear'. It is a method that would bring to an end those prolonged disputes among researchers and philosophers 'which no observations of facts could settle, and yet in which each side claims to prove the other side in the wrong' (1946: 296). Pragmatism is a method of ascertaining the meanings of intellectual concepts – those which essentially carry some implication concerning the general behaviour of people and so convey the 'would-acts', 'would-dos' of habitual behaviour – upon the structure of which arguments concerning objective facts may hinge (Feibleman, 1946: 297). Thus, when a proposition implies human conduct (e.g. the learning and planning actions of the Search Conference), pragmatism 'makes thought ultimately *apply* to action exclusively – to *conceived* action' (Peirce, 5.403).[3]

For the Emerys, in turbulent environments, a model of 'humans-as-machine' is inadequate (F. Emery, 1977: 69). What is adequate is a model of 'humans-as-ideal seeking' systems (open perceptual systems that learn from the environment). F. Emery (1997: 148) points out that the conception of a model of man as an ideal seeking system emerged when Ackoff and himself (Ackoff and F. Emery, 1972) 'got at the top of the problem' they had when they were 'struggling to formulate a model of man as a purposeful being'. Thus, the distinction lies in the sense that with purposeful systems the key is making choices between alternative goals that are simultaneously present. With ideal seeking systems, on the other hand, the key is to recognize that purposeful systems can be confronted by choice between purposes or objective of those purposes. Here lies the narrative relevance of the Emerys' model of humans.

The Emerys' model of man specifically incorporates Peirce's idea of meaning which involves reference to a purpose, a very natural idea for a pragmatist (Peirce, 5.166). From Peirce's perspective, a purpose is something that lies outside language. Purpose is referent to the external world thereby linking interpretation in accordance to a given meaning. Purpose is directly related to Peirce's term of 'lithium' which denotes 'prescribing what you are to do [your purpose] in order to gain a perceptive acquaintance with the object of the word' (Peirce, 2.330).

But where is the relationship to narrative? It is by means of Peirce's concept of 'unlimited semiosis' which Eco (1990: 37) asserts cannot be conceptually equivalent to 'the deconstructive drift'. This is because unlimited semiosis is confronted with something external to it in at least two cases. In one case we have the act of indication (for example, my purpose is …) whereby we point our finger toward a given object – indices are linked to the extralinguistic world. In the other case, we have the fact that the very semiotic act is determined by a 'dynamic object', a thought, an ideal, a feeling, a belief. Therefore, the text is uttered by the person according to his or her actual intention which is motivated by the dynamic object.

One more point which specifically relates to the Emerys' model of humans. For Peirce, the dynamic object can never be attained. It can only be known through the immediate object. This is what ideals are all about, they are 'endlessly approachable but unattainable in themselves' (F. Emery, 1997: 149). It is for this reason that Peirce views semiosis as perception whereby the world becomes understandable to us under the form of an immediate object. Here is where Peirce's endless series of representations are clarified. The dynamic object (e.g. humanity as an ideal) is always absent because we focus in the immediate one (e.g. acceptance of Aboriginal identity). Thus, we have an endless series of representations (diversity, understanding of ethnicity and so forth) each representing the one behind it (they are all geared towards humanity). Thus, the final logical interpretation involves 'habit'. That is, a disposition to act upon the world. This is why the Emerys assert that an ideal is 'an ultimately intended outcome', one that 'can never be obtained but can be approached without limit' (Ackoff and F. Emery, 1972: 57). Ideals, while ultimately unattainable, provide context and meaning for all planning activity. When doing active adaptive planning in complex environments, we can expect the effects of choice to be manifest in a core set of universal ideals from their related parameters of choice or decision making (F. Emery, 1977). Ideals enable people:

- to maintain continuity of direction and social cohesiveness by choosing another objective when one is achieved, or the effort to achieve it has failed; and
- to sacrifice objectives in a manner consistent with the maintenance of direction and social cohesion.

4. Congregational narratives. Hopewell (1987) was influenced by the structuralist and formalistic theories of Northrop Frye, Claude Levi-Strauss and Stith-Thomkins. Frye's work provided the narrative categories to classify romantic, comic, tragic and ironic plot structures. While White and Hopewell each use Frye's typology in conjunction with Pepper's world hypotheses typology, the renditions are quite different. And Hopewell's application is not the same as that of the Emerys. Hopewell makes the narrative connection to formism in Pepper's classification (see Table 7.2), while the Emerys connect their consulting approach (which includes story collection and construction) to contextualism.

Hopewell collected structural images and plot structures from local congregations so that he could classify them. As with White, Hopewell also explored their ideological differences. He also considered the nature of their congregational life by analyzing how their narrative (formalistic) worldview differed from other congregations. Hopewell (1987: 164) believed that church members identified with the 'plot of its corporate activity and also an attraction, through that history, to the Other whom the congregation proclaims its Lord'. Church members he argued, participated in 'narrative reflection and storied praxis' (164). The story life of each church 'even when it recounts pedestrian and trivial activity, is the legend of God's plan, if only its sounds and signs can be heard and read' (Wheeler, 1987: xiv).

In sum, a variety of narratology positions are being applied to organization consultation work. Pepper's (1942) typology has had a significant influence on the approaches of the Emerys and Hopewell in different ways. The Emerys focus on contextualism while Hopewell stays with formalism. Both adopt structuralist approaches, but the Emerys prefer the pragmatism of Peirce, while Hopewell seeks to use Frye's plot structures and Pepper's formalistic contrasts as a way to read God's plan. The other approaches reviewed were narrative therapy that is rooted in post-structuralist and appreciative inquiry in social constructionist narratologies. Appreciative inquiries like Hopewell's approach aims toward spiritual implications of the story consultation. In the next section we conclude with a brief contrast between approaches to organization story and narrative that cross several narratologies.

Part III: Comparing three cross paradigm narratologies

In this final section we apply what we have reviewed thus far in terms of the varied narratologies in Part I, and their various applications to organization consultation in Part II. We will contrast Czarniawska, Boje and Clair's approaches which each adopt at least three narratologies in their organization studies. Each seeks middle ground perspectives. In this sense their work is interdisciplinary in ways that blur boundaries between narratologies introduced in Part I and the applied work in Part II.

1. Narrating the organization. We see Czarniawska's (1997a) *Narrating the Organization* as integration between social construction, pragmatist and structuralist narratologies.[4] Her social construction approach builds upon Gergen (1991), Schutz (1972) and Weick (1995). She also relies upon combining the work of pragmatism (e.g. Rorty, Habermas and minor reference to Peirce) with social constructionism and the dramaturgical approach of Barthes (1966) and the scene-act ratio structure of Burke (1945).[5] Czarniawska (1997a: 57) mentions Peirce only briefly and not in the ways that the Emerys have applied his work in abduction (an alternative to both induction and deduction). Rorty (1980), who rejects the mirror or correspondence theory of truth, is a more featured pragmatist theorist in her work. But Habermas (1987), who seeks pragmatic rules for effecting workable speech communities, and was influenced by the work of Peirce, is also featured (1997a: 23, 45).[6] Czarniawska (1997a: 57) seeks to relate social construction to several aspects of pragmatism in order to reveal the 'reality' behind 'appearances'.

Several chapters are spent applying a formalistic frame to Swedish Public Administration, to read its narrative qualities. Table 7.3 is our integrative reading of Burke's (1945) scene-act ratio, and Henderson's (1988) plot types as applied by Czarniawska (1997a) to Swedish administration.

Henderson contributes the idea that act is related to realism, agent to idealism, scene to materialism, agency to pragmatism and purpose to mysticism. Burke of course has the typology of act, agent, scene, agency and purpose. In Act, Czarniawska applies contextualism in ways that are uniquely

Table 7.3: Burke and Henderson as applied by Czarniawska

1. **Act** (action)-focused plots = realism
   - ✓ Incessant action (movement) effect or constant talk and high mobility define community.
   - ✓ In contextualism, the context of action is an unfolding web of act to other act relationships without teleology.
   - ✓ Novelty and random events happen and account for change.
2. **Agent** (actor)-focused plots = idealism
   - ✓ I act in the interests of others, not my own or as my own agent.
   - ✓ Modern leadership theory assumes leaders (and entrepreneurs) act as their own agent, while managers act as the agent of their firm.
   - ✓ Leaders are the change agents.
3. **Scene**-focused plots = materialism
   - ✓ Static role structure (good guys/bad guys; progressives/conservatives) or changing alliances.
   - ✓ Modern organization assumes determinism of environmental factors (resources, technology, change and competition).
   - ✓ The environment (i.e. place) determines change.
4. **Agency**-focused plots = pragmatism
   - ✓ Follow unwritten rules, repeat successful tricks or constantly improvise and muddle along.
   - ✓ Modern leader theory assumes managers are agents of a 'super person' corporation, a legal person (or agent of anthropomorphic corporate-is-person).
   - ✓ Change is the result of the system of capitalism self-steering its invisible hand in the market (that is without place).
5. **Purpose**-oriented plots = mysticism
   - ✓ Simple, coherent, constant motives or more highly complex coping situations of enlightened or dark spirituality.
   - ✓ Modern management theory assumes people are purpose seeking, acting consistent with their motivations and values.
   - ✓ Change is a spiritual, visionary and even charismatic event.

different from what we describe of Pepper's work. She uses the typology outlined in Table 7.3 to generate several narrative insights into Swedish administration. She defines a 'story' as consisting 'of a plot comprising causally related episodes that culminate in a solution to a problem' and have 'a clear chronological structure, with a beginning and an end' (1997a: 78). Serials, on the other hand 'do not have any plot' and 'do not contain any solutions' and are 'continually adapted to meet new conditions and requirements' (78–9). Through what she terms 'company-ization' a story can become incorporated into the routine of an organization. For example, in her first story of Chapter 4, titled 'A new budget and accounting routine in Big City' the story begins that 'The Municipal Court decided that Big City was overcharging its citizens for energy and water' (79). The problem is an obsolete accounting system and Big City decides to clean up the problematic accounting system. The old accounting system did not control for cheating on the numbers at the end of the accounting period. The solution was training in registering dates of payment to resolve this story of catastrophic municipal finance routines. The serial takes a twisting turn when the Financial Council votes to abolish the changes being implemented. The changes proposed in the accounting systems were seen as too threatening.

As she proceeds she compares and contrasts this first story with two others (we shall not explore): 'In the first story, where the paradox was neatly incorporated into the design, the most likely outcome was a change that would improve the status quo' but in the third story change was co-opted; the second story reveals that 'those who constitute a certain order are the ones who try to change it' (99).

As the book proceeds the scene-act model of Table 7.3 is applied. For example, budget writers become 'script writers' on the 'stage-setting' of municipalities taking 'stage directions' from politicians. The concept of scene-act ratio is used: 'achieving a correct scene-act ratio can ... be seen as the main task of the stage directions: the scene directions must be coherent with acting instructions' (130). Actors need to be able to act on instructions, take stage directions, in order for the action to create a coherent scene. In this script, as the Swedish public employees imitate business company scripts, paradoxical effects happen: 'the action not only does not fit the scene but even appears to contradict it' (131). Budgeting is read as an act of 'collective writing'.

In her typology, she notes that modern leader theory assumes managers are agents of a 'super person' corporation, a legal person (or agent of anthropomorphic corporate-is-person). The organizations reviewed in her Chapter 7 are seen as 'actors trying to construct a new stage' as a 'control philosophy whereby the stage determines the actions and the actors' (159). When their actions remain intact, a new identity is hard to construct. Yet, an identity transformation is taking place onstage, in a setting in which other actors are authoring the identity-narrative. 'The new identity is to be "written" by somebody else, for example, the private sector' (160). She concludes by reasserting 'a need for normative narratives ... that they fulfill their function properly if they are loosely coupled to practice; if they legitimate (provide the legitimate rules for accounting for practice) rather than trying to influence practice' (164). And she moves from a pragmatist tracing of unfolding routines, plots and character-acts to a postmodern explanation, noting the postmodern traits of deconstruction, rejection of grand strategies, sensitivity to the multitude of small narratives with multiple interpretations indicative of plural and constantly renegotiated realties (162–3). Only in crisis does the Swedish administration contrive a single totalizing narrative. The crisis in Sweden happened as the 'institutional thought structure' was called into question. Adherents to that thought structure sought new narratives or stories to defend and resolve the attack. In sum, she seeks to show that 'narrative knowledge constitutes the core of organizational knowledge' (167). Through Burke's dramatistic method, 'people assume a dialectical stance in face of paradoxes, in order to achieve the dissolution of the paradox-induced drama' (167).

In Swedish organization-as-theatre, managers are expected to integrate their character and role in terms of agency and purpose, and not to act as their own self-promoting agent. Leaders of modern organization-as-theatre are expected to play the good guy in progressive (myth) scenes of material accumulation, achieving purpose in highly complex spectacles of production and consumption. The modern stage is set as progress or decline and the leader is expected to just play the prescribed role with 'the consistency required between the stage, the actor and the act' (Czarniawska, 1997: 35). The value of her eclectic approach that combines various aspects of formalistic Burkean narratology, socially constructed narrative, pragmatic tracing of material effects and causes of narratives, and even postmodern multiple and local narratives resisting totalizing accounts of Swedish organization administrators and politicians is that she is able to analyze the 'romanticist and modernist rhetoric ... that is so typical of contemporary life in large organizations' (141) as well as the postmodern tragic and ironic themes.

In sum, Czarniawska writes her narratives organized along theatric metaphors (or, inventing a word, she calls them ergonographic fictions) to interpret stories authored by practitioners and consultants as well as administrators and politics that construct the world of organizations-as-theatre in Sweden (Czarniawska, 1997a: 202–4). Her eclectic work balances between pragmatic-structuralism (this works), semiotic sign system (this is form), social construction (this is metaphor to read interactive narration) and postmodern local narratives. Her narrative analysis is an insightful and rigorous critique of the rhetorical moves of Swedish administrators.

2. Storytelling Organization Theory. Storytelling Organization Theory has been researched and theorized by Gephart (1991), Boyce (1995), Kaye (1996), Boje (1991a, 1995a) and Boje et al. (1999). My own work is a mix of folklore, social construction, post-structuralist and postmodern narratology (Boje, 1991a, 1995a). 'Storytelling organization' is a theory of organizations in which stories are the primary medium of interpretative exchange (Boje, 1991a: 100; 1991b). In the office supply study I kept a tape recorder running to study *in situ* collective story performance (Boje, 1991a, 1991b). The idea was to trace storytelling behaviours in their situated and embedded organizing contexts.

My study of Disney (1995a) used deconstruction and postmodern theory to demythologize the official founding stories of Walt and the Magic Kingdom by juxtaposing counter local narratives to the totalizing official accounts. For example, placing Disney's official story of harmony and benevolence in juxtaposition to marginal or excluded stories of strikes, reprimands and Tayloristic practices. The supplement narratives were not added to some 'pure' original or founding narrative, the counter-narratives occurred alongside the official story. The idea of an originary-founding story is a delusion of a realism narratology for Derrida. The founding story is a mythic point, since it bears the traces of past and future discourse contexts that register alternative readings. In short, it self-deconstructs as it is uttered.

From a postmodern narrative analysis, it is not just Walt Disney that dictates the Disney stories – it is the ground keepers, gag men, gang bosses, ink 'girls', story men, speed bosses, script writers, grips and animators. It takes all the people of a village to story and it takes all the people of the organization to do the narrative work of the storytelling organization. Disney is not all cartoons and theme parks; it has its strikes and communist witch-hunts.

As in Czarniawska's work, theatrics is an important frame for narrative analysis in Storytelling Organization Theory. The theatrical metaphor still in use at Disney has a traceable history. Before workers were 'cast members' in

Disney Theatre, and customers were 'guests', there was a different theatrics. Walt was the 'father' to his 'boys' (his term for male animators, storymen and gag writers) and to his 'girls' (his term for women doing the inking and more repetitive drawing work). Disney was 'one big happy family'. The family metaphor encouraged a paternalistic order, where boys were reprimanded or fired for cursing in front of the girls. Walt expected his family to be loyal to him as self-proclaimed father, and to work all hours of the day or night for their paternal hero. But, on 29 May 1941, 293 boys and girls went on strike. The Disney Theatre spectacle of 'one big happy, harmonious family' was shattered by 1,000 picketers and by stories of the dysfunctional family: unfair salaries, poor working conditions and a parochial code of behaviour. The family metaphor was no longer purchasing employee loyalty. Instead employees observed that an inner circle enjoyed more privileges, including better wages, while they worked like cogs in the machine, punching in and out to go to the lavatory or to sharpen a pencil. Babbit, for example, says his $300-a-week salary was inequitable in comparison to that of his female assistant who only received $50. The Cartoonist Guild union was organizing the unhappy family, and Walt fired anyone that joined, on the spot. He tacked his photos to his office wall, and fired everyone that he could identify.

In the storytelling organization other local stories, views and interpretations are perpetually deconstructing the official side of the story. And the storytelling organization is busily repairing its 'official' story with plot and character revisions. Deconstruction adds to the number of interpretations and readings and as such challenges any 'one' accepted or 'functionalist' (e.g. 'How stories sell Disney') reading. Story deconstruction analysis can re-examine several inter-connected aspects of organizational stories (adapted from Boje and Dennehy, 1993: 340; Boje, 1998b, 1998c).

At Disney, there are dualistic ways in which the employees become 'cast' members, while managers have fewer restrictions on dress codes and other behaviors. Reinterpretations and other sides of the story can be analyzed at Disney using Lyotard's (1984) theory of local accounts. For example, the official Disney tale is an example of modernist commodification in the way in which the story of Walt, Mickey and now Eisner have a dollar value, of the re-manufactured images Disney sells. From a Baudrillardian (1983, 1987) approach to postmodernism, there is much about Disney that is a 'creeping of surrealism' invading the modernist world of Taylor and the industrialization of the animated arts and the theme park (as factory), and the mass production of signs (Mickey) and stories (e.g. Snow White and the Seven Dwarfs) without attention to their roots and origins. In Baudrillard's postmodernism the differences between story, story scripts and the reality the stories and characters once represented has been obliterated. Yet, at Disney the scripts and plots set in motion are ways that employees and 'guests' are kept in Disney control. Disney is a 'simulation' presented to the guest, but one that has become more real than its obliterated historical referents. The spirituality of the stories has been obliterated by the Disney storytelling machine that seduces guests into suspending assessments of reality as they enjoy the shock of the theme park

Table 7.4: Story deconstruction analysis

1.	**Duality search.**	Stories contain binary terms such as positive/negative, male/female, manager/worker, organization/environment which can be explored. The initial term is presumed to have a hierarchical relation to the second (sometimes unstated) term. The story can be revised to suggest ways in which the reverse is true. This exploration allows the story to be 'resituated' in ways that transcend and balance the dualistic terms.
2.	**Reinterpretations.**	Stories can be retold to bring out other contexts, such as gender, class, race/ethnicity or ecology.
3.	**Voices.**	Besides the voices of the main characters, more marginalized voices can be given more space in a revised story. The relationship between the narrator's omniscient voice and the voice of the character, including the (silent) voice of the reader can be analyzed.
4.	**Other sides of the story.**	Explore and reinterpret the hierarchy (e.g. in the duality terms how one dominates the other) so you can understand its grip on other sides of the story. Besides one story being told, other stories can be told that are marginal, under-represented or even silenced in the telling of the dominant or official side of the story.
5.	**Plots.**	The plot (romantic, tragic, comedic or ironic) of the story, such as progress-through-technology or evolutionary attainment of a more ideal state can be analyzed and alternative plots proposed.
6.	**Exceptions.**	Stories have essentializing rules about human behaviour and universal principles about the way the organization, community, society or cosmos operate. These essentials and universals can be challenged with exceptions.
7.	**Trace what is between the lines.**	There are silences, things left unstated which those 'in the know' are aware of, and can fill in the blanks. Novices oftentimes do not know enough context, history or language to read between the lines.
8.	**Resituation.**	The point of doing 1 to 7 is to find a new perspective, one that resituates the story beyond its dualisms, excluded voices, hierarchies or singular viewpoint. The idea is to reauthor the story so that the hierarchy is resituated and a new balance of dynamic views is attained. In a resituated story there are multiple centres rather than one centre.

experience. Yet the employees that perform in the shows and maintain the rides do not see it as a postmodern, hyper-reality of simulation. The reality for Disney workers is 'smile or be fired' (Boje, 1995a; Van Maanen, 1991, 1992). And Disney is an example of Jameson's (1983) late multinational capitalism. Beneath the facade of Disney surrealism is the capitalist machine with conveyors and people movers, the animation, the merchandisers and the wardrobes. And beneath the postmodern façade shown to the public is the modernist storytelling machine that is Disney.

And the storytelling machine works its magic on the players. 'The CEO is like a father to us'; 'Our divisions are like cousins who gather at the annual company picnic' (Boje and Dennehy, 1993). The family trope can be used as a disciplinary process to cover the breach between the story of performativity and the story of familial self-disclosure. Department meetings are family-style 'self-initiated confessions' where folks confess their failures, mistakes and delays in production, and affirm their bonds of familial solidarity. People are in fear of having the shortcoming made the subject of the inquisition. As Foucault points out, they begin to gaze their performance to avoid such penal interview situations.

The analysis argues that Disney can be read as a contending plurality of premodern, modern and postmodern discourses. My study supports Jameson's (1983: 123) observation that organizations do not follow a course of era-to-era displacement, but rather that discursive elements shift in emphasis and in priority. In Storytelling Organization Theory organizations are theorized as simultaneous, multiple and contending discourses. This allows us to look at how modern totalizing, functionalist and universalizing discourses of organization history and identity (i.e. organization as person) are permeated with postmodern fragmented, local and resistant discourses. And within postmodern discourse, there are contending theories: from the affirmatives who posit a future beyond exploitation, a return to a spirituality that elevates ecology and democracy – to the sceptics who distrust all forms of enlightenment and progress-discourse.

Stage performers at Disney, the cast members, do their theatric performances in Disney Theatre, wearing their 'costumes'. The 'smile factory' manufactures 'friendly, courteous, fun' on a rigid assembly line (Eisenberg and Goodall, 1993; Van Maanen, 1991). In the theatre metaphor, employees are 'cast members', wearing 'costumes' instead of uniforms, playing 'roles' instead of doing jobs, playing to 'guests' not to 'consumers' (Smith and Eisenberg, 1987). The French workers at EuroDisney met the 'theatre metaphors' with cynicism and resistance. They did not want to be smiling robots, pretending to be stage-performers. Disney's theatric staging of work induces labour to believe that theatrical values define their value-added. In Marxist terms, use value gets defined as exchange value. We are seduced to forget the factory beneath the boardwalk.

In a Baudrillardian sense, there is no longer any detectable difference between theatre and work, story characters and workers, story scripts and job descriptions, guests and customers. People relate to Mickey Mouse and the Magic Kingdom as if they were real. 'Disneyland functions as an "imaginary effect" concealing that reality no more exists outside than inside the bounds of the artificial perimeter' (Fjellman, 1992: 301). The employees who developed the rides, inked the cartoons, sell the popcorn and perform in the shows do not see a postmodern hyper-reality. They see the modern factory. Their reality is 'smile or be fired'. The festive 'image' of having fun is consumed through commodity purchases in a spectacle of modern production. My point is that the modern and postmodern discourse of Disney is intertextual, or just plain connected. To see Disney as modern smile-factory is to miss its postmodern hyper-reality, and vice versa. The smile factory appropriates postmodern sensibility into its theatrical production, for all to consume. Van Maanen (1992) pointed out how Disney theme parks in Japan, France and the US differ. The Japanese have intensified the efficiency, cleanliness and safety aspects of Disneyland to fit their preference for order and harmony. Japan-Disney is more modernist than the US or EuroDisney theme parks.

In sum, both Czarniawska's *Narrating the Organization* and Storytelling Organization Theory use an eclectic array of narratologies, adopt a theatrics frame of stories and storytellers, and a dynamic model of how grand and local stories interact over time.

3. Equivalency Relations Theory. Taylor and his colleagues Cooren, Groleau, Robichaud and Van Every treat narrating and organizing as two sides of the same coin.[7] Their interdisciplinary approach is to combine formalistic speech-act and actor-network theory, a pragmatic focus on narrating in context, a post-structuralist focus on intertextuality and the life of texts beyond their initiatory speech acts and Schutz's theory of typification we reviewed as one of several approaches to social construction. Their work also builds on Giddens' structuration theory. With Czarniawska's *Narrating Organization*, Taylor and colleagues share a focus on theories of agency and agents, and also focus on the materiality of speech acts. While borrowing here and there from each of these narrative disciplines, they also make some unique adaptations. Fairhurst and Putnam (1999: 9) in summarizing this interdisciplinary nexus, summarize what is distinctive. Instead of a 'container' of physical structures or networks of communication, or a 'production' metaphor of organization being co-produced by talkers and conversationalists, Taylor and colleagues use an 'equivalency relationship' conceptualization of the relationship between narrating and organizing. To narrate at the conversational level is to organize and to organize is to narrate. They contend that the 'container' and 'production' metaphors sustain a dualizing primacy of organization over narrating. Fairhurst and Putnam (1999: 9) refer to the 'equivalency relationship' as a discursive metaphor due to its ties to conversation analysis.

Equivalency relationship breaks from the acontextual orientation of speech-act theory and early conversation analysis, such as in turn-by-turn conversation, and story-starting and story-finishing studies. Like Storytelling Organization Theory the focus is around multiple stories shared across multiple simultaneous conversation groups in patterns that constitute the organization as a whole. Like Narrating Organization there is some focus on the dramatics of agent, scene, back and front stage. Like Storytelling Organization Theory and Narrating Organization, Taylor and colleagues put Equivalency Relations Theory in a 'transorganizational' context (e.g. Cooren and Taylor, 1997). For Equivalency Relation Theory, the single paradigms do not allow an embedded understanding of speech acts or conversations in more macro contexts. 'Their solution is to conceptualize organizational communication as an interaction of two dimensions – conversations and text' (Fairhurst and Putnam, 1999: 10). In this move they point to the post-structuralist idea of intertextuality, to the life that texts (written or filmed) have beyond their speech acts in oral narration. But, unlike Derrida, they see narration (and communication in general) as mediated by Schutz's typifications in language. They move further away from a post-structuralist position and toward a pragmatic one in positing links between the trans-situational or transorganizational in the circulation of text-objects. The mediation performed in circulating such objects 'is the creation of an agent or agency of some subject's action (the subjective component) into material form or text (the objective component)' (Fairhurst and Putnam, 1999: 11). This has obvious overlay with Czarniawska's middle ground approach between social construction, dramatics and pragmatics. There is also a parallel to how the Emerys use the pragmatics of contextual exploration in their Search Conference narrative events. Like Czarniawska, Taylor and colleagues assert that 'speech acts are also objects, albeit symbolic ones' (Fairhurst and Putnam, 1999: 11). Yet, from a post-structuralist perspective the idea that texts, speech acts or narratives are put into material circulation by agents and agencies seems to imply both intentionality and positivistic reasoning (as we reviewed in realist narratives). However, Cooren and Taylor (1997) try to distance themselves from such criticism by focusing upon how meanings are socially constructed in conversations to create the typified meanings. They create 'macro-actors' with individual and collective agency so those individuals speak on behalf of collective bodies. The organization becomes a macro-actor and a text-agent with its narrative communication becoming the product of its relationships, rather than its origin. This does, however, seem to bring them close to the production (co-production) metaphor they seek to avoid. However, they do appear to move beyond a narrow focus on speech acts in conversations to look at how these are embedded in intertextual and transorganizational relationships. Taylor and colleagues try to overcome the duality between texts and conversation networks. They do this by invoking Giddens' structuration theory, that structure is both the medium and outcome. Like the other interdisciplinary models, they pose a dynamic and negotiated social approach to narrating in which knowledge is getting updated as well as forgotten. They argue that 'both text and conversation are necessary to understand organization-communication equivalency because of the constraints and enablements each imposes on the other' (Fairhurst and Putnam, 1999: 12–13). Unlike critical narratologies the equivalency relationship theory does not accept abstract analytic constructs such as the class struggle. Unlike social construction narratologies, it includes human and non-human communication and narration. However, we still stress the problem in assuming stable meaning contexts which do not grapple with the dynamics of shifting meanings in fragmenting contexts across time and place, as we explored in Narrating Organization and Storytelling Organization Theory.

Distinct from the first three models, the next approach to interdisciplinary narration takes a more multiple level approach to context and narration, including the relationships between person, group, organization and societal levels of narration.

4. Nesting organization in four narratives. Clair's (1993, 1994, 1996, 1997) approach is to nest organization in (1) personal narrative, (2) historical, (3) ancestral and (4) contemporary narratives. Like the first two approaches (Narrating Organization and Storytelling Organization), Clair's work is also eclectic. She draws upon the formalistic narratology work of narrative paradigm theory (Fisher, 1987), postmodern work about the voice, fragmentation and the body (Foucault, 1979), critical juxtapositions of multiple histories (voice and silence in material condition), and identity in terms of sexual harassment and hegemony (Clair, 1993, 1994, 1996). For us, her work (especially 1997) resituates Culler's (1981) duality we spoke of at the outset of the paper, the relation of narratology paradigms to living storytelling. Her approach is to tell personal and ancestor stories within embedded narratives. Her (1997) work looks, for example, at stories that name and fractionate in juxtaposed historical, ancestral, personal and contemporary narratives. This is her way, we think, to reclaim native epistemology and ontology.

Her theory is quite intertextual, 'no story stands alone' (1997: 323). Her juxtaposition of narratives is a way to focus on 'organizing silence ... how interests, issues and identities of marginalized people are silenced and how those silenced voices can be organized in ways to be heard' (323). In juxtaposing multiple and different narratives, new voices surface that were silenced in centuries of socioeconomic, political, cultural, aesthetic and spiritual oppression. For Clair (1997: 324), Fisher's (1987) narrative paradigm theory is a way to explain how historical narrative lets her own story of ethnic and ancestral identity unfold. What we see her doing is combing the structuralist narratology with a critical theory reading of multiple histories and narrations. It is like Currie (1998) who argues for treating formalism and postmodernism as two sides of discourse rather than privileging one over the other. Clair, we think, does this with formalism (structuralism), critical theory and in places postmodern narratology. For example Clair (1997: 324) calls on Foucault's (1979) work on how people's voices are physically muzzled in acts of torture and death. She extends it in a theory of the hegemony of silence, but not as a 'totalizing concept: within each practice oppressive silence is a possibility of voice'. As with narrative therapy, Clair (1997: 325) focuses on the importance of naming acts of oppression, and how the oppressors have named those same acts. For example, the dominant society has changed the name of the Cherokee people 'from Yunwiya to Chaluk, from Tsaragi to Cherokee, and recently to Native American' (326). Clair juxtaposes her own story of her own mixed ancestry and fractionated identity to trace the narratives of the oppressor and the marginalized. In the narrative telling of the Treaty of New Echota and the Trail of Tears relocation of the Cherokee, she articulates the organization and nation narratives, organizing all the four types of narratives into a collective narrative. She includes acts of hegemony, emancipation and resistance. Clair's (1997: 331) is critical theory because she embeds discursive practices 'in a material existence.' She is self-reflective on how her essay is a narrative in its own right, 'voicing several issues that have been silent', telling stories of the marginalized, reclaiming fractionated and fragmented membership, and juxtaposing historical and personal narrative and storytelling. In the process of her embedded and juxtaposed narrative work, Clair has reclaimed storytelling from its marginalized disembodiment in less interdisciplinary approaches to narratology (Table 7.1).

Discussion

We agree with Czarniawska (1997a: 17) that OT theory and practice 'can be seen as special genres of narrative situated within other narratives of modern (or postmodern) society, so that organization studies can focus on how these narratives of theory and practice are constructed, used and misused'. Our contribution has been to reclaim stories by following the work of Clair, TwoTrees and Toelken.

In Part I we argued that a varied set of narratologies are being applied to organization studies. Our thesis was that the living story of organization is made into forms and structures or deconstructions and constructions by the various narratologies. In Part II we compared alternative ways in which storytelling and narrating are being applied differently within and between narratologies. Specifically we contend that within the pragmatist approach of the Emerys as well as Hopewell there are different applications of Pepper's work on contextualism.

And these pragmatic approaches to narrative have different epistemological and ontological assumptions from Appreciative Inquiry and Restorying. The Restorying approach of White and Epston being applied to organization consulting and indigenous consulting is based in post-structuralism whereas the Appreciative Inquiry project applies a more social construction narratology that marginalizes deconstruction. We tried to make the point that restorying and appreciative inquiry approaches have much in common. In Part III, we contrasted several approaches, Narrating the Organization, Storytelling Organization Theory, Equivalency and Nested Narratives. The four narration approaches in Part III adopt a number of very different eclectic narratological positions. We think that this points to an important interdisciplinary trend, a move beyond the insulating disciplines of Parts I and II to more pluralistic approaches.

We conclude that there are many narratological turns happening in organizational consulting and the study of organizations (Best and Kellner, 1997). We have raised what we consider several provocative questions. Are the various narratological turns killing story? Can interdisciplinary approaches resituate the marginalization of folk and native stories by various narratologies? Is interdisciplinary study too eclectic with various analysts using story, narrative and organization in different ways and with different meanings?

We have claimed storytelling seems almost folkloristic, lowbrow, practical and not grand at all, something done around the water cooler. Even petit narratives do not seem as low class or indigenous as stories. 'Many analysts of the postmodern would have us believe that the legitimation of multiple small narratives is a valid means of resisting homologation of planetary proportions' (Francese, 1997: 4). Folklore has been studying storytelling for more than a century. Native storytelling refuses to give up the situating of individual stories in ancestral history and cosmos narration. In folklore, Kirshenblatt-Gimglett (1975), Hymes (1975), Jones et al. (1988) and especially Georges (1969, 1980a, 1980b, 1981) look at the undifferentiability of story and context. Yet, they do not go so far as to argue that stories live, as we have seen with TwoTrees, Clair and Toelken.

A focus on folklore, Clair's work, and the fables in Lyotard's (1997) *Postmodern Fables* undermines the Grand narratives that abound in organization theory with some old fashioned storytelling. Yet, we follow Best and Kellner (1997) in noting that Lyotard's total rejection of Grand narrative only serves to replace modern narratives with his own 'postmodern condition'

Grand narrative. We think a more fruitful set of approaches lies in looking at dynamic relations between macro and micro story as in the examples for Narrating the Organization, Storytelling Organization Theory and Nested Narratives.

The dynamic approach to reclaiming stories in organization narratologies and action science recognizes that narratives are self-deconstructing in dynamic ways. As such deconstruction is more than an analysts' tool. Culler (1981, 1982) also emphasizes the impossibility of a synthesis of story and narrative discourse because of the effect of self-deconstruction. 'A deconstruction involves the demonstration that a hierarchical opposition, in which one term is said to be dependent upon another conceived as prior, is in fact a rhetorical or metaphysical imposition and that the hierarchy could well be reversed' (1982: 183). In the approaches and studies we looked at in Part III, the self-deconstructing, be it from one view or its reverse, is an on going and embedded social process. We think narrative poses hierarchical opposition to story, at least that is our story of narratives. Telling our stories juxtaposed to narrative paradigms is a way to reclaim story from the emptiness of forms and naïve realism.

Notes

1   Pepper calls this general tendency Formism, but we wish to carry this sense wider and connect to other usages of the term. We will use lower case for this general sense of formalism, whilst Formalism will refer to linguistic (Russian) Formalism.
2   We are grateful to the editors for helping us craft this definition.
3   All numbers within parentheses refer to volume and paragraph of the *Collected Papers of Charles Sanders Peirce*, edited by Charles Hartshorne and Paul Weiss (1931–1935), Cambridge: Harvard University Press.
4   Czarniawska's (1997a: 6, 11, 18) narrative approach to organizations relies upon works we reviewed as formalistic work. In particular work by Barthes (1966) (structuralist analysis), Kenneth Burke (scene-act ratio) and Walter Fisher (narrative paradigm theory). She also includes Alasdair MacIntyre (moral philosophy) to modify Burke's typology and pragmatist aspects of Paul Ricoeur (literary hermeneutics) and there is some reference to Peirce, but not to the concepts of contextualism or abduction that are in the work of the Emerys. It also includes social constructionist work by Karl Weick (sense-making) and Jerome Bruner (narrative and logo-scientific modes of knowing) and formalistic work by Donald Polkinghorne (combining hermeneutics and the semiotics of how people narrate by putting events into a plot). There are also several postmodern references in the text, such as to Lyotard's (1984) distinction between Grand narrative and local stories and to Rorty's work. In short, the work samples many narratologies but we see Burke's as the primary application, in conjunction with social construction and pragmatism only in the sense that narratives have a material base, as in our review of Austin's speech-act theory.
5   Czarniawska (1997a: 29, 30) chooses drama as her all-encompassing metaphor, rather than theatrics because theatre constructs a problematic notion of 'authenticity' (or a 'true self') and the 'static' concept of a 'role'.

6   See Zanetti (1997, 1998) for a critical review of the roots of Habermas' theory of communicative action and the rules needed for effective speech communities in Peirce's pragmatism.

7   This section gratefully acknowledges the Fairhurst and Putnam (1999) review of Equivalency Relationship Theory. Our task is not to do a full review of the relation between communication and organizing, but to focus on the aspects of ERT that relate to narrating. We must, however, point out to the reader that Fairhurst and Putnam have a different profile of communication paradigms than the narrative approaches we have in Table 7.1. They use eight approaches: linguistics and sociolinguistics, conversation analysis (which we partially treat as formalistic), pragmatics, discourse analysis (which we treat in post-structuralism), cognitive psychology and artificial intelligence, semiotics, critical and postmodern language analysis (the last two we cover). We rely on their review of ERT in what follows.

References

Ackoff, R.L. and Emery, F.E. (1972) *On Purposeful Systems*. Intersystems. Chicago: Aldine.

AHC – Aboriginal Health Council (1995) *Reclaiming our Stories, Reclaiming our Lives*. An Initiative of the Aboriginal Health Council of South Australia. Dulwich Centre Newsletter, No. 1. New Zealand.

Alvesson, M. and Deetz, S. (1996) 'Critical theory and postmodernism approaches to organizational studies', in S.R. Clegg, C. Hardy and W.R. Nord (eds), *Handbook of Organization Studies*. London: Sage. pp. 191–217.

Alvesson, M. and Willmott, H. (1996) *Making Sense of Management: A Critical Introduction*. London: Sage.

Austin, J. (1962) *How to do Things with Words*. Cambridge, MA: Harvard University Press.

Barry, D. (1997) 'Telling changes: from narrative family therapy to organizational change and development', *Journal of Organizational Change Management*, 10 (1): 30–46.

Barry, D. and Elmes, M. (1997) 'Strategy retold: toward a narrative view of strategic discourse', *Academy of Management Review*, 22 (2): 429–52.

Barthes, R. (1966) 'Introduction to the structural analysis of narratives', trans. S. Heath in S. Heath, *Image – Music – Text*. Glasgow: William Collins. pp. 79–124.

Baudrillard, J. (1983) *Simulations*. New York: Semiotext (e).

Baudrillard, J. (1987) *Forget Foucault*. New York: Semiotext (e).

Berger, P.L. and Luckmann, T. (1967) *The Social Construction of Reality: A Treatise in the Sociology of Knowledge*. Garden City, NY: Anchor Books. (Original published 1966.)

Bergquist, W. (1993) *The Postmodern Organization: Mastering the Art of Irreversible Change*. San Francisco: Jossey-Bass.

Berry, T. (1988) *The Dream of the Earth*. San Francisco: Sierra Club.

Best, S. and Kellner, D. (1997) *The Postmodern Turn*. NY and London: Guilford Press.

Bhabha, H. (ed.) (1989) *Nation and Narration*. London and NY: Routledge.

Blumer, H. (1968) *Symbolic Interactionism: Perspectives and Method*. Englewood Cliffs, NJ: Prentice Hall.

Boje, D. (1991a) 'Organizations as storytelling networks: a study of story performance in an office-supply firm', *Administrative Science Quarterly*, 36: 106–26.

Boje, D. (1991b) 'Consulting and change in the storytelling organization', *Journal of Organizational Change Management*, 4 (3): 7–17.

Boje, D. (1995a) 'Stories of the storytelling organization: a postmodern analysis of Disney as "Tamara-land"', *Academy of Management Journal*, 38 (4): 997–1035.

Boje, D. (1995b) 'Teaching storytelling deconstruction skills'. Paper presented to Eastern Academy of Management, Storytelling Session, Cornell University, 5 May.

Boje, D. (1998a) 'Nike, Greek goddess of victory or cruelty? Women's stories of Asian factory life', *Journal of Organizational Change Management*, 11 (6): 461–80.

Boje, D. (1998b) 'The Swoosh goddess is a vampire: Nike's environmental accounting storytelling', in J. Bibberman and Abbass Alkhafaji, *International Business and Ecology Research Yearbook*. Saline, MI: IABD Publication. pp. 23–32.

Boje, D. (1998c) 'How critical theory and critical pedagogy can unmask Nike's labor practices'. Paper presented at the Annual Meeting of the Academy of Management San Diego. See http://cbae.nmsu.edu/mgt/jpub/boje/critped/

Boje, D. (1999) 'Is Nike Roadrunner or Wile E. Coyote? A postmodern organization analysis of double logic', *Journal of Business and Entrepreneurship*, Special Issue (March), Vol. 2: 77–109.

Boje, D. (2001) *Narrative Research in Communication and Organization*. London: Sage.

Boje, D. (2001 in press) *Spectacles and Festivals of Organization: Towards Ahimsa Production and Consumption*. Los Angeles CA: Hampton Press.

Boje, D.M. and Dennehy, R.F. (1993) *Managing in the Postmodern World: America's Revolution against Exploitation*. Dubuque, IA: Kendall/Hunt. (2nd edn 1994.)

Boje, D.M. and Luhman, J.T. (1999) 'Narrative theory and Pepper'. Unpublished working paper.

Boje, D.M., Fedor, D.B. and Rowland, K.M. (1982) 'Myth making: a qualitative step in OD interventions', *Journal of Applied Behavioral Science*, 18 (1): 17–28.

Boje, D. M., Gephart, R.P. Jr. and Thatchenkery, T.J. (1996) *Postmodern Management and Organization Theory*. Thousand Oaks, CA: Sage.

Boje, D.M., Luhman, J.T. and Baack, D.E. (1999) 'Hegemonic stories and encounters between storytelling organizations', *Journal of Management Inquiry*, 8 (4): 340–60.

Boyce, M. (1995) 'Collective centering and collective sense-making in the stories and storytelling of one organization', *Organization Studies*, 16 (1): 107–37.

Braverman, H. (1974) *Labor and Monopoly Capital: The Degradation of Work in the Twentieth Century*. NY: Monthly Review Press.

Burke, K. (1945) *A Grammar of Motives*. Berkeley, CA: University of California Press. (2nd edn 1969.)

Burrell, G. (1988) 'Modernism, postmodernism and organizational analysis 2: the contribution of Michel Foucault', *Organization Studies*, 9 (2): 221–35.

Burrell, G. (1997) *Pandemonium: Towards a Retro-Organization Theory*. London: Sage.

Clair, R.P. (1993) 'The use of framing devices to sequester organizational narratives: hegemony and harassment', *Communication Monographs*, 60: 113–36.

Clair, R.P. (1994) 'Resistance and oppression as a self-contained opposite: an organizational communication analysis of one man's story of sexual harassment', *Western Journal of Communication*, 58: 235–62.

Clair, R.P. (1996) 'Discourse and disenfranchisement: targets, victims and survivors of sexual harassment', in E. Berlin Ray (ed.), *Communication and the Disenfranchised: Social Health Issues and Implications*. Hillsdale, NJ: Lawrence Erlbaum. pp. 313–27.

Clair, R.P. (1997) 'Organizing silence: silence as voice and voice as silence in the narrative exploration of the treaty of New Echota', *Western Journal of Communication*, 61 (3): 315–37.

Clark, B.R. (1972) 'The organizational saga in higher education', *Administrative Science Quarterly*, 17: 178–84.

Clegg, S. (1990) *Modern Organizations: Organizational Studies in the Modern World*. London: Sage.

Cooperidder, D.L. and Srivastva, S. (1987) 'Appreciative inquiry in organizational life', in W.A. Pasmore and R.W. Woodman (eds), *Research in Organizational Change and Development (Vol. I)*. Greenwich, CT: JAI Press. pp. 129–69.

Cooren, F. and Taylor, J. R. (1997) 'Organization as an effect of mediation: redefining the link between organization and communication', *Communication Theory*, 7: 219–60.

Culler, J. (1981) *The Pursuit of Signs: Semiotics, Literature, Deconstruction*. Ithaca, NY: Cornell University Press.

Culler, J. (1982) *On Deconstruction: Theory and Criticism after Structuralism*. Ithaca, NY: Cornell University Press.

Currie, M. (1998) *Postmodern Narrative Theory*. NY: St. Martin's Press.

Czarniawska, B. (1997a) *Narrating the Organization: Dramas of Institutional Identity*. Chicago: University of Chicago Press.

Czarniawska, B. (1997b) 'A four times told tale combining narrative and scientific knowledge in organization studies', *Organization Studies*, 4 (1): 7–30.

Denzin, N.K. (1992) *Symbolic Interactionism and Cultural Studies*. Cambridge, UK: Basil Blackwell.

Derrida, J. (1978) *Writing and Difference*, trans. A. Bass. London: Routledge & Kegan Paul.

Derrida, J. (1981) *Positions*, trans. A. Bass. Chicago: University of Chicago Press.

Derrida, J. (1985) *The Ear of the Other*, trans. P. Kamuf. Lincoln: University of Nebraska Press.

Dixon, W.W. (1998) *The Transparency of Spectacle: Meditations on the Moving Image*. NY: State University of New York Press.

Eco, U. (1990) *The Limits of Interpretation*. Bloomington and Indianapolis: Indiana University Press.

Eisenberg, E.M. and Goodall, H.L. Jr. (1993) *Organizational Communication: Balancing Creativity and Constraint*. NY: St. Martin's Press.

Emery, F. (1977) *Futures We Are In*. Leiden: Martinus Nijhoff, Social Sciences Division.

Emery, F. (1993) 'The agenda for the next wave', in M. Emery, *Participative Design for Participative Democracy*. Canberra: Australian National University. pp. 30–9.

Emery, F. (1997) 'Active adaptation: the emergence of ideal-seeking systems', in E. Trist, F. Emery and H. Murray (eds), *The Social Engagement of the Social Sciences: A Tavistock Anthology (Vol 3: The Socio-Ecological Perspective)*. Philadelphia: University of Pennsylvania Press. pp. 147–69.

Emery, M. (1993) *Participative Design for Participative Democracy*. Canberra: Australian National University.

Emery, M. (1997) 'Open systems is alive and well'. Paper presented to the ODC division of the Academy of Management Meetings, Boston (August).

Emery, M. (1998) *Searching: The Theory and Practice of Cultural Change*. Amsterdam/The Netherlands: John Benjamins Publishing.

Epston, D. (1989) *Collected Papers*. Adelaide, Australia: Dulwich Centre Publications.

Fairhurst, G.T. and Putnam, L.L. (1999) 'Reflections on the organizational–communication equivalency question: the contribution of James Taylor and his colleagues', *The Communication Review*, (3) (1–2): 1–19.

Fayol, H. (1916) *General and Industrial Management*, trans. Constance Storrs. (First English edition 1949.) London: Sir Isaac Pitman & Sons Ltd.

Feibleman, J. (1946) *An Introduction to Peirce's Philosophy: Interpreted as a System*. New York: Harper & Brothers.

Fineman, S. and Gabriel, Y. (1994) 'Paradigms of organizations: an exploration of textbook rhetorics', *Organization*, 1 (2): 375–99.

Fisher, W.R. (1984) 'Narration as a human communication paradigm: the case of public moral argument', *Communication Monographs*, 51 (March): 1–22.

Fisher, W.R. (1987) *Human Communication as Narrative: Toward a Philosophy of Reason, Value and Action*. Columbia, SC: University of South Carolina Press.

Fjellman, S.M. (1992) *Vinyl leaves: Walt Disney World and America*. Boulder, CO: Westview.

Ford, J. and Ford, L. (1995) 'The role of conversations in producing intentional change in organizations', *Academy of Management Review*, 20: 541–70.

Foucault, M. (1979) *Surveiller et Punir: Naissance de la Prison [Discipline and Punish]*. Paris: Gallimard.

Francese, J. (1997) *Narrating Postmodern Time and Space*. New York: State University of New York Press.

Fulop, L. and Linstead, S.A. (1999) *Management: A Critical Text*. Melbourne: Macmillan Education Australia Pty Ltd.

Geertz, C. (1973) 'Thick description: toward an interpretive theory of cultures', in C. Geertz (ed.), *The Interpretation of Cultures*. NY: Basic Books.

Georges, R. (1969) 'Toward an understanding of story-telling events', *Journal of American Folklore*, 82: 314–28.

Georges, R. (1980a) 'A folklorist's view of storytelling', *Humanities in Society*, 3 (4): 317–26.

Georges, R. (1980b) 'Towards a resolution of the text/context controversy', *Western Folklore*, 39: 34–40.

Georges, R. (1981) 'Do narrators really digress? A reconsideration of "audience asides" in narrating', *Western Folklore*, 40: 245–52.

Gephart, R.P. (1991) 'Succession, sensemaking and organizational change: a story of a deviant college president', *Journal of Organizational Change Management*, 4: 35–44.

Gergen, K. (1991) *The Saturated Self: Dilemmas of Identity in Contemporary Life*. NY: Basic Books.

Gergen, K. (1994) *Realities and Relationships: Soundings in Social Construction*. Cambridge, MA: Harvard University Press.

Ginzburg, C. (1980) *The Cheese and The Worms: The Cosmos of a Sixteenth-Century Miller*, trans. John and Anne Tedeschi. Baltimore/London: The Johns Hopkins University Press. (Original in Italian, 1976.)

Glaser, B.G. and Strauss, A.L. (1967) *The Discovery of Grounded Theory: Strategies for Qualitative Research*. NY: Aldine Publishing Company.

Goodman, N. (1984) *Of Mind and Other Matters*. Cambridge, MA: Harvard University Press.

Habermas, J. (1987) *The Philosophical Discourse of Modernity: Twelve Lectures*, trans. F.G. Lawrence. Cambridge: MIT Press.

Hammer, M. and Champy, J. (1993) *Reengineering the Corporation: A Manifesto for Business Revolution*. London: Nicholas Brealey.

Harju, K. (1999) 'Protext: the morphoses of identity, heterogeneity and synolon', *Studies in Cultures, Organizations and Societies*, 5 (1): 131–49.

Hassard, J. (1993) 'Postmodernism and organizational analysis: an overview', in J. Hassard and M. Parker, *Postmodernism and Organizations*. London: Sage. pp. 1–24.

Hassard, J. and Parker, M. (eds) (1993) *Postmodernism and Organizations*. London: Sage.

Hatch, M.J. (1996) 'The role of the researcher: an analysis of narrative position in organization theory', *Journal of Management Inquiry*, 5 (4): 359–74.

Hatch, M.J. (1997) *Organization Theory: Modern, Symbolic and Postmodern Perspectives*. London: Oxford University Press.

Henderson, G.E. (1988) *Kenneth Burke: Literature and Language as Symbolic Action.* Athens, GA: University of Georgia Press.

Hopewell, J.F. (1987) *Congregation: Stories and Structures.* Philadelphia, PN: Fortress Press.

Hymes, D. (1975) 'Breakthrough into performance', in D. Ben-Amos and K. Goldstein (eds), *Folklore: Performance and Communication.* Paris: Mouton. pp. 11–74.

Jameson, F. (1983) 'Postmodernism and consumer society', in H. Foster (ed.), *The Anti-aesthetic: Essays on Postmodern Culture.* Port Townsend, WN: Bay Press. pp. 111–25.

Jones, M.O., Moore, M.D. and Snyder, R.C. (eds) (1988) *Inside Organizations: Understanding the Human Dimension.* Newbury Park, CA: Sage.

Kaye, M. (1996) *Myth-makers and Story-tellers.* Sydney, Australia: Business & Professional Publishing Pty Ltd.

Kilduff, M. (1993) 'Deconstructing organizations', *Academy of Management Review,* 18 (1): 13–31.

Kilduff, M. and Mehra, A. (1997) 'Postmodernism and organizational research', *Academy of Management Review,* 22: 453–81.

Kirshenblatt-Gimglett, B. (1975) 'A parable in context: a social interactional analysis of storytelling performance', in D. Ben-Amos and K. Goldstein (eds), *Folklore: Performance and Communication.* Paris: Mouton. pp. 105–30.

Levi, G. (1992) 'On microhistory', in P. Burke (ed.), *New Perspectives on Historical Writing.* University Park, PA: The Pennsylvania State University Press. pp. 93–113.

Lombardo, M.M. (1986) *Values in Action: The Meaning of Executive Vignettes.* Technical report no. 28 (November), Center for Creative Leadership, Greensboro, NC.

Ludema, J.D., Wilmot, T.B. and Srivastva, S. (1996) *Organizational Hope and Textured Vocabularies of Possibility: Reaffirming the Constructive Task of Social and Organizational Inquiry.* Weatherhead School of Management, Case Western Reserve University (July).

Lyotard, J.-F. (1984) *The Postmodern Condition: A Report on Knowledge,* trans. G. Bennington and B. Massumi. Minneapolis: University of Minnesota Press.

Lyotard, J.-F. (1997) *Postmodern Fables,* trans. G. Van Den Abbele. Minneapolis, MN: University of Minnesota Press.

Martin, J. (1982) 'Stories and scripts in organizational settings', in Albert H. Hastorf and Alice M. Isen (eds), *Cognitive Social Psychology.* NY: Elsevier/North-Holland. pp. 255–305.

Martin, J. (1990) 'Deconstructing organizational taboos: the suppression of gender conflict in organizations', *Organization Science,* 1 (4): 339–59.

Martin, J. and Knopoff, K. (1997) 'The gendered implications of apparently gender-neutral theory: re-reading Weber', in E. Freeman and A. Larson (eds), *Ruffin lecture series, Vol. 3, Business Ethics and Women's Studies.* Oxford: Oxford University Press. pp. 30–49.

Martin, J. and Meyerson, D. (1988) 'Organizational cultures and the denial, channeling and acknowledgment of ambiguity', in L.R. Pondy, R.J. Boland Jr. and H. Thomas (eds), *Managing Ambiguity and Change.* New York: John Wiley & Sons. pp. 93–125.

Martin, J. and Powers, M.E. (1979) 'Skepticism and the true believer: the effects of case and/or base rate information on belief and commitment'. Paper presented at the meetings of the Western Psychological Association, Honolulu, May.

Martin, J., Feldman, M.S., Hatch, M.J. and Sitkin, S.B. (1983) 'The uniqueness paradox in organizational stories', *Administrative Science Quarterly,* 28: 438–53.

Martin, J., Patterson, K. and Price, R. (1979) *The Effects of Level of Abstraction of a Script on Accuracy of Recall, Predictions and Beliefs.* Research paper No. 520. Graduate School of Business, Stanford University.

Martin, J., Patterson, K., Harrod, W. and Siehl, C. (1980) 'Memory for the content of scripts presented at varying levels of abstraction'. Paper presented at the meeting of the American Psychological Association, Montreal, September.

Marx, Karl (1867) *Capital: A Critique of Political Economy. Vol. 1. The Process of Capitalist Production,* ed. F. Engles, trans. S. Moore and E. Averling. NY: International Publishers. (First published 1867, English 1967.)

McCall, M.M., Lombardo, M.M. and Morrison, A.M. (1989) *The Lessons of Experience.* New York: Harper & Row.

McConkie, M.L. and Boss, W.R. (1986) 'Organizational stories: one means of moving the informal organization during change efforts', *Public Administration Quarterly,* 10 (2): 189–205.

Mills, A.J. and Simmons, T. (1995) *Reading Organization Theory: A Critical Approach.* Toronto: Garamond Press.

Muir, E. (1991) 'Introduction: observing trifles', in E. Muir and G. Ruggiero (eds), *Microhistory and the Lost Peoples of Europe,* trans. Eren Branch. Baltimore/London: The Johns Hopkins University Press. pp. vii–xxviii.

Mumby, D. (1987) 'The political function of narrative in organizations', *Communication Monographs,* 54 (June): 113–27.

Nietzsche, F. (1956) *The Birth of Tragedy* (1872) and *The Genealogy of Morals* (1887), trans. Francis Golffing. NY: Anchor Books (additions are original publication dates).

O'Connor, E.S. (1996) 'Lines of authority: readings of foundational texts on the profession of management', *Journal of Management History,* 2 (3): 26–49.

O'Connor, E.S. (1999a) 'Minding the workers: the meaning of "human" and "human relations" in Elton Mayo', *Organization,* 6 (2): 223–46.

O'Connor, E.S. (1999b) 'The politics of management thought: a case study of Harvard Business School and the Human Relations School', *Academy of Management Review,* 24: 117–31.

O'Connor, E.S. (2001 in press) 'Integrating Follett: history, philosophy and management', *Journal of Management History,* in press.

Parker, M. (1993) 'Life after Jean-Francois', in J. Hassard and M. Parker, *Postmodernism and Organizations.* London: Sage. pp. 204–12.

Parker, M. (1997) Unpublished book review of Boje, Gephart and Thatchenkery (1996), *Postmodern Management and Organization Theory.* Personal communication.

Peirce, C.S. (1940) *Philosophical Writings of Peirce,* ed. Justus Buchler. NY: Dover Publications, Inc. (2nd edn 1955.)

Pepper, S.C. (1942) *World Hypotheses: A Study in Evidence.* Berkeley, CA: University of California Press.

Peters, T. and Waterman, R. H. (1982) *In Search of Excellence: Lessons from America's Best-Run Companies.* NY: Harper Collins.

Pondy, L. and Mitroff, I. (1979) 'Beyond open system models of organization', *Research in Organization Behavior,* 1: 3–39.

Ricoeur, P. (1984) *Time and Narrative, Volume 1,* trans. K. McLaughlin and D. Pellauer. Chicago, IL: University of Chicago Press.

Rorty, R. (1980) *Philosophy and the Mirror of Nature.* Oxford: Basil Blackwell.

Schutz, A. (1972) 'On Multiple Realities', *Collected Papers I: The Problem of Social Reality.* The Hague: Martinus Nijhoff. pp. 207–59.

Schwandt, T.A. (1994) 'Constructivist, interpretivist approaches to human inquiry', in N.K. Denzin and Y.S. Lincoln (eds), *Handbook of Qualitative Research.* Thousand Oaks, CA: Sage. pp. 118–37.

Schwartz, H.S. (1994) Review of D. Boje and R.F. Dennehy 'Managing in the postmodern world: America's revolution against exploitation', *Academy of Management Review*, 20 (1): 215–20.

Siehl, C. and Martin, J. (1982) *Learning Organizational Culture*. Research Paper No. 654, Graduate School of Business, Stanford University.

Smith, R. and Eisenberg, E. (1987) 'Conflict at Disneyland: a root metaphor analysis', *Communication Monographs*, 54: 367–80.

Srivastva, S. and Cooperrider, D.L. (1999) *Appreciative Management and Leadership: The Power of Positive Thought and Action in Organizations.* San Francisco: Lakeshore Communications.

Stanfield, J.H.II. (1994) 'Ethnic modeling in qualitative research', in N.K. Denzin and Y.S. Lincoln (eds), *Handbook of Qualitative Research*. Thousand Oaks, CA: Sage. pp. 175–88.

Taylor, J.R. (1995) 'Shifting from a heteronomous to an autonomous worldview of organizational communication: communicaton theory on the cusp', *Communication Theory*, 5: 1–35.

Thatchenkery, T. (1992) 'Organizations as "texts": hermeneutics as a model for understanding organizational change', in W.A. Pasmore and R.W. Woodman (eds), *Research in Organization Development and Change*. Vol. 6. Greenwich, CT: JAI Press. pp. 197–233.

Thompson, P. (1993) 'Postmodernism: fatal distraction', in J. Hassard and M. Parker, *Postmodernism and Organizations.* London: Sage. pp. 183–203.

Toelken, B. (1996) 'The icebergs of folktale: misconception, misuse, abuse', in C.L. Birch and M.A. Heckler (eds), *Who Says? Essays on Pivotal Issues in Contemporary Storytelling*. Little Rock, AR: August House Publishers. pp. 35–63.

TwoTrees, K. (1997) 'Reclaiming stories of the Lakota'. Paper presented at the April 1977 International Academy of Business Disciplines conference, Case Western Reserve University, Cleveland, Ohio.

Tyler, S.A. (1986) 'Post-modern ethnography: from document of the occult to occult document', in J. Clifford and G. Marcus (eds), *Writing Culture: The Poetics and Politics of Ethnography*. Berkeley, CA: University of California Press. pp. 122–40.

Van Maanen, J. (1991) 'The smile factory: work at Disneyland', in P. Frost, L. Moore, M.R. Louis, C.C. Lundberg and J. Martin (eds), *Reframing Organizational Culture*. Newbury Park, CA: Sage. pp. 58–76.

Van Maanen, J. (1992) 'Displacing Disney: some notes on the flow of culture', *Qualitative Sociology*, 15 (1): 5–35.

Von Glaserfeld, E. (1989) 'Cognition, construction of knowledge, and teaching', *Synthese*, 80: 121–40.

Weick, K.E. (1979) *The Social Psychology of Organizing*, 2nd edn. Reading, MA: Addison-Wesley Publications.

Weick, K.E. (1995) *Sensemaking in Organizations.* Thousand Oaks, CA: Sage Publications.

Wheeler, B. (1987) 'Editor's Foreword', in J.F. Hopewell, *Congregation: Stories and Structures*. Philadelphia Press, PA: Fortress Press. pp. xi–xv.

White, H. (1973) *Metahistory: The Historical Imagination in Nineteenth-Century Europe*. Baltimore, Maryland: The John Hopkins University Press.

White, M. (1989) *Selected Papers*. Adelaide, Australia: Dulwich Centre Publications.

White, M. (1991) 'Deconstruction and therapy', *Dulwich Centre Newsletter*, 1: 6–46.

White, M. and Epston, D. (1990) *Narrative Means to Therapeutic Ends.* New York: W.W. Norton & Company.

Wilkins, A.L. (1979) *Organizational Stories as an Expression of Management Philosophy: Implications for Social Control in Organizations*. Unpublished doctoral dissertation: Stanford University.

Wilkins, A.L. and Thompson, M.P. (1991) 'On getting the story crooked (and straight)', *Journal of Organizational Change Management*, 4 (3): 18–26.

Wilmot, T.B. (1996) 'Inquiry and innovation in the private voluntary sector', *Global Social Innovations*, 1 (1): 5–12.

Zanetti, L.A. (1997) 'Advancing praxis: connecting critical theory with practice in public administration', *American Review of Public Administration*, 27 (2): 145–67.

Zanetti, L.A. (1998) 'On the problem of truth (with apologies to Horkheimer): challenging what's critical about public administration', *Research in Public Administration*, 4: 277–91.

PART 3

LANGUAGE, KNOWLEDGE AND POWER

8

The Prison-House of Language: the Penitential Discourse of Organizational Power[1]

Graham Sewell

Prologue

This chapter's purpose is to draw a parallel between a literary or narrative consciousness and a way of seeing organizations. Of course, this has been done superbly well before (e.g. Brown, 1977, 1987; Calás and Smircich, 1991; Czarniawska-Joerges, 1997; Czarniawska-Joerges and Guillet de Monthoux, 1994: *passim*; Jermier, 1985), often using techniques ultimately derived from literary criticism. This chapter, however, is *not* primarily an exercise in literary criticism. Rather than being an example of either Leavisite 'close reading' (Eagleton, 1983) or the perhaps more technical pursuit of Derridean 'deconstruction', this chapter is an exploration in the history of ideas (and, indirectly, a challenge to our idea of 'history' as a story of human progress[2]). More specifically, it is an exercise in the philology of our ideas concerning the 'rational' organization and their relation to a romanticized ideal of a 'natural' organizational order – ideas which deeply influence the way we still talk about organizations and, in particular, organizational power. I will show that a tension exists between these rational and romantic views which has important implications for how we might discuss power and resistance in organizations today.

Organizational power and the 'lingustic turn': beyond the agency/structure dualism

> [Words] may have several distinct meanings; several meanings connected with each other; several meanings which need one another to complete their meaning; or several meanings which unite together so that the word means one relation or one process ... It may be useful to separate these if you wish, but it is not obvious that in separating them at any particular point you will not be raising more problems than you solve. (Empson, 1930: 5–6)

Whether we are using them in a demotic or technical sense, we can easily find ourselves slipping between the two main idioms of organizational power (cf. Clegg, 1987) – power *in* organizations (i.e. relational power *between* individual organizational actors) and the power *of* organizations (i.e. enduring organizational structures which possess some kind of causal ability to shape lives therein). This idiomatic slippage resonates strongly with the toing-and-froing between the relative effects of 'determinism' and 'free will' or 'structure' and 'agency' found in much contemporary social theory. In the specialized arena of organizational theory the structure/agency dualism has recently received a good deal of attention (see, for example: Barley and Tolbert, 1997; Knights, 1997; Orlikowski, 1992; Reed, 1997; Willmott, 1987) and there has been a concerted effort by some theorists to use this development to wrest the initiative away from trendy, 'poststructuralist' relativism and reassert Enlightenment values of truth and progress. For example, it is Reed's (1997) conviction that so-called (although not necessarily *soi-disant*) post-structuralist organization theorists who have taken the 'linguistic' turn conflate the two distinct yet reciprocally related elements of agency and structure. In doing so, Reed considers that this severely limits their contribution to the discipline by confining it to a consideration of what might be called the 'little local difficulties' of everyday organizational life (and not much else besides, he might add). Reed is not alone here as his position reflects the well-established and persistent desire of philosophy and social theory to represent the world through dualistic oppositions (Dewey, 1960).[3]

The quest to unbundle the relationship between structure and agency can be seen, in a semantic sense, as an attempt to untie the Gordian knot of Empson's (1930) *Type II* ambiguity – when two or more alternative meanings are resolved into one. But how can we ever know where structure ends and agency begins, or *vice versa* of course? This form of ambiguity is evident in formal discussions of power in/of organizations, as well as being played out everyday through the language of self-reflexive understanding. Under these circumstances this ambiguity can be stated thus: '... to what *exact* extent are my own actions or the actions of others (my or their "agency") helped or hindered by the organization (its "structure")?' It is as if all we have to do in order to make sense of this form of sensemaking in organizations is to unravel the twin golden threads of agency and structure, in order to adduce their relative causal effects. For Reed, this separation avoids the conflationary tendencies of the post-structuralists and explains the experiences of organizational life in terms which, for him, extend beyond the parochial concerns of contingent and 'local' meaning, thus placing organizational theory firmly back where it belongs – within the broader progressive project of liberal/pluralist social theory.[4]

But Reed wants it both ways – he wants to combine the certainties which stem from revealing the causal powers of structure and agency in all their mechanistic glory with the suppleness derived from contingency and contextualization (see Reed, 1997: 32–3). Perhaps Reed anticipates the potential for self-contradiction here, getting around it by suggesting that accommodating contingency and contextualization is simply a matter of discerning how mediating structures are themselves mediated. By what? By agency of course! This tautological regress can be avoided, however, by repudiating the representationalist premises and axioms of orthodox organizational theory (Knights, 1997) and, instead of trying to untie the threads of indivisible ambiguity, we can try to develop interpretive devices which tackle it head-on. [5]

We can take some inspiration here from Foucault's discussions of Power/Knowledge, itself an ambiguous dyad which the author himself never felt compelled to disentangle. In this sense, this chapter does not constitute a rebuttal of Reed's normative views *qua* orthodox organizational theory and its relation to the 'linguistic' turn. Rather, it is an attempt to stand outside the orthodox structure/agency dualism as Reed presents it by showing the ambiguous nature of power in/of organizations. I do this by taking a philological and historiographical tour through the seventeenth, eighteenth and early nineteenth centuries in order to examine the romantic and rationalist antecedents of contemporary narratives of organizational power. To some it may appear, *prima facie*, that I have simply substituted one dualism for another here – in this instance romanticism versus rationalism rather than structure versus agency. It is my intention, however, not to present romanticism and rationalism as the extreme poles of a continuum but to demonstrate that, simultaneously, these intellectual traditions continue to influence our understanding of what it is to be subject to and bearer of power relations of a contemporary organization. In this sense, I am not proposing that we consider them as a *dualism* but a *duality*.

Of course this is much more in keeping with Giddens' (1984) conception of the reciprocal and recursive relationship between agency and structure, which avoids the incipient structural functionalist tendencies of Reed's account. Thus, the synchronic or idiographic duality of romantic and rationalist views of the organization is explored through the deployment of a rhetorical interpretive device – an examination of the organization-as-prison metaphor. The prison looms large as both a physical model and as a figurative emblem in both the rationalist and romantic traditions and serves to link them in this discussion of how we might construct a sense of the physical and psychological confinement of organizations. This linkage then serves as point of departure for a consideration of how this position might inform contemporary narratives of organizational power and resistance.

Imagining the penitentiary: the prison as a narrative of power relations[6]

> Prisons *mean* power and control... (Juan Rivera, New York Prisoners' Rights activist, quoted in Denborough, 1996 – my emphasis)

Why do prisons fascinate social theorists so, especially as they hardly seem, *prima facie*, representative of society as a whole? Although they serve as a constant reminder of the ultimate consequences if we find ourselves transgressing socially constructed rules, for many, prisons also provide the ultimate social laboratory. From an organizational perspective, at least, this seems a plausible consideration – a naïve observer might struggle to think of a better place to test new models of organization than in a setting where people are expected to do exactly as they are told. We can safely assume that the four master dimensions of classical social theory are to be found in the prison: power, control, legitimate authority and resistance. But in what configuration? As any first hand account of prison life will tell us, the interplay of these dimensions seldom follows the expectations of traditional organization theory and inmates rarely, if ever, do *exactly* as they are told (for example see Bettsworth, 1989; Smith, 1989). Indeed, some of the most interesting aspects of these stories are the ways in which prisoners subvert formal rules and procedures, forge their own hierarchies and create systems of social stratification founded on reputations for 'hardness' or ruthlessness, be they earned inside or outside the institution itself (Little, 1990).[7] The ingenuity shown by prisoners in subverting somebody else's rules is bound up with the assertion of self-fashioned identity. Take one vivid example.

> Scammin', always scammin'. The more rules, the more ways 'round them. If I go to the clinic, I can get over to Activities, unless that prick on the yard gate sees me. If I can make it to the library, I can get out to the field where the workers go through. If I get into the clinic yard with the methodonians, maybe Fred'll whack up his 'done, or I can stand over some cunt for his. Anyway, I can get some pills for me headache. I can get out to see the wing screw to get him to ring reception, so that I can get those trackpants out of me property. And when I get out for that phone-call, I'll see Bob in the workers' wing and maybe score some pot. (Anonymous prisoner quoted in Anderson, 1992: 217)

Tales of this sort can be extracted from almost any study of the harsh realities of prison life. Moreover, they bear a striking resemblance to stories of ingenuity displayed in subverting or resisting the rational organization that are to be found in the classical accounts of radical industrial sociology. In the face of this evidence one might wonder whether it is a manifestation of 'human nature' to react in this way to the strictures imposed by the play of power relations found in organizational life – be it in a prison, a factory or any other organization for that matter. Or, to put it another way, is this resistance a reversion to some natural state of being, despite the imposition of the strictures of rational organization? The triumph of some transcendent subjectivity or 'agency' over 'structure' if you will.[8] I shall argue that this view of the power of organization and the opposing force of agency through resistance is bound up in a historically embedded dialectic between narratives of the rational organization as a site of reformatory practice, on the one hand, and the Romanticization of what has been called by Clegg (1994) the 'resistant subject', on the other. In this fashion, the chapter proceeds by examining this apparent oppositional relationship between Romanticism and Rationalism in Western metaphysics as it relates to the representation of organizational life.

The rational will as a natural state

The potentially finely balanced tension between the triumph of the 'rational' will and the assertion of the forces of 'Nature' is a dilemma frequently encountered in the history of social theory. The common opposition of 'Nature' *versus* the 'rational' is now explored in relation to the organization-as-prison metaphor identified above.

There are many 'Natures' that we encounter every day. Indeed, the notion of 'Human Nature' itself – that is to say, an idealized state of being, based on an essentialist view of what it means to be human in terms of needs, desires and wants that, ultimately, can be translated into predictable patterns of behaviour – is not without ambiguity. Take, for example, the history of Western philosophy which contains, *inter alia*, two coherent streams of thought on the matter. On the one hand, there is the intensely pessimistic view of human nature found in the Judaeo-Christian myths of the Fall and original sin. This is, perhaps, epitomized by Locke's view of the 'State of Nature'. Here his philosophy and Christianity complemented each other through his belief in the retreat from an ancient and harmonious society caused by deviants who had challenged their position in this natural order (Cranston, 1965).[9] On the other hand and in direct contrast, the more radical and humanistic tradition, as exemplified by Rousseau and the ideals of the French Revolution, sees both man and society as being perfectible – a much more optimistic view that aspires to the construction of better social arrangements that would do justice to man's natural dignity and rationality. While both traditions are ultimately utopian, the former is regressive in its yearning for a return to a romanticized natural order where everyone knew their place. In the absence of this order, it is the job of institutions of the state to perform the 'holding' activity of preventing a descent into the rule of the mob. The latter tradition, however, is progressive in the sense that it exhorts us to reform those institutions – either through revolution or incremental change – so that we can realize the freedoms associated with the natural 'State of Man'.

Although the separate existence of the two metaphysical positions represented above is highly dubious – for example, Derrida (1976) argues that Rousseau was himself a Romantic rather than the clear headed rationalist pictured in most of his biographical accounts – presenting them as such provides the impetus for the rest of this discussion. Indeed, it is exactly because they exist in rhetorical opposition to each other as something of a false dichotomy that makes this history of ideas pertinent to the discussion at hand. For, like the relationship of Romanticism and Rationalism in Western philosophy, contemporary rationalist and romantic views of the organization share much common ground. This, I will contend, is especially the case in current discussions of organizational power and resistance.

On the origins of administrative rationalism: the organization as a well-run 'household'

At this stage it is helpful to make a brief philological digression within the main theme of the chapter by looking at how the origins of the term 'manager', as the steward of material and human resources within an organization, emerged through the activities of the Cameralist. This movement is interesting for the purposes of this chapter because it was instrumental in laying the foundations for the emergence of what might be called the early principles of rational management laid down by people like Jeremy Bentham and, later, Andrew Ure and Robert Owen – principles which are still evident today in managerial literature.

Although we can find the antecedents of modern management almost anywhere if we look hard enough (e.g. Lepawsky, 1949) I have chosen the Cameralists of Germany as the starting point for the codification of the 'science' of early modern public administration. This choice is not simply an arbitrary matter of convenience for, as we shall see, the deliberations of the Cameralist certainly pass the 'look-and-feel' test in terms of their formal similarity to many aspects of current administrative science. Moreover, the formation and consolidation of rational administrative principles and practices – *Cameral-Wissenshaft* or a science of 'management' if you will – by the Cameralists mirrored many other struggles associated with the development of early modern science and the emergence of Enlightenment thought in seventeenth century Europe (see Porter, 1997; Shapin, 1996). In this sense, the Cameralists were not a dominant movement who established hegemony over method or outlook. Rather, they took their place amongst various concurrent movements that were competing to establish modes of knowing or doing.

The classic historical text on the Cameralists (Small, 1909) would have us believe that they were some *Mitteleuropean* manifestation of the British Mercantilist and Utilitarian movements. This does them little justice as the movement reflected its singular German governmental and cultural context (Tribe, 1995). Much like management today, Cameralism displayed many of the features of a modern movement which links scientific research and scholarship with professional practice, however loosely (Spicer, 1998). It had its seats of learning at the universities of Halle and, later Frankfurt (an administrative science?). It had its individual heroes – pioneers like Florinus, von Seckerdorff, Becher and von Schröder and, later, Gasser, von Sonnefels and von Justi – all academics at German universities (management gurus?). It also had its canon of literature as each of these scholars was obliged to produce a treatise, based on their lecture courses, which formed the training materials for the officials of the courts or *Kammers* of the German principalities (management textbooks?). Some Cameralist thinkers even had experience of running things: for example, von Justi was director of mines and superintendent of a glass and steel works in Berlin (Spicer, 1998).

The analogy between the development of current management discourse and the establishment of professional public administration in seventeenth century Germany can be stretched too far but the important influence exerted by the Cameralists in establishing the etymology of the word *management* itself is beyond doubt. Tribe (1995) documents the gradual formalization of Cameralist discourse, from Florinus' contribution to *Hausväterliteratur* [10] [11] onwards, with its emphasis on the rational, efficient and orderly organization of productive activity. For example,

> Everybody knows full well/that the art of householding/which is also called *Wirtshaft*/is nothing but a proper and orderly organization/which the *Haus-Vatter* has to observe in material and temporal and material goods and means of subsistence: and is in this form also called *Oeconomia*/which is constructed from two Greek words/*Haus*/ and Law and Order [*Gesetz oder Ordnung*].
> (Florinus – translated and quoted in Tribe, 1995: 15)

This direct allusion in Cameralist discourse to something we now call management is further explored by Tribe in his discussion of the seventeenth and eighteenth century usage in Germany of the words, *menagieren* and *menage*. These build on the metaphor of the orderly and well-provisioned household synonymous with the hospitality of *Wirtshaft*. For example, von Rohr (1716) used the term, *menagieren*, to connote the activities of political administration whilst von Schröder (1752) used *menagie* as a form of good economic custodianship in its current sense (Tribe, 1995). These constitute a fusion and augmentation of the phonically similar French originating verbs – *mannège* (the Old French spelling convention) as in 'to train' or 'to lead' a horse using a single or lunging rein[12] [13] and *ménage* as in 'to husband' in the sense of the careful or the frugal stewardship of various aspects of a household.[14] This illustrates the continuing ambiguity of the verb infinitive 'to manage' – on the one hand, controlling the activities of subordinates within an organization whilst, on the other hand, impartially running the organization for the mutual benefit of all its members. It is this ambiguity of the idea of 'management' which links well with the rest of this chapter as the thinking of the Cameralists was mirrored here by other developments in the emergence of the prison as a prototype for the modern organization run under rational principles.[15]

From disorderly household to rational organization?: The origins of the modern penitentiary

The idea that government could become a science – indeed a science of management – was not confined to Germany. For example, in eighteenth century Britain, Rousseau's belief in the combined merits of 'Reason and Industry'[16] were having an impact on a number of formal and informal groups, including Whig political radicals, Nonconformist social reformers and, significantly, philosophers who were tempering the unadorned empiricism of the British tradition with their own interpretations of Continental thought.[17] These groups made intermittent common cause during the reformist zeal of the late eighteenth century over several matters of state. In addition to their almost universal concern for the advancement of rationally based general economic management these also included: the expansion of suffrage; the eradication of political patronage and nepotism; and religious freedom, including an end to the eligibility restriction of the Test Act which prevented all but members of the Church of England from holding any office of State. They were, however, at their most coherent and unified on the issues of crime and punishment. The belief that an organizational machine, running on rational principles, could be constructed to reform the dissolute habits of the criminal classes was becoming a popular belief amongst progressive thinkers. Moreover, it was becoming a pressing practical concern too as the loss of the American colonies meant it was more difficult to export British felons. In addition, the deterrent effect of transportation was becoming questionable as criminals became increasingly willing to take a punt on a new life in the colonies (Ignatieff, 1978).

The Cameralists' development of the analogy between the household and the organization is particularly striking here when it is considered that, even until the early nineteenth century, many prisons in Britain and Europe were themselves extended penal households, albeit unruly ones. Before the two Parliamentary Acts of 1774 (initiating the slow process of reform which eventually lead to the establishment of prisons as we know them today), warders were not salaried officers of state. Instead they extracted fees from their wards, much like an inn-keeper would from their guests. Some wealthy inmates would even have their own suite of rooms, staffed by servants, where they could receive visitors with little let or hindrance from their gaolers. For those less fortunate, material circumstances were far less comfortable and salubrious but they found themselves equally unregimented. For example, debtors, sometimes accompanied by their families, associated with convicted felons or those awaiting trial (Ignatieff, 1978). This chaotic depiction of the eighteenth century prison is vividly brought home through Bender's (1987) use of contemporary accounts of the Fleet[18] which show how inmates effectively ran the prison whilst their commercially minded custodians simply stood back and collected their fees.[19] No wonder the time was ripe for reform – there was a feeling that prisons must be rescued from the anarchy brought about by the collusion of the inmates *and* the warders.

The penal reforms of the late eighteenth century did much to increase the number of convicted criminals sentenced to custodial sentences, rather than transportation or execution. Although the so-called 'Bloody Code' (which made provision for people to be put to death for trivial crimes against property) was technically still in place until 1834, the number of capital offences was effectively in rapid decline, leading to a massively increased demand for long-term prison places. As a direct result, there was a transition from the spectacle of mass public execution to the hidden but ordered incarceration of offenders. But it was not only a matter of practicality. The changing of attitudes, shifting away from corporal punishment and towards the notion of penitence induced by incarceration, is famously captured by Foucault's (1979) epigrammatic use of the accounts from 1757 which graphically depict the torture and execution of the regicide, Damiens. This event can be interpreted as delineating a watershed in the development of the early modern period – a grotesque and atavistic enactment of the barbarism of Middle Ages before the Enlightenment has fully asserted itself. The graphic account of such a terrible spectacle signals the urgent necessity to replace public excess with private, yet transparent, containment and reform. The punishment of offenders, at once, becomes hidden behind closed doors and yet visible to all through the full ritualistic apparatus of the rational state.

In terms of penal policy, we celebrate this progressive transformation of the prison from a site of corporeal suffering and mental anguish to a setting of reformatory practice governed by rational rules. Here the prison comes to represent the penitential organization *par excellence*. Indeed, in the process of becoming the 'penitentiary', we find the apprehended felon increasingly subjected to the dubiously edifying effects of hard labour (Melossi and Pavarini, 1981) as well as contemplation, Christian dogma and an orderly and regular regime, preferably encountered in isolation from his (or, sometimes but not often, her) fellow inmates. But it is Foucault's ironic use of Damiens' spectacular demise which exposes a degree of hypocrisy at the heart of the Enlightenment project. Despite what might be the best of intentions, the experience of prison life in the modern period is still one characterized by misery, waste (both financial and human), recidivism and despair. Moreover, Foucault poses the question – is this form of punishment through incarceration any 'better' than those which proceeded it? This is not to say that, for the individuals involved at least (for example, the hapless Damiens), it is any better to go out in a blaze of gore and glory than to moulder away in some dank cell for the rest of their lives. Rather, Foucault opposes the self-congratulatory tone of 'progressives' who are, in effect, really conservatives supporting the normalizing tendencies of modern institutions.

The thrust of this argument becomes clear when we consider that, although punishment in the seventeenth century could be arbitrary, and undoubtedly brutal, the public spectacle of execution was also often the setting for dissent and protest against the exercise of sovereign power, as represented through the penal system (Emsley, 1987; Ignatieff, 1978). Additionally, the absence of any regime that smacked of rational management in the prisons themselves allowed prisoners to assert a degree of autonomy (although, if we go on Bender's word, this too was a far from edifying spectacle). In the modern organization, however, dissent and opposition become contained and manageable. Thus, the exercise of power is transformed from the grand gesture of the sovereign will to the micro-circuits of the institution where it may well be more opaque, more insidious, less contestable. In the light of these observations we must examine the basis for which the prison became to be seen as the model of rational organization and how narratives of struggle, resistance and the play of power relations have been inscribed upon this construct.

A play of fictions? The prison as a trope for the rational organization

> Though the wicked were fewer than the righteous, yet because we cannot distinguish them, there is the necessity of suspecting, heeding, anticipating, subjugating, self-defending, every incident to the most honest and fairest conditioned. (Thomas Hobbes quoted in Gert, 1995: 334)

How do we tell the difference between the 'righteous' and the 'wicked'? According to Hobbes, certainly not by outward appearances. For Hobbes, the price of social harmony is eternal vigilance. This view, still current today, is used to justify the subordination of individual liberty to the preservation of the *status quo*. There was, however, a moment in British intellectual history where ideas concerning individual liberty were, all too briefly, in the ascendant. The history of eighteenth century prison reform in Britain, somewhat ironically given its focus on incarceration and confinement, captures this moment. It is a history often told through the stories of the concerted efforts of two men. The unlikely character of this alliance becomes clear when we consider its two protagonists – Howard and Bentham – were an ascetic Christian moralist and an avowed atheist respectively. Whereas Howard's reformist inclinations were motivated by a compassionate paternalism borne of his Quakerism, Bentham believed in the perfectibility of man through the imposition of rational principles.

Howard and Bentham were both were well travelled in Europe and were familiar with Continental ideas concerning punishment and correction. In particular, the Italian utilitarian, Cesare Beccaria, exerted considerable influence on Bentham whose own ideas for a reformatory organization or 'penitentiary' represented an unsentimental and calculated attempt to construct the ultimate rational organization. This was to be a rationality that was transparent and unambiguous. Like many who have preceded the 'linguistic turn' in philosophy, Bentham yearned for a philosophical 'magic language' where one could precisely say what one meant and mean what one said. This is at its most evident in Bentham's writing on jurisprudence where he detected the 'pestilential stench of fiction' in the rhetorical trickery of lawyers (Harrison, 1983). In his design for the Panopticon,[20] however, Bentham hoped to by-pass the fictional operations of language to provide a direct, sensory rehearsal of reality (Bender, 1987). As a utilitarian, Bentham thought that nothing was more real than the sensory experience of pain and pleasure and all language, law and 'ordinary thought' were contaminated by fiction.

Although less zealous than Bentham in his desire to identify a universal set of unambiguous organizing principles, Howard was also acutely aware that the indeterminate categorization of prisoners was an obstacle to the imposition of discipline for, in the chaos of the seventeenth century prison, how could the authorities know who was a hardened criminal and who was simple debtor? (Ignatieff, 1978). Worse still, it could even become difficult to distinguish the gaolers from the gaoled! In this sense Howard, like Bentham, wished to wrest control of the prison from the colluding parties of inmates and warders, in whose mutual interest it was to keep the prison impervious to the rationalizing gaze of the modern scientific administration. Responsibility for running the prison would now be placed in the hands of impartial professional warders or 'managers' who would strictly abide by the rules determining the relationship between the gaoler and the gaoled. Thus, the time was ripe for the power of organization to exert itself, reforming its members by bringing about the structural context in which they could realize their destiny as rational subjects.

But is Bentham's Panopticon, even as he conceived it, an unambiguous and wholly rational machine? We must conclude that it is not for it does not even pass Bentham's own test of rational integrity – the transcendence of 'fiction'. As Božovič (1995) has demonstrated, as far as the Panopticon is concerned, fiction is at once an obfuscation of reality and an operational necessity. This is because it relies on the fiction of the apparent omnipresence of the gaoler in order to deter inmates from transgressing. Indeed, the irony of the Panopticon is that if the gaoler is ever seen then the apparent reality of their omnipresence is revealed as an illusion of fiction (Božovič, 1995). Despite this confounding observation, the Panopticon is often presented as the model of the ultimate and inescapable rational organization. Or, rather, this is often how Foucault's discussion of Bentham's model is interpreted with respect to current organizational settings – as exactly that, a model of domination creating an inescapable web of control enacted through material means (quite literally, a power 'machine').[21]

This not only does a disservice to Foucault's tropical use of the Panopticon to convey the desire of systems of knowledge to subsume individuals under a totalizing instrumental rationalism (Sewell, 1996), it even misrepresents Bentham's stated intention for the model prison. This was not to punish, control, repress or dominate *per se*, but to reform deviants by awakening the rational man within.[22] To be sure, as Jacques-Alain Miller has pointed out, the Panopticon *is* a materialized system of classification based on physical isolation (Miller, 1975). Nevertheless, equally as important as the physical constraints are the inscribed systems of classification – the figurative 'prison of words'. Indeed, as Bender (1987) explains, before the penal reforms of the late eighteenth century, prisons were characterized by randomness and irrationality. Futhermore, they neither assigned roles nor told 'stories' (Bender, 1987) – to an outsider it was difficult to distinguish a hardened criminal from an aristocratic debtor fallen on hard times; a starving vagrant caught stealing a turnip from a highwayman, pirate, or even a regicide. In contrast, in the Panopticon, inmates would be distinguished, not by their clothing or even their face (they were to have identical uniforms and remain hooded during the only communal activity – exercise) but by nominal instruments of 'biopower' such as age, height, weight, prison number, sentence length, time served, obedience record, etc. Here, at once, Bentham's rational organization is also a 'rationalizing' organization, imposing on the subjectivity of individuals any number of nominal and measurable categories. But the penitential ideals of organization are illusions of fiction itself for the inmates are not being gently coaxed toward some transcendental subjectivity representing the rational being within. Rather, the subjectivity of inmates is fluid and contested; for the individual, rationalized through systems of classification, may still be seen in a different light by peers or superiors (and also, of course, by subordinates in the informal pecking order of inmates). For example, an 'ideal' prisoner in the eyes of gaoler (obedient, dutiful, penitent?) may be seen as a 'turncoat' to many of their peers (supine, gutless, passive?). In this sense, there is no stable subjectivity – either self-fashioned or structurally determined – and even the most apparently rational of organizational designs cannot subordinate issues of identity and being to the power of organization. Put plainly, the Panopticon – the most unadorned expression of the ideal of the power of structure – is ultimately impotent, unable to awaken the immutable, singular and rational subjectivity within. If this is the case then what is the origin of the common misapprehension that organizations create an inescapable prison from which we should try to escape? I will argue that it lies in a Romanticized reaction against this fictitious presentation of the effects of the rational organization.

Constructing a Romantic vision of the prison: reinforcing the fiction

Now my friends emerge   20
Beneath the wide wide Heaven – and view again
The many-steepled tract magnificent
Of hilly fields and meadows, and the sea,
With some fair bark, perhaps, whose sails light up
The slip of smooth clear blue betwixt two Isles   25
Of purple shadow! Yes! They wander on
In gladness all; but thou, methinks most glad,
My gentle-hearted Charles! For thou hast pined
And hunger'd after Nature, many a year,
In the great City pent, winning thy way   30
With sad yet patient soul, through evil and pain
And strange calamity!

Excerpt from '*This Lime-Tree Bower My Prison (addressed to Charles Lamb, of the India House, London)*' by Samuel Taylor Coleridge, 1797 – this version from Beer (1974)

It is no coincidence that, at the same time as the formal rationalism of the Cameralists was beginning to assert itself in matters of administration, so the European Romantic movement was also gaining pace in art and literature. Again, Germany is our location for the start of our journey but, instead of the Princely courts, it is the *Sturm und Drang* literary generation of Goethe and Schiller that provides the impetus for the emergence of the Romantic counter-Enlightenment – the apparent antipode of rationalism. Even Hegel, a friend of the Romantic poet Höderlin and great admirer of Schiller, advocated Enlightenment principles whilst simultaneously harbouring grave concerns about the tendency of Modernity to bring forth new forms of repressive authority (Pippin, 1989).

Looking back on this period, Nietzsche – that self-appointed nineteenth century scourge of rationalism – displayed none of Hegel's ambivalence, choosing to champion the cause of the Romantics. For example, he saw Goethe's ascendancy as the (over)man of letters *par excellence* as having a significance that was not just confined to Germany but stretched well beyond, describing him as a 'European Event' (Nietzsche, 1976). For Nietszche, Goethe's pan-European credentials stemmed from his rejection of an idealistic 'Rousseauian morality'. Nietzsche detested the egalitarian ideals of the French Revolution as exemplified by Rousseau, dismissing the event itself as a seductive but hollow spectacle which had hoodwinked weaker minds into believing in the perfectibility of human society through the exercise of the common weal. This position was fuelled by Nietzsche's fear of the threat posed by an enfranchized *lumpen* mass to the reclamation of a 'natural' (but, nonetheless, mythologized) order – to him history had proved that the necessary outcome of the idealism of the French Revolution was the unbounded rule of the 'rabble'. This may well constitute an overstatement of the position of Goethe *contra* Rousseau on the part of Nietzsche but it does represent, *in extremis*, a kind yearning for a lost past – somehow simpler, less laden with problems – that is common to many streams of Romantic thought.

Again, like the Rationalists, the Romantic movement of late eighteenth century continental Europe similarly found a group of willing admirers ready to introduce their ideas to a British public. British Romanticism displayed a more limited, even prosaic, quality in comparison to the vast and ambitious socio-political sweep of Goethe (Paley, 1990).[23] This is ironic, for English Romanticism is primarily celebrated for its contribution to the *poetic* through the five canonical pillars – Coleridge, Blake, Byron, Keats and Shelley. Of these, for the purposes of this chapter at least, Coleridge is the most interesting. This is not because his poetry is any more sublime than his Romantic *confréres* – indeed, in lyrical terms Butler (1981) sees him as the most limited of the five – but because his life represents, in microcosm, the late eighteenth century contest fought out between rationalism and romanticism for the hearts and minds of the British intelligentsia.

Coleridge's transition from prodigious boy genius, through radical communitarian (he was a participant in an ill-fated attempt to set up a utopian community in the recently formed United States where he also acquired a loveless arranged marriage), to Christian apologist and conservative pamphleteer was rapid, even for a time of extreme intellectual flux and political turmoil. It is in this ultimate incarnation that Coleridge did most of his writing, although he had composed all of his great poems by then and had almost completely given up on poetry as a legitimate pursuit for a recently arrived member of the *haute bourgeoisie*. As the editor of the journal, *The Friend*, he poured his energies into swimming against the tide of constitutional, religious and political reform. Thus, Coleridge's retreat from radicalism culminated in a repudiation of all the great atheistic and rationalistic movements of the late eighteenth century, finding solace in the introspective yearnings for a bygone age so typical of Romanticism (Butler, 1981). This position led John Stewart Mill to describe Coleridge as the most conservative, even regressive, 'philosopher' of his time (Leavis, 1950).

A notable example of Coleridge's conservatism was his abiding concern that the emerging commercial spirit of the age was a threat to the 'constitution' of England (and, we can assume, the rest of the British Isles), both as a legal apparatus and as a symbolic representation of a ruling ideology. His fear and loathing of the commercial, and commercial organization running on rational principles in particular, as a threat to this romanticized purview is strikingly displayed in one of his greatest short poems, 'This Lime-Tree Bower My Prison' (see extract above). Here the dedication to Charles Lamb and the circumstances in which the poem was written each provide an important insight into Coleridge's distrust of organizations.[24] Lamb was a fellow charity boy and child prodigy at Christ's Hospital school – he reflected on these experiences in a celebrated later essay (Bloom and Trilling, 1973: 659–69) – who was in awe of Coleridge as a poet. Although they did collaborate on a number of Coleridge's early poems, Lamb later confined his literary activities to those of essayist and critic. Unable to make a living from what was then still a pursuit for the independently wealthy, or at least those who benefited from the support of a wealthy patron, Lamb was obliged to seek employment in one of the largest proto-modern organizations of his time, the East India Company. Between 1792–1825 Lamb was a clerk at India House, enduring what Coleridge clearly saw as a brutal and demeaning form of penal servitude (lines 27–32). Whether Lamb saw himself in the same light is debateable; he appears to have professed a strong aversion to the exalted countryside of the Romantic poets and clearly preferred life in London to the Lake District 'scene' of his friends (Bloom and Trilling, 1973: 656).

This is vividly brought home in 'This Lime-Tree Bower...' – Coleridge, himself a 'prisoner' of the bower as a result of scalding his foot, is unable to join Lamb and the Wordsworths on a country walk and he reflects on his incarceration in contrast to their emancipation (both literal and spiritual) by the verdant and lush Lake District countryside conjured up in his imagination. But it is also a reflection on the ultimate predicament of poor, 'gentle-hearted' Charles, for Lamb could be considered a prisoner twice over. First, his freedom in the country is only fleeting as he must eventually return to India House and the Great Wen in order that he resume his position as clerk. Secondly, he would have to return to care for his sister who became Lamb's ward after she killed their mother during a psychotic episode; a situation which prevented Lamb from ever marrying (Bloom and Trilling, 1973: 657–8). In this sense, Lamb is rendered powerless against the dominative strictures imposed by his life, especially his organizational life.

Nevertheless, organizational 'prisoners' like Charles Lamb who may be physically constrained can still let their minds run free, just as Coleridge does in the lime-tree bower. This is a theme which is frequently encountered in prison literature – confinement as an opportunity for emancipatory contemplation. For example, Duncan (1996) widely trawls French literature to illustrate a number of positive images of enforced confinement, including the prison as a refuge from the everyday and prosaic struggles of life or the prison as the location of spiritual rebirth in the face of great adversity. This is the romanticization of resistance at its most insidious – akin to saying 'They may break our bodies but they will never break our Spirit'.

As one might expect, other debates on our responses to imprisonment have been extensively played out in other literary texts. Take, for example, what is often thought to be the first 'modern' novel in the English language – Defoe's *The Life and Adventures of Robinson Crusoe*. Here we have a man unexpectedly wrenched from normality and marooned on an island. Unlike Coleridge though, Defoe does not unequivocally equate 'Nature' with 'Emancipation'. Indeed, his view is one of ambivalence in terms of Crusoe's unexpected reversion to a state of Nature – at once idyllic and harsh (a prison, if you will). Nevertheless, Crusoe uses the technology available to him to try and dominate Nature and, when he rescues 'Friday' from the attentions of slavers, Crusoe asserts his 'natural' order of domination by enslaving Friday himself. So we have a tension as Crusoe comes to terms with his lot on the island – separation from modern society and enforced communion with Nature versus the desire to emulate the society he has left behind. In attempting to resolve this dilemma on his prison-island, Crusoe is simultaneously attempting to resist the dominating forces of Nature while exercising power over Friday – making, one might say, the first prison novel displaying the ambiguity of organizational power relations. Crusoe is, at once, subject to and a bearer of power relations in a context where agency and structure are inextricably bound up.

Ever since *Crusoe*, studies of power relations inside 'total institutions' like prisons have continued to make compelling reading. This is, no doubt, why they translate into such good dramatic settings – from Hogarth's pictorial novella, *The Rake's Progress*, through Dumas' *The Man in the Iron Mask* to Willocks' *Green River Rising*. Moreover, when speaking of organizational life using a demotic idiom we often allude to the ways in which we are enmeshed in prison-like power relations. Thus, we invoke elements of structure and agency – the effects of pernicious structural arrangements (our 'employers', our 'jobs', our 'careers', etc.) or by the malevolent and irrational interventions of individuals (our 'bosses', our 'colleagues', etc.). But is it appropriate to speak of work organizations in any meaningful sense by deploying the organization-as-prison trope in this way? Or, to put it another way, do the power relations of organizational life actually imprison us, constrain us, condemn us to years of penal servitude?

To be sure, from the essentialist viewpoint of orthodox radical organization theory at least, resistance in the workplace is seen as a natural, even inevitable, response to the 'confinement' of the labour process. Some psychological approaches see the emergence of informal regimes of power and influence in real prisons in much the same way – as somehow reflecting the undeniable exercise of 'human nature'. The understanding of resistance in these terms is also present in literature, especially during the nineteenth century in the immediate aftermath of the first Romantics where writers such as Balzac, Stendahl, Dumas and Hugo celebrated the 'art' of convicts who exercise their intimate knowledge of carceral regimes in order to effect their masterful escape (Brombert, 1978).[25] It is almost as if it is the prisoner's moral duty – much like prisoners of war – to try and escape, or at least cause as much disruption as possible. This constitutes an appeal to the inmates' enduring human qualities of ingenuity and resistance in the face of inordinately powerful structural relationships.

Cords of love, fetters of iron:[26] the ambiguity of organizational power and resistance

Coleridge's depiction of Charles Lamb's organizational experience might appear depressingly familiar to those who consider themselves trapped or disempowered by their work or occupation. But those who feel this way should also be comforted by the content of current management texts. These contain a rhetorical retreat from the extreme rationalism of ultra-Taylorism with its ideal of directing an individual's every action through the exercise of managerial power, legitimated by a 'science' of management. Instead, they are rejecting the ideals of the penitential organization, with its apotheosis in Bentham's Panopticon, for a normative therapeutic discourse of emancipation based on mutual trust, employee autonomy, discretion, inclusion and the establishment of unitary interests (Barley and Kunda, 1992).

The emblematic word that is much bandied here to convey a sense of genuine change is 'Empowerment'. The view being represented is that, whereas the traditional strictures of organization would, at best, stifle agency or channel it towards acts of disruption and resistance, empowerment in the form of ceding autonomy and discretion enables agency to be directed at the positivities of 'continuous improvement' in any number of areas, be they quality, productivity, innovation, or learning. This constitutes a representation of the structure/agency dualism in one of its crudest manifestations – the playing out of the traditional oppositional forces of 'determinism' versus 'free will'. Under the circumstances of a loosened structure – a recognition of the need for an organization's members to express themselves creatively, if you will – then resistance takes on a new complexion. Who needs to resist when these strictures imposed by a penitential organization are dismantled, interests are mutual and power is diffused? In terms of the opposing forces of structure and agency, it is agency that is in the ascendant as we celebrate the power of individuals to effect change in the workplace – the 'fetters of iron' have been loosened, enabling the ingenuity of people to be directed, not towards resistance or disruption, but towards the benefits of 'continuous improvement'. Under these circumstances, what is presented as dissent or recalcitrance becomes even less acceptable than before, for it is no longer expected and certainly not tolerated, being the product of 'irrational' minds.

But are the rationalizing tendencies of penitential structures genuinely being ameliorated? Never before in the workplace have we been subjected to such a degree of enumeration and classification through the application of surveillance and performance measurement, undertaken by superiors and peers alike (Sewell, 1998). However, these are not presented as instruments of power and control. Rather, they constitute a reformatory therapy enacted through behavioural normalization. The irony is that, under the rhetoric of increased autonomy and empowerment, opportunities for the expression of elements of behaviour closely associated with agency – for example, dissent, difference and self-determination – are being closed off, pushed to the margins, labelled irrational. As the 'fetters of iron' are being discarded, so the tightening ligature of the 'cords of love' asserts itself.

Nowhere is the replacement of the 'fetters or iron' with 'cords of love' more apparent than in the current celebration of teamwork – an area of management discourse where usage of the term 'Empowerment' is at its most promiscuous. Here the Romantic spirit is evident as proponents seek to bolster the appeal of teamwork by suggesting that collective organization resembling teamwork is somehow the 'natural' way to coordinate human effort. Moreover, since the industrial revolution, orthodox forms of organization, especially those supporting standardized and formalized labour, have undermined this natural inclination to work in groups. Perhaps the most sophisticated representation of this position is contained in Jon R. Katzenbach and Douglas K. Smith's (1993) book, *The Wisdom of Teams*. Here the authors allude to an idealized period of pre-industrial manufacturing where production, unhindered by any disruption or disharmony stemming from conflicting interests, was undertaken by free and self-determining craft workers operating in loosely governed cooperative groups. This is used as a justification for the reassertion of these ideals in the contemporary organization through the implementation of teamwork.

The celebration of the power of individuals in the workplace to exert genuine influence on organizational processes and outcomes, simply by being members of a 'team', is not just confined to Katzenbach and Smiths' book – many other current texts echo these sentiments (see Sewell, 1998). But this influence cannot remain inchoate and unfocused. It must be supported, sustained and marshalled in order for it to make a contribution to the overall effectiveness of the organization. Hence, the recent proliferation of books on the implementation of change programmes. But how do these new organizational practices reproduce themselves?

Here, up to a point, I am in close agreement with Giddens (1984). He poses the question – in what sense is it that going about my daily business incorporates an enactment but also a reproduction of social practices? Here, he is well aware of the indivisibility of structure and agency through the constant writing and rewriting of 'rules' which are the constitutional fabric of these enduring social practices. As Giddens points out, rules act to shape meaning and establish a code of conduct. This is primarily a discursive process but the formulation of a rule is already an interpretation of it in an implicit sense. The basis for the rule prior to its formulation must exist in symbolic or material form. As such they are 'codified' interpretations of rules rather than rules *sui generis*.

Here I depart from Giddens in that I am placing more emphasis on the symbolic and discursive antecedents of rule formulation. We now see a romanticized discourse of therapy at play in legitimizing the production and reproduction of organizational practices. These practices are no longer embedded in the structure of a penitential organization but are derived from normative or what Rosen and Baroudi (1992) call 'ideational' forces such as mutual understanding, consensus, and unitary cultures. Using Giddens' nomenclature, the structural principles of an ideal-type rational organization such as the penitentiary are founded on rules that are formalized and visible and, as such, are ostensibly open to negotiation or challenge. Because they are legitimated in this way, any transgression of these rules can be strongly sanctioned. In contrast, the structural principles of an ideal-type romanticized organization are informal and tacit and, as such, are difficult to challenge. Nevertheless, and in a significant divergence from Giddens' framework, any transgression of these rules is still strongly (and formally) sanctioned, this time through therapy rather than punishment. The power of organization at once appears to recede into the background but – less obtrusive, harder to pin down – continues to impinge on the actions of individuals. Thus, the power of organization extends beyond the naïve structural functionalist view of a material arrangement that exists in externality to human action to include an appreciation of how going about one's daily business in an organization incorporates an enactment but also a reproduction of its structural properties. This avoids having to make a choice between the simplistic constructs – for example either 'agency' or 'structure' – by allowing us to represent issues of domination or power relations in a non-mechanistic form. This is important if we are to challenge the hegemony of the romanticized organization where resistance – i.e. the ability to transgress rules – becomes more difficult and where dissent is increasingly marginalized or labelled as irrational.

Epilogue

In a time when the power of organization is now celebrated as a liberator of the spirit, of all that is positive and beneficial, it may seem churlish to question the legitimacy of programmes which advocate increased autonomy, discretion and responsibility. However, at the heart of this all lies a pernicious fiction based on a romantic ideal – a reaction against the penitential organization. It is, moreover, a debased romanticism; little better than a misplaced nostalgia. At least the Romantics of the eighteenth and nineteenth centuries gave us a vocabulary by which we could challenge the unedifying aspects of Modernity (Rorty, 1989). However, such a challenge cannot be mounted with the meagre tools provided by the current crop of organizational Romantics, especially when the perennial ambiguity of organizational power does not allow us to pin it down and divide it up into equitable portions. Power is everywhere. It neither resides in the structure of the organization nor the hearts and minds of self-determining actors. It is not reducible to these things. This is not to say that there can be no genuine liberating or emancipatory spirit in the organization for there can be no relations of power without a degree of liberty (Foucault, 1994). To be sure, states of domination exist and asymmetries of power persist but they necessarily allow the possibility of resistance, of strategy, of reversal. This is why we must debunk the romantic fiction of empowerment as it further marginalizes the freedom to dissent as we are subjugated to a faceless tyranny of ideational control. Whereas 'fetters of iron' only constrained the human body, 'cords of love' now impose their strictures on the mind. To paraphrase Foucault (1978), if dissent, resistance and individuality are repressed or condemned to prohibition, non-existence or silence through dominant discursive forms of organizational empowerment then the mere fact that we are speaking about them has the appearance of a deliberate transgression from oppressive norms. Of course, speaking of them is not sufficient but it is a necessary component of meaningful resistance.

Notes

1 With apologies to Frederic Jameson.
2 Which is, of course, another of Derrida's projects.
3 This reflects the 'binary' thinking of Western epistemology where knowledge claims are true/false or Western ethics where actions are right or wrong (see Dewey, 1960).
4 Of course, Knights (1997), contra Reed, notes that the conflation which so displeases his protagonist is spurious as it could only take place if structure and agency stand in externality to each other as 'real' objects or phenomena.
5 Just as Alexander chose to repudiate the rule of King Gordius of Phrygia when he cut through his eponymous knot. Although others before him had accepted the challenge of untying the Gordian Knot and had failed, by simply cutting through it Alexander signalled his refusal to defer to the rule of Gordius.
6 *Imagining the Penitentiary* is the title of John Bender's (1987) book which has greatly influenced me, both explicitly and implicitly, in compiling this chapter.
7 In a setting where self-esteem is likely to be a scarce commodity, looking down at others plays an important role in asserting one's identity. The extreme contempt reserved for child sex offenders, police informants or convicted former police and prison officers can be seen as part of this process (Cohen and Taylor, 1972).
8 Such a view would reflect an almost 'Newtonian' sense of power and resistance – for every exertion of force expect an equal and opposite reaction.
9 This view translates well (at some distance, admittedly) into current discourses of self-interested economic behaviour where what is 'rational' behaviour and what is 'natural' behaviour are not necessarily at odds with other.
10 Although, at one level, a good *Haus-Vatter* could be taken literally to mean a good 'householder', it also conveys a much broader meaning, alluding to a ruler's effective government of their dominions.
11 Many aspects of the origins of the Cameralists are approaching mythological status. For example, Tribe (1995) reports that the authorship and provenance of Florinus' *Oeconomus prudens et legalis* of 1702 are uncertain.
12 A current usage of *manège* in colloquial French is intentionally to mislead someone, akin to leading them 'up the garden path' in English.
13 Conveying the verb 'to manage' in standard American Sign Language is still done by holding the hands as if they were gripping a horse's reins (Sternberg, 1994).
14 It is rather striking that one of former British Prime Minister Margaret Thatcher's favourite means of conveying the idea of good economic management was to invoke the idea of the well-run household.
15 Interestingly, the first extensive use of the verb 'to manage' in the context of early modern organizations was actually in asylums for the insane rather than prisons, although there were many similarities between the two at the time. The increasing use in eighteenth century asylums of therapeutics based on 'moral management', rather than sedation or confinement, is documented by Porter (1997).
16 In eighteenth century Europe the word 'industry' had yet to take on its current usage. Rousseau's usage is more meaningfully associated with the efficient co-ordination of human effort under the guidance of rational principles.
17 Robbins (1961) notes that, rather than creating the reformist zeal of eighteenth century Britain, the continental Enlightenment merely reignited the smouldering

radical tradition seen earlier in the seventeenth century.

18 Before the reconstruction of Newgate, the Fleet was Britain's most famous prison and the setting for many contemporary dramas.

19 There is a delicious irony here that we are returning to prisons as the site of commercial activity in many countries through the privatization of penal services.

20 The operating principles of the original Panopticon can be easily stated. Inmates were to be *sequestered* in individual cells constructed in a ring surrounding a central watchtower. The proposed arrangement would be such that inmates could only see outwards from their cells but all their possible actions would be constantly visible from the observation tower. Although inmates would be aware of the physical source of surveillance activity – the tower – the gaolers themselves must be invisible to them. This would be crucial to the Panopticon's operation for although, at any one moment, the inmate may not be under direct observation from the tower they should be aware that they *might* be under continuous surveillance. Thus, the disciplinary effect is constant even if the surveillance itself is not, allowing a small number of warders to exercise control over a large number of inmates. Under these conditions inmates would eventually become self-disciplining subjects through their expectation that any act of disobedience would be revealed to gaolers and sanctioned accordingly.

21 To be more precise, this is a favourite trick of those who wish to condemn its use as a hermeneutic device in current organizational theory – for example Thompson and Ackroyd (1995).

22 This is why Bentham was so sure that the Panopticon could be used as a model for almost any organization requiring the coordination of human activities in time and space.

23 Goethe served as Prime Minister of the Weimar court between 1775–1785.

24 It might appear that I am committing the 'crime' of adducing Coleridge's original intent here. In my defence I call on the support of Stanley Fish who states that, '"originalism" is not the name of a distinct style of interpretation but the name of interpretation as practised by anyone; since meaning cannot be determined apart from (the prior and simultaneous) assigning of intention, everyone who is an interpreter is in the intention business, and there is no methodological cash value in declaring yourself (or even thinking yourself) not to be an intentionalist because you couldn't be anything else' (Fish, 1994: 184).

25 Brombert (1978) notes that these authors frequently allude to the 'art' of the master prison escaper Benvenuto Cellini.

26 This refers to an extract of John Brewster's eighteenth century pamphlet, *On the Prevention of Crimes*. In noting that 'There are cords of love as well as fetters of iron' Brewster was suggesting that those who remained unbowed by the tyrannies of corporal punishment and physical isolation could be won over by 'more tender impressions'.

References

Anderson, T. (1992) *Take Two: The Criminal Justice System Revisited*. Sydney: Bantam.

Barley, S.R. and Kunda, G. (1992) 'Design and devotion: surges of rational and normative ideologies of control in managerial discourse', *Administrative Science Quarterly*, 37: 363–400.

Barley, S.R. and Tolbert, P.S. (1997) 'Institutionalization and structuration: studying the links between action and institution', *Organization Studies*, 18 (1): 93–117.

Beer, J. (ed.) (1974) *Samuel Taylor Coleridge: Poems*. London: J.M. Dent & Sons.

Bender, J. (1987) *Imagining the Penitentiary: Fiction and the Architecture of the Mind in Eighteenth-Century England*. Chicago: University of Chicago Press.

Bettsworth, M. (1989) *Marking Time: A Prison Memoir*. London: Macmillan.

Bloom, H. and Trilling, L. (1973) *The Oxford Anthology of English Literature: Romantic Poetry and Prose*. Oxford: Oxford University Press.

Božovič, M. (1995) 'Introduction: an utterly dark spot', in Jeremy Bentham, *The Panopticon Writings*. London: Verso.

Brombert, V. (1978) *The Romantic Prison: The French Tradition*. Princeton, NJ: Princeton University Press.

Brown, R.H. (1977) *A Poetic for Sociology: Towards a Logic of Discovery for the Human Sciences*. Chicago: University of Chicago Press.

Brown, R.H. (1987) *Society as Text: Essays on Rhetoric, Reason and Reality*. Chicago: University of Chicago Press.

Butler, M. (1981) *Romantics, Rebels and Reactionaries: English Literature and its Background, 1760–1830*. Oxford: OUP.

Calás, M.B. and Smircich, L. (1991) 'Voicing seduction to silence leadership', *Organization Studies*, 12 (4): 567–602.

Clegg, S.R. (1987) 'The language of power and the power of language', *Organization Studies*, 8: 61–70.

Clegg, S.R. (1994) 'Power relations and the constitution of the resistant subject', in John M. Jermier, David Knights and Walter R. Nord (eds), *Resistance and Power in Organizations*. London: Routledge.

Cohen, S. and Taylor, L. (1972) *Psychological Survival: The Experience of Long-term Imprisonment*. Harmondsworth: Penguin.

Cranston, M. (1965) 'Introduction', in Maurice Cranston (ed.), *Locke on Politics, Religion and Education*. London: Collier.

Czarniawska-Joerges, B. (1997) *Narrating the Organization: Dramas of Institutional Identity*. Chicago: University of Chicago Press.

Czarniawska-Joerges, B. and Guillet de Monthoux, P. (1994) *Good Novels, Better Management: Reading Organizational Realities*. Chur: Harwood Academic Press.

Denborough, D. (1996) *Beyond the Prison: Gathering Dreams of Freedom*. Adelaide: Dulwich Centre Publications.

Derrida, J. (1976) *Of Grammatology*. Baltimore: John Hopkins Press.

Dewey, J. (1960) *The Quest for Certainty: A Study of the Relation of Knowledge and Action*. New York: G.P. Putnam.

Duncan, M.G. (1996) *Romantic Outlaws, Beloved Prisons: The Unconscious Meanings of Crime and Punishment*. New York: NYU Press.

Eagleton, T. (1983) *Literary Theory: An Introduction*. Oxford: Blackwell.

Empson, W. (1930) *Seven Types of Ambiguity*. London: Chatto & Windus.

Emsley, C. (1987) *Crime and Society in England, 1750–1900*. London: Longman.

Fish, S. (1994) *There's No Such Thing as Free Speech (and it's a good thing too)*. Oxford: OUP.

Foucault, M. (1978) *The History of Sexuality (Vol. I): An Introduction*. Harmondsworth: Penguin.

Foucault, M. (1979) *Discipline and Punish*. Harmondsworth: Penguin.

Foucault, M. (1994) 'The ethic of care of the self as a practice of freedom', in James Bernauer and David Rasmussen (eds), *The Final Foucault*. Cambridge, MA: MIT Press.

Gert, B. (1995) 'Hobbes', in Robert Audi (ed.), *The Cambridge Dictionary of Philosophy*. Cambridge: Cambridge University Press.

Giddens, A. (1984) *The Constitution of Society: Outline of the Theory of Structuration*. Berkeley, CA: University of California Press.

Harrison, R. (1983) *Bentham*. London: Routledge and Kegan Paul.

Ignatieff, M. (1978) *A Just Measure of Pain: The Penitentiary in the Industrial Revolution, 1750–1850*. New York: Columbia University Press.

Jameson, F. (1972) *The Prison-House of Language: A Critical Account of Structuralism and Russian Formalism*. Princeton, NJ: Princeton University Press.

Jermier, J. (1985) ' "When the sleeper wakes": a short story extending themes in radical organization theory', *Journal of Management*, 11 (2): 67–80.

Katzenbach, J.R. and Smith, D.K. (1993) *The Wisdom of Teams: Creating the High-Performance Organization*. Boston: Harvard Business School Press.

Knights, D. (1997) 'Organization theory in an age of deconstruction: dualism, gender and postmodernism revisited', *Organization Studies*, 18 (1): 1–19.

Leavis, F.R. (1950) 'Introduction', in F.R. Leavis (ed.), *Mill on Bentham and Coleridge*. Cambridge: Cambridge University Press.

Lepawsky, A. (1949) *Administration*. New York: Alfred A. Knopf.

Little, M. (1990) *Young Men in Prisons: Criminal Identity Explored through the Rules of Behaviour*. Aldershot: Dartmouth.

Melossi, D. and Pavarini, M. (1981) *The Prison and the Factory: Origins of the Penitentiary System*. Totowa, NJ: Barnes & Noble Books.

Miller, J.-A. (1975) 'Le despotisme de l'utile: la machine panoptique de Jeremy Bentham', *Ornicar?* 3 (May): 1–10.

Nietzsche, F. (1976) 'Twilight of the idols: skirmishes of an untimely man – §48–§51', in Walter Kaufman (trans. and ed.), *The Portable Nietzsche*. Harmondsworth: Penguin.

Orlikowski, W.J. (1992) 'The duality of technology: rethinking the concept of technology in organizations', *Organization Science*, 3: 398–427.

Paley, M.D. (1990) ' "These promised years": Coleridge's "religious musings" and the millenarianism of the 1790s', in Keith Hanley and Raman Selden (eds), *Revolution and English Romanticism: Politics and Rhetoric*. Hemel Hempstead: Harvester Wheatsheaf/St. Martin's Press.

Pippin, R.P. (1989) *Hegel's Idealism: The Satisfactions of Self-consciousness*. Cambridge: Cambridge University Press.

Porter, R. (1997) *The Greatest Benefit to Mankind: Medical History of Humanity from Antiquity to the Present*. London: Harper Collins.

Reed, M.I. (1997) 'In praise of duality and dualism: rethinking agency and structure in organizations', *Organization Studies*, 18 (1): 21–42.

Robbins, C. (1961) *The Eighteenth Century Commonwealthman*. Cambridge: Cambridge University Press.

Rohr, J.B. von (1716) *Compendieuse Haußhaltungs-Bibliothek*. Liepzig.

Rorty, R. (1989) *Contingency, Irony, and Solidarity*. Cambridge: Cambridge University Press.

Rosen, M. and Baroudi, J. (1992) 'Computer-based technology and the emergence of new forms of managerial control', in Andrew Sturdy, David Knights and Hugh Willmott (eds), *Skill and Consent: Contemporary Studies in the Labour Process*. London: Routledge.

Schröder, W. von (1752) *Fürstliche Schatz- und Rentkammer*. Königsberg (first published 1686).

Sewell, G. (1996) 'Be seeing you: a rejoinder to Webster and Robins and to Jenkins', *Sociology*, 30: 785–97.

Sewell, G. (1998) 'The discipline of teams: the control of team-based industrial work through electronic and peer surveillance', *Administrative Science Quarterly*, 43 (2): 397–428.

Shapin, S. (1996) *The Scientific Revolution*. Chicago: University of Chicago Press.

Small, A.W. (1909) *The Cameralists*. Chicago: Chicago University Press.

Smith, K. (1989) *Inside Time*. London: Harrap.

Spicer, M.W. (1998) 'Cameralist thought and public administration', *Journal of Management History*, 4 (3): 149–59.

Sternberg, M.L.A. (1994) *American Sign Language Concise Dictionary*. New York: HarperPerennial.

Thompson, P. and Ackroyd, S. (1995) 'All quiet on the workplace front? A critique of recent trends in British industrial sociology', *Sociology*, 29: 615–33.

Tribe, K. (1995) *Strategies of Economic Order*. Cambridge: Cambridge University Press.

Willmott, H. (1987) 'Studying managerial work: a critique and proposal', *Journal of Management Studies*, 24: 249–70.

9

After Knowledge: the Language of Information

Rolland Munro

[Information] … is less the evolution of technical efficiencies in communication than a series of arenas for negotiating issues crucial to the conduct of social life: among them, who is inside and outside, who may speak, who may not, and who has authority and may be believed. (Marvin, 1988: 4)

Introduction

It has become a commonplace to suggest that we live in an information society. But what could this mean? Currently there is the creation of a world-wide web and the building of super-highways, major projects towards the dream of creating a global village, to use Marshall McLuhan's term. But compared, say, to the goal of getting a man on the moon, or the attempts in the 1960s to end world famine, these are projects that turn society inwards. Putting everybody on (m)e-mail seems less a case of unproductive expenditure, or even a potlatch, and more 'improvement' by way of funding what Strathern (1997) has called self-enhancement.

This chapter is about the *language* of information. The aim of the chapter is to help explicate some of the ideas and key terms which sustain our images of information. The discussion therefore is concerned less with technical detail of projects, and much more with understanding how projects conducted in the name of information come to seem more relevant and practical than others. For example, I will explore how contemporary discourse has come to be dominated by certain motifs, such as the idea of passing on information on a 'need to know basis'. In this respect, the concern is with the *moral* imperatives implicit in all this talk of information. Should we pass on information? Why? Whose knowledge/information is it anyway?

The focus of the chapter is on how talk of information structures and shapes the very society that comes to speak its language. The point is to understand the different ways in which the language of information incites us to change, especially when our experience of each other becomes 'wrapped up' electronically. For example, in his analysis of the 'wrapping of language' around the new communication modes of the twentieth century, Mark Poster (1990: 8) suggests:

> What is at stake are new language formations that alter significantly the network of social relations, that restructure those relations and the subjects they constitute.

Indeed, in some obvious ways this is already happening. Many young people feel more familiar today with Michael Jackson than with their next door neighbour. Nor is a vicarious experience altogether new, since the invention of print – and painting – made the figure of Jesus of Nazareth more familiar to some families than perhaps some fathers, involved as they might be in travelling away from home as merchants, sailors or even shepherds.

I will consider the language of information in three ways. *First,* there is the question of information itself. What is it we are talking about when we use the term information? When do we talk about information and when should we talk more about knowledge? If information sounds perhaps more temporary than knowledge, it also sounds much more vital and pressing. Why is this?

Second, there are institutional questions. What are the various relations between information and organizing? Information carries with it all the virtues of economy, efficiency and effectiveness. But how does the language of information – as vital and pressing – shape and guide current thinking about the *organizing* of society. For example, does current talk of information affect our receptivity to different organization theories? Or is it more the case that well-entrenched dogmas of organization have been shaping our ideas of information?

Third, there are questions about individuality. How does talk of information position us as persons? How does the language of information prefigure our understandings about who and what we are? Does the 'wrapping of language', as Poster would have it, so change society that identity is 'dispersed in the electronic network', making one's identity 'imaginary' (Poster, 1990: 117)?

After discussing some elementary links between moral arguments and information, I will summarize and explain the basic ideas of Shannon and Weaver's information theory. It will be helpful then to broaden this discussion by elaborating and contrasting two quite different theories of knowledge – the production and the consumption view – before going on to consider Lyotard's reworking of the concept of information in a postmodern society. I will conclude by extending Lyotard's analysis to consider how the 'wrapping of language' affects how we think of persons.

The moral burden

One aspect of the information society is the piecemeal and partial integration of various forms of electronic media, including computer databases, television and cable networks, together with advertising and publishing houses. This integration is made possible through a digital reproduction of image, text and sound, but much of the appearance of integration is simulated, in that data have to be stored before they are called up as information. For reasons of cost, as well as practicality, most data will continue to be stored off the superhighways, rather than on them.

The consequences of all this information technology are usually highlighted in two ways. *First*, in respect of databases and superhighways, it is recognized that these huge forms of capital will have to be developed and maintained. So it is thought that many occupations of the future will be limited to what is called knowledge work. Some knowledge workers will help to translate knowledge of events into storable forms of data, thus making it stand 'in advance' of needs. In so much as this standing 'in advance' is inevitably coded in particular and specific ways, other workers will help to retrieve data in the form of information, as and when needed. *Second*, acts of storing and retrieving are envisaged as becoming our main form of interaction. It is anticipated here that many of our most important relationships will therefore be with machines. Even where interaction continues to take place with other persons, this will (increasingly) become electronically mediated. Instead of conversation taking place face to face, discussion will take the long way round, with each of us communicating through our screens (and virtual reality equipment) rather than in physical proximity.

However, the story of information is not all one of humans being reduced to 'bits' to feed the cybernetic machine. As will be explained in the next section, a principle, if little understood, impact of information theory has been the 'subjectification' of knowledge. Far from knowledge seeming meaningful in its own right, it has become perceived increasingly as a property of persons. This aspect to the 'exteriorization' of knowledge is perhaps entirely unexpected. Rather than imagining the world as working through knowledge being first produced, then pushed on people, we have to imagine information being created as it is pulled through by a process of consumption.

Although not everything is as it appears, this subjectification of knowledge might seem to intensify the moral burden on persons. This is because, in very specific, rather than general circumstances, a giving of information could imply grave consequences. For example, consider the situation in which you are captured by the enemy and where the information you have, if revealed, would lead to the loss of several hundred lives. Or, again, imagine that two people who have asked you to lunch turn out to be executives for a rival corporation and are offering you a large sum of money in cash in return for information on your company's latest product.

Receiving information also has ethical consequences. Suppose a colleague tells you that they just made up some of the details on the form that you are about to process. Had you not been told this, you could have just carried on, even if the details on which you would have been relying were fallacious; but now the question is whether you should report your colleague, or redo their work? Or you hear screams and a loud crash next door, followed by the sounds of a car leaving quickly – should you investigate and make sure your neighbour is all right? Or carry on with your DIY, or watching your favourite cable or television programme?

Such examples are virtually endless, a matter that has been exploited by such analytical approaches as 'game theory' and information economics. But they also suggest the most obvious way in which moral implications enter all this giving, and receiving, of information. Whatever information's characteristics are, surprisingly, neutrality is not one of them. Indeed, information, it is more generally assumed, is power. Whenever there is an exchange of information, someone may be making a great deal of money and others may get hurt or killed.

Conversely, the everyday experience of information is not of this order. Information does not usually burn in the hand, dry in the throat, or creep in the pit of the stomach. The image of information is exactly one of neutrality: impersonal, factual, technocratic, boring. Minutes of the last meeting, product specifications and company recruiting policies, none of these may seem either to benefit or harm anyone. Railway timetables, for example, are usually consulted only in rather specific and immediate occasions, such as when we want to catch a train. Handbooks, guides, WWW pages, all these are chock full of information and yet so little seems to be of interest.

It is as if knowledge has been split in two. On the one hand, there is a general production of knowledge, a process of 'commodification' in which, as will be discussed further below, some forms of knowledge are transformed into signals. These are stored, or are put into transmission, and are known generically as 'data'. On the other, there is the highly specific consumption of knowledge, whereupon these signals, in the form of a reduction of uncertainty, become re-interpreted into understandings. In-between data and understanding is information, a transient, intermittent and instantaneous material that, somehow, creates the knowing subject. This formulation suggests we should look more closely at one of the key theories associated with the term information.

Information theory

Information theory was greeted as a revolution, its potential for thinking about communications being compared to the impact of the heliocentric theory on the physical sciences. Developed as a combination of Claude Shannon's theorems and ideas popularized by Warren Weaver, and published together as *The Mathematical Theory of Communication*, the key idea is that information is surprise, with surprise being defined formally as a reduction in the uncertainty of the receiver.

Weaver's introduction hedged bets on the importance of Shannon's theorems. Weaver suggests that, in focusing on the efficiencies of transmission, the theorems might only be addressing the first of three levels. Since their prime concern was the accuracy of a transmission of symbols (the technical problem), this seemed to leave untouched two deeper levels of communication: the precision of conveying meanings (the semantic problem) and the desire to affect conduct (the effectiveness problem) (Shannon and Weaver,1949: 4).

At first sight, this stress on its limits seems right. In so far as Shannon's theorems were aimed at maximizing efficiencies of transmission, and reducing 'noise', they address only the problem of accuracy in transporting signals. Here, for example, is how Poster (1990: 8), frames what he sees to be the heart of the matter:

> For the issue of communicational *efficiency* ... does not raise the basic question of the *configuration* of information exchange, or what I call the wrapping of language.

Yet this explanation can hardly account for either the excitement that greeted Shannon and Weaver's work, or explain the fact that, for almost two to three decades afterwards, the ideas colonized almost every academic discipline across both the physical and the social sciences. Thus, before too quickly dismissing information theory, and the cybernetic paradigm (Wiener, 1949), which also informed it, a closer examination will be helpful.

The following diagram illustrates the key assumptions lying behind Shannon and Weaver's analysis. Importantly, the decoder is a mirror of the encoder, each containing an identical set of messages.

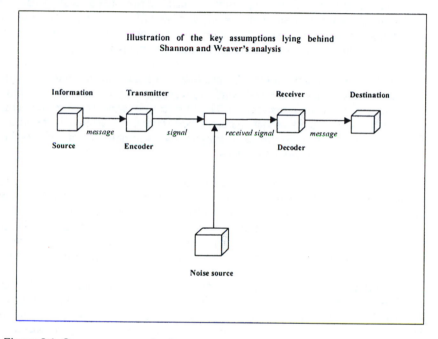

Illustration of the key assumptions lying behind Shannon and Weaver's analysis

Figure 9.1 One-way communication

Uncertainty for the receiver – in these specific circumstances – is restricted to knowing which of the pre-set messages the sender specifically wishes to activate. For example, if the set of stored messages in the decoder is all twenty six letters of the alphabet, then the sender only needs to send a signal that will help the receiver elicit the desired letter. And so on.

There are of course well established, if very specific, circumstances in which it is desirable to send only a signal, rather than send a message, such as when an army has a plan of attack and only waits on the order to attack. Yet much more is at stake. A corollary of Shannon and Weaver's idea of information being a surprise, is the finding that it is *generally* more efficient to send a signal to elicit a pre-coded message, than it is to send a message itself. Given the problem of noise, it appears better to employ redundancy and send two identical sets of signals to first elicit, and then confirm, the pre-stored messages 'send reinforcements', and 'we are going to advance', than risk a new message arriving in the form of 'send three and fourpence, we are going to a dance'.

As a 'technical' solution, this finding was radical enough. However – and it is this very leakage that makes Poster's discussion of the mode of information possible – the implications of the technical solution spill over into what Weaver had separated off as the semantic and effectiveness levels. Specifically, the idea of sending a signal to elicit a precoded response sets up two further challenges to extant ideas about communicating meanings.

1   The first challenge affects the idea of a diffusion of knowledge. It evolves from Shannon and Weaver's dictum that signs do not 'carry' meanings. Strictly, therefore, it is *never* possible to 'send' a message as such. Meanings are always, and no more than, what is 'read off' signs. Thus, the idea of signals eliciting pre-coded messages is of more general importance to understandings of communication than was first thought.

2   The second challenge affects the production of knowledge. It involves the idea that there may be no base level of messages. Signals merely elicit other signals, which elicit other signals. The implication is that there are no actual 'meanings' as such, and that signals, albeit recursively arranged, are all that there is. It is the *arrangement* of signals that is important – an idea picked up implicitly by the notion of DNA.

While both these challenges thoroughly undermine a traditional picture of knowledge, both in terms of its diffusion and in terms of it being built up from basics, it is important to stress that both of these ideas were potentially available from other sources. For example, the importance of language bracketing 'meaning' was already implied in Saussure's twin precepts of linguistics: *difference* between signs (e.g. 0 and 1) and the *arbitrary* nature of any sign in relations between signifier and signified.

For the information theorist, data only turn into information when they are *used.* Henceforth, knowledge is split into data, which are travelling in the signals of the world, and information, which has its creative impact only on the internal biography of 'individual' persons. What seems missing, however, in this initial story of information is any moral force that could ensure a constant *circulation* of data beyond its dissemination on a 'need to know' basis. What could sustain a circulation of knowledge, over and beyond that driven only by users, merely extracting information for their individual needs? What, indeed, are the ethics for each of us in adding to, and not interrupting, a *general* circulation of data? Before developing this point in light of the work of Lyotard, the idea of knowledge requires some further discussion.

The production of knowledge

Talk about information signals the end of knowledge, at least in the form of its production being a central dynamic of Western civilization. In this section, I shall explain how the traditional idea of knowledge carries a different world view to that which is embraced by the idea of information. Whereas knowledge has been conventionally understood as something that has to be produced – as real – I will argue in the next section that knowledge can also be generated in a *consumption* view of reality.

Coming from twin footholds in the libraries of the monasteries and master-apprentice relations of the craft guilds, knowledge has long been viewed as an incremental process (Kuhn, 1962: 2). Whether embodied in books, literally embodied in persons, or increasingly built into machines, the view that knowledge is both real, and cumulative, is a view that carries on uninterrupted through the inception of universities, the rise of knowledge based professions, like medicine and law, and the emergence of the factory.

Metaphors about knowledge are notoriously architectural. Areas of knowledge are divided up into fields or grounds, on which theories are erected. The foundations allow further building and development. Various views can be taken, depending on the perspective, and so on.

Yet as fast as knowledge is being built, it is also on the verge of collapse. The architectural metaphors turn into archaeological images. For knowledge to grow, new orders emerge, causing the building of the past to turn to rubble and collapse into ruins. In the eye of Foucault (1970), the courses of knowledge, the different layers in building, can be read off as breaks and discontinuities. But even Foucault, for all his care not to impute progress into all this growth of knowledge, also historicizes. Adopting the theme of incommensurability, which he shares with Thomas Kuhn, he eschews the assumption of accretion, the growth of knowledge, yes, but he still assumes deletion, an actual abandonment of 'past' orders of ideas.

What passes as knowledge in one generation certainly can come to seem little more than a heap of nonsense to the next. But, when considering what passes for knowledge, the crucial term, surely, is as much 'passes', as it is knowledge. As Latour (1987) has argued, things do not hold because they are true; things are taken to be true *because* they hold. This suggests that any analysis of knowledge needs to pay close attention to cultural context in order to ascertain exactly who, or what, is 'passing', and it is exactly this approach that distinguishes the sociology of knowledge from both a traditional writing of science as a series of discoveries and its critique.

Adopting Bourdieu's (1984) idea of cultural capital, the concern in this idea of 'passing' is with a *circulation* of particular forms of cultural capital. There are two points here. First, it might be better to talk about increases and decreases in the velocity of circulation of forms of cultural capital, rather than their elimination. Second, we have to accept a plurality in institutions. There are many circulations of cultural capital, although not all of these will have the same locality or scale.

Foucault, the historian, overlooks the rise of other institutions, in which a deletion of previous forms of knowledge may be neither attempted, nor culturally necessary. While Foucault takes account of everyday practice *within* sciences, such as medicine and psychiatry, his positivism reflects nonetheless the general tendency to mistake the mores of academic learning for culture more generally. Whereas academic knowledge is often normative, in suggesting that nothing less than certainty will do, other institutions may be much more permissive over what passes for knowledge. For example, where a farmer has always grown cabbages, or rice, then they may go on so doing. They grow what they know. Or if a clerk processed a form this way last week, she will try to process it the same way this week. But there are also institutions in which 'old' forms of knowledge are never quite deleted (see Munro, 1995). Even where a clerk may adopt a new procedure, he has to be ready to return to the previous procedure next month. Outside of the academy, it is not only habit and precedent that continue their long slow proliferation, it is also the stubborn existence of pragmatism.

It is not an exaggeration to suppose that whatever has passed for knowledge, is still passing as such, somewhere in the world. Nor need we look far, say to the exotic of Japan, or to the Amazonian rainforest for the presentation of oddities. As David Hume noted, the sceptics who doubt the existence of objects, like buildings, still take the stairs, rather than walk out of windows. Indeed, it is not only academics who show such contrarieties. Most Euro-Americans display the peculiar myopia that lets them go on talking about the sun rising, long after they have understood the implications of heliocentric theories.

The consumption view

For a wider understanding of knowing than that made available by the production view, it is helpful to turn now to consider the consumption view, as set out by Mary Douglas. Against some *deus ex machina*, like progress, or an abstract idea, like truth, Douglas suggests that people 'show' what they think through what they exchange; that is, knowledge is spread through their consumption of goods. Whereas others like Thomas Kuhn, and the early Michel Foucault, seek to demonstrate 'internal' changes *within* science over time, thus merely weakening the metanarratives of truth and progress, Douglas begins with a potentially much more pluralist view of knowledge as being whatever 'passes'.

In making her questions explicitly social, rather than merely epistemological, Douglas does not so much eschew the possibility of a growth in knowledge, as she begins by asking the very different question: how is it that knowledge is shared and reproduced? Thus, rather than decide ahead what knowledge is, Douglas' focus is over what *passes* for knowledge among a group. The key metaphor here is that of 'circulation'. To understand how knowledge circulates, Douglas focuses on the circulation of goods. Here is how Friedman (1990: 327) develops the thesis:

> Following a line of argument that began with the recognition that goods are building blocks of life-worlds, we have suggested, as have others, that they can be understood as constituents of selfhood, of social identity.

Instead of attempting to go on to explain how knowledge grows or changes, incrementally or not, Douglas asks a much more basic question. How is knowledge – any form of knowledge – performed, or even presented to each other at all?

Douglas and Isherwood (1980: 76) insist that 'any choice between goods is the result of and contributes to, culture'. There are three aspects that are central here. First, the expressive nature of materiality is crucial for understanding the consumption view. The consumption view makes a 'sharing' of knowledge possible by drawing attention to the *expressive* nature of materiality, particularly goods. Arguing therefore that goods are consumed because they are good to think, Douglas and Isherwood (1980: 65) thus *ground* the continuance of social knowledge in its display:

> Goods, in this perspective, are ritual adjuncts; consumption is a ritual process whose primary function is to make sense of the inchoate flux of events.

As Douglas and Isherwood (1980: 67) express the matter: consumption 'uses goods to make firm and visible a particular set of judgements in the fluid processes of classifying persons and events'. Douglas is primarily concerned here to turn around the dismissal of much consumption as irrational. In an extension of the ethnomethodological approach (Garfinkel, 1967), which stresses the methods by which participants make themselves and their work visible to each other, our consumption of goods not only helps make our knowledge visible, this 'show' of knowledge also makes us accountable to each other as members of an 'us'. As will now be discussed, the penalties for a failure to display 'where we stand' may be *exclusion* from the group.

Second, and of equal importance, is the related matter of inclusion and exclusion. It is important to note how intimately for Douglas and Isherwood (1980: 88) exclusion is tied to the consumption thesis:

> Sharing goods and being made welcome to the hospitable table and to the marriage bed are the first, closest fields of inclusion, where exclusion operates spontaneously long before political boundaries are at stake.

Indeed, since we consume each other through goods, it is possible to see that people's consumption of each other is also subject to the tenets of the consumption thesis. In this way, Douglas and Isherwood (1980: 88) theorize 'the social' as being active in the sharing of goods:

> No one likes to recognize that the capacity to share all three [bed, board and cult] is socially endowed, a result of current decisions, and not an ineluctable fact of nature.

In emphasizing matters of inclusion and exclusion as one of the recursive effects of meanings, Douglas points to the *effects* which are sustained as a consequence of the tie between identity and consumption. Who sleeps with whom, who feeds with whom and who is whom, these are not matters only for economics. These matters are recursively organized through the social:

> Studies of the ancient Israelites ... contemporary Thai villagers ... and contemporary Lele tribesmen in the Congo show how the world is organized in a recursive system of metaphors dealing with admission to bed, board and cult.

Against Lévi-Strauss' division of social life into three communication systems of goods, women and words, Douglas and Isherwood (1980: 88) aim to synthesize these into a theory of consumption:

> The meanings conveyed along the goods channel are part and parcel of the meanings in the kinship and mythology channels. Trading persons, goods or words not only reveals the social which constitutes them. The social is itself instantiated by the knowledge that comes through such tradings.

Finally, and critically, more than exclusion is entailed. The 'naturalness' of any exclusion has also to be asserted:

> ... whenever exclusion is operated to define a category of outsiders, the segregated category tends to be accredited with a different nature ...

Exclusion, at least to those in the know, always seems 'natural'. For example, drawing on Trollope, Douglas gives the example of the wealthy and complacent Wharton: how could he let his daughter marry a man he didn't know? Knowledge circulates within its own circles and the consumption thesis helps to explain this.

In contrast to the production view, Douglas' analysis is particularly helpful in re-instating the importance of 'implicit knowledge'. Such a picture of knowledge circulating through exchange, of course, is very different from the current idiom where, for example, the *added* value of information raises the ogre of the 'cost of information'. In what follows, we turn now to a different writer, Jean-François Lyotard, to discuss the transformation of knowledge that is heightening our 'need to know' on the one hand and, at the same time, making natural our increasing exclusion from the majority of information flows.

The transformation of knowledge

Subtitled 'a report on knowledge', Jean-François Lyotard's *The Postmodern Condition* has been seen as providing the definitive epitaph on traditional views of knowledge. Its summary statements over the 'end of knowledge' have been widely understood to sum up what Lyotard calls the 'obsolescence of the metanarrative apparatus of legitimation'. In particular, his three word definition of postmodernism as 'incredulity towards metanarratives' not only underlines 'the crisis of metaphysical philosophy', it also brings into question the 'university institution which in the past relied on it' (Lyotard, 1984: xxiv).

Early in *The Postmodern Condition*, Lyotard addresses how technological transformations are having a considerable impact on knowledge. His analysis here proceeds on the idea that the nature of knowledge is changing, as it is now processed through different media than before. *First,* in respect of research, he identifies how many disciplines, such as genetics, owe their theoretical paradigm to cybernetics. *Second,* in respect of the transmission of required learning, Lyotard (1984: 4) holds that 'it is common knowledge that the miniaturization and commercialization of machines is already changing the way in which learning is acquired, classified, made available, and exploited'. However to understand Lyotard's thesis that the nature of knowledge cannot 'survive unchanged within the context of general transformation' his points about research and the transmission of learning need to be taken together.

Lyotard draws attention to how these twin aspects of research and transmission of learning together form a *language of information* that is reshaping knowledge. His claim is that knowledge can fit the 'new channels and become operational' only if 'learning is translated into quantities of information [bits]'. He predicts an abandonment of 'anything in the constitutional body of knowledge that is not translatable in this way'. This prediction should not be mistaken, however, for the more common idea that the use of computers has become obligatory. Much more is at stake.

Lyotard's version of what I will call the 'cyber pass' – the formation of an 'obligatory passage' through which knowledge must pass to be accorded the status of knowledge – is at once more complex and profound. He can be better understood as noticing how cybernetic theorizing and computer languages have begun to act as a *network*, increasingly entwining research together with the transmission of learning. As Lyotard (1984: 4) says, 'along with computers comes a certain logic' and, with this, a set of prescriptions 'determining which statements are accepted as 'knowledge' statements'.

Lyotard defines this transformation of knowledge as a process of 'exteriorization' and identifies three closely interrelated aspects. First, the process of *legitimation* involves a thorough exteriorization of knowledge, driven by 'the ideology of communicational "transparency"' ' (Lyotard, 1984: 5). Second, the process of exteriorization goes hand in hand with a commodification of knowing in which the goal is exchange of information as goods. As Habermas (1971) has also stressed, knowledge ceases to be an end in itself: it loses its 'use-value' for 'exchange-value'. Third, there is the question of *performativity*, of people inhabiting knowledge processes. The process of exteriorization proceeds not only 'with respect to the "knower"'. More crucially for Lyotard (1984: 4), exteriorization takes place 'at whatever point the knower may occupy in the knowledge process'.

In terms of a trend towards the 'exteriorization of knowledge', Lyotard perceptively suggests that practitioners of science enjoy their legislative function over truth most happily behind its closed doors, but are embarrassed when scientific discourse is called upon to legitimate its own reasoning. The point, even though it is not obvious, as Lyotard (1984: 8) admits, is that there is a 'strict interlinkage' between the 'kind of language called science and the kind called ethics and politics':

> Knowledge and power are simply two sides of the same question: who decides what knowledge is, and who knows what needs to be decided? In the computer age, the question of knowledge is now more than ever a question of government.

In respect of the issue of what is included and excluded as knowledge, Lyotard is explicitly raising the question of monopoly power and the ways in which institutions can affect discourse. This point requires some further comment.

Information within institutions, Lyotard sees as differing from a conversation. A modern institution, at least in an overly 'reifying view', always requires 'supplementary constraints' for statements to be declared admissible. These constraints filter 'discursive potentials'; there are 'things that should not be said'. Institutions also privilege certain classes of statements in that there are 'things that should be said, and there are ways of saying them' (Lyotard, 1984: 17). Yet perhaps in this respect things are also changing. Against the tradition of a nation-state, or for that matter the 'scientific estate' (Galbraith, 1967) enjoying privileges over the production and distribution of learning, Lyotard (1984: 5) points out the increasing strength of the opposing principle – transparency – according to which society only exists and progresses if 'the messages circulating within it are rich in information and easy to decode'. The rules for the production of knowledge are being put into abeyance by rules for its consumption.

Turning now to the theme of commodification, Lyotard suggests that the ideology of communicational transparency goes hand in hand with the commercialization of knowledge. The goal is no longer knowledge, but exchange. Knowledge is produced in order to be sold and it is consumed to be valorized in a new production:

> The relationship of the suppliers and users of knowledge to the knowledge they supply and use is now tending, and will increasingly tend, to assume the form already taken by the relationship of commodity producers and consumers to the commodities they produce and consume – that is, the form of value. (Lyotard, 1984: 4)

As Lyotard adds, it is not hard to see information circulating along the same lines as money. The pertinent distinction would no longer seem to be between knowledge and ignorance, but between 'payment knowledge' and 'investment knowledge' (Lyotard, 1984: 6).

This commodification raises the further question of 'performativity' and Bourdieu's (1984) distinction between 'symbolic capital' and 'cultural capital' seems to explicate almost just such a division. But Lyotard's is hardly just a distinction between 'objective knowledge' for sale and 'subjective knowledge' for prestige. Instead, Lyotard (1984: 6) imagines flows of knowledge:

> ... travelling along identical channels of an identical nature, some of which would become reserved for 'decision-makers', while the others would be used to repay each person's perpetual debt with respect to the social bond.

The world of exchange, knowledge and values is the same world of reciprocity, uncertainty and ethics. These are not two separate worlds. Lyotard's insight is to understand how it is that the *same* flows of knowledge can have, simultaneously, two quite separate functions. In this respect, *The Postmodern Condition* paints a picture of knowledge as not only transformed by the cybernetic paradigm, but *occupied* in a way that gives a double meaning to his comment on the occupation of knowledge becoming 'the principal force of production' (Lyotard, 1984: 5).

Having discussed some of Lyotard's insight on institutional arrangements, I shall now clarify this matter of occupation by discussing how these transformations affect people. In Lyotard's view, persons perform themselves in the context of 'language games'. As we will now see, Lyotard's (1984: 21) questioning of the 'right to occupy' knowledge, what he calls a post in these language games, brings together all three themes, legitimation, commodification and performativity.

Up the Cyber Pass

In a careful reading, *The Postmodern Condition* is as equally important for Lyotard's imaginative rewriting of the communications paradigm, as it is for its ability to draw attention to trends that heighten a relativization of knowledge.

While careful not to claim that 'the *entirety* of social relations' (Lyotard, 1984: 15) is caught within language games, he is equally careful to develop, rather than reject the cybernetic paradigm. As the analysis in the previous section made clear, he understands that both the research and transmission of learning functions of society have been institutionalized, and hence transformed, by 'flows of information'.

What may make *The Postmodern Condition* one of the most visionary books since Plato's *Republic* is Lyotard's implanting of language games – an idea from Wittgenstein which accepts agonistics as a founding principle – into a theory of communications. As Lyotard notes, the trivial cybernetic version of information theory misses the 'agonistic' aspect of society, the tendency for persons to wrestle with each other, often in a non-antagonistic way (Lyotard, 1984: 16):

> Each language partner, when a 'move' pertaining to him is made, undergoes a 'displacement', an alteration of some kind that not only affects him in his capacity as addressee and referent, but also as sender.

This steers a course (the original meaning of cybernetics) between pessimistic images of societies as giant machines, being fed on information to maximize their performance in terms of pre-programmed goals, and over-optimistic images of human conduct, where conversations over justice, truth and beauty transcend the mundane circulation of data.

Instead of holding on to a 'humanist' view of persons, who can take or leave information as we find it, Lyotard sees knowledge as that which has to be 'posted' by an utterance [a form of words shaping up a line], through what can be called, conveniently, a 'cyber-net' of communications. He positions each of us at *posts* through which 'various kinds of messages pass'. Young or old, man or woman, rich or poor, a person is always located at 'nodal points' of specific communications circuits, however tiny these may be. Like Mary Douglas, Lyotard accepts our embeddedness in the social. Critically, therefore, messages cannot just be relayed, but have to be 'passed' on. However, he develops the circulation metaphor with a difference. As a consequence of the 'transformation of knowledge' detailed earlier, he sees each of us as always being located within the cyber-net *at a post*.

Importantly, this positioning at a post gives persons discretion over what they 'pass' on. No-one, in Lyotard's view, is entirely powerless over the messages that 'traverse and position' a person at the 'post of sender, addressee or referent' (Lyotard, 1984: 15). This is Lyotard's key insight, to place persons and their wrapping of self in language games, *within* the cyber-net. People exist not only at the 'crossroads of pragmatic relationships', they also are 'displaced' by messages that traverse them, in perpetual motion. And to each move that they are subject, they can respond with a counter-move.

The mistake, perhaps, of those who sought to follow the thinking of Shannon and Weaver was not to take it far enough. It is not so much that a consumption view of knowledge is *de facto* superior to production views, as it is the circulation metaphor that was missing from early versions of information theory. Each receiver, by virtue of their position 'at the post', also gets a chance to be a sender. This raises the question of 'translation' in a fundamental way quite missing from Shannon and Weaver's analysis. As Latour (1987: 117) defines translation, there is a double movement involved:

> Translating interests means at once offering new *interpretations* of interests and *channelling* people in different directions.

Channelling people in different directions is effected by offering new interpretations of interests. Instead of conceiving ourselves as mere receivers, in a passive picture of messages being dumped on us, the language of information can be reconfigured to admit persons as potentially active in flows of knowledge.

Lyotard's adoption of the circulation metaphor admits everyday conduct back inside the transmission image, although not quite in the way Mary Douglas imagined conduct. This is the difference. In the cybernetic world of machine to machine conversation, each decoder can be made identical in the image of a central coder. But this is not possible with persons. The basic assumption of Shannon and Weaver, the decoder being a mirror image of the encoder, does not hold in the realm of persons. We have no idea of another person's decoder. Indeed, all we can ever check are signals (expressions) and never messages (meanings). Thus, even the very existence of each of us as a 'post' can only ever be a simulation.

This ability to simulate a 'post', although Lyotard does not go this far, can be related to the accumulation of cultural capital. Specifically, Lyotard is arguing that we are not only increasingly in actual occupations that determine the flow of information – becoming so-called knowledge workers – he also identifies that each of us has to go on earning our right to so 'occupy' a post (1984: 21). What is at stake, so to speak, at the post, is a display of 'competence' in either research, or the transmission of knowledge. This competence is never an accomplished fact (1984: 24), but depends on the creation of a peer group who will judge the competence of the sender, simultaneously as they judge the truth of the statement.

Critically, within this cyber-net, each post becomes entangled in its own incommensurate language games with any other post. Our very inclusion in one language game may thus make it 'natural' for our being excluded from other language games.

Discussion

In this chapter I have argued the importance of understanding the language of information. Talk about information usually privileges concern about information handling, the storage and transport problems of circulating signs through space and time, and downplays the importance of *interpreting*, the construction and consumption of meaning through sign work. What I hope to have shown is how these problems must be considered together.

On Lyotard's analysis, being at a post gives a person discretion over what passes through that post. The crux of the matter is one of circuits: at each post, each receiver may in turn become a sender. Even if the circuits are tiny, this discretion offers much more potential for play than seems possible in a naive reading of information theory. What the occupant can post through to other posts, goes beyond making a meagre 'copy' – to adopt terms deployed by Michael Taussig (1993) – being at a post involves a 'contact' with other persons. It is this contact, however abbreviated and detached, that animates the circulation of data in the form of language games.

Yet it is important to see that this discretion does not quite add up to *control* over what is posted through the transmission circuits. We have come a long way from communication being simply a matter of conveying one's 'intentions' in the form of a commonly understood speech act. In a consumption mode, there are no intentions; only goods, including words, are exchanged. So it is not intentions that are interpreted, but 'moves'. Further, 'moves' are subject to the surveillance of a peer group, who are also reading the move in order to judge the sender's competence. Thus, typically, the 'right to occupy' a post, is being settled simultaneously with the formation and development of the various language games. These conditions create and sustain the agonistics which fully 'occupy' those at the post.

While Lyotard's analysis is considerably more sophisticated than Shannon and Weaver's, it would be a mistake to underestimate the importance of the earlier work in either reflecting, or even helping to create something of the postmodern condition. While Lyotard's own contribution explicitly comes from his building on the cybernetic model (and incidentally revealing 'game theory' to be just one very specific language game), his analysis often treats information theory as being only concerned with passing 'messages'. But, in attending to the problems of transmission, the proponents of information theory explicitly rejected the notion of just sending 'messages'. It is in this particular respect, as has been discussed, that the influence of information theory went well beyond its solving of purely technical problems and spilled over into the semantic and effectiveness levels.

It seems likely, nevertheless, that any revolution brought about by information theory was less a direct consequence of the theory itself, so much as its *formulation* began to alter two basic preconceptions about knowledge. First, in terms of what Lyotard calls the 'transmission of required learning', information theory began with the question of what did the *receiver* need to know? In so much as this question set aside a traditional concern with the 'intentions' of the sender, this formulation is an *inversion* over the traditional direction of knowledge. By putting the traditional assumptions of philosophy and science round the other way, information theory has helped to alter how we think about knowledge. In an age of customerization, this is also an inversion that is hard to resist. Instead of privileging stories of knowledge beginning with an idea, or a discovery of truth which then of necessity *needs* to be disseminated, information theory has helped reconfigure the directional effect of necessity itself. It imagines persons, as 'receivers', who start with a *need to know*. Or rather, more specifically, as having certain 'needs' in respect of knowledge.

It is the appearance of a 'user', therefore, with individuated and specific information needs, who gives value to data in the moment of consumption. The picture is one of individual persons giving value to data; and perhaps holding the moral key in their decision to give, or receive, information. Yet this picture is surely misleading? As the agonistics of language games suggests, the idea of persons only using data when they need it seems at once too limited and too passive. Could each of us ever have all the information necessary to act morally? Or would our ability to act be forever submerged in an endless quest for further information?

Second, in terms of what Lyotard calls the 'research' function, this individuation of a need to know involves, in turn, a *relativization* of knowledge. Once information is defined formally as a reduction in the uncertainty of the receiver, greater attention becomes focused on *differences* between what people already know. Depending on what has already been encoded, different signals may be necessary. Knowledge is no longer knowledge, all of a piece, so to speak. Or even remaining the product of multiple and contesting disciplines. Now knowledge – to proceed as knowledge – first has to be broken into 'bits' of information. What 'every person needs to know' is no longer a universalizing quest, but becomes a relative matter of individual 'needs'. Critically, this is a process that stops being a matter of logic; instead it becomes a process of *disassembly* that is driven by the putative needs of specific receivers (users).

In these circumstances, the logic of knowledge is no longer something 'external' dependent on an idea of the existence of truths, so much as what *counts* as knowing is being made variable to 'information needs'. Indeed, in the new order, only some information counts.

Unlike Mary Douglas' view of consumption, where every choice of a word, partner or good, contributes to culture, only a limited amount of data ever seems to qualify for the status of information. This paucity in our own use, of course, undercuts the idea that information, more generally, is vital and pressing; and further reduces our interest in either adding to, or reducing, the circulation of information.

What we should not overlook, however, is that the circulation of information has itself been commodified. As Lyotard, among others, observes: use-value is prefigured by exchange-value. Or, rather, exchange-value has itself been pre-figured. In an information society, the only source of real information is seen to be that of the market. It is not only that 'use-value' becomes excluded, the point is that the very existence of the market begins to make it *natural* to disregard any other forms of information. Flows of information are increasingly settled on a 'need to know' basis by the market. In this way it is likely that it will be moves which reference the market that come increasingly to inhabit, and dominate, language games.

Conclusion

The purpose of this chapter is not to consider whether visions of an information society are utopian or dystopian. Nevertheless, it is possible to say that the future for people, even those lucky enough to be employed as knowledge workers, seems highly problematic. Far from an information society being a solution to problems of alienation and anomie, the transition from manual to mental labour may yet bring further exploitation and a 'terminal' unhappiness for many, whether they are students or 'self-employed' office workers in tomorrow's cottage industry.

Indeed, visions of cybernetic societies conjure up images of robotic worlds in which people no longer have any place, unless wired up in the form of cyborgs (see Parker and Cooper, 1998). Yet claims about the disappearance of the subject are not entirely fanciful. For example, Poster (1990: 116) discusses the definite effects that forms of computer writing appear to have on the subject:

1 they introduce new possibilities for playing with identities
2 they degender communication by removing gender cues
3 they destabilize existing hierarchies in relationships and re-hierarchize communications according to criteria that were previously irrelevant; and above all
4 they disperse the subject, dislocating it temporally and spatially.

On this analysis, Poster (1990: 117) argues that identity becomes 'imaginary'. But, if we take the problem of signs, discussed earlier, seriously, was this not always so?

What the earlier analysis of information in this chapter makes clear is that there is no base level of 'messages', or meanings, to which we can return. If this is so, Poster's argument is better restated in terms of a 'wrapping of identity' shifting from more familiar forms of language generated by the body, in sound, smell and gesture, to the flatter, if nuanced, surfaces of electronic print. In ways that Derrida (1978) has discussed in respect of writing, 'signature' already depends less on what he calls 'presence'. In electronic print, self and style have to be crafted into the text through a distribution of idiosyncrasies, an identity work that will likely increasingly expose the hazards of ever assuming that people share a 'natural' language, like English.

Whatever is the case here, it needs to be stressed that the 'wrapping of language' is no mere dressing up of identity. Identity is precisely what is at stake. Of course, since it usually excludes persons from its production at the same time as it claims to centre them as 'customers', talk of information certainly seems somewhat artificial and illusory. However, on Lyotard's analysis of multiple language games, many of which may be open only to a few players, talk of information definitively marks a transformational shift in identities. Our very place in society has begun to depend less upon what is distributed to us by consensus (*Gemeinschaft*), and its associated discourse of human rights, and much more upon an actual occupation of 'posts' within the 'flows of information'. The mode of information, rather than being – as many suppose – a social bond between persons, has come to rupture the social.

If Lyotard is right, any impression of belonging to an information society is a mere gloss on the multiplicity of language games. The agonistics of language games are such that these fully 'occupy' knowledge workers in an intensive surveillance over each other's moves – countermoves are necessary either to thwart moves that create 'a new argument' within the language game, or respond to moves that attempt to 'change to a new game' (1984: 43). The potential consequences of persons being situated as 'cultural intermediaries' in this way is that each of us, as knowledge workers, is condemned to an endless participation in a multiplicity of incommensurable moral debates.

We are all, in this form of individuality, after knowledge. The language of information is the language of individuals with their rights to know, but what I have argued in this chapter is that there is more to this language than it seems. Across different localities and folds in the cyber-net, each of us is so involved in the ethical niceties of individual language games, that we can miss the larger moral order. That is, parasitic on our very activities passing locally as knowledge, is the circulation of 'data'.

References

Bourdieu, P. (1984) *Distinction: a Social Critique of the Judgement of Taste.* London: Routledge.

Derrida, J. (1978) *Writing and Difference*, trans. A. Bass. London: Routledge and Kegan Paul.

Douglas, M. and Isherwood, B. (1980) *The World of Goods: Towards an Anthropology of Consumption.* Harmondsworth: Penguin.

Foucault, M. (1970) *The Order of Things: An Archaeology of the Human Sciences.* London: Tavistock.

Friedman, J. (1990) 'Being in the world: globalization and localization', *Theory, Culture and Society*, 7 (2–3): 311–28.

Galbraith, J.K. (1967) *The New Industrial Estate.* New York: Signet.

Garfinkel, H. (1967) *Studies in Ethnomethodology.* Englewood Cliffs, NJ: Prentice Hall.

Habermas, J. (1971) *Knowledge and Human Interests*, trans. J. Shapiro. Boston: Beacon.

Kuhn, T.S. (1962) *The Structure of Scientific Revolutions.* Chicago: University of Chicago Press.

Latour, B. (1987) *Science in Action: How to Follow Scientists and Engineers through Society.* Milton Keynes: Open University Press.

Lyotard, J-F. (1984) *The Postmodern Condition: A Report on Knowledge*, trans. G. Bennington and B. Massumi. Manchester, UK: Manchester University Press.

Marvin, C. (1988) *When Old Technologies Were New: Thinking about Electronic Communication in the Late Nineteenth Century.* New York: Oxford University Press.

Munro, R. (1995) 'Managing by ambiguity: an archaeology of the social in the absence of management accounting', *Critical Perspectives on Accounting*, 6: 433–82.

Parker, M. and Cooper, R. (1998) 'Cyborganization: cinema as nervous system', in J. Hassard and R. Holliday (eds), *Organization and Representation: Work and Organization in Popular Culture.* London: Sage.

Poster, M. (1990) *The Mode of Information: Poststructuralism and Social Context.* Cambridge: Polity Press.

Shannon, C.E. and Weaver, W. (1949) *The Mathematical Theory of Communication.* Illinois: University of Illinois.

Strathern, M. (1997) 'From improvement to enhancement: an anthropological comment on the audit culture'. Founder's Memorial Lecture, Girton College, University of Cambridge.

Taussig, M. (1993) *Mimesis and Alterity: A Particular History of the Senses.* New York: Routledge.

Wiener, N. (1949) *Cybernetics and Society: The Human Use of Human Beings.* Boston: Houghton Mifflin.

10

Rhetoric and Organizational Control: A Framework for Analysis

Stephen Linstead

Introduction

In this chapter I will examine the features of rhetoric in relation to forms of control within and affecting organizations. In the first part I will consider some recent treatments of language and rhetoric, especially two significant contributions by Gowler and Legge, and map some relations between key dimensions of linguistic analysis in organizations – linguistic features, textual strategies, rhetorical themes, discursive resources and discursive fields, animated by the rhetorical processes of mystification, play and the symbolic resources of context. These are illustrated by classifying different aspects which have emerged from the study of managerial rhetoric and management control.

Having situated the discussion, I will then take the idea of the rhetoric of control, as one aspect of rhetoric, and develop from Gowler and Legge's analysis of the rhetoric of bureaucratic control a general model of rhetorics of organizational control. This identifies additional rhetorics of social control, humanistic control, technological control, self-control, objective control, altruistic control and linguistic/symbolic control. Finally I take up the issue of critique and follow Foucault in arguing that rhetorics of control, as masks, operate through technologies which can be revealed by analysis. Each form of technological analysis, associated with a characteristic form of power, then acts as a line of critique, and opens up dimensions along the lines of operation of technologies of surveillance, technologies of the self, of subjective power, authoritarian power, ideological power, cultural power, representational power and ethical power.

In pursuing this analysis, it may become clear that I am attempting to reconcile some analyses which appear to be modernist – Gowler and Legge are operating with notions of surface and depth, for example – with some which are postmodernist or post-structuralist. I admit neither to naïve confusion nor to any grandiose claims of making commensurate the incommensurable. One of the most important features of rhetoric is that it reconciles opposites through mystification, creating powerful and persuasive associations between contending forces. As such, and insofar as it is persuasive, my analysis is itself rhetorical – as we know from a burgeoning literature, no use of language can escape rhetoric because language and object can never be isomorphic. As Gowler and Legge (1996) alert us, the idea of 'plain speaking' is itself rhetorical. Indeed, as Tony Watson (1996) graphically illustrates, even silence and the failure of language – situated in time and context – can perform rhetorical functions. Rhetorical tools can be used to control and oppress, but they can also be used to resist and oppose, and I hope I am using those I deploy here with sufficient reflexivity to avoid the charge of sleight-of-hand. I am using them in order to provide a framework for understanding how some lines of analysis – both modern and postmodern – current in critical organization and management studies, could be seen to relate to each other, what they might be said to expose and how they might be developed. Any framework of this nature has to be undertaken in the light of Lyotard's observation that postmodern thought leaves us no option other than to be incredulous of metanarratives. Yet this statement, taken out of context, is often deployed as though Lyotard, and Derrida, Foucault or even Baudrillard, thinks or thought that we can avoid using metanarrative entirely, or that it doesn't have some usefulness in living our lives. Of course, my metanarrative is not as genuinely Grand as that of Hegel, the chief target of such postmodernist statements – indeed it is much closer to a local, *petite* narrative – and its aims are relatively modest. So perhaps it might be allowed some room to exercise. One thing that the study of rhetoric emphasizes – and this the postmodernists all recognize if they are not always in practice as wary of it as they announce in theory – is that language is a treacherous medium in which to work, which will betray both itself (as artifice) and our purposes (by falling short of them) eventually. Following Derrida, then, the task that confronts us is choosing the better form of betrayal (see Linstead, 1993). This responsibility is not an easy one to discharge – for Derrida it more or less encapsulates the human predicament – so the analysis I offer here makes no grand claims to offer solutions in reconciling oppositional forms of analysis. But I hope it will make the choices clearer.

Rhetorical analysis and management and organization studies

Rhetorical analysis has received increased attention in the social sciences over the past two decades. Defined broadly as persuasive language, an inescapable component of human argument, it weaves a texture of fact and metaphor, constructed within logical and narrative frameworks (McCloskey, 1988). Considered as 'the science of argumentation conceived of as contextual persuasion rather than formal proof or abstract demonstration' (Nelson, 1987:

209; Leith and Meyerson, 1989) it has become a central concern for some economists critical of the lack of reflexivity in economic studies regarding the ways in which economic argument achieves its effects (Henderson, 1982; Henderson et al., 1983; Klamer and McCloskey, 1988; Klamer et al., 1988; McCloskey, 1985, 1990). The rhetorical nature of the wider human sciences has been considered (Brown, 1989; Nelson et al., 1987; Simons, 1989, 1990) and the concept of 'rhetorics of enquiry' (Angus and Langsdorf, 1993; Nelson et al., 1987) has also encompassed the natural sciences including mathematics (Myers, 1985, 1991; Rorty, 1987) and the process of reasoning itself (Brown, 1987). In general the concentration has been on the more formal styles of argumentation adopted in scientific or social scientific writing (Schwegler and Shamoon, 1991).

Although some attempts have been made to relate rhetoric as persuasion to oral argumentation, or 'talk', in the study of politics (Nelson, 1987: 209), and Brown (1989: 123–70) discusses the consequences of rhetorical analysis for formal organization and social planning, there have until recently been relatively few attempts to examine how rhetoric works as part of the process of meaning construction in and around organizations, especially when organizational meaning itself 'goes public'. Exceptions to this are several contributions to Czarniawska (1995), especially her introduction which maps the field incisively, and Watson (1996), who illustrates through a serendipitous field occurrence how rhetorical functions may be performed by inarticulate and overtly non-persuasive attempts at utterances, grunts or even silences. Important here also is the unfortunate distinction which Czarniawska-Joerges notes that is commonly made between rhetoric and reality, or talk and action – the former being mere surface appearance or verbiage, form rather than substance. Even Legge (1995), whose work on rhetoric is otherwise ground-breaking in the field of human resource management, is not immune from making this popular distinction.

Although much of the literature on organizational culture considers stories to be an important part of the creation and transmission of such cultures (Boje, 1995; Martin, 1982; Wilkins, 1983, 1984) the emphasis is overwhelmingly on types of story and how they are deployed symbolically rather than on the rhetorical features of such stories and their significance as discursive practices. Despite also the recent resurgence on an emphasis on metaphor (Grant and Oswick, 1996; Putnam et al., 1996), this relative neglect of rhetorical processes is particularly odd if we consider the widely acknowledged significance of oral communication, from the transmission of information and preferred meanings in everyday transactions to the evangelical deliveries of visions and missions, in most studies of management after Mintzberg (1973; Hales, 1993; Thomas, 1993).

Managerial rhetoric and textures of meaning

Nevertheless, this neglect is relative and not absolute. Signal contributions from the work of Gowler and Legge (1981; 1983; 1996) provide both the earliest and most thorough application of the theory of rhetoric to an organizational context through the examination of supervisory story-telling and managerial argumentation. For them, rhetoric is

the use of language to
a) justify and legitimize actual or potential power and exchange relationships;
b) eliminate actual or potential challenges to existing power and exchange relationships

and, at a deeper level
c) express those contradictions in power and exchange relationships that cannot be openly admitted, or, in many cases, resolved.
    (Gowler and Legge, 1981: 245)

They observe that management is an oral tradition and that managers are members of a self-defining species. As such, managers frequently communicate to themselves and each other as a collectivity in negotiating and establishing their subjectivity, their distinctiveness as a collective, and the nature of the managerial enterprise. They generate managerial cultures, maintain and transmit their significant symbolic and structural features, and even produce their own rationality (Czarniawska, 1997; Czarniawska-Joerges, 1992, 1993). In the process they also change, develop and extend meanings according to the purpose in hand, expanding the indexical scope of managerial talk (Manning, 1971). They often espouse a speech style which is unadorned with tropic embellishments, elaborate constructions or ambiguous or evocative language, concerned with fact rather than persuasion (plain speaking) yet adopt a style which on examination is anything but plain (rhetoric) whilst attempting to give the appearance of plain speaking (see also Simons, 1989: 3; 1990). This feature is especially prominent in public accounts of managerial action.

In the earliest of their seminal contributions to the study of rhetoric and organization Gowler and Legge (see Figure 10.1) identify a reciprocal relationship between the *linguistic* determinants of rhetorical categorization and its *social* determinants, which recognizes, with Foucault and at a perhaps more ontological level, Derrida, the inseparability of power and language. Linguistically and socially meanings can be clear and *differentiated* (that is to say brought into the foreground of our knowledge and usually well understood) or unclear, inconsistent and *undifferentiated* (pushed into the background of knowledge and poorly understood). This is not inconsistent with deconstructionist arguments about undecidability – it recognizes that although it may be in the nature of language to be undecidable in any final sense, language at work is capable of conveying consistent and determinable meanings in most situations (Linstead, 1984, 1993; Norris, 1990).

When the background of assumptions upholds what is verbally explicit, meanings come across loud and clear. Through these implicit channels of meaning, human society itself is achieved, clarity and speed of clue-reading ensured. In the elusive exchange between explicit and implicit meanings a perceived-to-be-regular universe establishes itself precariously, shifts, topples, and sets itself up again. (Douglas, 1975: 4 – emphasis in original)

Linguistic Discrimination

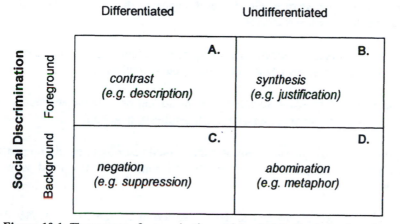

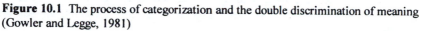

Figure 10.1 The process of categorization and the double discrimination of meaning (Gowler and Legge, 1981)

Gowler and Legge (1981) argue that the interaction of social and linguistic features gives rise to four *textures of meaning*: contrast, synthesis, negation and abomination. The differentiated textures of contrast (foreground) and negation (background) represent digital communication, functioning by means of sharp descriptive distinctions in the former case, by suppression or denial in the latter. Meaning is on/off, either/or. In the undifferentiated case of synthesis (foreground) and abomination (background), analogical communication is represented by ambiguities which blur the boundaries of digital communication but also intervene in the gaps and interstices which it leaves. Multiple meanings, ambiguous words, phrases and symbols are deliberately used to lubricate communication, to bend, deflect and conflate meaning on a more/less dimension. Shades of meaning and *double entendres* are common. Synthesis is exemplified by justification, abomination by metaphor.

Similar distinctions are made by Cooper and Fox (1989: 247) in distinguishing between control and nomadic modes of organization, following Bohm's (1980) discussion of the implicate and explicate orders in the physical world (Morgan, 1986: 233–4). The argument that the visible forms and structures of the organized world emerge from the flux of the world-in-process, elements of which can be found in philosophy from Heraclitus to Deleuze, complements the distinctions made by Gowler and Legge and further alerts us to the promissory dimension of rhetoric – that meaning in any utterance is always *at stake* (Goffman, 1959). Rhetorical forms are not always attempts to impose a predetermined structure on the world, but are just as frequently ad hoc attempts to keep interest at play in emergent situations, in order to stay in touch with whatever may develop.

The management of meaning: accounts and ideology

In the first of their studies, Gowler and Legge (1981: 269) identify three independent functions of rhetorics:

i   *Attributions* made by leaders in conditions of extreme uncertainty (contrast and synthesis, possibly negation but foreground emphasis)

ii *Cautionary tales* used to socialize new personnel or introduce outsiders to the nature of the organization (contrast, synthesis, negation)

iii *Myths* that permit the statement of 'what would be difficult to admit openly and yet what is patently clear to all and sundry that the ideal is not attainable'.

This typology is complementary to the discussion of Lyman and Scott (1970), who additionally distinguish between explanations and accounts, an account being for them:

> a linguistic device employed whenever an action is subjected to valuative enquiry. Such devices are a crucial element in the social order since they prevent conflicts from arising by verbally bridging the gap between action and expectation. Moreover, accounts are 'situated' according to the statuses of the interactants, and are standardized within cultures so that certain accounts are terminologically stabilized and routinely expected when an activity falls outside the domain of expectations. (Lyman and Scott, 1970: 112)

An account as defined here might therefore be as brief as 'It was an accident' or 'I was only joking' (Emerson, 1969). Even explanations will in part possess some of the qualities of an account, as in their presentation they will usually attempt reflexively to account for their own history and present, their existence and necessity. By implication they will also need to cope with their own contradictions. Additionally they will have an interest in setting the pattern and parameters for future occasions when accounts may be necessary, when excuses or justifications of action are called for, or in setting the conditions for avoiding having to give accounts in the future.

Lyman and Scott's discussion implies a degree of separation between plain speaking (explanation) and rhetoric (accounting), yet we have so far argued for their interpenetration. Elsewhere, Gowler and Legge (1983) also address the issue of this practically blurred relation by distinguishing between the meaning of management (intentional meanings comprising the *techno-social* order) and the management of meaning (the implicational meanings comprising the *moral-aesthetic* order). The former, they suggest, exist on the surface level, the latter at a deeper level. They argue that the boundaries between the two are deliberately blurred by rhetoric, in order for managerial activity to achieve easier, and apparently more 'objective', justification:

> the rhetoric of bureaucratic control conflates management as a moral order with management as a technical-scientific order, whilst submerging the former ... and contributes to management as a political activity concerned with the creation, maintenance and manipulation of power and exchange relations in formal work organizations. (Gowler and Legge, 1983: 199)

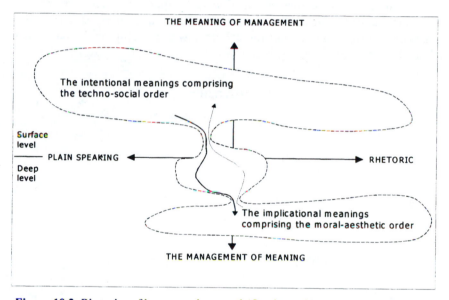

Figure 10.2 Rhetorics of bureaucratic control (Gowler and Legge, 1983/1996)

Discrimination and rhetorical forms

It is now possible for us to combine some of the features of both of Gowler and Legge's papers discussed so far into one diagram, which will illustrate their interconnection. Figure 10.3 superimposes some of the elements of the attribution of meaning and the discriminatory process with the management of meaning and identifies the emergence of particular rhetorical styles. For example, where the meaning of management is foregrounded, with the emphasis on digital communication and thus contrast, we would expect that explanations would be the dominant expressive form achieved through the 'plain-speaker's' recourse to fact, logic and rationality. This emphasis on the features of the techno-scientific order produces what I have called a *scientismic* rhetorical form. If we maintain our emphasis on the meaning of management in the foreground, but move into a more emphatic rhetorical mode with the analogical form of expression, we find that synthesis and justification become dominant. Cautionary tales, where the partial and local comes to signify the whole system, are the typical means of communication in what I have called the *metonymic* rhetorical form. If we background the meaning of management in favour of the management of meaning, then the blurred boundaries of analogical communication produce functional accounts, stories which operate through abomination or the creation of silences, and which employ mythic and symbolic expressions within the *metaphoric* rhetorical form. Where the management of meaning remains the concern, but plain-speaking and digital forms of communication predominate, then the dominant texture of meaning will be the more blunt one of negation and suppression, and the form of expression adopted will be that of assertion. This mode, given as it is to one-dimensional exaggeration, typically delivered with a thump on the boardroom table, I have termed the *hyperbolic.*

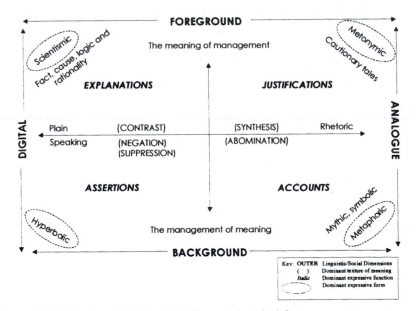

Figure 10.3 Socio-linguistic discrimination and rhetorical forms

Ideology and control

As we have seen, for Gowler and Legge the management of meaning is not a rational but an ideological process, and as such frequently involves appeals to the 'right to manage' (Golding, 1980a, b, 1991; Storey, 1981, 1983). This is so especially in conditions where managerial authority is being eroded, or where division and conflict are seen to undermine attempts to establish 'corporate culture' (Young, 1989). Salaman (1979: 199–212) identifies five 'ideologies' at work in sustaining and legitimating managerial control. These 'ideologies' can also be understood as themes which emerge in managerial rhetoric, which may complement each other, as a common stock of reinforcing discursive resources upon which managers draw according to their perception of the occasion. The first of these themes, *structuralism,* emphasizes organization as an outcome of politically neutral management principles, functional necessities and achievement based on merit. *Psychologism* develops this theme and relates organizational performance to individual responsibility and behaviour, with the application of 'scientific' or objective and neutral assessment procedures arbitrating who rises and falls within it. *Consensualism* sees division and differentiation as necessary to the pursuit of organizational goals and attributes organizational survival to the existence of an underlying broad consensus about these goals and the means of achieving them. Conflict is recognized only as an aberration, a product of mischief or miscommunication, and is remedied either by punishment or better internal information flows. *Welfareism* offers the velvet glove, seductively binding members to the organization through apparent concern for their happiness and contentment, having an obvious connection to the corporate culture approach and its antecedents. The last of these themes, *legalism,* emphasizes the contractual basis of the employment relationship, and seeks to exploit implied member consent to the legitimate authority of those who manage.

In a slightly different but complementary approach, Ray (1986) concentrates less on the rhetorical themes but more on the types of control which they may be said to express. The early twentieth century was dominated by *bureaucratic control,* where tight specification of tasks, performance reward and regulation of behaviour led to improved performance. The years following the Second World War were dominated by *humanistic control,* in which welfaristic practices and the provision of a pleasant and supportive work environment were held to lead to improved productivity. From the 1980s, *cultural control* emerged which attempted to engender a love of the organization and its goals, a collective feeling of belonging, which would lead to improved performance. A fourth type of control, *subjective control,* has effectively been added by the work of analysts such as David Knights who observe how the individual becomes a 'self policing subject' through the operation of a combination of subtle techniques of surveillance and pervasive discursive positioning. In what follows I extend these analyses by expanding both the consideration of types of control and their rhetorical forms, and the possibilities presented for resistance, but first it is necessary to consider the additional dimensions to the understanding of 'discourse' presented by neo-Foucauldian analysis.

Rhetoric and discourse

Before developing our argument further it is necessary to clarify the relationship between rhetoric and other associated concepts, particularly that of discourse, a concept prominent in the work of Michel Foucault (1972) which as we have indicated has influenced a school of neo-Foucauldian organizational analysis. In a general sense, a *discourse* can be any regular and regulated system of statements, and discourse analysis therefore would properly focus upon the relations within the system. Foucault directs our attention beyond the system of rules governing the discourse internally, to relate them to the conditions of power and knowledge which influenced not only the form of the discourse, but which favoured its appearance at a particular point in time rather than an alternative, and its specific relations with other forms of discourse as it changed over time. What a discourse does, then, is structure the rules and procedures by which different forms of knowledge are determined. Further, it defines different fields of understanding as legitimate objects of that knowledge. Foucault, for example, studies illness, madness and criminality as examples which define the boundaries of the normal, healthy, sane and honest. Within these fields, the discourse will also establish relationships between repertoires of concepts which in the case of madness, for example, might include somatic (symptom-oriented) or therapeutic procedures as appropriate responses to specific types of illness signified by particular behaviours. The discourse also determines criteria for the establishment of acceptable 'truth' and the creation of 'truth-effects', and further delimits what can and cannot be said, the normal, the abnormal, the standard and the deviation and hierarchizes the field of these relations. It also opens up discursive spaces or *'subject – positions'* to which it both tries to lay claim and offers to recipients through *inter-pellation* (an implicit invitation to take them up).

Discourse is not dominated by language alone. The argument of discourse analysis is not that words determine reality. It does, however, recognize that 'the practices which constitute our everyday lives are produced and reproduced as an integral part of the production of signs and signifying systems' (Henriques et al., 1984: 99). There is no world which exists entirely outside the forms of its representation, otherwise it would not be knowable, in which sense Derrida's controversial statement 'il n'y a pas de hors texte' (there is nothing outside the text, or there is no outside-text) only reiterates Kant. World and text, reality and representation, are interconnected, irreducibly interpenetrable, but not coterminous (Selden, 1991: 59). Discourse therefore also relates to non-discursive practices and these are an important focus for discourse analysis. A *discursive formation* then will be identified by defining 'the system of formation of the different strategies that are deployed in it', by showing 'how they all derive ... from the same set of relations' (Foucault, 1972: 68).

What then is the difference between a discourse and a *text*? Fairclough (1992) argues that discourse analysis links the systematic analysis of spoken or written texts to systematic analyses of social contexts, taking into account formative contexts and extra-discursive effects. Textual analysis in his view strengthens discourse analysis, subsuming linguistic analysis and intertextual analysis. Where linguistic analysis shows how texts selectively draw upon, rely on, or exploit *linguistic systems*, intertextual analysis shows how they draw upon *orders of discourse* which are the particular configurations of conventionalized practices (genres, discourses, narratives etc) which are available to text producers in particular social circumstances. (Fairclough, 1992: 194)

This also involves conscious or unconscious drawing upon other texts, so that the text is itself an *intertext* (Barthes, 1977; Calás and Smircich, 1991; Linstead and Grafton-Small, 1992). Thus a discourse may relate specific features of several individual texts, while any individual text may draw upon several discourses, and several other texts. Fairclough's (1992: 195) contention is that 'the linguistic and intertextual heterogeneity of texts ... is a particular feature of periods and areas of intense social and cultural change' or as Jean Baudrillard might put it, a condition of hyper-reality.

What then is the relationship between text, discourse and rhetoric? Rhetoric is a feature of texts, which may or may not be rhetorical.[1] In meeting their rhetorical, or persuasive, objectives, texts will draw on the sort of linguistic features which have been identified by rhetoricians since Aristotle. They will also draw on one or more discourses which warrant the truth of their arguments. Specific rhetorics, such as the rhetoric of bureaucratic control identified by Gowler and Legge, will emerge to effect the link between particular discursive fields (e.g. the moral-aesthetic and the techno-social). A rhetoric of ethical control, as another example, could be posited as effecting the link between the moral-aesthetic and the socio-political, and several other examples are possible, as we shall demonstrate. Rhetorics of control are not the only possible forms of rhetoric, as rhetorics of resistance or emancipation also exist. Importantly however, *rhetoric is the means by which closure is attempted over the spaces between discursive fields*, usually in the direct or indirect furtherance of a political object.

What I now want to consider is the expansion of the concept of discursive fields and their linkages, which provides the basis for the identification of other rhetorics of control.

Rhetorics of bureaucratic and social control

Gowler and Legge, as we have seen, have emphasized that rhetoric elides the distinctions between discursive fields. Working broadly along one diagonal of their diagram (Figure 10.5), we can see that the 'moral-aesthetic' field is that which ontologically privileges *idealism* and orients itself towards issues such as truth and beauty through the use of implicational meaning. The *realist* approach of the techno-social order, constructed through intentional and purposeful meaning, orients toward 'objective' organizational, commercial and economic interests, whether bowing to the laws of physics or the logic of the market. The rhetoric of bureaucratic control, when successful, collapses them into each other such that a moral burden of rectitude is imported into practical arrangements, which are not just necessary, but constructed as virtuous and proper too - indeed beautiful in the sense that they are a form to be reproduced and hence desired.

Linguistic Features	Textual Strategies	Rhetorical Themes	Discursive Resources	Discursive Fields
e.g.		(characterization)	(ideologies)	
Classical forms		Hierarchy	Structuralism	Moral-aesthetic
Description	Address	Accountability	Psychologism	
Narrative		Achievement	Consensualism	Techno-social
Metaphor	Argument	(membership)	Welfareism	.
Synthesis		(masculinity)	Legalism	
< ---------------	------------------	*Mystification*	------------------	*r* ------------- >
				h *p*
				e *r*
< ---------------	------------------	*Play*	------------------	*t* ------------- >
				o *o*
				r *c*
< ---------------	*Symbolic*	*Resources*	*Of Context*	*i* ------------- >
				c *e*
				a *s*
				l *s*

Figure 10.4 Features in the analysis of the rhetoric of management control

(*Sources*: Burke, 1969; Fairclough, 1992; Gowler and Legge, 1981, 1983; Leith and Meyerson, 1989; Salaman, 1979)

But what would happen if we chose to link the other two discursive fields that we have identified in the neglected quadrants of the diagram? What kind of rhetoric would result? At one end of the diagonal, the sense of a natural order is conveyed through common-sense assumptions and meanings oriented towards individuality, personality and practicality, with a sense of getting through the day with whatever is at hand. At the other end of this plain-speaking *naturalism* we find a more rhetorical *collectivism*, where negotiated meanings are contested and worked through to produce a politico-social order, oriented towards the law, government, power and the civil collective interest.

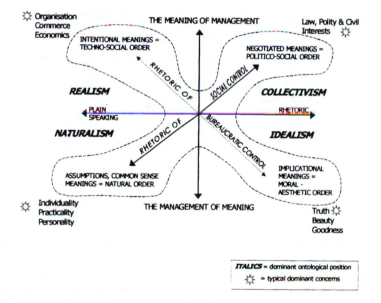

Figure 10.5 Rhetorics of bureaucratic and social control

The rhetoric of *social control*, the expression of the civilizing process identified by Freud, links the individual to the collective, despite the fact that individual freedoms are frequently sacrificed for the perceived public good, both by implying that this is best for everyone *and* that it is natural, common-sense to be so persuaded. Both rhetorics may work together – indeed because social life is intertextual we expect several rhetorics to be in play simultaneously. In Thatcherism, for example, the specific constructions of the rhetorics of bureaucratic and social control served to attempt a moral elevation of the pragmatics of business and corporate interests, whilst deploying the ideology of the common individual and their freedoms to mask increasing social intervention by the government. In any particular period, the forms of the same rhetorics will be characteristically different and their relative weight will form a distinctive relation.

We could simplify our previous diagram and perhaps illustrate the point further by considering the identities of specific rhetoricians who might speak from the four quadrants – or epistemological spaces – we have identified, although unless they are attempting to bridge the quadrants they are more properly to be regarded as ideologues rather than rhetoricians.

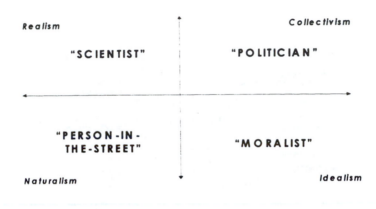

Figure 10.6 Typical rhetoricians

The ideal-type speaker of the idealist quadrant would be the *moralist*, opposed in the realist quadrant by the more objective *scientist*; while the *person-in-the-street* would talk plainly from the naturalist quadrant, opposed by the oratory of the *politician* from the collectivist pole. Here I am deliberately using popular stereotypes for the purpose of illustrating the argument more clearly, and I won't therefore pause to debate the varieties of orientation around each pole – such as the empirical varieties of science in action. I am taking this rather simplified time out to crystallize what we have discussed so far because I am about to explore the rhetorical implications of the other possible vectors on the diagram, and thus make the scheme considerably more complex.

More rhetorics of control

As I have hinted, the possibilities of formation of discursive fields are not fully captured in considering them as only being formed at the extremes of the diagonals of the diagrams we have so far considered. Indeed I would like to propose that they can usefully be represented as also being formed along vectors which link the midpoints of the vertical and the horizontal, and also by vectors which do not cross the centre point of the diagram, but travel along the sides. In making this move, however, I should draw attention to the importance of Gowler and Legge's device of using dotted wavy lines to indicate the constant blurring and shifting, formation and collapse of meaning and the loose and ambiguous nature of what might appear to be linear relationships. For the sake of clarity I will drop this device from this point, but we should remember that its caveats still apply – these representations, however useful, can only ever bear a loose relationship to the flux of reality.

Turning to the vertical and horizontal axes, we find positioned somewhere between plain-speaking and rhetoric the mild *rhetoric of humanistic control* which Ray (1986) implied; and somewhere between the foreground and the background, depending on how strong the culture is, the *rhetoric of linguistic/symbolic control*, which equates to Ray's idea of cultural control. In the former, the techno-social and the politico-social orders merge in the formation of organizational functions, whilst the natural and moral-aesthetic orders merge in the concept of personal skill. What the rhetoric of humanistic control did, as Ray and other commentators note of the Hawthorne studies and the post-Hawthorne Human Resources movement, was to elide the poles and make personal skills and attributes merge with organizational functions, turning the former into human capital and the latter into an apparent avenue for human growth and self-actualization. The rhetoric of linguistic/symbolic or cultural control bridges between the objective manifestations of that which is shared but perhaps on the borders of articulation, such as behaviour, ritualized patterned actions, even the artefacts produced by that behaviour and the more subjective dimensions of belief and values. Culture thus becomes a consistent continuum of behaviours that are similar, and hence become good, because beliefs and values are shared; and because beliefs and values are shared, behaviours will continue to be good. 'Strong' cultures will be further shifted towards the upper end of the vertical axis, 'weak' ones the lower.

Each of the two rhetorics discussed above can, however, be thought of as itself the midpoint between two more extreme outlying rhetorics. The rhetoric of humanistic control has both a more dehumanized variant, and a more spiritually elevated variant. The rhetoric of linguistic/symbolic control has a more personal and individualized variant, and a more technicized and disciplined variant. Let us now consider these more closely.

The *rhetoric of objective control* emphasizes the human being as a unit, with individual behaviour as the defining variable. At the one end of the continuum is alienation, the somewhat uncomforting demand that we just grit our teeth and get on with the job regardless of how unpleasant it is, because it is necessary. At the other end of the continuum is self-identity, where the individual naturally expresses who they are through the work they do, possibly, but not necessarily, with high intrinsic motivation as the options are not extensive – that is to say, the range of work available is a natural consequence of and determined by the prevailing state of affairs and the characteristics of the individual. In this rhetoric, the individual is caught between externally determined, but perhaps challengeable, necessity and natural inevitability. The greatest triumph of this rhetoric then, in its own terms, is to convince individuals that they are engaged in identity building activity when they are in fact engaged in its opposite, even to incorporate subjective difference into objective sameness, turning dehumanizing work into character-building process as the artificial arrangements of work become the natural order and the individual takes their proper place therein. F.W. Taylor's construction of the 'high-priced man' to persuade the Bethlehem steelworkers to perform to his principles is an example of this rhetoric at work.

The *rhetoric of altruistic control* sees alienation as neither natural, inevitable nor particularly functional. Here individuals become bound on the one hand to a social ideal of service, and on the other to an ideal of self-perfection. The rhetorical trick here is to apparently effect the latter through the processes of self-effacement that usually characterize the former, which is a fundamental characteristic of the Protestant ethic. In Reaganism, this rhetoric developed its quasi-religious elements explicitly to bind the right-wing 'moral majority' into its rhetoric of social control, and bolstered this with a more secular and social emphasis on self-control. Emotional labour is an example of this rhetoric at work, backgrounding the self in order to delight the customer, smiling in the most trying of circumstances.

The *rhetoric of self-control,* as we have observed, also links easily to the concept of self-perfection. The encultured attenuation of the individual urge to self-gratification found in linguistic/symbolic control here is individually internalized – the individual has become self-policing, self-governing with a greater/lesser degree of effectiveness and freedom. Professionals may be found toward the right hand side of this continuum, as one example, whilst at the other end the combination of self-identifying individuality and self-gratification creates a situation which is almost ungovernable. The situation much in the news in the UK in recent years, the predicament of professional football clubs with highly talented, highly paid players who are developing bad disciplinary records both on and off the field is a case in point. Paul Gascoigne, perhaps Britain's most talented soccer player for decades, after several years spent in and out of drying-out clinics and courts for violent behaviour, recently suffered the double ignominy of simultaneously being cited for unfair play and carried off injured, breaking his own arm trying to elbow an opponent in the face – ironically for the second time in his career.[2] Stan Collymore, another extremely talented star, has been thrown out of several football clubs who were unable to work with him because of his drinking, depressions and violent behaviour. Given a last chance by Leicester City, it took him 131 hours before he turned a fire extinguisher on guests at a hotel where the team were staying whilst on a training break in Spain.

The *rhetoric of technological control* jettisons the idea of the self-disciplining subject for discipline through the medium of technology. It spans the distance between the environmental determinism of assuming there is no other way to carry out the work as a disciplinary force, and the active need for surveillance, inspection and measurement of performance. Human behaviour and needs are subordinated to the demands of a technological system, and machines themselves may be used to monitor the degree to which the required adjustments of the human system are being made.

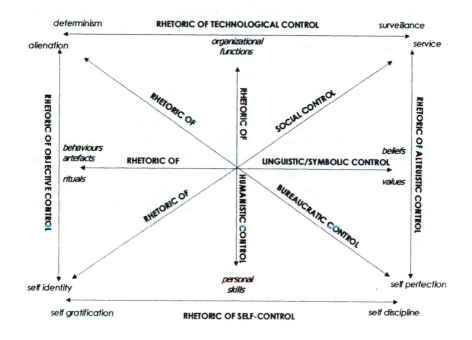

Figure 10.7 Other possible rhetorics of control

Technologies of power

Each of the rhetorics we have identified above, can of course be made the subject of critique. But the particular interest of the rhetorician is to examine how these rhetorics work in the first instance, and to use that as the basis for critique. Both Foucault and Derrida, in their different ways, allow us to examine closely *how* these rhetorics achieve their effects, and the *technologies of power* which they employ, in order to reveal these effects as effects, and not phenomena to be taken for granted.

The rhetoric of bureaucratic control, as Gowler and Legge demonstrated, works through a *technology of ideological power*. Through the mechanisms of accountability, used to monitor and control on a day to day basis; hierarchy as a means of structural control; and achievement, as a means of using the past to legitimate the present, the moral-aesthetic order is imperceptibly collapsed into the techno-social order, making the contingent, belief and interest-based appear to be natural and necessary. In a circular movement, because it is accepted as natural and necessary, the contingent finds its own moral justification – i.e. it becomes *right*. It becomes the only way for us to *become* that to which we must aspire. Often working in support of this, the rhetoric of social control works through the *technology of cultural power*. Here the socio-political and negotiated elements of culture, often negotiated in a context of considerable power differentials, are presented as consensual, and hence binding on individuals. A rhetoric here, rather than seeking to justify the benefits accruing to dominant groups in terms of the exercise of power, justifies them as a result of the workings of common sense, of individuals making their own decisions according to their own interests, acting collectively but out of a sense of self-interest. Disadvantageous differentials may be accepted then, from this perspective, because although we may all be individuals, we are all part of the same cultural collective, and believe in the same processes for achieving reward, advancement, enlightenment etc. Democracy, for example, might not be the perfect system, or even a Panglossian one, but it is the one we share and believe in.

The rhetoric of technological control links the intersubjective elements of social control – i.e. that our actions are available to the inspection and approval of our peers, regulated and condemned via a mechanism that appears to be consensual and rhetorically presented as such – with the deterministic elements of technology, which means that what technology *can* monitor, will be monitored. The continuum varies from the ever-watching screens of Orwell's *1984* to the peer surveillance of teams which may restrict or prevent restriction of output, and its social manifestations are represented in a variety of contemporary forms, from the Japanization of the production-line to the genre of 'real' TV in which the surreptitious observation of the general public – even to the point of the public doing it themselves – becomes entertainment. Nevertheless, the particular emphasis here is on the tying of the determinism of technology to the social, so this can also extend as far as the relations between *market* technologies (which are, in late capitalism for example, held to increase market efficiency and are hence both legitimate and desirable) and *political* systems (where for example in capitalism again, *democracy* is the most effective system for maintaining the appearance of equity and the level of trust that is necessary for market transactions to become efficient). Technological determinism, again represented in capitalism by the argument that we must move at the fastest pace of which we are capable, and typified by the growth of the Internet, becomes political determinism which makes representative democracy not just the preferred political system, but the necessary one, the one which new forms of organizing and doing business in a virtual world *demand*.

The rhetoric of objectification, or objective control, operates through what I have called the *technology of authoritarian power*. Here the bridging task of rhetoric is between the alienation of technological determinism and the self-identity of the subject. It achieves this at one end of the continuum by breaking

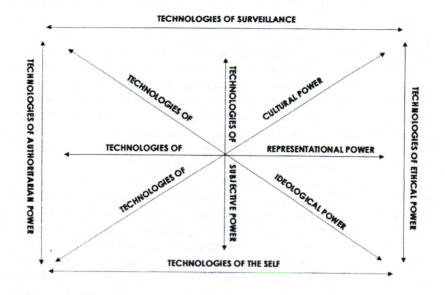

Figure 10.8 Lines of critique

the subject down into constitutive elements, defined in terms of their interface with technology – one is what one does, is defined by that, and indeed is regarded as a prosthesis of the technology rather than the other way round. At the other end of the continuum the role of technology dwindles – self-identity is a given, a common-sense category, taking the form 'I am what I am'. The role of authoritarian power then is to close the gaps that open up here by fiat, and if necessary by force. This is not necessarily problematic, as long as an alternate rhetoric of social control does not develop to organize resistance among these fragmented and subaltern selves. But self-identity can never be far from self-gratification, and the bottom left corner of the diagram, far from authoritarian strictures and social consensus, is its most anarchic, and where the self is most sovereign.

Selves, of course, are made subject by more than social or technologically based forces, and moving along the diagram the link is made again to the moral and ethical dimensions of such subjugation through the rhetoric of self control operating through what Foucault has so aptly described as *technologies of the self*. Here the self as given becomes increasingly unsatisfactory, and the subject must work to control, discipline and hence improve, and indeed, construct the self as a reflexive project. Along this continuum the emphasis is on mastery of the self, but as we link more with the moral-aesthetic this translates into self-perfection and betterment, and through the rhetoric of altruistic control, *technologies of ethical power*, which may be religious or secular, bind the self into a path of spiritual improvement increasingly through social performance in the service of others.

The two rhetorics which link the vertical and horizontal midpoints of the diagram are on the horizontal, where the rhetoric of linguistic/symbolic control works through *technologies of representational power*, and on the vertical where the rhetoric of humanistic control works through *technologies of subjective power*. Regarding the first, we are back to Gowler and Legge's distinction – which they admit is reversible and tentative – between plain-speaking and rhetoric, and the representational strategies which are employed at either end of the continuum can be thought of in organizational terms as on the one hand, the issuing of commands, and on the other, the quasi-religious discourses of many corporate culture initiatives which may be supported by multi-media representational capabilities. Regarding the second, here is where the individual is most fully incorporated into organizational objectives, where self-development is harnessed and channelled by organizational needs. The self, at the higher end of the continuum, develops in order to do the job required; at the middle, the self is developed more strategically to cover for future possibilities; whilst at the bottom, the disciplined self is more self contained and self reliant, prepared to put its skills at the service of the organization or indeed society as long as this suits its purposes, but prepared to move or resist if it does not. Rhetoric here operates to collapse the issue of individual identity into that of the organization, so that organizational requirements become, as far as possible, uncontested.

Final thoughts

The purpose of this chapter has not been to provide a model which is fully explanatory, but one which usefully maps relations and can enable developments of analyses which might tend to confine themselves normally to one area of the relational nexus to more readily bring other areas into focus. Gowler and Legge's early work opened up enormous possibilities for rhetorical analysis which have not yet fully been taken up. They concentrated on carefully exposing the workings of one form of rhetorical control, that of bureaucratic control, and devised a model for understanding the workings of rhetoric that can be applied to other rhetorics of control. By identifying these key features, they opened up a space for extending their model to identify other rhetorics of control which work alongside the rhetoric of bureaucratic control, and make up together the texture or nexus of a discourse of control that characterizes a particular social and temporal setting. What they did not emphasize was that their analysis of the rhetoric of bureaucratic control was characteristic of Western late capitalism. Capitalism, of course, has many forms; and there are other alternatives to capitalism. The key terms of bureaucratic control – achievement, accountability and hierarchy – would have very different forms in the kind of Communist system represented in the work of novelists like Kundera and Skvorecky, for example, and indeed achievement would hardly be recognizable at all. And yet, Aktouf (1996) provides an illustration of how close these two systems may in fact be in the criteria actually applied in performance appraisal and promotion decisions, rather than those which the systems profess are applied. But what is beyond argument is that some form of bureaucratic control is central to both systems.

In this chapter I have sketched in outline what other rhetorics may work alongside the rhetoric of bureaucratic control, and suggested that the relations between these rhetorics may also be both formative of and formed by prevailing discourse/s of control. There remains much work to be done, on the lines of Gowler and Legge, in identifying the key concerns or 'charter myths' of these other rhetorics, and in identifying the technologies through which they achieve their effects. At the macro-level, the relations between rhetorics and discourses remain to be fully explored. However, we need to be mindful that in common with other human communications, these rhetorics are messy, ambiguous, often unclear, contradictory and ever-shifting as Gowler and Legge constantly emphasize. They are also not homogeneous. So although this chapter has sustained Gowler and Legge's interest in control, not only are there other rhetorical fields awaiting further exploration – for example the rhetoric of emancipation – but elements of these other rhetorics can always be found within the intertext of the rhetoric of control. Finally, where concentration on linguistic forms in organization studies has often been criticized for taking a micro-approach which loses sight of the organizational level, reducing it to the interpersonal, it should be clear by now that rhetorical analysis is more than capable of moving both inward and outward, both in the direction of a deconstructive hermeneutics and of socio-political critique.

Notes

1 And as Watson (1996) points out, rhetoric may not be textual either.
2 Piling irony upon irony, an elbow to the face is now colloquially known as 'Gascoigne's kiss' and a cocktail has been given the same name because of its reputed quality of being able to render the drinker senseless in one movement.

References

Aktouf, O. (1996) 'Competence, symbolic activity and promotability', in S. Linstead, R. Grafton Small and P. Jeffcutt (eds), *Understanding Management*. London: Sage.

Angus, I. and Langsdorf, L. (1993) 'Unsettled borders: envisioning critique at the postmodern site', in I. Angus and L. Langsdorf (eds), *The Critical Turn: Rhetoric and Philosophy in Postmodern Discourse*. Carbondale and Edwardsville: Southern Illinois University Press. pp. 1–20.

Barthes, R. (1977) *Image-Music-Text*, trans. Stephen Heath. London: Fontana-Collins.

Bohm, D. (1980) *Wholeness and the Implicate Order*. London: Routledge.

Boje, D. (1995) 'Stories of the storytelling organization: a postmodern analysis of Disney as "Tamara-land"', *Academy of Management Journal*, 38 (4): 997–1035.

Brown, R.H. (1987) *Society as Text*. Chicago: Chicago University Press.

Brown, R.H. (1989) *Social Sciences as Civic Discourse*. Chicago: Chicago University Press.

Brown, R.H. (ed.) (1990) 'The postmodern in sociological theory'. A special section of *Sociological Theory*, 8 (2).

Brown, R.H. (1992) 'From suspicion to affirmation: postmodernism and the challenges of rhetorical analysis', in R.H. Brown, *Writing The Social Text*. New York: Walter De Gruyter. pp. 219–27.

Burke, K. (1969) *A Grammar of Motives*. Berkeley, CA: University of California Press.

Calás, M. and Smircich, L. (1991) 'Masquerade: organizational culture as metafiction', in P. Frost et al. (eds), *Reframing Culture*. London: Sage. pp. 311–26.

Cooper, R. and Fox, S. (1989) 'Two modes of organization', in R. Mansfield (ed.), *The Frontiers of Management*. London: Routledge. pp. 247–61.

Czarniawska, B. (1995) 'Rhetoric and modern organizations' in *Managerial and Organizational Rhetoric*, a special issue of *Studies in Cultures, Organizations and Societies*, 1 (2): 147–52.

Czarniawska, B. (1997) *Narrating the Organization: Dramas of Institutional Identity*. Chicago: University of Chicago Press.

Czarniawska-Joerges, B. (1992) 'Rationality as an organizational product', *Administrative Studies*, 11 (3): 152–62.

Czarniawska-Joerges, B. (1993) *The Three Dimensional Organization*. Lund: Studentlitteratur/Chartwell Bratt.

Douglas, M. (1975) *Implicit Meaning*. London: Routledge.

Emerson, J.P. (1969) 'Negotiating the serious import of humour', *Sociometry*, 32: 169–81.

Fairclough, N. (1992) 'Discourse and text: linguistic and intertextual analysis within discourse analysis', *Discourse and Society*, 3 (2): 193–217.

Foucault, M. (1972) *The Archaeology of Knowledge*. London: Tavistock.

Goffman, E. (1959) *The Presentation of Self in Everyday Life*. New York: Anchor Books.

Golding, D. (1980a) 'Authority, legitimacy and the "right to manage" at Wenslow Manufacturing Co.', *Personnel Review*, 9 (1).

Golding, D. (1980b) 'Establishing blissful clarity in organizational life: managers', *Sociological Review*, 28 (4): 763–82.

Golding, D. (1991) 'Some everyday rituals in management control', *Journal of Management Studies*, 28 (6): 569–83.

Gowler, D. and Legge, K. (1981) 'Negation abomination and synthesis in rhetoric', in C. Antaki (ed.), *The Psychology of Ordinary Explanations of Human Behaviour*. London: Academic Press.

Gowler, D. and Legge, K. (1983) 'The meaning of management and the management of meaning: a view from social anthropology', in M.J. Earl (ed.), *Perspectives on Management*. Oxford: Oxford University Press. pp. 197–233.

Gowler, D. and Legge, K. (1996) 'The meaning of management and the management of meaning', in S. Linstead, R. Grafton Small and P. Jeffcutt (eds), *Understanding Management*. London: Sage. pp. 34–50.

Grant, D. and Oswick, C. (eds) (1996) *Metaphor and Organizations*. London: Sage.

Hales, C.P. (1993) *Managing through Organization*. London: Routledge.

Henderson, W. (1982) 'Metaphor in economics', *Economics*, 18 (4): 147–57.

Henderson, W., Dudley-Evans, T. and Backhouse, R. (1983) *Economics and Language*. London: Routledge.

Henriques, J., Hollway, W., Walkerdine, V. and Venn, C. (1984) *Changing the Subject: Psychology, Social Regulation and Subjectivity*. London: Methuen.

Klamer, A. and McCloskey, D. (1988) 'Economics in the human conversation', in A.

Klamer, D. McCloskey and R. Solow (eds), *The Consequences of Economic Rhetoric*. Cambridge: Cambridge University Press. pp. 3–20.

Klamer, A., McCloskey, D. and Solow, R. (eds) (1988) *The Consequences of Economic Rhetoric*. Cambridge: Cambridge University Press.

Legge, K. (1995) *Human Resource Management: Rhetoric and Reality*. London: Macmillan.

Leith, R. and Meyerson, G. (1989) *The Power of Address: Explorations in Rhetoric*. London: Routledge.

Linstead, S.A. (1984) 'Ambiguity in the workplace'. Unpublished PhD thesis, CNAA/Sheffield City Polytechnic.

Linstead, S.A. (1993) 'From postmodern anthropology to deconstructive ethnography', *Human Relations*, 46 (1): 97–120.

Linstead, S.A. and Grafton-Small, R. (1992) 'On reading organizational culture', *Organization Studies*, 13 (3): 331–55.

Lyman, S.M. and Scott, M.B. (1970) *The Sociology of the Absurd*. New York: Appleton-Century-Crofts.

McCloskey, D. (1985) *The Rhetoric of Economics*. Madison, WI: University of Wisconsin Press.

McCloskey, D. (1988) 'The consequences of rhetoric', in A. Klamer, D. McCloskey and R. Solow (eds), *The Consequences of Economic Rhetoric*. Cambridge: Cambridge University Press. pp. 280–94.

McCloskey, D. (1990) *If You're So Smart: The Narrative of Economic Expertise*. Chicago: University of Chicago Press.

Manning, P.K. (1971) 'Talking and becoming: a view of organizational socialization', in J. D. Douglas (ed.), *Understanding Everyday Life*. London: Routledge. pp. 239–56.

Martin, J. (1982) 'Stories and scripts in organizational settings', in A. Hastorf and A. Isen (eds), *Cognitive Social Psychology*. London: Routledge. pp. 255–305.

Mintzberg, H. (1973) *The Nature of Managerial Work*. New York: Harper and Row.

Morgan, G. (1986) *Images of Organization*. London: Sage.

Myers, G. (1985) 'Text as knowledge claims: the social construction of two biologists' articles', *Social Studies of Science*, 15: 593–630.

Myers, G. (1991) 'Stories and styles in two molecular biology review articles', in C. Bazerman and J. Paradis (eds), *Textual Dynamics of the Professions*. Madison, WI: University of Wisconsin Press. pp. 45–75.

Nelson, J.S. (1987) 'Stories of sciences and politics: some rhetorics of political research', in J.S. Nelson, A. Megill and D. McCloskey (eds), *The Rhetoric of the Human Sciences*. Madison, WI: University of Wisconsin Press. pp. 198–220.

Nelson, J.S., Megill, A. and McCloskey, D. (1987) 'Rhetoric of inquiry', in J.S. Nelson, A. Megill and D. McCloskey (eds), *The Rhetoric of the Human Sciences*. Madison, WI: University of Wisconsin Press. pp. 3–18.

Nelson, J.S., Megill, A. and McCloskey, D. (eds) (1987) *The Rhetoric of the Human Sciences*. Madison, WI: University of Wisconsin Press.

Norris, C. (1990) *What's Wrong With Post-Modernism?* London: Harvester/Wheatsheaf.

Putnam, L.L., Phillips, N. and Chapman, P. (1996) 'Metaphors of communication and organization', in S.R. Clegg, C. Hardy and W. Nord, *Handbook of Organization Studies*. London: Sage.

Ray, C.A. (1986) 'Corporate culture: the last frontier of control?', *Journal of Management Studies*, 23 (3): 287–98.

Rorty, R. (1987) 'Science as solidarity', in J.S. Nelson, A. Megill and D. McCloskey (eds), *The Rhetoric of the Human Sciences*. Madison, WI: University of Wisconsin

Press. pp. 38–52.

Salaman, G. (1979) *Work Organizations: Resistance and Control*. London: Longman.

Schwegler, R.A. and Shamoon, L.K. (1991) 'Meaning attribution in ambiguous texts in sociology', in C. Bazerman and J. Paradis (eds), *Textual Dynamics of the Professions*. Madison, WI: University of Wisconsin Press. pp. 45–75.

Selden, R. (1991) 'The rhetoric of enterprise', in R. Keat and N. Abercrombie (eds), *Enterprise Culture*. London: Routledge. pp. 58–71.

Simons, H.W. (1989) 'Introduction', in H.W. Simons (ed.), *Rhetoric in the Human Sciences*. London: Sage. pp. 1–9.

Simons, H.W. (ed.) (1990) *The Rhetorical Turn: Invention and Persuasion in the Conduct of Inquiry*. Chicago: University of Chicago Press.

Storey, J. (1981) *The Challenge to Management Control*. London: Business Books.

Storey, J. (1983) *Managerial Prerogative and the Question of Control*. London: Routledge.

Thomas, A.B. (1993) *Controversies in Management*. London: Routledge.

Watson, T.J. (1996) 'Rhetoric, discourse and argument in organizational sense-making: a reflexive tale', *Organization Studies*, 16 (5): 805–21.

Wilkins, A. (1983) 'Organizational stories as symbols which control the organization', in L.R. Pondy, P. Frost, G. Morgan and T.C. Dandridge (eds), *Organizational Symbolism*. Greenwich, CT: JAI Press. pp. 81–92.

Wilkins, A. (1984) 'The creation of company cultures: the role of stories and human resource systems', *Human Resource Management*, 23 (Spring): 41–60.

Young, E.D. (1989) 'On the naming of the rose: interests and multiple meanings as elements of organizational culture', *Organization Studies*, 10 (2): 187–206.

PART 4

ORGANIZING SILENCE

11

Appropriating the Other in the Discourses of Comparative Management

Robert Westwood

Introduction

In this chapter I want to suggest that cross-cultural or comparative management/organization studies display some continuity with the knowledge/power strategies of the colonial project; in particular, the strategies of the appropriation and re-presentation of the Other. Such strategies have run a line from Napoleon's Egyptian 'encyclopaedia', through the dark machinations of orientalism, to the representation of the constructed imaginary of Japanese and Confucian management. In the case of Japanese management for example, the presentation has been driven by Western interests, and has primarily been an attempt to capture the threat of the interpolating otherness of a successful economy, and to transduce it into a form that is comprehensible and therefore manageable – to the West. In the process and along the way, what is actually being dealt with is a re-presentation of an imaginary and exoticized Japan.

The language of alterity was an inevitable part of the colonial experience and of anthropology, but it remains pervasive in comparative management. The Other is gazed upon, researched, measured and then re-presented in forms accessible, understandable and palatable to a Western audience. The language of comparative management seeks to represent the management systems of the Other. It pretends to an objective presentation of those systems, but it can only talk about them in a language informed by its own localized and historically situated ontologies, epistemologies and moralities. It is a Western (primarily US) perspective and interpretation. The re-presentation is a construction by Western researchers and theorists *for* a Western audience. The Other is re-presented as an imaginary, concocted through the interpretative strategies of a Western purview. The motive is to transduce the Other into something comprehensible so that the Western interlocutor can more efficaciously deal with the Other. Comparative management is a strategy in 'governmentality' through which the West apprehends, appropriates and incorporates the Other so as to, in one move, create the difference and make the difference manageable. Pragmatically it is a strategy that is designed to enable Western business to interact and compete more effectively with other business systems.

In these strategies and practices the West re-presents and positions the Other, in doing so the Other is constructed in particular ways. It has been extremely common to use essentializing language in so doing. This pretends to apprehend the Other in their totality and further to reveal their (hidden) true nature. The Other in some generalized form (say the 'Indian') is labelled and then various essentializing qualities and characteristics are attributed. The Other is captured in this homogenizing and totalizing language. This was a ploy at the heart of the discourse on race, but more latterly the language games around culture have trodden a similar track. Comparative management frequently accounts for the Other and their management systems in these essentializing ways, as we will see.

Another feature of the appropriating discourse of the West is to engage in practices in which the Other is re-presented in negative terms. The Other is depicted as deficient, backward, primitive or in other ways denigrated and diminished. It has been common for the colonial and neo-colonial discourse to depict the Other as suffering from a lack. This is, naturally, always in comparison to the West's plenitude. This chapter deals with the language of deficit as a pervasive device in the West's re-presentations of the Other, but more specifically in the comparative management discourse from Harbison and Myers (1959) to Hofstede (1991). A binary or set of binaries is frequently constructed, one side of which valorizes the West whilst the other denigrates the Other. A particularly common form of this in comparative management is to contrast Western principles of democracy and participation, which are said to inform management style and leadership, and to contrast this with the authoritarianism and autocracy of the Other. This chapter explores this binary and its pervasiveness in the comparative management literature.

The capacity to re-present and appropriate the Other in these ways is dependent on power/knowledge systems and practices. The early part of the chapter points to the massive dominance of the US in the discourse about management. It holds a hegemonic position with respect to this discourse, and polices it, not only through an intellectual imperialism but also through an extensive institutional apparatus constituted in and by the academy. There is a discourse and an apparatus here that works an inclusionary–exclusionary practice. The US-centred corpus marks out a discursive space that is defining, powerful and delimiting. Those outside are available to be scrutinized, captured and re-presented, but their participation is sharply circumscribed. Participation by the Other in this discourse is subject to their sublimation to the defined rules of the game, including ontological, epistemological and methodological ones. Those unwilling or unable to conform have their versions of management marginalized, massively attenuated or simply ruled out.

'Northern' science makes claims to truth and universalism, despite the fact that it is a particular, localized, historically situated form of knowledge (Harding, 1998). For a long time US management discourse functioned in splendid isolation, barely acknowledging the rest of the world. Its emissions were positioned as universalistic, it claimed to speak for all, whilst being constructed on the relevancies and understandings of a particular nature – those germane to the aspirations of a politically dominant champion of modern capitalism and a burgeoning economic rationalism. Even with the birth of comparative management and the inevitable acknowledgement of other management systems, the tendency to use the language of universalism did not recede. A particularly vital and formative version of such totalizing universalism driven by a specific politico-economic discourse was the convergence thesis. This proposed a particular trajectory for economic development which, it argued, was universally applicable to all states embarking on the industrialization/modernization pathway. These early positions markedly framed and continue to inform the comparative management discourse.

Ignoring and homogenizing the Other: the language of universalism and other exclusionary strategies in management discourse

Made in America: the hegemony of US management discourse

Management theory is a North American invention. The origins of a formal, theorized discourse about management and organization cannot really be situated anywhere other than the US at around the turn of the century. No other nation had deemed it necessary to make management[1] the subject of scholarly attention and bring its investigation into the academy. Since those origins US management theory has sustained a position of dominance both by carving out and policing the discourse about management and by providing an institutional frame which supports that project. The impact on the rest of the world has been profound and far-reaching. As Jamieson (1980: 16) puts it

management theory is largely an American artefact and has been heavily exported throughout the world by management consultants, American run or inspired management educational institutions and most powerfully of all, by successful American companies.

Harris and Moran (1991)[2] suggest the existence of a 'universal subculture of management'. This represents a new version of the convergence thesis, one no longer promoted in the grand terms of a global homogenization, but as a more localized and specific, sub-cultural assimilation. There is some sense in this argument given the overwhelming dominance of US-based management theory and its global promulgation through the education and mass media industries. Managers around the world are increasingly socialized, *qua* managers, via the machinations of US-centred MBA programs and the like.

At the institutional level, Boyacigiller and Adler (1991) have documented the dominance of US business schools and journals. Whilst the Harvard Graduate School of Administration was established in 1908 (Harbison and Myers, 1959: 105), the growth and impact of US management theory is mostly post-World War II. The influential journals of the *Administrative Science Quarterly* and the *Academy of Management Journal* were established in 1956 and 1958 respectively. The timing is not incidental since it mirrors the economic and political dominance of the US in the immediate post-war period and an explosion in its business activities, particularly on a new international scale. Despite these international concerns and the massive weight of research and writing emanating from the US management academic institutional apparatus, the thrust was, and remains, parochial and domestic.

The book publishing business is part of the institutional apparatus. US texts have, until recently barely acknowledged management practice, let alone theory, from outside. Accounts of the history of management pay scant reference to the rest of the world. For example, Holt (1993) makes a cursory reference to the longevity of management *practice* and the organizational competencies of past societies. His only reference to the pre-modern is a brief mention of the achievements of Rome and Athens. He immediately jumps from there to a resolutely Anglocentric account that begins with Robert Owen and segues through the usual suspects – Taylor, the Gilbreths, Gantt and Urwick. Occasionally, other texts acknowledge something outside of the Anglo-American tradition – a trivial reference to the organizational capacity signalled by the Great Wall of China perhaps, or the Mayan cities of Mexico and Guatemala. This neglect is apparent in Ronen's (1986) more scholarly comparative management text which, whilst referring to the trading practices of the Egyptians, Phoenicians and Greeks, really only begins the account in the 1500s with Columbus. There is no mention of China or anything east of Greece.

Contemporary texts make much of globalization and often provide examples of international business operations. However, the overriding aim is to draw the attention of would-be American managers to the fact of international competition and the 'development of a worldview that accommodates the marketing of products and services in other cultures' (Holt, 1993: 64). The motive is to appropriate knowledge of Others to put at the disposal of US business managers. Despite the global rhetoric and the illustrative material dealing with business practice outside of the US, there is barely any theory, model, concept or theorist that is not of Anglo-American origin.[3] Readers are sometimes made aware of cultural differences and shown examples of culturally informed differences in practice, but there is no presentation of a theoretical position from outside the Anglo-European corpus and no critique of the veracity, culture-boundedness or limitations of that corpus. The theory and language of management and organization remains unashamedly Anglo-American.

Adler's (1983) survey of business/management journals for the period 1971–1980 revealed less than five per cent dealt with cross-cultural or international issues. Godkin et al.'s (1989) and Peng et al.'s (1991) surveys showed little increase. A recent review of over 3,500 articles in 16 leading international management-related journals concludes that research in the field is: a) predominantly conducted by scholars from the US and a limited number of European countries, b) focuses on management issues in the US, Europe or Japan – or on generalized and deterritorialized conceptions, and c) draws overwhelmingly from sources published in the US or, to a lesser degree, from Western Europe (Wong-Mingji and Mir, 1997). This latter draws attention to the circular, self-referential nature of Western-dominated management discourse.

Speaking for the world: the language of universalism

As noted, until recently management texts barely acknowledged non-US theories, conceptualizations or, indeed, practice with respect to management. Either there was a wilful disengagement from any mode of organizing and managing outside of the US or an assumed universalism – either explicit or implicit. Universalistic claims for management theory and practice were present at the outset – for example in Burnham's *The Managerial Revolution* (1941). The universalist case was most forcefully put by the Industrialization thesis (Haire et al., 1966; Harbison and Myers, 1959; Kerr et al., 1960). It is a position that has continued, albeit in a more implicit or default fashion, down to today.

Various commentators (Boyacigiller and Adler, 1991; Lammers and Hickson, 1979; Osigweh, 1989) have noted management theory's assumed universalism. It has been challenged at one level on the grounds that theory construction itself is culture-bound. It is argued that the values and assumptions of the theorist will reflect those prevailing in the wider culture that he/she inhabits. Such values and assumptions will colour the perceptual and cognitive processes that the person brings to bear on the research and theory construction processes (Boyacigiller and Adler, 1991; Harding, 1996; Hofstede, 1980). This process was recognized by Merton (1968) in noting the influence of social structure and culture on scientific knowledge. Social structure and culture not only provide a specific focus but also 'enter into the conceptual phrasing of scientific problems'; a point echoed by Harding (1996). This phrasing includes the impact of the mythic elements of US culture such as the pioneer and the frontier (Prasad et al., 1997: 21). These in turn are manifest in values such as utilitarianism, pragmatism, rationality, self-reliance and independence, masculinity, aggressiveness which frame conceptions of business and management practice. The language of theoretic management discourse is imbued with these mythic and value-based elements.

Boyacigiller and Adler (1991: 278) conclude by suggesting that organizational science 'has become trapped ... within geographical, cultural, temporal and conceptual parochialism'. The US positions and promotes itself as at the centre, as keeper and protector of the knowledge and discourse about management. Research and theory from non-US countries are required to attenuate what they report and discuss with specificities of location and context. That is, research from, say Turkey, must specify the localized context of the research – in terms of economy, culture or other aspects of the social formation depending on the issue addressed. There is a requirement to provide caveats that place limits on the generalizability of what is reported: 'this may be true of the Turkish context, but that is all'. Papers dealing with research and theory emanating out of the US context are not so bound; there is no requirement for such contextual specificity. The findings are presented *as if they were universal in nature*.

Valorizing self and assertions of efficacy

Along with presumptions of universalism comes a valorization of the Western worldview and a belief in the efficacy and veracity of its methods. Prasad (1997: 295) contends that this is informed by Hegelian teleological conceptions of history under which the West has moved further along history's track towards a developed state and 'imagines the rest of the world to be fated to follow in the wake'. There is an accompanying assumption that the West's historical categories have universal applicability. This is inextricably linked to a view of Western science and its ontological, epistemological, methodological and ideological dominance. Even today some parts of the world are still viewed as 'living *laboratories* of mankind's past cultural stages' (Harris and Moran, 1991: 118, my italics).

At any point in time certain discourses and modes of representation assume positions of authority, dominance, veracity and legitimacy. They do so by claiming a privileged position – epistemologically, ontologically and often morally. Such positionings are clothed in a tropological framework that masks the will to power and elides the arbitrary and contingent nature of the claim. The language of culture and cultural difference provides a rich terrain upon which to parade such rhetorical and metaphorical practices. But such a claim to a privileged position rests on an exclusionary practice that denies the legitimacy, veracity and authority of other (and Others') claims. Western management discourse has accomplished such a positioning. It has achieved a closure (at least a partial and temporary one) under which alternate representations are seen as aberrant departures – cast out as irrelevant, marginal, circumscribed, particularized, illegible, confused or simply unintelligible. It is this project that Sardar (1985) refers to as the 'epistemological imperialism of the West'.

Chakrabarty (1992) refers to this trap of discursive dominance in the context of speaking on India's past. He notes that writing about India must always really be writing about the West since the West has dominated historical analysis and all claims to historical writing perforce get refracted through the cognitive/theoretic lens of the West. As he puts it,

> Insofar as the academic discourse of history ... is concerned, 'Europe' remains the sovereign, theoretic subject of all histories, including the ones we call 'Indian', 'Chinese', 'Kenyan'...There is a peculiar way in which all these other histories tend to become variations on a master narrative that could be called 'the history of Europe'. (1992: 1)[4]

Past social structures are accessed and assessed through the presents' most powerful and successful. Hence modernization, development and industrialization as categories of historical momentum constructed by the Western academy become the vehicle for any discourse about the past (and the future) of those – and what else can we say – less developed and pre-modern societies. Generations of Western historians, philosophers and sociologists have constructed their accounts in ways that claim universality, that claim to speak for all humanity – despite rank ignorance of large portions of that humanity. Recognizing that does not displace the dominant discursive place – it is there and remains – the issue is how to deal with it. The categories of that discourse are the ones available. Thus, India's history, claims Chakrabarty, has always been constructed within the categories provided in the first instance by the West. Often these are invidious binaries – such as despotic-constitutional, medieval-modern, feudal-capitalistic – within which India is always suffering a lack or deficit. The discourse of comparative management plays the same game. Other's management systems can only be discussed (sensibly and in an accredited space) in terms of Western categories and conceptualizations.

As we have seen, an institutional apparatus supports US hegemony with respect to management discourse. An 'intellectual technology' (Miller and Rose, 1990) of institutions and their practices, pedagogical practice, publishing institutions, the 'business' of management education, the methodologies of research, the orthodoxies of management theory and the practices that sustain them. The technology transduces phenomenon into information – research papers, reports, textbooks, training packages, statistics, graphs etc. – and allows the phenomena to be apprehended and controlled. This is akin to Foucault's notion of governmentality (Foucault, 1979a, 1979b) which has been applied directly to the practices of colonialism[5] and, I would argue, is still present in contemporary comparative management practice. Governmentality requires a system of surveillance and discipline, but this is not merely a mechanism for punishment and control, it is 'a procedure ... aimed at knowing, mastering and using' (Foucault, 1979a: 143). The observer, in this case a management researcher, comes to command a knowledge of the Other, and this knowledge is linked to systems of comparison and classification that positions the practices of the Other as inferior and in need of intervention and management. The Other – their management styles and systems – are observed, recorded, submitted to the West's 'intellectual technology', captured in codes and classifications, pinned down within an alien discursive space, and re-presented in information systems that are accessible to and comprehensible by the Western audience. This practice, at the same time, reaffirms the value and power of the appropriator.

Harris and Moran (1991) indicate the presumptive efficacy and legitimacy of the Western management system to intervene and modify the situation in foreign contexts – 'innovators [innovative international managers] may respect the established system [of the local culture], while working to bend or beat it to make it more responsive to satisfying human need' (Harris and Moran, 1991: 119). This paternalism and interventionism is again pervasive in the literature. The comparative management literature describes foreign management and business systems but always from within a Western theoretical frame and always with a view to enhancing Western business practice vis-à-vis those foreign economies.

Exclusion and marginalization

Contemporary Western management theories are constituted by abstracted and reified realities. Following a cannibalized conception of positivistic science, the discourse is radically de-contextualized from the relevancies and specificities of any concrete set of organizations or the people that populate them. This enables the theoretic treatment of management as 'unsituated' thereby bolstering the universality claims (Wong-Mingji and Mir, 1997: 354). More particularly, such theoretic representations are ineffably detached from the contexts constituted by the social differentiations of class, culture, ethnicity and gender (Nkomo, 1992). Only very recently has explicit attention been paid to the erasure of gender in organization theorizing (Calás and Smircich, 1991; Hearn et al., 1989; Martin, 1990, 1994; Mills and Tancred, 1992). Even more recent has been a turn to reveal the erasure of race and ethnicity (Cox and Nkomo, 1990; Holvino, 1996; Nkomo, 1992).

Nkomo (1992) points to the intellectual and professional marginalization of research and theory related to racial minorities, even within the US. Race is barred from serious inclusion as a major analytical category and is marginalized. Studies based on minority (or foreign) samples are rarely accepted for developing and generalizing organizational theory. Such results will be delimited and held to be only valid for that group. She argues that 'Western' knowledge is positioned as superior and universal, but goes further in stating that it is white males who define and police the discourse. Such claimed universalism rests on specific and limited samples – typically white, Anglo-Americans, frequently male dominated. The delimits placed on research on minority groups are not applied to this group. She agrees with Minnich (1990) who points to a fundamental error in such knowledge production wherein a process of faulty generalization occurs leading to non-inclusive universalization. Nkomo argues that such faulty generalizations and false universalism leads to a 'hierarchically invidious monism' (Nkomo, 1992: 489) where the dominant group define the discourses' parameters, police it and elevate themselves to positions of superiority. But, more importantly, in that move all other groups are positioned in a way that means they 'must be defined and judged solely with reference to that hegemonic category' (ibid.).

There is a relationship between the desire for universal theorizing and the suppression of others' experience (Nkomo, 1992). The claim for universality from within a domain that is actually limited and particular, is clearly an exercise of power, an act of inclusion–exclusion that carves out and occupies a discursive space. Non-Western scholars of management are held intellectual captives. All conceptualizations of management are perforce refracted through the intellectual lens of Western discourse and its knowledge/power nexus. Only those voices resonating with that hegemony are acknowledged, accorded legitimacy and given access to the fortress of institutional academia. Accounts, interpretations and theories from non-Western contexts failing to participate in the dominant game are condemned to silence or marginality. Those that do attempt to participate in the dominant discourse end up presenting a denatured, distorted representation of localized realities. Harding (1996: 498–9) maintains that modern 'northern' science is a historically achieved, particular, 'local knowledge system' (see also Harding, 1998; Wong-Mingji and Mir, 1997). A knowledge system that has pursued a vigorous inclusion–exclusion practice and whose dominance and claims to universality result from a knowledge–power practice in which European colonial expansion was fundamentally implicated. These practices involved acts of knowledge and information appropriation from the colonized that are transformed into modes amenable to the Western scientific purview. The dominant group, through the language of universality, appropriates and incorporates others and denies their difference and independent voice.

The positioning of dominance and claim to speak universally engenders various strategies. These include: a) incorporation, which drags the Other into the dominant discourse and causes a mis-representation of their worldview; b) refraction and filtering through the dominant discourse which entails a re-representation of the Other within the discursive space of the dominant group. This means that the Other is represented in a way that enables the dominant group to capture, lay out and make sense of the Other. It is an act of violent translation or transliteration. The Other is recast in the image of the dominant group in ways that make the Other accessible and comprehensible to the dominant group and potentially controllable by them. Finally, c) strategies of silencing and marginalization which repress and oppress the Other and deny the existence of any counterpoint to the dominant group.

Culture free? – Universalism in comparative management

In texts that address directly comparative management issues, assumptions of difference and similarity are, naturally, at the foreground. In these texts the Other has at least to be acknowledged. However, even in this part of the Western management discourse, universalistic aspirations are still evident, for example in England, Negandhi and Wilpert's (1979) influential text. The intention is clear at the outset when they declare that the aim of comparative management studies is to develop universals that apply everywhere. As they say 'the science of organizations seeks to establish propositions that apply universally across time and space' (p. 8). This reprises Sjoberg's (1970) argument that to study the effects of culture on management one must develop a culture-free classification system and identify the etic.[6] 'Certain invariant points of reference or universal categories are required which are not merely reflections of the cultural values of a particular social system' (Sjoberg, 1970: 25). The notion of universal categories of culture was at the heart of Parson's pattern variables.[7]

The culture-free hypothesis reached its nadir with the positivistic empiricism of the Aston studies (Hickson and McMillan, 1981; Hickson et al., 1974; Pugh, 1969; Pugh et al., 1968) which claimed value-free, objective measurements of organizations. However, as Jamieson (1980) points out, analysis is actually driven by an implicit theory or model of economic functioning and assumptions about organizational goals that are deeply rooted in the features of one economic system, that of modern European industrial capitalism. The Aston account cannot escape that framework and the language that goes with it. They attempt, in effect, to find a meta-language that avoids cultural specifics – avoids reference to particular countries or companies – by constructing abstracted categories, patterns or combinations of variables that can be objectively measured. It is similar to the Parsonian project in that regard. There is a claim to 'get outside' the language game, outside the concepts in terms of which we think about the world. Just as the Aston groups' analysis is in fact imbued with a particular understanding of economic systems and their organizations, so the categories of Sjoberg and Parsons are ineluctably informed by *particular* historical conditions that enabled the development of modern industrial capitalism. Indeed, Habermas, commenting on the universalistic and culture-free claims for the pattern variables notes that 'if one examines the list, one can scarcely overlook the historical situation of the inquiry on which it is based. The four pairs of alternative value orientations ... which are supposed to take into account *all* possible fundamental decisions, are tailored to an analysis of *one* historical process' (Habermas, 1972: 353). This depiction of Western knowledge and science as but one essentially local variant has gained ground in the post-colonial literature; it is captured admirably by Harding (1998).

Re-presenting the Other in comparative management

Tracking the emergence of the comparative management project is not easy. British and other European commissioners visited the US in the 1850s to report on the American 'system' of management and manufacturing. It is noteworthy that their analysis identified cultural factors as critically accounting for system differences (Sawyer, 1954). But these were not widely accessible reports. It was not really until the post-World War II period that academic attention focused on differences in management systems. Prior to that interest was focused more at the macro, abstracted and universalistic level of nomothetic economic theory. Indeed, much early US management theory was driven by nineteenth century economic theory of this type (Jamieson, 1980). The earliest formally comparative texts were those of Harbison and his colleagues (especially Harbison and Myers, 1959), but also Haire et al. (1966), Farmer and Richman (1964, 1965) and Kerr et al. (1960).

Another notable early contribution was the work of Abegglen (1958) in describing factory organization and management in post-war Japan. This is significant since it insinuates, right from the start, one of the West's pre-eminent Others at the centre of the discourse. It is Japan more than any other country that has had its business and management system pored over, represented, reconstituted and in other ways worked over by the West's management discourse. It is also with the Japanese that we encounter the most complex interstices of Western-Other discursive entanglements. This engagement has moved beyond simple appropriation and representation to more complex interrelationships of counter-position, turn and hybridity. We shall return to these issues subsequently.

The discursive space these texts shared at the time is certainly not coincidental. They entered a space already constructed by a triumvirate of interrelated projects. The first of these is a crystallization of anthropological concerns with culture in the work of Kluckhohn and colleagues (Kluckhohn, 1951b, 1962; Kluckhohn and Strodtbeck, 1961). This is highly significant. Firstly in view of the general, historical project of anthropology as an explicit confrontation with the Other. A project marked by modernist, rationalist attempts to categorize, explain and adduce to the knowing gaze of the West all exoticized 'Others'. Secondly, because comparative management expressly co-joins with that project in pursuit of culturalist explanations of differences in management phenomenon. Also of significance were those more ideographic anthropological concerns with personality and national character exemplified by Benedict's (1946) *Patterns of Culture.*

The second element of the discursive space is that constructed by the Parsonian functionalist project, particularly his theories of societal evolution and development and the role of cultural values in that (Parsons, 1951, 1977; Parsons and Shils, 1951). Parson's views on the functionality of cultural elements, especially values, in the constitution of stable social systems, have been foundational for many culturalist explorations of management systems differences. His position on social development precipitated a view of development that rests on assumptions of modernizing values and social formations that were ultimately Anglocentric and positioned non-Western societies as 'underdeveloped' – as being at various stages of the pre-modern and as suffering therefore from a deficit. The Parsonian pattern variables of culture and Kluckhohn and Strodtbeck's dimensionalizing of cultural values, are the direct foundations for successive constructions of general explanatory frameworks for culturally derived differences in management. Indeed, they have been the almost exclusive source for the most popular models in the comparative management literature such as Adler (1991), Hofstede (1980, 1991), Triandis (1982/3), Trompenaars (1993) and most recently Maznevski and DiStefano (1995) and Maznevski et al. (1993).

The third and closely related element was engendered in the debates around modernization, development and industrialization. This multi-disciplinary project was comprised of Western economists, sociologists and political scientists. Core constituents of this textual space included Bendix (1964), Inkeles and Smith (1974), Levy (1966) and Lewis (1955). A critical contribution was McClelland (1961) and his theories of how the psychologistic achievement need and motive varies across cultures with implications for economic development. Positions in these debates were formative of the more focused convergence thesis which postulated that as societies go along the path of development and industrialization they would converge to a commonality of structures, institutions, practices and even value sets.

What should not be forgotten is the analysis of Weber (1970a, 1970b) in his attempt to explore processes of rationalism and the emergence of industrial capitalism and bureaucratic organizational forms. Whilst not expressly comparative, Weber does provide commentary on other countries, notably China and India, constructing positions that have been part of a continued debate about the cultural, historical and institutional conditions for the emergence of these aspects of the social formation in the 'West' and inhibitions to their emergence in the 'East'. We will return to those debates later in the chapter.

This densely interwoven and heavily ideological discursive space was one that emergent comparative management studies entered and participated in. It is an intellectual legacy that continues to inform comparative management. Each of these will be considered either explicitly or implicitly, in what follows.

Positioning the Other: converging to the modern

A critical point in assessing the comparative management discourse occurs when one asks for what purposes it is constructed. The rhetorics of motive here are multiple and complex. They range across the varied terrain of the modernist project. First, as noted, comparative management is located in the developmental debates of the 1960s where the central question was 'why is it that certain nations/cultures have demonstrated an intractability in terms of embracing modernization and the march of contemporary industrial development?'. Answers appealed to aspects of political economy, but often included a culturalist analysis which suggested that the underdeveloped suffered under cultural systems not conducive to the requirements of the modernization-development process. A sub-text, though, is the West's desire to see modernization and development spread so as to incorporate underdeveloped nations into the world economy, make them participate in an uneven international division of labour, and make their resources available in a more controllable and systematic manner. It must be noted that the very idea of *development* was rooted in the colonial project. As Ludden (1992: 250) summarizes 'Development was linked in instrumental ways to the growth of the modern state, the preoccupations of colonial rule, and a general commitment to economic progress'. Colonial states needed to 'manage' their colonies and apply their own political economy regimes. Modes of production and productivity, revenue generation and collection, data collection, analysis and dissemination, and general administration are transported to the colonies. Disparities between the colonizers' conception and expectations of these issues of governmentability, and the perceived situation in the colonized locations, marks out the 'development' space. Put another way, the gap provides a rhetoric of motive for the discourse and practices of development.

An alternate or additional motive is that a process of incorporation reduces the uncertainties and threat posed by an alien Other. Here the motives may be psychological as well as pragmatic. As already noted, the Other has commonly been represented as a danger or threat. Appropriating and incorporating the Other is a mechanism for reducing this threat by representing the Other to Self in knowable ways.

A third motive concerns the old anthropological project of bringing the Other under the gaze of the Western scientific apparatus thus making it amenable to the machineries of categorization, tabulation and order. Anthropology was implicate in the colonial project. It provided the knowledge/power by which the Other could be represented in intelligible ways for the West. The colonial governments, their diplomatic armouries, and the trading bodies that represented the pragmatic interests of those governments, such as the East India Company, were able to deploy that knowledge/power so as to effect administrative control. This project is on-going; taken up by the paraphernalia of comparative management and international business. As Harris and Moran (1991: 24) put it 'Culture knowledge provides insights into people, so both managers and other professionals benefit when we understand both culture general and specifics to facilitate intercultural communication, client relationships, and productivity. .... Culture astuteness enables us to comprehend the diversity of market needs, and to improve strategies with minority and ethnic groups at home, or foreign markets abroad'. The 'we' is, of course, US corporations. Comparative and international management is also Western – and primarily US-centred. It too is rooted in a socially, politically and ideologically particular discourse glossed as universalistic. This epistemic history holds it captive and excludes any alternative discursive position the Other might proffer. As Prasad et al. (1997: 24) suggest, there is a deeply 'sedimented parochialism in international management'.

The incorporatist rhetoric had significant expression in the convergence thesis that worked at the same time and in the same discursive space. This posited that there were forces at work – not least of which were rationalism, industrialization and modernization – that would impel systems, and specifically modes of organizing economic activity, along a common trajectory (Harbison and Myers, 1959; Kerr et al., 1960; Moore, 1965). The industrialization thesis of Harbison and colleagues can be seen as the foundation for comparative management studies, configuring the discourse and the language within which the issues have been cast (Jamieson, 1980).

The convergence thesis was crystallized in the impactful *Management in the Industrial World: An International Analysis* (Harbison and Myers, 1959). The central argument is stated explicitly

> Industrialisation is an almost universal goal of modern nations. And the industrialisation process has its own set of imperatives: things which all societies must do if they hope to conduct a successful march to industrialism. This is what we call the logic of industrialism. (p. 117)

Early in the book they make a similar statement, but with vital additional elements 'The logic of industrialisation ... leads to uniformity rather than diversity among industrial organizations and organization builders' (p. 5). The last phrase is critical, since it asserts not only that economic systems and institutions are compelled down a path of uniformity, but persons are too. This is not just an industrialization imperative but also a managerialist imperative.

Harbison argues that for the requisite type of economic development, a cadre, indeed a class, of business owners and managers needs to develop. These people require capabilities, values, skills and even personalities that model those seen to be effective in the US. Haire et al. (1966: 15) make a strong case for this in arguing that training foreign nationals for business leadership is not merely a matter of 'injecting our techniques', but also '... help(ing) him to develop the whole view of life that goes with certain kinds of managerial philosophy. In a sense you can't make a manager without making a man'. This amounts to constructing the subjectivity of a group of people in 'developing' countries to whom can be accorded the label, status and identity of 'manager' – such accordance being granted by the West. This process is seen as part of the 'universal imperative' of the industrialization process (ibid: 39). The 'manager' is seen as displacing the old figures of authority within existing social systems – the head of the family, tribal chief, communal leader. As power and knowledge accrues to the management cadre within this new socio-economic order, they inevitably become '... an elite of brains. They become an intelligentsia' (ibid: 120).

So much weight is placed on the need to develop a managerial elite that it is argued that it should precede the tackling of universal education and a drive against illiteracy. This remarkable conclusion warrants a lengthy quotation:

> A substantial proportion of the community must be literate in any progressing society, but industrialisation does not require at the outset that the majority of peasants, factory workers, porters or servants have the rudiments of an education ... Resources need to be invested in appropriate institutions of higher education even at the expense of some delay in providing universal general education. (Harbison and Myers, 1959: 107)

They urge political leaders to persuade people that education is an *economic investment*, a driver of economic growth, and not a benefit that all community members should enjoy. Thus were sown the seeds of rampant economic rationalism and managerialism!

By interpolating this language of the universal imperative Harbison and Myers condemn as redundant, anachronistic, deficient and backward modes of organization and authority that do not fit with the industrialization and managerialist thesis. Inevitably they use a language reflecting this positioning of the Other in their analysis. They comment (1959: 33) on the inefficiencies of organizations and point to the wasteful expenditure of energy on '*illogical or non-productive* activities'. In the next sentence they imply that this is true of France where the businessmen are 'as much interested in using the firm as a means of maintaining or building the family name as in amassing a large fortune'. This is a language of deficit, a construction of the Other as being in lack and regressive relative to the industrializing West that has set up the standards, established the criteria and applied the judgements. A most critical aspect of this language of deficit reverberates around notions of shifts in power and authority and their associated structures. According to Harbison and Myers, industrialization amounts to the erosion of traditional relations and structures which are uniformly positioned as primitive, outmoded, authoritarian and deficient. We will tackle this representation of the Other in more depth shortly.

In similar vein, consider this quote from Farmer and Richman (1965: 41) – considered by many as the fathers of comparative management – 'There are only a limited number of rational ways to make steel and a country does not get output in this sector by *using prayer rugs, doctrinaire slogans or wishful thinking*' (my emphasis). Further, Japan's system is described as based on feudalism, paternalism and family rule. Terms such as primitive and illogical also pepper the text. Even European management systems were not protected from this incipient disparagement.

The industrialization thesis has strong structural-functionalist inclinations and the debt to Parsons is overt in places. This opens up another realm of representation and appropriation. It is argued, for example, that

> The reorganization of society (from non-industrial to industrial) can be analysed in terms of four of Parson's pattern variables. The thesis advanced here is that an increase in universalism, achievement, suppression of immediate emotional release (affective neutrality) and specificity all accompany industrialisation in the long run. (Theodorson, 1953: 481)

The language of convergence and industrialization also demands, therefore, that the values and behaviours of the Other change in line with Western expectations. This citation of Parsons is significant given that the analytic categories have been deployed consistently in the comparative management discourse. They have been accorded empirical referent status such that comparative studies have pursued differences on these categories. They are apparent, as indicated earlier, in most of the leading attempts to discuss and/or measure and dimensionalize culture in management theory.

The convergence thesis presumes this effect on values and behaviour, but also suggests more macro-level effects in terms of urban drift, mobility, changes in occupational structure and thus class structures, and ultimately changes in the role of the State. The trajectory of these effects appears to be from the introduction of technology as the driver of industrialization, and thus to the macro-level changes (see Theodorson, 1953: 481). As Jamieson (1980) suggests, the chief criterion of *techne* is efficiency and it is this predominant instrumental value of efficiency that is the principal force for change. Jamieson and other detractors of the industrialization thesis have argued that the changes it is said to bring are not inherent in the process and that it has no definite social effect, including no *necessary* efficiency imperative (Blumer, 1960; Nash, 1966). There is no universal or inherent logic here. What is being described are the values underlying industrial capitalism – the language of capitalism. It is not the technology that demands efficiency or rationality; it is the capitalist (Jamieson, 1980: 4). As he further points out, Weber's (1970a) thesis in *The Protestant Ethic and the Spirit of Capitalism* dealt with an ideal type – bourgeois capitalism – not the general category of capitalism. It was the nomothetic and systematizing sociology of Parsons and Durkheim that took analysis away from the particularistic and ideographic to the universalistic and decontextualized. There has more recently been a challenge to core notions of how capitalism itself functions and recognition that it is not monolithic but varied (Berger, 1986; Clegg and Redding, 1990; Hamilton, 1997; Redding, 1990).

The notion of convergence begs the question 'convergence to what'? And actually the answer suggests more of a 'coming to' than a convergence. A 'coming to' the forms of economic rationalism, industrialization and management developed in the West and discursively positioned as synonymous with being modern and developed and thus only a small step from civilized. In Webber's (1969) summary there was at least the proposal that the game was not yet up since forces for divergence were still at play. This sets up an interesting binary in which the forces for convergence – in Webber's terms, economics, technology, education, pragmatism and elites – are aligned against the forces for divergence, the most notable of which is culture. He discusses culture as a type of relaxant that discourages the energy necessary to accomplish the change into the modern. Thus, his metaphors include 'the more somnolent societies' who have not climbed the ladder of dynamic hierarchical needs, and culture as a 'warm, comfortable, supportive and protecting *sea*'.

Cultures, he argues, are robust and persistent, but will eventually be overrun by the exigencies of the economic imperative. 'Bare bottoms are an issue in Tanzania' Webber informs us – referring to the continued preference for semi-nudity among the Masai – but that, *in the end,* the pressures of economic necessity will overcome the Masai tribe's '*vanity*' and they will cover their 'nature'. The reference to the Masai is interesting since they have in more recent times entered into one of the major economic growth areas of late capitalism – the marketing of cultural goods. You can now pay to enter their villages, pay to photograph them in traditional dress (bare bottoms have an economic value now), pay to witness their songs and dances in a hotel-as-safari-camp. Webber's anticipated covering did not occur, at least not in the expected way. There is no simple appropriation and incorporation here, no straightforward convergence to a Westernized homogeneity. True, the economic imperative has achieved its penetration, but there is a turn, a re-appropriation. The Other exploits its 'Otherness', mirrors back the gaze on the exotic and markets it.

Appropriating the 'Other': the language of (cultural) difference

Taxonomies of the Other

Comparative management is, by definition, an investigation of differences and similarities in management practice. Culture has formed the prime vehicle for this investigation and the universalistic categories provided by Parsons and Kluckhohn have been the foundation. Parson's functionalist project pursued a positivistic taxonomy for categorizing and explaining social phenomena. Indeed, Gouldner refers disparagingly to Parson's 'taxonomic zeal'. In many respects this resonates with the eighteenth and nineteenth centuries' scientific preoccupation with classification, categorization and taxonomy which sought to reduce phenomenal complexity to the ordered rationalities of scientific labelling.

Throughout its short history comparative management has doggedly pursued systems of classification which aspire to fix perceived cultural differences. The most widely cited is Hofstede's (1980, 1991) five dimensions of work-related value differences: large to small power distance, individualism-collectivism, masculinity-femininity, high to low uncertainty avoidance and long-term versus short-term orientation.[8] These gross categories are deployed to provide 'cultural maps of the world' showing the relative dimensional position of fifty plus countries and regions. The system provides a totalizing language in which it is presumed one can speak of 'large power distance cultures', or of Asian cultures being collectivist. A second popular schema is Trompenaars' (1993) with his seven universal problems adopted from Parsons.[9] There is an attempt to operationalize these categories and lay out the position of various countries on a table or graph of differences. Inferences, often wildly speculative, are then drawn to make statements about aspects of management/business practice in different locations. Particular aspects of management are first fixed to an analytic category and then discussed. As such they are reified and decontextualized from the specificities in which they are actually enacted.

A recent addition to this taxonomic practice is the work of Gatley et al. (1996). This idiosyncratic book divides the world into four 'paradigm views of the world' – Eastern, Western, Northern and Southern cultural paradigms. This establishes a Four-World taxonomy that makes the following crude differentiations: we are introduced to 'the pioneering, action-oriented cultures of the West, to the cool rational cultures of the north. We then travel south to the traditional, family-oriented cultures and then move on towards the reflective, idealist cultures in the east' (p. 8). Each area has its defining orientation, both negative and positive as depicted below:

Table 11.1 Gatley et al.'s cultural taxonomy

	Positive orientation and key resource advantage	Negative orientation
North	Rationalism Information management	Nationalism
East	Holism Process management	Mysticism
South	Humanism Relationship management	Tribalism
West	Pragmatism Resources management	Materialism

What is East and what is South, for example, does not always match a sheer geographic delineation. Within Europe they discuss more specific differences making use of de Madarianga's work (1922, 1966). Here, France, metaphorically aligned with Air, is characterized by thought and intellectualism, and has *Le droit* as a defining metaphor. It is in the northern cluster. England, in the Western cluster, linked with Earth, is characterized by materiality and action, and has *fair play* as a defining metaphor. The south is represented by Spain whose motif is *El honor*. It is represented by Fire and has passion and universality as guiding values. This is not only a stunning example of 'taxonomical zeal', but continues a long tradition of trading in stereotypes and essentialisms. They conclude with the idealistic argument that modern management needs to find synergistic blends of these different orientations.

A related aspect of the taxonomic project is various attempts to cluster countries, either statistically or conceptually. The semiotics of these tabular presentations is interesting. One of the earliest versions is the clustering of Haire et al. (1966). They divide the world into five clusters. The labels are revealing: Nordic-European, Latin-European, Anglo-American, Developing countries, and Japan as an outlier (as it often is).[10] The developing countries get an economic position rather than a geographic/cultural location. It is their state of economic underdevelopment that provides the rationale for a label and defines their presumed collective identity. In Hickson and Pugh (1995) Africa is also undifferentiated and economically defined along with India and South East Asia as 'developing countries'.

The rationale for such clustering, even when based on statistical analysis, is always dubious and often rests on notions of ethnic or racial type and national character or, more solidly, on language group. What, in substance, has Germany got in common with Norway? What information or understanding does the generic label 'Latin-European' provide when laid across four diverse European states. When Ronen and Shenkar (1985) provide a cluster analysis of past studies some odd things happen. In Haire et al.'s study (1966) 'India' appears in the Latin American cluster; for Sirota and Greenwood's (1971) study India appears in the Anglo cluster along with Austria and Switzerland; and Hofstede's (1976) has Sweden in the Anglo cluster whilst Switzerland is in the Latin European. There are odd games of sameness–difference being played out here.

The essential Other: the language of essentialisms and exoticisms

A pervasive feature of comparative discourse is the tendency to essentialize the Other. That is to assume to be able to identify and capture the defining qualities and the real or true essence of the Other. The practice tends towards assumptions of pre-figured, deterministic and inherent qualities that supersede differences due to history, materiality, social change or other externalities. In this context specifically essentialism refers to a reductive strategy wherein the 'Other's' subjectivity is constructed by a Western discourse which claims to speak authoritatively and definitively about what constitutes that subjectivity. It is a strategy that claims to tell us what the essential nature of a particular group of people – say Chinese – is.

It is suggested that there is a 'preoccupation in Western analysis with disclosing an assumed underlying essence' (Smart, 1996: 183). It is assumed that a group of people can be summarized with a label such as 'the Chinese' and that their essential nature, characterized by certain specific qualities, can be meaningfully captured (Thomas, 1994). This makes the Other a 'knowable Other'. The notion of 'race' uses this practice – an attempt to construct particular races as definite entities with known and specific qualities; latterly, 'culture' has been used in a similar fashion. As Thomas (1994: 89) puts it 'Each of these concepts [race, nation, culture] privileges differences – understood at different moments primarily in temperamental, physical and now cultural terms – and rendered the essentialized entities through an array of attributes that are supposedly peculiar to them.' He sees modernity as, in part, an epoch of anthropological typification. Rushdie tellingly describes essentialism as 'the respectable child of old-fashioned exoticism' (Rushdie, 1992: 67).

The tendency to exoticize is also a salient feature of the West's representations of its Other. In this case the perceived cultural differences are amplified, exaggerated and distorted – made more different. It often results in somewhat more positive images, but not necessarily. An exoticizing practice has certainly been present in literature and art, but is also prevalent in anthropology. In accounting for anthropological practice Keesing notes that

> ... our goals and expectations in representing Otherness – push us to overinterpret. Our professional roles as dealers in exotica may impel us to seek deep and cosmologically salient meanings where native actors may find shallow, conventional and pragmatic ones: to discover non-existent philosophies. (1989: 459)

He argues that the theoretical and methodological inclinations of anthropology lead to the seeking out of the most exotic cultural 'texts' and to read and present them in the most exotic way. This inevitably results in the representation of other people's worlds as 'more radically different from one another and from our own than they are' (p. 469). In comparative management this practice is pervasive. There is a wilful focus on what is sharply different and a neglect of what is similar. The practice impacts on the perceived value and validity of 'scientific' work emanating from locations exoticized by the West. 'The historic exoticization of large parts of the world and a corresponding distrust of the 'scientific' validity of their work contributes to their marginalization' (Wong-Mingji and Mir, 1997: 361).

The language of comparative management is replete with essentialisms, indeed, most of the culturalist perspectives rests on them. One hardly knows where to start since almost any text in the field has recourse to one essentialism or another, and we have encountered a number already in this chapter. Below we present a rather random selection of others. It has become a common strategy to identify and attribute an 'Other's' difference to some essential quality and then infer differences in management practice based on that.

Japan has been a prime candidate for the essentializing project. The representations of Japan in the West have been as varied and tied to economic and geo-political relations as those of China. The various representations of Japan in line with economic conditions have been documented by Wilkinson (1990). He notes that the ascribed qualities that at one point in time have positive valence in the West, come, at a different point to have negative valence. Thus when the global economic structures turn problematic the images of Japan shift so that the positive 'efficient' gets recast as 'ruthless' or 'aggressive'; 'pragmatic' turns into 'unprincipled', 'group norms' become 'conformity', 'discipline' becomes 'regimented', 'paradox' becomes 'contradiction'. Analysts for the CIA only recently concluded that 'Japan is like no other nation-state known, as its people are "creatures of an ageless, amoral, manipulative and controlling culture ... suited only to this race, in this place" ' (Najita, 1993: 13). There are many instances of an essentializing tendency in influential texts on Japanese management such as Pascale and Athos (1982) and Ouchi (1981).

Harbison and Myers' (1959) work has many essentialisms – they talk, for example, of low levels of trust in Italy, British 'aristocratic values', German 'authoritarianism', 'unquestioning loyalty' in Japan, authoritarianism and paternalism in India, Chile and Egypt and so on. Similarly in Weinshall's (1977) influential text there are innumerable instances. An interesting example is the assertion that the French approach to problems is 'Cartesian', exemplified by a 'systematic, quantitative assault on all aspects of a problem'; this is contrasted to a US pragmatic approach (p. 172). In Harris and Moran (1991) we find another spate of essentialist declarations such as 'The Hispanic attitude towards fatalism reduces the appeal of product guarantees and warranties' (p. 4), and 'Middle Easterners are introverted and shy' (p. 52). The damaging effects of essentializing practice are indicated by the following quote from a report of the International Bank for Reconstruction and Development (1953: 523, my emphasis): 'All employees interviewed – both Ceylonese and foreign – agree that the Sinhalese is not *naturally* inclined toward hard physical labour'.

Hickson and Pugh (1995) provide a recent attempt at accounting for management differences around the world. It too is full of essentialistic statements, although the language is more circumspect with frequent recourse to rhetorical questions rather than the declarative language found in earlier texts. Here are some examples. They assert that 'Generally speaking, economically more developed nations tend to be more abstractive, the less developed more associative' (p. 38). There is, however, no explanation of why this should be so, how such a difference could develop, and, most importantly, no substantiating evidence. They also claim that people in developing countries make decisions that are more *ad hoc*, 'even inconsistent' (p. 230). There is also a claim that Arabic language is one of persuasion and 'of the moment', not of 'cold reasoning' (p. 199). Arabic culture is described as authoritarian and personalistic. There is a range of disparaging and essentialist representations of the Other here: as an inferior thinker – intuitive versus logical thinking; the concrete versus the abstract, ad hoc and inconsistent versus systematic and consistent.

In Gatley et al.'s (1996) text there are boundless numbers of both essentialisms and exoticisms. Indeed the whole frame of the book is permeated with these practices. I will note only one particularly odd example here. A key cultural contrast they draw is between Western 'atomism' and Eastern 'holism'. The former is implicitly tied to notions of universalism and the West's scientific practice. From this follows ideas about the West's inner-directed, assertive, mechanistic approach to things, which is contrasted, naturally, to the East's outer-directed, responsive and organic approach. However, the odd turn is taken with a link to split brain theory: 'These two orientations [atomism and holism] have been attributed to the relative dominance of the two brain hemispheres, the analysing reductive left brain, which seems to dominate the Western world and the synthesizing, visio-spatial right brain which seems to dominate in the East' (p. 13). This is the first time that cultural differences have been expressed in such an extreme form so as to suggest that whole cultures are half-brained!

The Other has sometimes been represented in oddly stark and abstracted terms. Harris and Moran (1991) present a table of value differences that they say can be used to analyse sources of inter-cultural misunderstanding. It represents a tabulated summary of some important US cultural values put alongside a set of alternative cultural features that are contrastive, often oppositional. What is notable is the construction of this absurdly generalized Other that is positioned as counter-point to the cultural relevancies of the US.[11] What is offered is a decontextualized US/non-US contrast with no meaningful specificity attached to the Other. Note the language and tone used in this table. The implications are clear: there is a set of US cultural values and beliefs that underpin and support an approach to management. That these are in tune with accepted practice within the US discourse on management and organization is not surprising and does not need to be made explicit. By inference, the alternative is at least problematized both in terms of that discourse and the practices it supports. Just to take one or two examples. 'Competition stimulates high performance' (US model – good) versus 'Competition leads to unbalances and leads to disharmony' (Other model – bad). 'Commitments should be honoured' (US model – good) versus 'A commitment may be superseded by a conflicting request or an agreement may only signify intention and have little or no relationship to the capacity of performance' (Other model – bad).

In some work there is a psychological reductionism, often fuelled by the technologies of Western psychometrics. Thus it was reported that, using TAT measures, subjects from developing countries were more insecure, conforming, tradition bound, conventional and resistant to change than those from developed (Josh, 1965: 101). Similar examples with respect to Chinese personality can be found in Bond (1986) and the whole cross-cultural psychology project inescapably, and often unreflexively, pursues the same project (e.g. Segall et al., 1990). Lynn's (1971) work was a key element in the discourse that associated personality with national character.

Redding has made a vital contribution to understanding Overseas Chinese[12] management practice, however, he too has recourse to a marked essentializing. In early articles (Redding, 1982; Redding and Martyn-Johns, 1979) an overview is provided of a different Chinese worldview traced to implications for management style. The thesis is starkly based on the premise that the Chinese 'think differently' (p. 103). The suggestion is that Chinese cognitive frames are different with respect to how they think about causality, time, self, probability and morality. To focus on just one of these, it is claimed that the Chinese conception of causality is not uni-directional but mutually causal. It is further claimed that Chinese thinking does not incorporate abstract logic, but rather is rooted in a 'radical empiricism' where concepts of reality are purely based upon concrete perception. This is seen as a reason for the failure of transition to Western scientific theorizing. This is a line of reasoning apparent in Husserl (1970) when contrasting 'oriental philosophies' with 'Greek-European science'. He argued that the latter was capable of 'absolute theoretical insights', or proper theory, whereas oriental philosophy was tied to a 'practical-universal' and 'mythical-religious' orientation. This orientation meant a 'naïve' and 'straightforward' approach to the world, the world as concrete and particular. For Redding the link to organization practice is thus: 'It is possible that people do not get organised because the process of thinking in abstract terms about the elements of organizations does not come naturally' (p. 114). The empirical organizational referent is that Chinese organizations are, objectively, typically small in scale and non-complex in structural terms, and that management in such organizational forms is thereby also different. The talk is of the 'Oriental mind' and of 'Oriental culture' and in both cases there is an assumption of radical essential differences in ways of thinking.

In Redding's major opus *The Spirit of Chinese Capitalism* (1990) the tone is more sober but essentializing practices are still present. There is somewhat less psychological reductionism, rather the argument proceeds by essentializing Chinese culture. Contemporary management/business practices are tracked back through values' socialization to historical, philosophical and religious antecedents, especially Confucianism. These antecedents provide a 'psycho-social legacy' still impactful in framing the cognitions, values and behaviours of contemporary business people among the overseas Chinese communities.[13] This is a significant acclamation of the post-Confucian hypothesis that has been a widely deployed analytic in explaining East Asian management and business latterly.

The Post-Confucian Hypothesis was a term originally used by the futurologist Kahn (1979) to explain the notable economic growth of Asia's Four Dragons (Hong Kong, Taiwan, Singapore and South Korea). It argues that certain aspects of the Confucian legacy have provided values, behavioural orientations and social systems conducive to economic development given the conditions prevailing in the latter quarter of the twentieth century. Despite the obvious diversity among the Chinese communities across Asia, it is presumed that a shared Confucian heritage has instilled a common set of values that translates into a distinctive approach to business/management with core commonalities. The Post-Confucian thesis has been taken up by numerous scholars (Hofstede, 1991; Hofstede and Bond, 1988; Oh, 1991; Redding, 1990; Redding and Hsiao, 1990). Others, whilst not explicitly invoking the hypothesis have pursued similar culturalist explanations with similar essentializing elements (see Berger and Hsiao, 1988; Chen, 1995; Clegg et al., 1986; Hicks and Redding, 1983; Westwood, 1997; Wong, 1985; Yoshihara, 1988).

One of the most outrageous assertions of essential differences derived from cultural value orientations in recent times has been made by Hofstede and Bond (1988). Following Bond's Chinese Value Survey (CVS) and subsequent analysis, a fifth dimension is added to Hofstede's original four. It is labelled initially 'Confucian Dynamism' and subsequently 'Long Term Orientation'. The language is dubious. For example, if Confucianism is interpreted broadly *all* the items in the CVS could be construed as Confucian not just those under this dimension. The assertion that the first set of items loading on one pole of the dimension are 'dynamic' and 'future-oriented' and those at the other end 'static' and 'short-term' is questionable. Clearly 'thrift' and 'persistence' imply a 'long-term orientation' but in what way is dynamism implied? The other two items – 'ordering relationships by status' and having a 'sense of shame' – would seem to have little that is either dynamic or long term. At the other end of the pole, surely 'respect for tradition' implies a long-term, rather than short-term orientation (albeit focused on the past). 'Reciprocation' is a social 'rule' that helps to govern stable relationships. In some manifestations it has a short time horizon – for example in the British tradition of buying 'rounds' of drinks in a pub – but it can also have long term implications, governing a pattern and network of relationships through a lifetime and even across generations. This is especially true of the operation of reciprocation (*bao*) in Chinese contexts. It also does not connote a static situation, reciprocation is embedded in a stream of activities in an ongoing exchange relationship and is clearly future oriented – based upon the assumption of future returns being given for an offer provided now. Similarly, 'protecting your face' is a central mechanism for the maintenance of stable order in Chinese society, it is not a short-term, egotistical expediency, but has embedded resonance for the perpetuation of a social system or set of relationships. It is also hard to see how 'personal steadiness and stability' is short-term; it reflects the Confucian ideal of the 'Golden Mean' and is something to be cultivated over a person's lifetime. These conceptual difficulties and matters of interpretation are important given the extravagant claims made for the dimension.

Hofstede (1991) goes on to make some extraordinary claims about 'Western' and 'Eastern' values and cognitions. A 'Western' cognitive paradigm is proposed, dominated by the search for Truth, religiosity and analytical thinking. The 'Eastern' paradigm is constituted of the search for Virtue, practical ethics and synthetic thinking. This leads to the outrageous claim that the CVS research, by showing the link between Confucian Dynamism and recent economic growth, 'has demonstrated the strategic advantage of cultures that can practice Virtue without a concern for Truth' (1991: 172)!

Denigrating the Other: the language of lack and deficit

The West's representations of the Other have typically engaged in a practice which denigrates, belittles, disparages or demonises the Other. Indeed, it has been argued – following Foucault and Irigary – that linguistic and structural practices always entail that difference is interpreted as 'less than' (Oseen, 1997). This is clearly expressed by Bhabha (1986: xviii): 'The Other must be seen as the necessary negation of a primordial identity ... that introduces the systems of differentiation which enables the "cultural" to be signified as a linguistic, symbolic, historic reality'. This is apparent, for example, in early histories of civilization such as Buckle's *History of Civilisation in England* (1904 – original vol. 1857–61) and Guizot's *General History of Civilisation in Modern Europe* (original vol. 1857–81). Note in both cases the 'localization' of civilization. Both refer to the progressive, evolutionary development of Europe and present images of the non-Western Other as both temporally and typologically different. That is, lagging behind and doing so because they have a deficiency in their make up. They are depicted as barbarous, lawless, unreasoned, uncultivated and unfree. According to Buckle, Asia is oppressed by nature and by slavery. Guizot depicts Asia as characterized ineffably by immobility and lack of freedom. The binary is the West's freedom, movement and change versus Asian stasis, autocracy and slavery. Western representations of the Other have not been uniform or fixed but rather have varied as discourses have altered across epochs and epistemes (Mackerras, 1989; Thomas, 1994). Early representations depicted a lack of religiosity (and therefore a need of salvation – or defeat), these were replaced in the eighteenth century with images of ignorance, untruth and deficiency. This in turn was altered by the evolutionary discourse that represented the Other as backward, as lagging in the evolutionary race. Other discourses depicted deficiencies in personality and character (see Thomas, 1994: 68–71).

The Other has also frequently been depicted as dangerous, as a threat – to the West – and so demonised or vilified. At the same time the orientalist and various other Western representational practices have sought to reduce the threat by capturing the Other, by constructing the Other in a form that makes it accessible, understandable and hence controllable. This is an appropriating strategy that constructs the Other as a known alterity – a re-presentation on the West's terms. It is a depiction of pure difference, but one that can 'nonetheless, be assimilated by the totalising narratives of Western history' (Prasad, 1997: 295).

The Other's representation as in some way being deficient, backward, primitive, disordered, barbarian, despotic or in other ways suffering from a lack is pervasive and invidious. With reference to the histories of India, Chakrabarty (1992: 6) maintains that the ' "Indian" was always a figure of lack'. This discursive space in which the Other is positioned is, of course, constituted in relation to, indeed, in reflection of, the West. The West positions itself as a plenitude – as possessing all the things in which the Other is deficient. It was Said's (1978) 'Orientalism' that most brilliantly revealed this discursive practice and its devastating impact. In summarizing the Orientalist project Dirks (1992: 9) indicates how in constructing and representing the Orient, there is an inherent denigration. Orientalism is a '... sophisticated body of scholarship, embodied in such practices as philology, archaeology, history and anthropology, all glorifying the classical civilizations of the East (at the same time as they glorify even more the scholarly endeavours of the West that makes possible their recuperation) by suggesting that all history since the classical age was characterized by *decline, degradation and decadence*' (my emphasis). Said (1978) argued that the Orientalists' discourse represented the Orient as ontologically distinct and opposite to the West and characterized as comprising a litany of (largely) negative attributes: 'despotism ... splendour, cruelty, sensuality' (p. 4); untruthfulness, lack of logic, absence of energy and initiative, intrigue, cunning, unkindness, lethargy and suspicion (pp. 38–9); eccentricity, backwardness, indifference, feminine penetrability, supine malleability (p. 206). Sakamoto (1996: 115) argues that the Western Orientalist practice of positioning the Orient as the West's Other has signified its primitiveness, stagnation and unreason. The Other is marked by absences in relation to the West's plenitude.

Western discourse about Asia and Africa also commonly represents a lack in the Other. Within the ideological formulations of modern capitalism, India is portrayed as an example of aborted or failed capitalist modernity. The discourse frames India and offers various negative alterities: pre-capitalist (not capitalist), protoindustrial (not industrial), semi-feudal (not post-feudal), traditional (not modern), underdeveloped (not developed) (O'Hanlon and Washbrook, 1992: 142). There is no identity other than the one provided in relation to the West's modern, capitalist positioning. British administration in India was an imposition that proceeded on the basis of defining indigenous organizational systems as tyrannical, disorderly and/or improper. A strategy, Dirks (1992) argues, based on a fictive interpretation of Indian modes of organization, one that profoundly misunderstood its hierarchical relations, systems of patronage and reciprocation of land-ownership.

China has for a long time formed a quintessential Other for the West. As noted, it has frequently been negatively represented in the West. These negativities have taken various forms from stagnant and backward through to despotic, authoritarian and cruel. More than anything else, perhaps it has been represented as mysterious, quixotic, exotic, strange – often fed by the language of inscrutability. However, as Mackerras (1989) makes clear in his detailed analysis of the West's images of China, these representations have not been homogenous and uniform. The images have been various, often depending upon the relative power position of the West vis-à-vis China, and by particular geo-political and social interactions. This follows the classic Orientalist representation of the glorification of a 'golden age' followed by decline and stagnation. Thus China has, at times, been represented as highly civilized, advanced, inventive and dynamic. In more recent times, and certainly since its communist revolution, the images have been more negative – heightened by its ideological postures. Today its business systems are often held up for ridicule. The state owned enterprise system is uniformly depicted as inefficient and archaic. Business practices are frequently represented as underdeveloped, lacking in rationality and corrupt.

The management and business systems of Japan have also long puzzled and intrigued the West. There has always been a struggle to find a language to capture the system from a Western perspective. But it is always a language that positions Japan in relation to the West. In doing so it is almost impossible to avoid the recurring binaries which carry Western positivities and Eastern negativities. Thus from the outset Harbison and Myers (1959) discussed the Japanese *zaibatsu* and could only find Western categories to describe them. They were described as having 'carried the ideas of feudalism, paternalism and family rule into the new industrial society' (p. 4). They recognize that 'patrimonial management can be an effective spur in the early days of industrialisation' (p. 70), but cannot be sustained and is only a first stage. There needs to be the separation of management and ownership and the developed of a 'professional' management ethos. Again the imposition of a Western model of economic development is foisted onto another culture – despite its obvious economic progress.

The language Harbison and Myers use to describe other management/business systems is also replete with intimations of deficiency, lack and negativity. With respect to India they refer to 'abuses' in the management system, the seeking of 'speculative profits at the expense of others', the occurrence of 'illegal activities', 'thrusting, unscrupulous management', all of which have put 'Indian management in the doghouse' (p. 151). With respect to Egypt they are more subtly but damagingly negative. They argue that there are both progressive and 'primitive' management systems in Egypt, but the former, those 'under foreign management', is where one finds 'a rational organizational structure' and other accoutrements of modern (Western) management practice. In the primitively managed enterprises, which are controlled by a 'strong willed individual or family clique', one finds 'a personal rather than a functional type of organization, a complete absence of rational management procedures, and a dearth of competent professional and supervisory personnel' (p. 158). Only those managers with Western training and education are properly equipped since this makes them 'sophisticated' (p. 162).

The West's Other is often represented in the language of stagnation. This is a dominant trope. It implies that the rest of the world has not been able to match the dynamic changes of the West. And in contemporary discourse change is always progressive. By not moving, by stagnating, the Other is seen as regressive, backward and inferior. Harris and Moran (1991) make much of change in their advice to international (read US) managers. They must be proactive change agents and not just within the organizational sphere, but in the community since 'in a time when nation states seemingly falter, world corporations prosper' (p. 111). Managers need to initiate change to 'correct obsolescence'. They need to be innovative change managers and the West must take the lead since 'some cultural systems are more open and accepting of change' (p. 117). 'The complexities of Western cultural living would appear to stimulate creativity without inordinate attention to detail. On the other hand, change in Eastern culture, as in Third World nations, is often accompanied by painstaking concern for its effect on relationships, so there is a preference for bending the cultural bonds within the existing system to avoid radical alterations' (pp. 117–8). Note that the Other is not only change resistant but also less complex.

Weinshall (1977) argues that resistance to change is common in the developing world, impeding economic progress. With respect to India, particularly, he argues that change resistance is largely due to culture. The logic again assumes the Western view that change is progress and good. The Other is deficient in not recognizing this logic and in having a culture unable to embrace the type of change advocated by Western modes of organization/business. Later he argues that attitudes in Africa and Asia towards private enterprise and business generally are deficient (note the absurdity of lumping all of Asia and Africa together), and that people and businesses in those locations need to be more closely supervised and controlled. The whole tone of the book is one in which foreign companies and workers have deficiencies that are in need of rectification through Western training or other modes of intervention.

Carsons, in Weinshall (1977), proffers supposed 'Anthropological Insights', but actually trades in a tirade of neo-Orientalist and essentializing representations. Throughout there is the explicit assumption that the cultural values and behaviour patterns of the 'developing world' are antithetical to economic progress and modern management practice. He argues that the traditional emphasis on non-material values retards the growth of systematic business management 'in the American sense' (p. 240). His quote of Lauterbach's study of Latin America is indicative; 'Where leisure, contemplation, or merely an unhurried way of going about things and avoidance of worry about the future represent dominant values in life, clockwise, split-second decisions or rigid datelines, even for loan repayments, may be at odds with cultural assumptions' (Lauterbach, 1962: 383).

Richman (1977), who suggests cultural variation in conceptions of science, offers a radical assumption of difference. He infers that the scientific method is necessary for effective modern management and thus, certain cultures again have a deficit. He, and both Farmer and Richman (1964) and McClelland (1961) invoke Calvinism as an ethos supportive of the scientific method. Providing an anecdote about American business in Saudi Arabia, Richman goes further than pointing to a deficit with respect to the scientific method by suggesting that the Arab staff had difficulty working out causal relationships. He says that they were unable to see the logic of 'if tyre pressures are not checked regularly, tyre damage is likely'! (Richman, 1977: 30). This attribution of differences in notions of causation and in other modes of cognition has been made elsewhere, including, as noted, by Redding (Redding, 1980, 1982; Redding and Martyn-Johns, 1979).

McClelland's (1961) culturalist conceit was that certain societies had developed a higher Need for Achievement, that this fostered entrepreneurial activity which, in turn, spurred economic development. In other societies the Achievement need was weak thus hampering the engine of growth. This is a psychologistic example of the rhetoric of deficit. A Western sense of efficacy and power permits the assumption that interventions can rectify this deficit, as McClelland's practice expressly set out to do. The language of rectification and redemption has, of course, been central all the way through the West's engagements with its Other(s): from missionary salvation to IMF economic restructurings. The language here is alarming. Richman (1977), supporting McClelland's contentions, argues that the culture, ideology and religious beliefs of some countries means that, 'the general population tends to have a fairly low achievement drive' (p. 28). Furthermore, the values inherent in Protestantism and Calvinism give rise to a higher need for achievement motive 'than those who behave in accordance with the orthodox Hindu, Moslem, Buddhist and even Catholic religious values and doctrines'. Huge swathes of humanity are castigated by the deficit principle. The fact that McClelland's thesis has been shown to be empirically flawed is incidental to the significant role he played in debates about development and his participation in some of the critical rhetorics of deficit and rectification in the neo-colonial discourse.

Perhaps most damaging was the argument that places like Taiwan and China were low in the achievement motive. Indeed, it was claimed that they had a need structure – high in power and affiliation and low in achievement – 'typical of traditionalist, stagnant, authoritarian cultures'. There is clearly something radically wrong with the conceptualization here. A relatively short period of time – too short for 'the general population' to suddenly acquire large doses of the achievement need – saw the economies of East Asia boom with entrepreneurial flair apparently in abundance. It has been argued that 'McClelland's conceptualisation of the achievement motive as a well internalised predisposition in the self-reliant individual as a result of independence training is probably only one variety' – a Western individualist one (Yang, 1986: 113). Yang says that Asian achievement orientation is simply different, a 'social-oriented achievement motive rather than an individual-oriented one' (Yang, 1981).

This small parcel of the discourse echoes another, larger segment. Following Weber, a language was constructed that positioned China as an exemplar, *via negativa*, for the efficacy of the West's model of political economy and the values presumed to underpin it. China was the prime candidate for the deficit principle – seen as festering in a stagnant state brought about by persistent adherence to archaic traditional values and structures rooted in Confucianism and a ruinous flirtation with the blighted dogmas of Marxism–Leninism–Maoism. From Weber onwards there was an assumption that the Confucian heritage was an impediment to modernist economic development. But, as we have seen, there has been an interesting turn latterly as Confucian-influenced states have registered some of the world's most dramatic growth figures. These events have precipitated a reversal of logic wherein the Confucian heritage, once castigated as the cause of stasis, is now being attributed with the value base responsible for driving the economic boom from the 1970s to the mid 1990s. This led to the promulgation of the Post (or neo-) Confucian Hypothesis.

Lest the impression be given that this language of lack is only present in earlier management texts, here are examples from a more recent text. Hickson and Pugh (1995) have as much recourse to essentializing, stereotyping and negative representations as any of these earlier writers. In commenting on the Middle East they firstly refer to the economies of the region as 'oil-distorted' (p. 190) and then to inadequacies of the management system, which unsurprisingly they largely lay at the door of Islam. They oddly declare that 'if Arab culture can be said to have an abiding duality, then Arab management has many paradoxes' (p. 195), as if no Western culture has dualities and paradoxes! The paradoxes are said to include the pursuit of individual interests, but through collective means – through personal relationships. One is tempted to declare this a universal paradox – certainly the norm in large parts of the world. Whose paradox is it then? There is reference to historically situated corruption practices and inherent submissiveness. The place of personal feelings and obligations in organizational affairs is lamented as a pre-modern aberration juxtaposed to supposed Western abstract rule governance and objective impersonalism.

The collusion of scholars from the 'developing' world with these representations needs to be acknowledged. Thus the Arab management scholar Ali Abbas castigates the contradictions inherent in Arabic management, themselves resting upon the wider dualities between the modern and the traditional, the religious and the secular and the ideal and the pragmatic:

> the influence of these forces is exemplified by: 1. The establishment of a huge number of administrative laws and regulations while no attempt is made to implement them – they are just signs of modernity; 2. Designing systems for selection and promotion according to qualification and merit, but hiring and rewarding according to social ties and personal relations; 3. Setting up

organizational structures and designs that remain as decoration, while abiding by them only on an exceptional basis. (Ali Abbas, 1990: 21)

Such collusion often reflects the reality that if foreign scholars want to participate in the modern management academy they must deploy this language. Kiggundu (1989) has also been a critic of management in the developing context and provides a tabular summary of their deficiencies. Hickson and Pugh (1995: 231) make reference to this and conclude that in developing contexts 'Managements do manage, and organizations do work, but they often depart from – or is it 'fall short of' – the model of impersonal organization' that the West presents. Managers in these other contexts are also represented as imitators, people incapable of functioning autonomously, dupes acting out another system's parts – 'there is a risk that when on the job in a system imitating impersonal organizations elsewhere, people will too often be mere "performers" of roles' (pp. 230).

The language of power and authority: authoritarianism

A recurrent re-presentation of non-Western management is in relation to the West's socio-political discourse and its assumptions concerning the veracity and performativity of its liberal-humanist, democratic postures. This rhetoric establishes another trenchant binary: democratic/participative versus autocratic/authoritarian. The West has consistently portrayed the leadership and authority patterns of the Other as authoritarian, even despotic. This is certainly the case with respect to China, where it goes back at least as far as Quesnay and Montesquieu (see Mackerras, 1989). More recently even the sinologist Pye (1985) refers to Chinese 'virtuocracy' which acknowledges an authoritarianism, albeit ameliorated by a moral sensibility.

This binary is at the heart of Harbison and Myers (1959). Early in their book they lay out their stall: 'successful motivation of the workforce requires effective exercise of leadership in a democratic setting where leadership is based largely on consent' (p. 32). In a later chapter they denigrate all other systems for having the impediment of an authoritarian culture and mode of organization. They argue that successful management and enterprise organization is based on the leadership of a professional management elite that leads through a rule governed system based on democratic values. In contrast, the most 'primitive system of authority ... is the sovereign rule by a single person or a single family' (p. 40). Under such a system the ruler leads with an 'iron hand' in ways that are 'defensive, enervated and static' (p. 41). If sovereign rule persists 'it will retard and eventually strangle successful industrialisation' (p. 44). In contrast, and only in the most 'advanced' societies, is 'management by objectives based on personal initiative, consent and self-direction'.

Part of the logic of industrialization, it is argued, is the inevitable increase in organizational size and complexity, and as this occurs, sovereign rule by individuals and families becomes untenable. Harbison and Myers agree with Etzioni (1958) that when traditional systems prevail people accept such leadership since it is an extension of authority relationships with fathers, teachers, community elders and religious leaders. But once industrialization gets under way these authority systems are inappropriate. 'Modern' management as an authority system displaces these older forms. Furthermore, modern management requires three responses from employees: subordination, loyalty and productivity. Autocratic management is not stable and sustainable without coercive support and can only achieve subordination, not loyalty and productivity. They launch a sustained attack on traditional authority systems labelled as authoritarian and/or paternalistic. Such systems have roots in the feudal system of lord and serf and are based on paternalism, dependence, gratitude and reciprocal obligation, but as a mode of functioning are not productive or sustainable if industrial growth is the aim. They can be transferred into the industrial enterprise in the early stages of industrialization, as in the case of Japan, such that 'the industrial *pater*' takes the place of the family *pater* or village head. All but a few modern economies (specifically the USA, Britain and Sweden) are taken as deficient in terms of the authority system required for modern management.

However, there is an odd, almost contradictory subtext in the thesis. They point out that 'the primary concern of most management is to establish and maintain its authority'. If free to make independent choices about its management–worker relationships, management would pursue one of two strategies, either dictatorial or paternalistic. However, they continue, 'outside pressures force management to share authority and/or modify its approach towards a constitutional or democratic/participative mode' (p. 50). Thus, it appears democratic management is not a morally chosen direction but merely an expedient response to external pressures, particularly from political forces and from trade unions.

Richman (1977) also explicitly sets up these autocratic–democratic binaries in his tabulated classification of key elements in the management process that he then links to various cultural determinants and constraints. Richman cites as examples of cultures which impel an authoritarian management practice Saudi Arabia, Peru and 'even' Germany and contrasts this with the more participative US, Canada and Yugoslavia. The pragmatic message is that [US] companies should not invest in trying to introduce more participative styles in those countries where authoritarian practices are accepted and effective. He gives the same warning to companies transacting with the paternalistic management systems of Japan and Latin America. As he says 'it may be very costly and possibly dangerous – in terms of efficiency and productivity – for the international firm to deviate substantially from such a pattern of management' (Richman, 1977: 26).

This type of language has a common thread in the comparative management literature, right down to the present. It is forcefully present in Hofstede's (1980, 1991) Power Distance dimension where cultural antecedents are held to constitute and legitimize inherently hierarchical structurings and authoritarian or paternalistic leadership patterns across most of Asia, Latin America and other parts of the world. In the literature on Asian leadership for example, the style is invariably referred to as autocratic (Chen, 1991, 1995; Cho, 1991; Hamzah-Sendut et al., 1989; Komin, 1990; Redding, 1990; Redding and Richardson, 1986; Redding and Wong, 1986; Wong, 1985).

Relocating self: agency, reversals and hybridities

There has been a turn in the post-colonial project wherein there is a rejection of the notion that colonialism can be depicted as a monolithic and homogenous project that was uniform in its practices and effects (Dirks, 1992; Loomba, 1998; Thomas, 1994). There is also a rejection of the notion that colonialism was always an exclusively dominating strategy and uniformly a zero-sum game wherein the colonizer had all the power and effect and the colonized none. These older positions always position the colonized as passive subjectivities, as disempowered dupes. There has been, in general, a turn to a recognition of the agency of the colonized and away from the older conceptions of unidirectional colonial imposition and determinacy (Dirks, 1992; Parry, 1987; Thomas, 1994). Stoler (1992), for example, urges that colonialism is the creator of both the colonizer and the colonized. She also points to the wide diversity in the colonial project itself, both in terms of motives, goals, practices and interactions, and in terms of effects. In particular there was often a fragmentation between what was planned, perceived and interpreted at the metropolitan centre in the home country and the relevancies and practices on the ground in the localized context of colonial administration.

What needs to be acknowledged – and it can be no more than that here as more detailed analysis of these issues will have to await another time and place – is that the interaction between the colonized and the colonizer is more complex, multi-dimensional and multi-directional than it has sometimes been represented in the past. Similarly, comparative management cannot, and should not be seen as a monolithic, one-sided discourse with only one centre of knowledge/power. This does not devalue the preceding analysis in this chapter, but does indicate that it is a partial analysis lacking in sophistication. The Other has and always has had strategies of resistance, of denial, of re-appropriation of mirroring, of imitation and hybridity, of return and of repositioning. The post-colonial challenge to Western dominance is no longer simply to point to its repressive, dominating appropriating and controlling effects but to explore: the ways in which the West has itself been constituted in those processes, the localized variations in colonial practice and varied interactions between colonizer and colonized, and, the Other has had agency in reacting to the colonial experience – no longer the passive recipient.

The strategies of the Other have been varied and of varying efficacy. A radical position has been taken by the African writer Ngugi wa Thiong'o, who gave up writing in English to write only in his own language. He recognizes that language not only describes but also organizes – it organizes our thinking and the way we construct the meanings that are held to constitute 'our world', including a sense of self. He sees the invasion and persistence of English in Africa as a 'cultural bomb'. He sees it eroding African history, culture and identity, including his own sense of self. Language and culture are inseparable – if one is lost then so is the other. He wants to remain focused on the specificities of his own language and what it represents, eschewing any attempt to embrace language as a universal vehicle (see Ngugi wa Thiong'o, 1981). This is an extreme form of resistance to the language of dominance; there are other strategies.

From an Islamic position Tibi (1995) discusses the possibility of a de-Westernized science, one not founded on Cartesian dualism and Weberian notions of rationality, objectivity and instrumental intervention. He argues that Western science rests on assumptions on humanity's capacity and right to objectify the natural and the social environment in order to apprehend and control it. This is a secular project and antithetical to Muslim religiosity – to notions of the omnipotence of god, the sacred and the immutable. Muslim knowledge systems are held to be 'knowledge for living', whereas 'when a Westerner thinks of knowledge, it is mainly of "knowledge for power", that is such knowledge that enables one to control natural and material objects and human individuals and societies' (Watt, 1988: 13). The rejection of Western epistemologies by Islamic scholars partly rests on the view that its claim to universality is false, that its knowledge is only a localized construction produced in and for a particular context (historical, social and geo-political). For example Lepenies (1981: 256) argues that Merton's classic distinction between science and belief is no longer valid and that (Western) scientific knowledge should be viewed 'as a specific kind of belief which is only part of the larger belief-system of a given culture'.

Bhabha (1995) has pursued the notion of hybridity. On the one hand colonial practice creates, in many situations, a mimetic response, wherein 'locals' take on and mimic the colonial – aping Western modes of dress and behaviour, modelling Western administrative practices, taking up rowing and so on. V.S. Naipul has referred disparagingly to 'mimic men' and 'black skin/white masks' and in Asia the term 'banana' has similar connotations. Bhabha maintains, however, that hybridity has a positive element since the colonized is partly appropriating the colonizer. In mimicry there is no direct correspondence, no perfect reproduction, the hybrid is, just that, it remains different. Bhabha points out the paradox by showing that mimic men, whilst being in a sense an authorized version of otherness 'end up emerging as inappropriate colonial subjects'. They are not a proper reproduction, so they unsettle, they mirror and distort, they are autonomous. Sakamoto (1996) reflects on the attributions and images of Japan that the West trades in. It has been common to depict Japan as a mimetic society, especially with respect to Western products and modes of design. However, Sakamoto uses a similar type of hybridity thesis to suggest that mimicry cannot be viewed in such a simplistic manner. The hybrid escapes the prison of the dominant discourse, it is not a mere 'copy', it slips away, attains its autonomy and comes back to confront and challenge the dominant party.

The rise of the Asian economies precipitated a confident challenge to the Western hegemony. There was much talk of 'Asian Values', of the 'Confucian League' (Kao et al., 1994) and of the Post-Confucian Hypothesis. Asian business people and academics began to articulate an indigenously constituted account of management and business practice. It may have had heavy Western influences, it may have been compelled to use the language and the apparatus of the Western management orthodoxy to find a voice, but it began to mark out a fresh space. It may have had hybridic qualities, but it was taking on an increasingly autonomous tone. The 1997 economic crash has retarded that project. The West has somewhat gleefully watched the economic crisis and has taken the opportunity to reassert the efficacy of its management system. There is a danger that a once strident alternative voice has been muted...

Notes

1   Throughout the text, where reference is made to 'management' or management studies/theory, it should also be read to include 'organization' and/or business.
2   Harris and Moran's top-selling book *Managing Cultural Differences* had its first edition in 1979.
3   Some of the very few exceptions include Weber and Ouchi.
4   It is important to note that Chakrabarty sees the categories of 'Europe' and 'India' as aspects of the imaginary, as aspects of hyper-reality.
5   Indeed, Thomas (1994) depicts colonial discourse as a governmentalization of culture.
6   This emic-etic distinction is still at the heart of methodological debates in comparative management (see Punnett and Shenkar, 1996).
7   The pattern variables are: affectivity/affective neutrality, specific/diffuseness, achievement/ascription, particularism/universalism, collectivism/individualism. Note these are the central categories in Trompenaars (1993) schema.
8   The fifth dimension was actually developed by Michael Bond (The Chinese Culture Connection, 1987) following his Chinese Values Survey and was originally labelled 'Confucian Dynamism'.
9   The dimensions are: universalism versus particularism, individualism–collectivism, emotionality–emotional neutrality, specificity–diffuseness, achievement–ascription, monochronic/sequential versus polychronic/diachronic views of time and internals versus externals with respect to orientations to the environment. The labels are sometimes different in different published forms.
10 Nordic-European included Sweden, Norway, Denmark, Germany. Latin-European included Belgium, France, Italy and Spain. Anglo-American included England and the US. Developing countries included Argentina, Chile and India. These were countries included in the investigation and don't represent an attempt to classify all countries.

11 Note that parts of this cultural tabulation also owe a debt to Kluckhohn and Strodtbeck.
12 A term used by Redding and others to refer to ethnic Chinese communities outside of Mainland China in Hong Kong (and still applicable despite the reunification), Singapore, Taiwan, around Southeast Asia and elsewhere in the Chinese Diasporo.
13 In Hong Kong, Taiwan, Singapore.

References

Abegglen, J.C. (1958) *The Japanese Factory: Aspects of its Social Organization.* Glencoe, IL: Free Press.
Adler, N.J. (1983) 'A typology of management studies involving culture', *Journal of International Business Studies*, 3: 29–48.
Adler, N.J. (1991) *International Dimensions of Organizational Behaviour*, 2nd edn. Boston, MA: PWS-Kent.
Ali Abbas (1990) 'Management theory in a transitional society: the Arabs' experience', *International Studies of Management and Organization*, 20 (3): 7–35.
Bendix, R. (1964) *Nation Building and Citizenship.* Englewood Cliffs, NJ: Prentice-Hall.
Benedict, R. (1946) *Patterns of Culture.* New York: Penguin.
Berger, P.L. (1986) *The Capitalist Revolution.* New York: Basic Books.
Berger, P.L. and Hsiao, H.-H.M. (eds) (1988) *In Search of an East Asian Development Model.* New Brunswick, NJ: Transaction.
Bhabha, H. (1986) 'Remembering Fanon: self, psyche and the colonial condition', foreword to F. Fanon, *Black Skin, White Masks.* London: Pluto Press.
Bhabha, H. (1995) *Location of Culture.* London: Routledge.
Blumer, H. (1960) 'Early industrialisation and the laboring class', *Sociological Quarterly*, 1: 1–24.
Bond, M.H. (1986) *The Psychology of the Chinese People.* Hong Kong: Oxford University Press.
Boyacigiller, N.A. and Adler, N.J. (1991) 'The parochial dinosaur: organizational science in a global context', *Academy of Management Review*, 16 (2): 262–90.
Burnham, J. (1941) *The Managerial Revolution.* Westport, Conn: Greenwood Press reprint.
Calás, M.B. and Smircich, L. (1991) 'Voicing seduction to silence leadership', *Organization Studies*, 12 (4): 567–601.
Carsons, D. (1977) 'Anthropological insights', in T. Weinshall (ed.), *Culture and Management.* Harmondsworth: Penguin. pp. 239–60.
Chakrabarty, D. (1992) 'Postcoloniality and the artifice of history: who speaks for "Indian" pasts?', *Representations*, 37: 1–26.
Chen, C.H. (1991) 'Confucian style of management in Taiwan', in J.M. Putti (ed.), *Management: Asian Context.* Singapore: McGraw-Hill.
Chen, M. (1995) *Asian Management Systems.* London: Routledge.
Chinese Culture Connection, The (1987) 'Chinese values and the search for culture-free dimensions of culture', *Journal of Cross-Cultural Psychology*, 15: 417–33.
Cho, D.S. (1991) 'Managing by patriarchal authority in Korea', in. J.M. Putti (ed.), *Management: Asian Context.* Singapore: McGraw-Hill.
Clegg, S. R. and Redding, S.G. (eds) (1990) *Capitalism in Contrasting Cultures.* Berlin: De Gruyter.

Clegg, S.R., Dunphy, D.C. and Redding, S.G. (eds) (1986) *The Enterprise and Management in Southeast Asia*. Hong Kong: Centre of Asian Studies, University of Hong Kong.

Cox, T. and Nkomo, S.M. (1990) 'Invisible men and women: a status report on race as a variable in organization behaviour research', *Journal of Organizational Behaviour*, 11: 419–31.

De Madarianga, S. (1922) *Englishman, Frenchman, Spaniard*. Oxford: Oxford University Press.

De Madarianga, S. (1966) *The Spirit of Europe*. London: Hollis and Carter.

Dirks, N.B. (1992) 'From little king to landlord: colonial discourse and colonial rule', in Dirks, N.B. (ed.), *Colonialism and Culture*. Ann Arbor, MI: Michigan University Press. pp. 175–208.

England, G., Negandhi, A. and Wilpert, B. (1979) *Organizational Functioning in a Cross-Cultural Perspective*. Kent, OH: Kent State University Press.

Etzioni, A. (1958) 'Human relations and the foreman', *Pacific Sociological Review*, 1 (1): 33–8.

Farmer, R.N. and Richman, B.M. (1964) 'A model for research in comparative management', *California Management Review*, VII (2): 55–68.

Farmer, R.N. and Richman, B.M. (1965) *Comparative Management and Economic Progress*. Homewood, IL: Irwin.

Foucault, M. (1979a) *Discipline and Punish*. New York: Viking.

Foucault, M. (1979b) 'On governmentality', *Ideology and Consciousness*, 6: 5–21.

Gatley, S., Lessem, R. and Altman, Y. (1996) *Comparative Management: A Transcultural Odyssey*. London: McGraw-Hill.

Godkin, L., Braye, C.E. and Caunch, C.L. (1989) 'US-based cross-cultural management research in the eighties', *Journal of Business Economic Perspectives*, 15 (2): 37–45.

Habermas, J. (1972) 'Science and technology as ideology', in B. Barnes (ed.), *Sociology of Science*. Harmondsworth: Penguin.

Haire, M., Ghiselli, A. and Porter, L. (1966) *Managerial Thinking: An International Study*. New York/London: John Wiley.

Hamilton, G.G. (1997) *Chinese Capitalism? The Economic Organization of Chinese Societies*. London: Routledge.

Hamzah-Sendut, Tan Sri Datuk, Madsen, J. and Thong, G.T.S. (1989) *Managing in a Plural Society*. Singapore: Longman.

Harbison, F. and Myers, C.A. (1959) *Management in the Industrial World: An International Analysis*. New York: McGraw-Hill.

Harding, S. (1996) 'European expansion and the organization of modern science: isolated or linked historical processes', *Organization*, 3 (4): 497–509.

Harding, S. (1998) *Is Science Multi-Cultural?* Bloomington & Indianapolis, IN: Indiana University Press.

Harris, P.R. and Moran, R.T. (1991) *Managing Cultural Differences*, 3rd edn. Houston: Gulf.

Hearn, J., Sheppard, D., Tancred-Sheriff, P. and Burrell, G. (1989) *The Sexuality of Organization*. Newbury Park, CA: Sage.

Hicks, G.L. and Redding, S.G. (1983) 'The story of the East Asian economic miracle. Part 1 and 2: the culture connection', *Euro-Asia Business Review*, 2/3 (4): 18–22.

Hickson, D.J. and McMillan, C.J. (eds) (1981) *Organization and Nation: The Aston Programme*, IV. Farnborough, Hants: Gower.

Hickson, D.J. and Pugh, D.S. (1995) *Management Worldwide*. London: Penguin.

Hickson, D.J., McMillan, C.J., Hinings, C.R. and Schwitter, J. (1974) 'The culture-free context of organization structure: a tri-national comparison', *Sociology*, 8 (1): 59–80.

Hofstede, G. (1976) 'Nationality and the espoused values of managers', *Journal of Applied Psychology*, 61 (2): 148–55.

Hofstede, G. (1980) *Culture's Consequences: International Differences in Work Related Values*. London: Sage.

Hofstede, G. (1991) *Cultures and Organizations: Intercultural Cooperation and its Importance for Survival*. London: McGraw-Hill.

Hofstede, G. and Bond, M.H. (1988) 'The Confucius connection: from cultural roots to economic growth', *Organizational Dynamics*, 17: 4–21.

Holt, D. (1993) *Management and Principles*. Englewood Cliffs, NJ: Prentice Hall.

Holvino, E. (1996) 'Reading organization development from the margins: outsider within', *Organization*, 3 (4): 520–33.

Husserl, E. (1970) *The Crisis of European Sciences and Transcendental Philosophy*, trans. D. Carr. Evanston, IL: Northwestern University Press.

Inkeles, A. and Smith, D. (1974) *On Becoming Modern*. London: Heinemann.

International Bank for Reconstruction and Development, The (1953) *The Economic Development of Ceylon*. Baltimore, OH: Johns Hopkins Press.

Jamieson, I. (1980) *Capitalism and Culture: A Comparative Analysis of British and American Manufacturing Organizations*. Farnborough, Hants: Gower.

Josh, V. (1965) 'Personality profiles in industrial and pre-industrial cultures: a TAT study', *Journal of Social Psychology*, 66: 98–114.

Kahn, H. (1979) *World Economic Development: 1979 and Beyond*. London: Croom Helm.

Kao, H., Sinha, D. and Ng, S.H. (eds) (1994) *Effective Organizations and Social Values*. London: Sage.

Keesing, R. (1989) 'Exotic readings of cultural texts', *Current Anthropology*, 30 (4): 459–79.

Kerr, C., Dunlop, J.T., Harbison, F.H. and Myers, C.A. (1960) *Industrialism and Industrial Man: The Problems of Labor and Management in Economic Growth*. London: Heinemann.

Kiggundu, M.N. (1989) *Managing Organizations in Developing Countries*. Delhi: Kumarian Press.

Kluckhohn, C. (1951a) *Toward a General Theory of Action*. Cambridge, MA: Harvard University Press.

Kluckhohn, C. (1951b) 'The study of culture', in D. Lerner and H.D. Lasswell (eds), *The Policy Sciences*. Stanford, CA: Stanford University Press.

Kluckhohn, C. (1962) 'Universal categories of culture', in S. Tax (ed.), *Anthropology Today*. Chicago: University of Chicago Press.

Kluckhohn, F. and Strodtbeck, F.L. (1961) *Variations in Value Orientations*. Evanston, IL: Row, Peterson & Co.

Komin, S. (1990) 'Thai value system and its implication for development in Thailand', in D. Sinha and H.S.R. Kao (eds), *Social Values and Development: Asian Perspectives*. New Delhi: Sage. pp. 151–74.

Lammers, C.J. and Hickson, D.J. (eds) (1979) *Organizations Alike and Unlike: International and Inter-institutional Studies in the Sociology of Organizations*. London: Routledge and Kegan Paul.

Lauterbach, A. (1962) 'Managerial attitudes and economic growth', *Kyklos*, 2: 383–5.

Lepenies, W. (1981) 'Anthropological perspectives in the sociology of science', in E. Mendelsohn and Y. Elkana (eds), *Sciences and Cultures: Anthropological Studies of the Sciences*. Dordrecht: Reidel. pp. 245–61.

Levy, M. (1966) *Modernisation and the Structure of Societies*, Vol. 1. Princeton, NJ: Princeton University Press.

Lewis, W.A. (1955) *Theory of Economic Growth*. London: Allen and Unwin.

Loomba, A. (1998) *Colonialism/Postcolonialism*. London: Routledge.

Ludden, D. (1992) 'India's development regime', in N.B. Dirks (ed.), *Colonialism and Culture*. Ann Arbor, MI: Michigan University Press.

Lynn, R. (1971) *Personality and National Character*. London: Pergamon.

Mackerras, C. (1989) *Western Images of China*. New York: Oxford University Press.

Martin, J. (1990) 'Deconstructing organizational taboos: the suppression of gender conflict in organizations', *Organizational Science*, 1: 339–59.

Martin, J. (1994) 'The organization of exclusion: the institutionalization of sex unequality, gendered faculty jobs, and gendered knowledge in organizational theory and research organization', *Organization*, 1: 401–31.

Maznevski, M.L. and DiStefano, J.J. (1995) 'Measuring culture in international management: the cultural perspectives questionnaire'. Paper presented at the Academy of International Business Annual Conference, Seoul, Korea.

Maznevski, M.L., Nason, S.W. and DiStefano, J.J. (1993) 'Fourteen faces of culture: a new instrument for understanding cultural differences'. Paper presented at the Academy of International Business Conference, Hawaii.

McClelland, D.C. (1961) *The Achieving Society*. Princeton, NJ: Van Nostrand Reinhold.

Merton, R.K. (1968) *Social Theory and Social Structure*. Glencoe, IL: Free Press.

Miller, P. and Rose, N. (1990) 'Governing economic life', *Economy and Society*, 19: 1–31.

Mills, A.J. and Tancred, P. (eds) (1992) *Gendering Organizational Analysis*. Newbury Park, CA: Sage.

Minnich, E.K. (1990) *Transforming Knowledge*. Philadelphia: Temple University Press.

Moore, W.E. (1965) *The Impact of Industry*. Englewood Cliffs, NJ: Prentice-Hall.

Najita, T. (1993) 'Japan's industrial revolution in historical perspective', in M. Miyoshi and H.D. Harootunian (eds), *Japan in the World*. London: Duke University Press.

Nash, M. (1966) *Primitive and Peasant Economic Systems*. Chicago: University of Chicago–Chandler Publishing Co.

Ngugi wa Thiong'o (1981) *Decolonising the Mind: The Politics of Language in African Literature*. Portsmouth, NH: Heinemann.

Nkomo, S.M. (1992) 'The emperor has no clothes: rewriting "race" in organizations', *Academy of Management Review*, 17 (3): 487–513.

Oh, T.K. (1991) 'Understanding managerial values and behaviour among the Gang of Four: Korea, Taiwan, Singapore and Hong Kong', *Journal of Management Development*, 10 (20): 45–56.

O'Hanlon, R. and Washbrook, D. (1992) 'After Orientalism: culture, criticism and politics in the Third World', *Comparative Studies in Society and History*, 34: 141–67.

Oseen, C. (1997) 'The sexually specific subject and the dilemma of difference: rethinking the different in the construction of the non-hierarchical workplace', in P.

Prasad, A.J. Mills, M. Elmes and A. Prasad (eds), *Managing the Organizational Melting Pot: Dilemmas of Workplace Diversity*. London: Sage.

Osigweh, C.A.B. (1989) 'The myth of universality', in C.A.B. Osigweh (ed), *Organizational Science Abroad*. New York: Plenum Press.

Ouchi, W.G. (1981) *Theory Z: How American Business Can Meet the Japanese Challenge*. Reading, MA: Addison-Wesley.

Parry, B. (1987) 'Problems in current theories of colonial discourse', *Oxford Literary Review*, 13: 25–58.

Parsons, T. (1951) *The Social System*. London: Routledge & Kegan Paul.

Parsons, T. (1977) *The Evolution of Societies*. Englewood Cliffs, NJ: Prentice-Hall.

Parsons, T. and Shils, E.A. (1951) *Towards a General Theory of Action*. Cambridge, MA: Harvard University Press.

Pascale, R.T. and Athos, A.G. (1982) *The Art of Japanese Management*. London: Penguin.

Peng, T.K., Peterson, M.F. and Shyi, Y.P. (1991) 'Quantitative methods in cross-national management research: trends and equivalence issues', *Journal of Organizational Behaviour*, 12: 87–107.

Prasad, A. (1997) 'The colonising consciousness and representations of the Other: a postcolonial critique of the discourse of oil', in P. Prasad, A.J. Mills, M. Elmes and A. Prasad (eds), *Managing the Organizational Melting Pot: Dilemmas of Workplace Diversity*. London: Sage. pp. 285–311.

Prasad, P., Mills, A.J., Elmes, M. and Prasad, A. (eds) (1997) *Managing the Organizational Melting Pot: Dilemmas of Workplace Diversity*. London: Sage.

Pugh, D.S. (1969) 'The context of organization structures', *Administrative Science Quarterly*, 14: 94–114.

Pugh, D.S., Hickson, D.J., Hinings, C.R. and Turner, C. (1968) 'Dimensions of organization structure', *Administrative Science Quarterly*, 13: 33–47.

Punnett, B.J. and Shenkar, O. (1996) *Handbook for International Management Research*. Cambridge, MA: Blackwell.

Pye, L. (1985) *Asian Power and Politics*. Cambridge, MA: Harvard University Press.

Redding, S.G. (1980) 'Cognition as an aspect of culture and its relation to management process: a exploratory view of the Chinese case', *Journal of Management Studies*, 17 (2): 127–48.

Redding, S.G. (1982) 'Cultural effects on the marketing process in Southeast Asia', *Journal of the Market Research Society*, 24 (2): 98–122.

Redding, S.G. (1990) *The Spirit of Chinese Capitalism*. Berlin: Walter de Gruyter.

Redding, S.G. and Hsiao, M. (1990) 'An empirical study of overseas managerial ideology', *International Journal of Psychology*, 25: 629–41.

Redding, S.G. and Martyn-Johns, T.A. (1979) 'Paradigm differences and their relation to management, with reference to Southeast Asia', in G.W. England, A.R. Negandhi and B. Wilpert (eds), *Organizational Functioning in a Cross-Cultural Perspective*. Kent, OH: Comparative Administration Research Institute.

Redding, S. G. and Richardson, S. (1986) 'Participative management and its varying relevance in Hong Kong and Singapore', *Asia Pacific Journal of Management*, 3 (2): 76–98.

Redding, S.G. and Wong, G.Y.Y. (1986) 'The psychology of Chinese organizational behaviour', in M.H. Bond (ed.), *The Psychology of the Chinese People*. Hong Kong: Oxford University Press.

Richman, B.M. (1977) 'Significance of cultural variables', in T.D. Weinshall (ed.), *Culture and Management*. Middlesex, England: Penguin. pp. 15–38.

Ronen, S. (1986) *Comparative and Multinational Management.* New York: Wiley.

Ronen, S. and Shenkar, O. (1985) 'Clustering countries on attitudinal dimensions: a review and synthesis', *Academy of Management Review*, 19: 435–54.

Rushdie, S. (1992) *Imaginary Homelands: Essays and Criticism 1981-1991.* New York: Granta.

Said, E.W. (1978) *Orientalism.* New York: Random House.

Sakamoto, R. (1996) 'Japan, hybridity and the creation of colonialist discourse', *Theory, Culture and Society*, 13 (3): 113–28.

Sardar, Z. (1985) *Islamic Futures: The Shape of Ideas to Come.* London: Mansell.

Sawyer, J.E. (1954) 'The social basis of the American system of manufacturing', *Journal of Economic History*, XIV (4): 370–84.

Segall, M.H., Dasen, P.R., Berry, J.W. and Poortinga, Y.P. (1990) *Human Behaviour in Global Perspective: An Introduction to Cross-Cultural Psychology.* Boston: Allyn and Bacon.

Sirota, D. and Greenwood, J.M. (1971) 'Understand your overseas workforce', *Harvard Business Review*, 49 (1): 53–60.

Sjoberg, G. (1970) 'The comparative method in the social sciences', in A. Etzioni and F.L. Dobow (eds), *Comparative Perspectives: Theories and Methods.* Boston: Little, Brown and Co.

Smart, B. (1996) '(Mis)Understanding Japan', *Theory, Culture and Society*, 13 (3): 179–92.

Stoler, A.L. (1992) 'Rethinking colonial categories: European Communities and the boundaries of rule', in N.B. Dirks (ed.), *Colonialism and Culture.* Ann Arbor, MI: Michigan University Press. pp. 319–52.

Theodorson, G.A. (1953) 'Acceptance of industrialisation and its attendant consequences for the social pattern of non-Western societies', *American Sociological Review*, 18 (5): 476–85.

Thomas, N. (1994) *Colonialism's Culture: Anthropology, Travel and Government.* Cambridge: Polity Press.

Tibi, Bassam (1995) 'Culture and knowledge: the politics and Islamisation of knowledge as a postmodern project? The fundamentalist claim to de-Westernization', *Theory, Culture and Society*, 12: 1–24.

Triandis, H.C. (1982/3) 'Dimensions of cultural variations as parameters of organizational theories', *International Studies of Management and Organization*, 132 (4): 139–69.

Trompenaars, F. (1993) *Riding the Waves of Culture: Understanding Cultural Diversity in Business.* London: Nicholas Brealey.

Watt, W.M. (1988) *Islamic Fundamentalism and Modernity.* London: Routledge.

Webber, R.A. (1969) 'Convergence or divergence?', *Columbia Journal of World Business*, 4 (3): 75–83.

Weber, M. (1970a) *The Protestant Ethic and the Spirit of Capitalism.* London: George Allen and Unwin [original 1930].

Weber, M. (1970b) *Essays in Sociology*, ed. H.H. Gerth and C.W. Mills. London: Routledge and Kegan Paul [original 1948].

Weinshall, T. (ed.) (1977) *Culture and Management.* Harmondsworth: Penguin.

Westwood, R.I. (1997) 'Harmony and patriarchy: the cultural basis for "paternalistic headship" among the overseas Chinese', *Organization Studies*, 18 (3): 445–80.

Wilkinson, E. (1990) *Japan Versus the West: Image and Reality.* London: Penguin.

Wong, S.L. (1985) 'The Chinese family firm: a model', *The British Journal of Sociology*, 36 (1): 58–72.

Wong-Mingji, D. and Mir, Ali H. (1997) 'How international is international management? Provincialism, parochialism and the problematic of global diversity', in P. Prasad, A.J. Mills, M. Elmes and A. Prasad (eds), *Managing the Organizational Melting Pot: Dilemmas of Workplace Diversity*. London: Sage. pp. 340–64.

Yang, K.S. (1981) 'Social orientation and individual modernity amongst Chinese students in Taiwan', *Journal of Social Psychology*, 113: 159–70.

Yang, K.S. (1986) 'Chinese personality and its change', in M.H. Bond (ed.), *The Psychology of the Chinese People*. Hong Kong: Oxford University Press.

Yoshihara, K. (1988) *The Rise of Ersatz Capitalism in Southeast Asia*. Oxford: Oxford University Press.

12
Telling It Like It Is? Gender, Language and Organizational Theory

Joanna Brewis

The argument that organizational theory ignores, occludes or marginalizes gender difference, and therefore renders the subjugation of women in organizations invisible, is now well established in feminist-oriented analyses of organizational life. Indeed, in a review of texts dealing with gender and organization, Grey claims that

> What seems to be emerging (or to have emerged) ... is a new 'grid of intelligibility' within which it is not possible to make sense of organizations without recourse to concepts of gender ... That is to say, gender has always been an issue in organizations, but one which was occluded by the fact of male-domination of organization studies and society more generally. Thus the new grid of intelligibility is seen as desirable ... *it provides a more accurate picture of organizations.* (Grey, 1995: 49 – emphasis added)

Many of these (pro-)feminist commentators (for example, Mills and Tancred, 1992a, 1992b; Parkin, 1993) argue that a failure to recognize the differences between men's and women's experience of work results in the misleading assumption that organizations are gender-neutral environments – the claim here is that the language used by organizational theorists tends to neglect gender disparities. Consequently, the increasing trend towards a 'gendering' of organizational analysis – a deliberate attempt to make such language more inclusive – is seen as a step forward. This kind of analysis is seen to represent a better truth than conventional 'malestream' organizational analysis, which does not acknowledge gender as a highly influential organizing principle in human interaction.

It may seem odd that orthodox organizational analysis has been tagged '*male*stream', given the alternative argument that we need to gender our analysis of organizations. Might we not argue that the tag 'malestream' indicates that this form of organizational language *is* gendered? Indeed, as Grey (1995: 47) points out, so-called malestream organizational analysis is gendered in the sense that it speaks of *masculine* concepts such as reason, objectivity, logic, order and structure as central to efficient and effective organized life. These concepts can be considered to be masculine because women historically have been associated with the passions, the emotions and the instincts, given their capacity to carry and give birth to children:

> women are [seen to be] intrinsically closely involved with the family where so many 'natural', 'bodily' (and therefore lower) functions occur, whereas men are [seen to be] intrinsically involved with the world of work where (at least for some) 'cultural', 'mental', and therefore higher functions occur. (Martin, 1989: 17 – see also Hearn, 1993)

The salient point here, perhaps, is that orthodox organizational analysts do not *explicitly acknowledge* the gendered character of the language they use. As Grey (1995: 50) suggests, 'previous discursive formulations have included gender but in marginalized or misogynized form'. Paradoxically, then, malestream organizational theory can be seen to fail to account for gender difference in organizing in practice, whilst at the same time using tacitly gendered concepts of organizing which are mirrored in this practice.

Weber's classic bureaucratic model might be seen to be a case in point.[1] As Thompson and McHugh (1995: 147) suggest, in (pro-)feminist writing on organizations, Weber 'is placed firmly in the centre of this "malestream" organisational analysis'. The characteristics of Weber's (1970: 196–8; 1994: 226–8) ideal type model of bureaucracy include a clearly defined hierarchy, within which officials are positioned on the basis of merit, paid according to rank and have a specific area of jurisdiction. Further, bureaucratic officials' work within the bureaucracy is their sole or primary occupation and represents a career, within which judgements about promotion are made by their seniors. In the Weberian ideal type, these officials are also subject to discipline in the form of strict rules and procedures; and the authority of senior officials rests on the acceptance of bureaucratic rules and those officials' right to enact such rules. Thus their authority adheres to the office, not to the official themselves. Weber also points out that

> The theory of modern public administration ... assumes that the authority to order certain matters by decree ... does not entitle the bureau to regulate the matter by commands given for each case, but only to regulate the matter abstractly. This stands in extreme contrast to the regulation of all relationships through individual privileges and bestowals of favor [sic], which is absolutely dominant in patrimonialism .... (Weber, 1970: 198)

Feminist and pro-feminist organizational theorists, however, have suggested that Weber's foregrounding of reason, objectivity, logic, order, structure and an upwardly progressive career in his analysis of bureaucracy is *masculine,* and translates into the derogation of women in such organizations in practice. That is to say, these theorists have sought to explicitly gender Weber's original analysis. Kanter's (1977) liberal feminist stance in *Men and Women of the Corporation,* for example, makes the point that bureaucracies are often, indeed typically, characterized by gendered inequality of opportunity, and the glass ceiling in particular. For Kanter, the problem is women's powerlessness. Her point is that women ought to be socialized and developed differently (that is, in a more masculine mode) within such organizations so as to be able to accede to positions of power, and to redress the existing gender imbalance. Ferguson (1984: 9), writing in the radical feminist tradition, suggests that bureaucracy represents the 'scientific organization of inequality'. She rejects the way in which masculine bureaucracy, as she sees it, subjects its participants to a process of feminization, so that they become slaves to their superiors' wishes and commands.[2] Ferguson suggests that this is more problematic for women than it is for men because women are already produced as subservient by their experience in the family – thus there is a 'doubling' of their subordination in bureaucracies. Her conclusion is that bureaucracy can never be democratic, and therefore has to be replaced with alternative modes of organization which are non-hierarchical and process focused, as opposed to being goal or outcome focused (Ferguson, 1984: 190).[3,4]

Despite their theoretical differences, both Kanter and Ferguson suggest that, in order to understand organizations properly, we need to look for gender difference in organizational processes, rules, systems, interactions, cultures and procedures – that is, we need to employ gender in the language that we use to characterize organizational life. What is also implied here is a need to attend to participants' accounts of organizational life (especially accounts from women) which reveal gender difference rather than homogeneity; that a focus on gender difference in listening to the language used by those who take part in organizations in our empirical work will lead to more sophisticated theorizing of the gendered ways in which organizations work.

The same views are expressed in (pro-)feminist work on sexual harassment. In particular, much of this analysis abides by the tenet that the phenomenon of workplace harassment has been identified as a result of listening to what women have to say about their working lives. For example,

> Did the relations that constitute sexual harassment exist before they were named, and did the women in those relations have an experience? Is not that pre-discursive experience the reason that women wanted to take the personally risky and politically fundamental step of giving the experience a name? (Cain, 1993: 89)

As is evident in the quotations above, sexual harassment is usually depicted in harassment literature as a phenomenon that has existed as long as women have engaged in paid labour outside of the home, but one that has only recently become a topic for public discussion. Cain clearly evokes the understanding that sexual harassment as a pattern of behaviour existed prior to any form of linguistic representation or problematization of that behaviour as harassment. MacKinnon (cited in Benson and Thomson, 1982: 236) is also emphatic that working men harassed working women before this behaviour was labelled as harassment – the problem she identifies is specifically one of there not being a language available to understand or express such experiences prior to the Williams case. Hoffman (1986), in her analysis of harassment in academia, extends these claims to suggest that harassment has been 'discovered' – that is to say, recognized as an already present phenomenon and inserted into language – by commentators such as herself (see also Brewer and Berk, 1982; Ellis et al., 1991; Maypole and Skaine, 1983; Ross and England, 1987; Taubman, 1986). Further, Cain in particular suggests that the recognition of harassment has been achieved through individual women insisting that their mistreatment be publicly voiced, even in the absence of a linguistic framework through which to make sense of the claim that male members of organizations systematically and continually seek to oppress their female colleagues. That is to say, in general these commentators imply that the recognition of harassment has been achieved through sensitivity to gender difference in empirical accounts of organizational life, and that the voicing of gender differentiated experiences represents a hitherto repressed and unheard language of that life (also see Brewis, 2001; Brewis and Linstead, 2000: Ch. 3).

In both the harassment literature and the feminist analyses of bureaucracy, then, we see the emphasis on taking (women's) accounts of organizational life which identify gender difference seriously, in order to build a more satisfactory and inclusive language which fully captures the ways in which organizations work. The emerging theme in this and other organizational theorizing is that, to put it crudely, whether one is male or female *matters* at work – and such an understanding of organizational life is disruptive in a very real sense. By paying attention to gender, it affirms that men and women are likely to experience organizations in different ways. Thus, gendered organizational analysis does deviate from the asexual and ungendered representation of organizations characteristic of the malestream orthodoxy. In short, it resists this hitherto dominant paradigm in the study of organized life.

However, let us consider the stance of those organizational analysts who seek to gender organizational theory in the ways suggested above – by looking for gender in organizational processes, rules, systems, interactions, cultures and procedures – in more detail. This seems important given the growing number of texts which insist that the insertion of gender into academic language is indispensable in our understanding of how organizations work, and the corollary that the organizational orthodoxy appears to be shifting in order to include, as Grey (1995: 46) puts it, 'gender as a grid of [organizational] intelligibility'. As already stated, these analysts seem to see the knowledge they produce as more accurate than the claims made by malestream organizational theorists. Their more or less explicit thesis appears to be that, in its omission/occlusion/marginalization of gender difference, malestream organizational theory throws up a linguistic smokescreen which conceals the prevalence of male dominance in organizations. Are we to accept these claims as unproblematic, as a notable advance in the field of organizational analysis?

To answer this question, it is pertinent to employ the work of Foucault (especially 1980), whose analysis is premised on the identification of what he refers to as discourses; sets of ideas, theories, symbols, institutions and practices which underpin and reproduce specific ways of knowing and behaving in the world (also see Brewis, 1998: especially 60–7; Brewis, 2000: especially 72–5; Brewis, 2001). The relevant instances here are the discourse of gender difference which positions men and women as possessing distinct characteristics, abilities and traits, and the discourse that interprets the workplace as an environment in which rationality and objectivity must prevail at all costs, which elsewhere has been labelled scientific modernism (Geuss, cited in Reed, 1985: 80–1; Brewis, 1996, 2000).[5] Consequently, specific forms of 'talk, rule-following, behavior-patterning [sic], writing, reading, image creation, interrogation and thought …' (Brewis et al., 1997: 1277) in particular parts of our lives represent discursive regimes. Foucault argues that discourses create subject positions, spaces for individuals to locate themselves within and to define themselves through. He suggests that we settle ourselves amongst the subject positions available to us, as produced by existing discourses, and therefore come to understand ourselves and to know how we should go about our lives. For example, as we generate knowledge about what we think it means to be human, we simultaneously consume this knowledge; we learn about who we are, and behave accordingly. Thus we are lived embodiments of discourse; the operations of discursive regimes act to structure the field of our possibilities as humans. Only through the effects of these regimes do we come to know about ourselves, becoming self-aware subjects capable of particular forms of action. Foucault refers to this as the process of subjectification, or *assujetissement*.

Discourse, then, is *powerful* – it has material and concrete effects. As Foucault puts it, '"Truth" is linked in a circular relation with systems of power which produce and sustain it, and to effects of power which it induces and which extend it' (Foucault, 1986: 74). Importantly, he goes on to suggest that discourse is also contingent – that our current behaviours, ideas and structures are nothing more, and nothing less, than a series of historically and culturally located interpretations of what it is to be human. That is to say, we as human agents create 'truths' about the world, and the objects and people within it, by thinking, being and doing in particular ways; but Foucault (1986: 46) argues that there are other ways of being, thinking and doing, which are no more or less 'true' than those which we currently practise. As we talk, follow rules, behave, write, read, create symbols, ask questions and think in particular ways, then, we place artificial limits around ourselves. The power of discourse, however, is one that produces us as active and self-conscious agents, not a power which distorts, represses and conceals the truth of who we are and how we should live (Foucault, 1980: 98).

This is not to say that discourse does not operate in such a way as to make certain forms of talk, rules, behaviour, writing, reading, symbol creation, questioning and thinking possible, and others impossible, within specific historical and cultural epistemes. Discourse works so as to include and exclude simultaneously. Indeed, when MacKinnon says that sexual harassment was 'unspeakable' prior to *Williams v Saxbe*, she captures something of this inclusive/exclusive effect, although her position is very much that the dominant patriarchal/masculinist discourse obscured the *truth* that is harassment up until this point, rather than the Foucauldian alternative that harassment as a phenomenon has been produced by the ways in which particular feminist discourses work. That is to say, for Foucault (cited in Sheridan, 1980: 98), 'discourse is not about objects, rather discourse constitutes them'.

A question which inevitably arises from this presentation of Foucault's analysis of discourse points to the ways in which powerful discourses – such as scientific modernism – achieve their dominance, and in so doing exclude ways of knowing the world which do not sit within their confines. Indeed, his own work has focused in detail on the ways in which individuals classified and constructed as 'mad', 'sick', 'criminal' and sexually 'deviant' have been marginalized, pathologized, and simultaneously created as legitimate targets of medical, legal and governmental intervention, by particular constructions of what it is to be human (Foucault, 1967, 1973, 1977, 1979). A lengthy discussion of this issue is beyond the scope of this chapter, but it is worth alluding to Foucault's focus on the micro-relations of power to suggest how certain discourses come to be privileged over others. In his analysis of the operations of discourse, he is concerned less to suggest an over-arching theory of what power is than to offer an 'analytics' of power – to examine how power actually works in the specific sites in which it is exercised (Foucault, 1980, 1982; see also Knights and Vurdubakis, 1994). It is this interest in sites where individual subjects are produced which underlies Foucault's work:

> I am attempting ... to *open up* problems that are as *concrete* and *general* as possible, problems that approach politics from behind and cut across societies on the diagonal, problems that are at once constituents of our history and constituted by that history; for example the relation between sanity and insanity; the question of illness, of crime, or of sexuality. (Foucault, 1986: 375–6)

Foucault, then, does not so much ignore structures of power (something of which he is frequently accused) as conduct an ascending, 'bottom-up' analysis of the workings of power. As he explains,

> the important thing is not to attempt some kind of deduction of power starting from its centre and aimed at the discovery of the extent to which it permeates down to its base, of the degree to which it reproduces itself down to and including the most molecular elements of society. One must rather conduct an *ascending* analysis of power, starting, that is from its infinitesimal mechanisms, which each have their own history, their own trajectory, their own techniques and tactics ... (Foucault, 1980: 99)

A Foucauldian approach would not, therefore, start from the empirical fact that it is men who tend to be in positions of power in organizations and in society more broadly to infer the production and sustenance of discourses such as scientific modernism which privilege men above women in the language that they use and the practices that they encompass. Rather, it would argue that the systematic conferring of such privilege results from a 'swarming' (Rouse, 1994: 106) or 'codifying' of subjectifying micro-practices which is politically and economically expedient at this level. For example, Foucault (1986: 182–3) explains how localized eighteenth century disciplines such as training soldiers to hold and use their bodies in a particular way were initially developed to meet specific needs such as the invention of new forms of weaponry, but eventually emerged as 'general forms of [bodily] domination'. These specific techniques, he suggests, were imitated in other sites where similar exigencies existed so as to 'gradually produce the blueprint of a general method ... being totally inscribed in general and essential transformations ...'. The discursive regime of scientific modernism, we might argue, has therefore 'swarmed' out of highly specific and contingent reactions to, for example, new industrial technologies, political problems such as increased geographical mobility of populations (Bauman, 1983) and particular religious transformations, all of which demanded certain forms of organizing in their wake. The power that this discourse affords to men (or, more precisely, masculine subjects) 'should not at all be seen as a simple projection of the central power' (Foucault, 1980: 201). The reproduction across the early modern social of local forms of organizing which demonstrated their 'political [and/or economic] usefulness' in specific sites has instead, we might suggest, generated ways of thinking, being and doing which generate and consolidate that power, so that organizing more generally now tends to be done in ways which favour men (masculine individuals).

Foucault's position is therefore substantially different from the work of commentators like Kanter, Ferguson, Cain et al., who seem to believe that 'the truth is out there', to coin a phrase, and who argue that gender difference is central to an inclusive (that is to say, true or accurate) language of organizational life. Power for them is oppressive; the power ascribed to men in organizations and in society in general produces inaccurate and obscuring (malestream) representations of how organizations work. Foucault (1986: 61), on the other hand, asks 'If power were never anything but repressive, if it never did anything but to say no, do you really think one would be brought to obey it?' Power for him is not a possession which we can share, acquire or seize. Rather it is relational, we subjugate ourselves within it, we actively reproduce power through our own thoughts and actions (Foucault, 1979: 94). Consequently, the claim that malestream organizational analysis is inaccurate, power-tainted and ideological, and that gender ought to be a central component in the analysis of organizations, can be re-considered using a Foucauldian perspective.

We can start this re-consideration by reiterating that theorizing which takes the above position is part of an alternative discourse which *resists* scientific modernism, the discourse to which malestream organizational theorizing belongs. However, from a Foucauldian point of view, the discourse to which gendered organizational theorizing belongs is no more 'true' than the orthodox perspective of organizations as gender-neutral environments. Taking this analysis further implies that this alternative discourse may generate power effects of its own. Might it not, for example, produce a sense on the part of working men and women that their genderedness is irrevocably influential over their organizational experience; that it represents one of the defining characteristics of their experience as humans, and as workers? More specifically, this discourse can be seen perhaps to constitute women in particular as believing that the organizational world sets them up to fail, that their working lives are *necessarily* impeded and made more difficult by their gender. Is this understanding any more liberational than an understanding on the part of these same women that organizational failure is due to their personal flaws (as opposed to anything more structural), an understanding which might be seen to be an effect of scientific modernist discourse?

As can be inferred from the above discussion, much of the re-reading of organizational life as gendered does not chime with Foucault's requirements for intellectual analysis (one form of the production of knowledge, of certain languages which speak of how the world works). He bases these requirements on the inextricable bonds that he identifies between power and discourse. For Foucault, intellectual analysis should provide at least some impetus for what he calls the 'critical ontology of self' (Foucault, 1986: 50); that is to say, for a relationship to self in which we have become attuned to the operations of power through us, and have realized that it is misguided to understand particular discursive regimes as reflecting some kind of unassailable truth. Foucault's argument is that our current preoccupation with truth prevents us from identifying the ways in which we continually place artificial barriers around ourselves; that it prevents us from experimenting with the ways in which we think and behave. Thus for Foucault there are opportunity costs attached to every way of being/thinking/doing because every way of being/thinking/doing is simultaneously a way of not being/thinking/doing (and all ways of being/thinking/doing, as Foucault (1986: 343) himself puts it, are 'dangerous').

Knights and Vurdubakis (1994: 188) suggest, then, that 'Foucault embarked on a project of estrangement from that identity [the way we currently understand ourselves] by rendering visible the various costs involved in how we become "who we are" ...'. Freedom for Foucault is an active, reflexive *process* of being, thinking and doing; it is based on us choosing how we relate to ourselves and to others, without being bound by some unfounded belief in the truth of who we are and how we should live. In other words, Foucault counsels that we examine all of our beliefs, texts, practices, images, rules, institutions and systems for the possibly dangerous implications they may have, in line with his dictum that there are always other ways of being, doing and thinking. It is, therefore, transgression that characterizes his conceptualization of freedom; the idea of going beyond what we had always thought was inevitable, the seeking out of what Foucault calls 'limit experiences'. These involve living in as risky a fashion as possible so as to uncover the 'constructedness' of our fears. It necessitates a defiance of the constraints we have placed around ourselves to reveal them as having no firm metaphysical or ontological grounding. Foucault calls on us to undertake limit experiences in order to challenge the ways in which we have been constituted to be, do and think ourselves (Foucault, 1986: 50).[6]

In order to impel this kind of practice amongst individual subjects, Foucault argues that a particular kind of intellectual work is required; not the confidence of those who proclaim that gender is a crucial and not-to-be-overlooked aspect of organizational life, but the kind of analysis that holds all so-called truths up for scrutiny in such a way as to reveal them for the historically and culturally located interpretations that they are. Given that discourses cannot be definitive, any claim to the contrary, from a Foucauldian point of view, either consolidates the operations of existing discursive regimes, or installs a new kind of regime, with an accompanying set of subjectifying effects (Gandal, 1986: 129; Knights and Vurdubakis, 1994: 192). The intellectual role of guru, of teacher, is, therefore, displaced by Foucauldian analysis (Sheridan, 1980). The foremost consideration that Foucault puts forward for this rethinking of the functions of the intellectual is that their role should

> not [be] a matter of emancipating truth from every system of power (which would be a chimera for truth is already power) but of detaching the power from the forms of hegemony, social, economic and cultural, within which it operates at the present time. (Foucault, 1985: 94)

The intellectual here is asked to question truth claims; to challenge prevailing conceptualizations of the truth, but to make it clear at the same time that there is no better truth than what is already available, merely different interpretations; to use language in such a way as to mark fluidity and ambiguity rather than attempting to fix what takes place in the world around us:

> I dream of the intellectual who destroys evidence and generalities, the one who, in the inertias and constraints of the present time, locates and marks the weak points, the openings, the lines of force, who is incessantly on the move, doesn't know exactly where he [sic] is heading nor what he will think tomorrow for he is too attentive to the present. (Foucault, 1988: 124)

Those who adhere to the position which puts gender at the centre of organizational analysis are, from this perspective, insufficiently self-reflexive; they seemingly prefer to assume that they have attained a 'better truth' by resisting the allegedly distorted 'truths' peddled by malestream organizational theorizing, that the language they use to represent organizations is more inclusive than that used by malestream writers.

Nonetheless, a Foucauldian analysis of organizations would not reject out of hand any attempt to read organizations through the lens of gender; it would not dismiss attempts to listen to women's own accounts of organizational life to ascertain the differences between their experiences and those of men. This is because the inclusive/exclusive effects of prevailing discursive regimes necessarily '[push] back a whole teratology of knowledge beyond [their] margins' (Foucault, cited in Barrett, 1991: 143), such that a reactivation of marginalized voices demonstrates that what passes for truth has really only succeeded in achieving intellectual ascendancy. That is to say, the resurrection of the marginalized reveals the historical and cultural character of prevailing discourse and undermines its status as truth. With regard to gender and organizations, then, we might use Foucault to suggest that women's experiences of organizational life have, in the modern West, been marginalized by that which has come to be accepted as the truth of organizations (that they are neutral, non-discriminatory environments in which relations are governed by objectivity and rationality so as to ensure that there is no reward for anything other than individual merit). This has some limited parallels with the approach taken by Kanter, Ferguson, Cain et al. However, and importantly, Foucault refuses to acknowledge that what has been marginalized is somehow a more authentic truth, a more inclusive language, than that which is accepted wisdom, as earlier discussion of MacKinnon's claim that harassment historically was 'unspeakable' suggests. Rather, he sees this focus on previously silent voices, as suggested above, as revelatory; that there are other ways of interpreting human existence:

> One does not have to maintain that these confused voices sound better than the others and express the ultimate truth. For there to be a sense in listening to them and in searching for what they say, it is sufficient that they exist and that they have against them so much which is set up to silence them. (Foucault, cited in Smart, 1986: 171)

The 'sense in listening' to these 'confused voices', these other languages, then, lies in the fact that they point to the unfoundedness of prevailing discourses; they are no more true than what is currently accepted as true, but they do indicate that there are alternative ways of knowing the world (McNay, 1992). Furthermore, in listening to these voices, we become able to identify the implications of their omission from or marginalization in prevailing organizational discourse given that prevailing discourse, in the way that it constructs the world, either prevents us from noting this omission/marginalization or explicitly justifies it.

A Foucauldian approach might suggest, then, that we listen to accounts of women's lives in organizations, that we attend to the language that they use to construct their experiences, in such a way as to proclaim the ways in which their experience differs from that of men, whilst also being sensitive to the ways in which it does not. As already established, the former function is to some extent performed by the perspective on organizations which sees gender as central – including the feminist analyses of bureaucracy and of sexual harassment. However, a Foucauldian perspective would also have as an important tenet of its argument the idea that it is prevailing discourses which constitute us as 'men' or 'women', much as they place boundaries between the 'sane' and the 'mad', the 'healthy' and the 'sick', the 'law-abiding' member of society and the 'criminal', the sexually 'normal' and the sexually 'deviant' (Brewis et al., 1997). Consequently, listening to women's voices from this point of view *does not* imply the 'rounding out' of an organizational picture which historically has been one-sided or truncated. It is not a matter of closing the theoretical circle, of making academic language about organizations more inclusive, having firstly invited all parties involved to contribute, as is implied by commentators such as Kanter, Ferguson and Cain. If we accept that gender is a discursive category[7] – i.e. that there is no biological or essential basis to masculinity and femininity as sets of behaviours, attitudes and experiences – then we must accept that there is nothing authentically 'feminine' about women, that they are constituted as such by discourse. Any differences between men and women's behaviours in, attitudes to and experiences of organizations are therefore produced by discursive regimes. That is to say, if women experience discrimination in organizations, this is because the prevailing discourse of gender difference constitutes women as less rational, less objective and less capable of logical thought (Cixous, 1988; Hines, 1992; Martin, 1989), not because men are somehow incapable of recognizing what women can really do. This is not just a matter of women being produced as women, however. It is also a matter of organizations being produced, as already suggested, as masculine through the discourse of scientific modernism; that the workplace is understood to be and structured as an environment in which rationality, logic and objectivity must prevail at all costs. Scientific modernism therefore works in tandem with the prevailing discourse of gender difference, arguably bringing about the following effects:

(i)   It produces understandings and representations of organizations as places which should not be 'tainted' by the irrational – the irrational becomes the antithesis of organizational life.

(ii)   It produces understandings and representations of women as less suited to organizational life, given their positioning within the discourse of gender difference as irrational, emotional and inevitably subjective in decision making.

In a Foucauldian analysis, listening to women talking about organizations therefore allows us to explore the ways in which their discursive positioning *may* ensure, in *certain* organizational situations, that they are degraded and denigrated, or at least treated differently; to reveal the powerful character of the discursive regime around gender difference where it operates alongside, indeed implicitly genders, scientific modernism. What is being aimed at here is a more reflexive understanding of organizations; one which acknowledges that the prevalence of any single organizational language is potentially dangerous, especially for those whom that language disenfranchises. Crucially, then, a

Foucauldian approach differs from the perspective which positions gender as central to organizational life in its intellectual approach – it is not an attempt to replace one 'truth' with another but, instead, to point to how particular ways of knowing the world inevitably operate in inclusive and exclusive ways. How, then, might we actually apply Foucault to accounts of organizational life from men and women in this regard? How might these accounts reveal to us that women being discursively constituted as women *potentially* results in them being derogated in organizations? How might these accounts be used to afford us another way of seeing which allows a different, if not necessarily more true or more accurate, picture of organizational life, the better to assess the implications/opportunity costs of the ways in which we currently organize? To attempt to answer these questions, this chapter now turns to data gathered from qualitative interviews undertaken in a UK university and in a UK financial services organization.[8]

At the University of Smithtown, interviews were carried out in the engineering department (E) and the chemistry department (C). Both engineering and chemistry can be identified as scientific in emphasis, and individuals in these departments could therefore be argued to work in the very apotheosis of a 'man's world', certainly numerically and, as the data reveal, also discursively. Interviews were conducted with male and female academic and support (that is, administrative and technical) staff at all levels. Department E is a large department spread across several buildings on campus, the history of which dates back to the origins of the university in the early nineteenth century. At the time of the interviews, the department employed something of the order of 70 academic staff, of whom only three were female. Support staff, on the other hand, tended to be female on the administrative side and male on the technical side. Of the 750 students studying for undergraduate and postgraduate qualifications, approximately 10% were female. Department C is much smaller and much newer – indeed its standing as a research and teaching centre in its own right dates back only as far as the early 1970s. It is contained within a single building. At the time of the interviews, there were some 35 academic staff employed in department C, and some 160 postgraduate students studying for various qualifications. As in department E, only a minute proportion of the academic staff, and an only slightly larger proportion of the students, were female. The gender split amongst support staff was also similar to that found in department E. All senior staff in both departments, whether academic or support, were male.

The second organization, Minerva Financial Services, employs more than 10,000 staff nationwide; roughly half of which sell the company's products (for example, insurance policies). The other half administer the products which have been sold. More than 2,000 staff work at Minerva headquarters, the location where the interviews were held, and all were in the latter capacity. Interviews at Minerva again were conducted with male and female staff at all levels, and these men and women worked in three different departments – Human Resources, Car Insurance and Home Insurance. Minerva did not display quite the same degree of horizontal and vertical segregation as was evident at Smithtown. There were, for example, many female supervisors (in charge of small teams numbering perhaps 10 individuals within departments). However, there were few women in evidence in the more senior positions, and it is also worth noting that in Human Resources, where the majority of staff were women, the HR Manager was male. Moreover, the clerical work which many of the respondents here were employed to do is traditionally seen as 'women's work'; although, as already stated, men still attained the higher organizational echelons in Minerva in greater numbers.

As suggested above, the language used by respondents in these interviews implies that the prevailing discourses in both Smithtown and Minerva are scientific modernism (organizations are rational, logical and objective environments with no room for sentiment and emotion) and the discourse of gender difference (men are rational, logical and objective; women are irrational, illogical and subjective). This is unsurprising, given the powerful character of both discourses and the fact that they can be seen to predominate in our understandings and practices across the modern West.

For example, male academic staff at Smithtown were reported as having a tendency to treat their female colleagues very differently from the way in which they treated each other, seemingly based on their discursively constituted understanding of what women are and can do. Indeed, one female lecturer had, she claimed, suffered from a serious stress-related illness as a result of the treatment meted out by her male colleagues, which behaviour she explained as follows:

> I think there are two aspects to prejudice ... gender and race, and it is very difficult to fight against that ... I've not taken much action; they have taken action against me, I've not taken action against them. It's upsetting me now because I feel that maybe I should have [taken action] ...

In general, this woman described her department (E) as having a highly sexist culture, as compounded in her case by racist attitudes (she is a woman of colour). Her colleague, working in a different section of department E, similarly implied that sexist attitudes prevailed amongst male academic staff. This emerged in a comment that this respondent had not been asked to apply for the lectureship that she held at the time of the interviews, even though she had been a Research Associate in the department when the vacancy had arisen. She believed that this omission was due to her male colleagues' belief that she, as a young married woman, would inevitably be considering a break from work in the near future to have children, and also commented that

> [my male colleagues] don't see that what's sauce for the goose should be sauce for the gander. Like sometimes I do wonder if I came in, you know, in the morning and said 'I'm pregnant', you know, 'I'm going to have twins', you know, 'I'm very happy about this, how about me going part-time, chaps?' they'd all be 'Oh, er, ah, this is going to be so difficult' and they've all got four

children, they're allowed to have four children.

Here, this woman implies that, not only was it sexist for her male colleagues to assume that she wanted children, but also that, in the event of her becoming pregnant, this would not be seen by her male colleagues as in any way commensurate with them having families. In other words, the men in her section would automatically assume that she would want to stay at home and care for her child full-time, because their wives take the bulk of domestic responsibility in their families. This points us, firstly, to the way in which women may be constituted by the discourse of gender difference – as properly responsible for most of the delivery of care within the family, and for the greater proportion of domestic labour – and simultaneously by the discourse of scientific modernism – as therefore less suitable for organizational life. In critiquing such assumptions, Eisenstein (1993) takes issue with the term 'working mother', because she argues that it positions women who have children as mothers first and workers second; and promotes the understanding that they are working *despite* having children. The term 'working father', by way of contrast, does not have common currency. Barrett (1980: 157) also points out that the way in which women are understood in society more generally – as care providers – can be seen to explain the location of women within the workforce (see also Hartmann, 1981; Mitchell, 1971).

The above, however, has implications for men just as it does for women. Walton (1998), for example, describes how the fathers in her research, which focused on men who worked in 'flexible' ways such as job share and part-time, told her that they had all taken time off from work at the time when their children were born, but that in no instance had they been able to do this through formal organizational channels. Whereas maternity leave for women is an established statutory right in the UK, these men had had to take unpaid leave or sick leave, or use up part of their holiday allowance at these times. Given that the Maternity and Parental Leave Regulations (1999), which have their origins in the EU Parental Leave Directive, have now come into force in the UK, this situation has now changed, at least to some extent.[9] Nonetheless, as Walton also argues, for legislative changes to have any real effect fatherhood needs to become part of men's 'defining role' just as motherhood is part of women's 'defining role'. There is evidence that suggests that men have, in the main, yet to embrace fatherhood in this way; for example, Kivimäki (1998) points out that, in Finland, where 'right to care' leave has been a feature of employment law provisions for some time, very few men actually take their full entitlement – due, we might surmise, to concerns that to do so would somehow compromise their standing as men and as organizational participants. Harlow (1999: 5), in a similar vein, reports research undertaken at Edinburgh University which suggests that working British fathers, especially those in executive or professional positions, spend as little as 15 minutes a day with their children. This compares to an average of 90 minutes for women in equivalent jobs. Although researcher Lynn Jamieson attributes part of this phenomenon to increasing job insecurity, her data also suggest that many men enjoy the social kudos of fatherhood more than the actuality of looking after their offspring. Thus the twin discourses of gender difference and scientific modernism can be seen to work together to construct and maintain gendered patterns in the division of labour at home and at work – which could be seen to be dangerous for both men and women.

Further to the above, a female secretary, who worked in department C at Smithtown, commented on a male academic's surprise that she was able to put together a high-quality report, that she was capable (it was implied) of a task demanding reason, rigour and accuracy. She stated that

> I think ... [Smithtown is] quite a chauvinistic institution and I think women's ability, I suppose I'm thinking of myself here, I can only speak for myself, you have to really prove that you can hold up in certain areas.

This woman also reported a similar incident, which she again attributed to sexism and which involved a male academic refusing to believe that she could operate the university computer system. Furthermore, another female member of department C suggested that this kind of treatment was characteristic of her experience of work per se, that 'sometimes I've been made to feel less intelligent than my male counterparts'. This respondent was a doctoral student, and told the following story about an experience she had had at a conference:

> Recently I went to a conference abroad with my, well, not with my supervisor, but he was there ... and his son was there and it was a [chemistry] conference and his son's not an expert in [chemistry] or anything, and [her supervisor] tried to introduce me and his son to this male, this expert in [chemistry] and basically [the expert] didn't even look at me, let alone acknowledge me ... he thought I was [the son's] girlfriend ... I did actually make a point of saying, you know, 'I'm at this conference, basically I do know what I'm talking about'.

What is interesting here is the reported assumption that the woman speaking could only have been attending the conference as a guest of one of the male delegates – and the assumption that she was another man's girlfriend is arguably even more significant, defining her as it did both through her relationship to the men also present and her sexuality. Here the implication is clear – that women's proper role is as a (sexual) adjunct to men.[10]

In their own language of organizational life, then, the Smithtown women quoted above all suggest that they have experienced sexist treatment at the hands of their male colleagues; according to them, these men believe that men and women have different capabilities and that women, on the whole, cannot be expected to behave in the rational, logical and intelligent way which organizational participation demands.

Other respondents, both male and female, *themselves* used language about women which criticized them for being less rational or logical, and more subjective, than men – indeed some of these comments were offered by the very women who complained of the sexism displayed by their male colleagues. One set of observations, offered by Minerva respondents, centred on the fact that women are less likely to display the impersonal 'toughmindedness' required to make decisions at work:

> [I]t depends how assertive you are, a lot of women are not very assertive ... (female senior employee relations officer)

> Mostly the supervisors are women ... I think they may give a softer approach if [staff] step out of line. I wouldn't know for certain, it just may appear that way. (male clerk)

> I think [management are] trying to encourage more men to come in. I think they generally prefer male supervisors, whether they've got a bit more authority I don't know. I think the women are generally more lenient towards letting customers off paying money whereas a man'd argue down the phone, say 'No, you're not having this, we are going to take you to court', whereas a woman might say, particularly my supervisor would say 'Oh, they can have it'. (male senior clerk)

Aspersions were also cast on women's judgement, particularly as connected to their apparent predilection for bitchiness, for attacking co-workers on grounds unrelated to their work performance. For example:

> there is quite a bit of infighting among the girls upstairs, you know, and they watch each other ... I don't like it. I mean, I used to mix a lot more with the girls but since they started all the catty infighting I've come out of it because I don't like it. But I think when you get a group of women together you always get that – one watches what the other's got, doesn't like it ... (female technician, Smithtown)

On the other hand, female interviewees were, sometimes simultaneously, just as damning of women who had seemingly gone *too far beyond* their 'natural' femininity. For instance, one female academic was represented by other women in department C at Smithtown as 'bolshy' and 'pushy'; adjectives which were not used to describe men. Indeed, this woman was seen as having 'something to prove'. An example given was her refusal, upon her promotion from a postdoctoral research position to a lectureship, to share an office – even though the impression gained from the data collection was that the *male* lecturers in the department all had sole occupancy offices. Other relevant comments were offered by a secretary in department E – she suggested that female undergraduates, after entering the university, underwent a transformation to become much more like their male colleagues. After a few months on the engineering degree course, it appeared to her that there was little to differentiate the female undergraduates from the male undergraduates 'apart from their boobs'. Importantly for the argument here, the tone with which this respondent delivered this evaluation, as well as the language she used, strongly suggested that this was not a transformation of which she approved.

In the above data, then, a general understanding and representation of women and work through the twin discourses of gender difference and of scientific modernism is apparent – both in what respondents actually say and do and in what they report others as having said and done. The women at Smithtown and Minerva might therefore be seen to be caught in an organizational double bind; it appears that they must, on the one hand, not appear overly feminine, because otherwise they will not be taken seriously but, on the other, they must be careful not to stray too far into the domain of the masculine, lest they be seen as unnaturally assertive, 'pushy' or 'bolshy'. The problems identified by Sheppard (1989) that women can experience in managing gender identity at work, and the judgements that they are subject to if they do not 'succeed' in this endeavour, are apparent here. Sheppard makes reference to the fact that her women managers had to be careful to tread a 'tightrope' of impression management; that they felt compelled to balance their appearance and their behaviour so as to give off a mixture of signals to the effect that, whilst they were able to be masculine enough to 'do the job', they had not in any way abandoned or compromised their femininity. Otherwise, they worried about, for example, attracting punitive labels such as 'lesbian' and 'castrating bitch' (see also Bartky, cited in Martin, 1989: 21; Brewis, 1999: 91–2, 93; Brewis and Sinclair, 2000: 201; Gherardi, 1995: 135). Alvesson and Billing (1997: 98), likewise, recognize the difficulties of identity management for working women:

> Domesticity and sexuality as images of women still exist and facilitate some self-understandings and behaviours and make others, including those that facilitate careers, less viable. But in large sectors of contemporary society, they do not dominate any longer. The modern, professional, career-oriented woman is certainly a legitimate social identity – *although potentially a problematic one for women to adopt if it breaks too strongly with traditional ideas of femininities associated with sexual attractiveness and family orientation* (emphasis added). (See also Brewis et al., 1997; McDowell and Court, 1994)

Moreover, language which implies an acceptance of the double bind was used, as we have seen above, mainly by *women themselves* in Smithtown and Minerva. This 'buying in' to the discourse of scientific modernism and the discourse of gender difference by women leads us back to Foucault's claim that we subjugate ourselves within discourse, that power is not exercised over us so much as through us, such that we subject ourselves to the effects of discourse:

> He [sic] who is subjected to a field of visibility and knows it, assumes responsibility for the constraints of power; he makes them play spontaneously upon himself; he inscribes in himself the power relation in which he simultaneously plays both roles; he becomes the principle of his own subjection. (Foucault, 1977: 202–3)

Discursive regimes can only be sustained by human beings because they are cultural and historical constructs which we perpetuate through specific ways of thinking, being and doing. That is to say, 'power is only exercised over free subjects and only insofar as they are free' (Foucault, 1982: 221). Consequently, here we can make room for the argument that disadvantage suffered by women at work might not in its entirety be something that men do to women; it is also something that women do to themselves and to other women (Alvesson and Billing, 1997: 204–5). This is not a position that would be accepted by Kanter, Ferguson, Cain et al. – indeed, as Lloyd points out, what looks like a patriarchal conspiracy is understood in Foucauldian analysis to be

> the accidental coalescence of a multiplicity of sometimes mutually reinforcing and sometimes contradictory tactics, the outcome of the 'local cynicism' of power ... [understanding the workings of power involves] abandoning the idea that the intelligibility of patriarchy derives from the conscious decisions of men (as a unified group); and, as such ... the rejection of the notion of some kind of 'headquarters that presides over its rationality' ... (Lloyd, 1993: 444)

To return to the questions originally posed, then, these data have been analysed, not as representing a fully rounded portrait of organizational life at Smithtown and Minerva, but in such a way as to highlight other representations of organizations beyond those which position them as objective, rational and meritocratic environments, and to emphasize the ways in which powerful discourses work to include and exclude. Indeed, these data reveal fairly evocatively that the ways in which the discourses of scientific modernism and gender difference are reproduced at micro-level in accounts from the Smithtown and Minerva respondents mean that structures, images, ideas and behaviours which denote women's relative unsuitability for organizational life apparently continue to prevail in both organizations. That is, women's constitution as women to some extent seems to result in their derogation in these organizations, although it is women just as much as men who constitute women in these ways. This derogation also points us to the opportunity costs of this way of organizing, of the particular approach produced by the twin effects of the discourses of scientific modernism and of gender difference, for women *and* men.

Having engaged in the above analysis, it is important to restate the thesis that, when women experience differential and arguably less satisfactory treatment in organizations than do men, this is not, from a Foucauldian perspective, the result of a distorted or inaccurate understanding of what women can actually do. Instead it is a form of practice characteristic of the discourse of gender difference which constitutes women as irrational, emotional and subjective (and men as the opposite), and of the discourse of scientific modernism, which represents and therefore constitutes organizations as rational, impersonal and objective. Furthermore, this perspective also allows us to make better sense of the claim that working women's voices are not homogenous (Hutcheon, 1988; Jaggar, 1983; Martin, 1989; Moore, 1988), as we have seen in the data analysis. Just as men and women's experiences differ from each other by virtue of the gendering of human beings through the operations of prevailing discourses, so do the experiences of women differ from each other. Our constitution through a variety of different discourses, including those concerning class, sexuality, ethnicity, age, religion, health, criminality, sanity, physiology and so on, means that we understand ourselves as much more than just gendered. These aspects of our identity, the multiple ways in which discourses cross and criss-cross us, mean that our experience is also layered in particular ways. As we have seen in one of the Smithtown respondents' accounts, for example, it will probably make a difference to her organizational life if a woman understands herself and is understood by others to be a member of an ethnic minority as opposed to defining herself and being defined as a member of an ethnic majority.

Consequently, as Alvesson and Billing point out, the relationship between gender and organizing processes is highly variable and complex. Although it is perhaps true broadly speaking that women are disadvantaged relative to men in the modern organization, the claim cannot be made that this is true of all working women everywhere. For Alvesson and Billing, moreover, gender is not always the 'fundamental organizing principle' in work scenarios – other factors may be more significant in specific sites (1997: 191). A Foucauldian analysis of gender, therefore, allows us to acknowledge that discourses simultaneously produce us as working class, middle class or upper class; heterosexual, homosexual or bisexual; ethnically in the majority or the minority; young, middle-aged or elderly, and so on, *as well as* producing us as gendered. Gender here, as Bordo suggests, 'never exhibits itself in pure form, but in the context of lives that are shaped by a multiplicity of influences which cannot be neatly sorted out' (1990: 114). It intersects with class, sexuality, ethnicity, age etc., to produce different – at times, radically different – experiences of what it is to be a woman or man, such that it is difficult to speak of gender as some kind of unified or defining experience (McNay, 1992: 65) as theorists such as Kanter, Ferguson and Cain tend to do.

Thus, while a Foucauldian perspective *can* be used to identify a subjugated experience common to 'femaleness' in the organization, to identify the regularized effects of a pattern of male domination, it is also useful for attending to the ways in which other differences may loom large in our organizational behaviours, attitudes and experiences. We can, as a consequence, acknowledge gender, but *not* as a monolithic force which shapes docile human bodies in predictable and standardized ways, and consequently produces predictable and standardized patterns of disadvantage – the Foucauldian focus on discourse explains the experience of marginality (and of centrality) in what Rubin (cited in Fraser and Nicholson, 1990: 28) calls its 'endless variety'.

Moreover, using Foucault also facilitates a more micro-level, engaged resistance to gender iniquities in the modern organization than that envisaged by those who seek to gender organizational theory – such as Ferguson's argument that only non-bureaucratic forms of organization are legitimate. The understanding that we are products of an active engagement with the prevailing discourses of our time and place simultaneously permits us *as individual actors* to make sense of how we have become what we are, to assess its opportunity costs, and to make some progress towards changing or challenging it. Foucault argues that we feel the effects of power in our own lives, at the level of our individual experience, in the sense that the effects of discursive regimes are apparent in our beliefs and practices, the images and ideas that we are exposed to, and the structures and systems that we interact within. Consequently, we should question and resist the effects of discourse at the 'most basic levels' (Foucault, 1980: 99), because this is where its power impacts (also see Brewis, 1998: 64–7, 71–2; 2000: 74–5, 83). That is, we should engage in the critical ontology of self; examining who we think we are and experimenting with other ways to think, be and do, so as to produce different and *perhaps* (for us as individuals) preferable discursive effects. This suggests that we need to listen to all the potential 'voices' which seek to represent the world – but to hear them as evidence of the variety of perspectives available to us through which to view the world and our existence within it, to reveal that the 'truth', the language to which we subscribe as accurately representing the world, is nothing more than a particular perspective which has succeeded in marginalizing all other claims to know that world.[11] To do otherwise is to risk placing, for example, gender in a position where its inclusion becomes as imprisoning and oppressive as its omission. As Grey points out:

> it is conceivable that the gendering of organizational analysis could become a shibboleth which critical thinkers would wish to de-bunk. This is not somehow to claim that gender should *not* be a central concept and object of study for organizational analysis, but that, in constituting it as central, power is being exercised in ways which would repay further analysis, perhaps in the form of a genealogy of gender. (Grey, 1995: 50)

In sum, then, part of a Foucauldian theorizing of the organization would be to pay attention to women's accounts of organizational life. Such an approach, as established, undoubtedly disrupts the claims of malestream organizational orthodoxy. From a Foucauldian point of view, however, attention should not just be paid to *women's* voices. Moreover, attention to organizational voices should be sensitive to the ways in which *other* forms of difference appear to affect working life. The overall objective of this kind of analysis would be to theorize the ways in which various discursive regimes generate specific, complex and potentially problematic effects for individual working subjects.

Notes

1   However, it is important to remember here that Weber has arguably been widely

misinterpreted as an advocate of this form of organizational structure. His careful differentiation between *Zweckrationalität* (formal, instrumental or means rationality) and *Wertrationalität* (substantive, material or ends rationality) can be expressed in the sense that he sees bureaucracy as an effective *means* of organizing human action, but not necessarily one that achieves substantively rational *ends* (Weber, 1968). Indeed, Weber (1994: 231) argues that formal and substantive rationalities may well be contradictory tendencies – for example, the 'formalism' required of bureaucratic officials may be difficult to sustain if these individuals seek to work for the interests and welfare of those under their jurisdiction. Another instance of this is provided by Merton (1957: 202–3), who cites the tension between client demands (the substantively rational ends of an organization) and the requirement for the bureaucrat to at all times behave impersonally and according to the rules (the formally rational means of delivering that organization's service or product).

In fact, because of his conclusion that formal and substantive rationalities are to some extent incompatible, Weber talks of trying to oppose the machinery of bureaucracy, of trying to resist its mastery of human lives (also see Turner, 1992: 11–12; Brewis, 2000: 78–9).

2   As Billing (1993) states, Ferguson is careful to separate 'femininity' from 'femaleness'. The former, she argues, equates to passivity and subordinacy, whereas the latter embraces caring and connectedness. In her differentiation of different aspects of the feminine, Ferguson echoes earlier radical feminists such as Daly (1984).

3   As endnote 1 implies, this is an argument which to some extent resonates with Weber's own claims – he suggests that the problems which are 'opened up' by the tension between formal and substantive rationalities 'belong in the theory of "democracy" ' (1994: 231).

4   If Ferguson's work can be seen as an attack on Weber's ideal type, Kleinman's (1996) empirical study of healthcare organization Renewal could be seen as an implicit attack on Ferguson's modelling of the alternative organization, although Kleinman never mentions her predecessor by name. Kleinman's analysis demonstrates that alternative organizations like Renewal may fail to live up to their democratic, non-sexist ideals in practice.

5   In order to demonstrate the existence and power of the discourse of scientific modernism, and of the discourse of gender difference, some examples from everyday practice are required. In terms of the former, obvious instances include commonalities of organizational life such as the employment contract which sets out rights and responsibilities on each side; guidelines specifying the steps to be followed when generating particular reports, drawing up job descriptions and person specifications, conducting appraisals, calculating performance related pay, and running recruitment initiatives; the existence of dress codes and other restrictions on individual behaviour at work such as a ban on decorating one's workspace; definitions of disciplinary offences and the ways in which such breaches are to be systematically addressed, and so on. Such taken-for-granted practices speak of the emphasis that is placed on a particular organizational orientation – standard, impersonal, unemotional, structured and logical. In terms of the latter, the discursive emphasis on gender difference is nowhere so obvious as in the initial attempt to specify sex at (and indeed sometimes before) birth. That is to say, *even in the face of physiological ambiguity*, medical personnel will label a baby as either

male or female, and surgery or the use of hormones may be recommended to resolve any enduring 'problems'. As O'Donovan (1985: 62) comments, 'These case histories not only show how error can occur in sex assignment, but also how the social construction of gender and the consequent development of gender identity differentiates human beings who are not necessarily biologically differentiated'.

Nonetheless, as Foucault also argues, discourses are not solid and monolithic. That is to say, the discourse of scientific modernism does not absolutely and without exception produce the ways in which we think of and actually go about organizing. Examples include individuals working for their own personal gain in ways that are actually detrimental to the organization as a whole, such as the alleged defrauding of Foyles, one of the oldest bookshops in London, of millions of pounds over nearly two decades, as widely reported in May 2000. Neither does the discourse of gender difference ensure that all individuals are 'successfully' differentiated as male or female. Gender ambiguity as a deliberate identity choice is more and more widely reported at the current time (see, for example, Smyth, 1995). This is because there are always a number of discourses in operation at any one time, such that the effects of one may counter the effects of another and, in relation to this, there is the ever-present possibility of resistance.

6   Further clarification of what Foucault means by transgression of limits is needed at this juncture. For Foucault, power is productive in a very specific sense – it literally produces us as individual subjects, makes us able to think, speak, act and intervene in the world around us. 'Productive' here is intended in its narrowest possible sense of *producing something* – it does not have the more positive connotations of the term in its common usage. However, the productive nature of power as Foucault sees it also entails the inevitable *and necessary* placing of limits so that the 'I' becomes possible – and there is therefore a gulf of difference between his argument that the 'I' is historically and culturally situated and suggesting that it ought to be renounced altogether. To posit the former is to acknowledge the fluidity of any one subject position, the absence of any kind of authentic or enduring subjectivity, which permits existing subjects to come to act in ways which embody a *reflexive* relationship with self, to begin to fashion themselves, to choose the ways in which they want to be. In other words, to recognize the situatedness of the self is to allow subjects the possibility of *selecting their own limits* such that the 'I' remains available, if always on an until-further-notice basis. To renounce the subject, on the other hand, as writers such as Baudrillard (1983, 1984, 1993) seem to do, is to refuse the possibility that subjectivity can be anything other than constraining and therefore to deny human beings the capacity to act proactively, to make choices, to move forward and to make changes. For Foucault, this renunciation would render us passive, mere receptacles of experience, able only to live in the intensity of the moment. As McNay (1992: 135) puts it,

> For Foucault, then, the exploration of the self always takes place in the space of coherent identity ... [otherwise] one has no way of explaining how the limits of the actual can be systematically investigated in order to open up the realm of the potential ... [he] recognizes that the closure that occurs around the notion of the self is arbitrary or fictional, but at the same time, this closure is necessary to enable the individual to act in an effective fashion.

Moreover, whilst it is precisely the opportunity costs of the limits that we presently live within that Foucault bids us pay attention to, he is also adamant that there is no ideal self, no self without such costs, given that, as already established, every way of being/doing/thinking is precisely and simultaneously a way of not being/doing/thinking – and this of course equally applies to those selected as a result of the critical ontology of self. However, as he somewhat acerbically points out, 'to say that one can never be "outside" power does not mean that one is trapped and condemned to defeat no matter what' (Foucault, 1980: 141–2).

7   Following Foucault demands that we see gender in this way, because it allows us to explain historical and cultural variations in what it means to be a man or a woman. It is also true that his own work makes little space for gender, but this can be seen as an aporia in his work as opposed to a genuine and significant deficiency (McNay, 1992: 32–8). That is to say, as I have argued elsewhere (Brewis, 2001; Brewis and Linstead, 2000: 89–90), just as Foucault's own work allows us to see the effects of the modern discourse of, say, sexuality, it is also possible to give a Foucauldian account of the *en-gendering* of the human subject – of humans constituted not simply as sexual subjects but also as gendered subjects. See, for example, Butler (1990, 1993), Kerfoot and Knights (1993, 1996) and Brewis et al. (1997).

8   These data were originally gathered for my doctoral thesis (Brewis, 1996). They have also been reported in part in Brewis (2000).

9   Provided they have a child that was born on or after 15 December 1999, or adopted a child on or after this date, and have completed one year's continuous service with their employer, British parents of both sexes are now entitled to be absent from work on the basis of parental leave. The total leave available per child is 13 weeks (for each parent), and the right to take such leave expires either on the child's fifth birthday or (in the case of adoption) five years after the child was placed with the parents. Parents who have disabled children are excepted from this limit – they are permitted to take their leave up to the child's 18th birthday. It is also worth noting that the Employment Relations Act (1999) enshrines the right for parents to take 'reasonable' time off to care for dependants, as also required by the Parental Leave Directive, although neither type of leave has to be paid (*IDS Brief*, 1999).

   Furthermore, a legal challenge launched by the Trades Union Congress, which has now been referred to the European Court of Justice, claims that more than 2.7 million working parents who have children under five are being unlawfully excluded from the right to take parental leave, given the qualifying birth date that the Regulations impose. The TUC argues that parents of all children who were under five years old on the 15 December 1999 should be entitled to the leave. Interestingly, the Irish government, who also tried to deny parental leave to workers who were already parents, were advised by the European Commission that they were mistaken in their interpretation of the Directive, and have now amended their original stance. Indeed the High Court judges who referred the TUC's case suggested that they would probably prevail in the ECJ (Pook, 2000).

10   The respondent quoted here is a lesbian and so in any case would have had no sexual interest in her supervisor's son. However, none of the men present knew that this was the case.

11   Nonetheless, such practice does not in any way guarantee that the prevailing discourse will be overturned, at least in the sense that it no longer predominates as the one truth about any particular issue, given that in finding a position of intelligibility in a marginalized discourse one is acting as an individual subject, and not automatically or even necessarily encouraging others to abandon their ideas of

what is true and what is not. Negative reactions to those who have transgressed what are popularly assumed to be our limits – male transvestites, for example (Brewis et al., 1997) – are evidence of this. It is also apparent from Foucault's own work that for the individual subject to challenge prevailing discourse and explore his or her own limits requires not inconsiderable tenacity – his own experiments with LSD and sado-masochistic sex (see Simons, 1995) suggest the somewhat extreme means by which an unsettling of identity may be achieved. However, his idea of 'swarming' as applied to revolutionary movements such as Solidarity also implies that addressing oneself to the specific nuances of power as experienced in one's own situation *may* develop into a larger scale movement – that is, resistance can become codified in much the same way as can power (Foucault, 1986: 377).

References

Alvesson, M. and Billing, Y.D. (1997) *Understanding Gender and Organizations.* London: Sage.

Barrett, M. (1980) *Women's Oppression Today: Problems in Marxist Feminist Analysis.* London: Verso Editions/New Left Books.

Barrett, M. (1991) *The Politics of Truth: From Marx to Foucault.* Cambridge: Polity Press.

Baudrillard, J. (1983) 'The ecstasy of communication', in H. Foster (ed.), *Postmodern Culture.* London: Pluto Press.

Baudrillard, J. (1984) 'Game with vestiges', *On the Beach,* 5: 19–25.

Baudrillard, J. (1993) *Symbolic Exchange and Death.* London: Sage.

Bauman, Z. (1983) 'Industrialism, consumerism and power', *Theory, Culture and Society,* 1 (3): 32–43.

Benson, D.J. and Thomson, G.E. (1982) 'Sexual harassment on a university campus: the congruence of authority relations, sexual interest and gender stratification', *Social Problems,* 2 (9): 236–51.

Billing, Y.D. (1993) 'Gender and bureaucracies'. Conference paper presented to the 11th Standing Conference on Organizational Symbolism, EADA, Barcelona, Spain, 28 June–1 July.

Bordo, S. (1990) 'Feminism, postmodernism and gender-scepticism', in L.J. Nicholson (ed.), *Feminism/Postmodernism.* New York: Routledge. pp. 134–53.

Brewer, M.B. and Berk, R.A. (1982) 'Beyond nine to five: introduction', *Journal of Social Issues,* 38 (4): 1–4.

Brewis, J. (1996) *Sex, Work and Sex at Work: A Foucauldian Analysis.* Unpublished PhD thesis, University of Manchester Institute of Science and Technology.

Brewis, J. (1998) 'Who do you think you are? Feminism, work, ethics and Foucault', in M. Parker (ed.), *Ethics and Organizations.* London: Sage. pp. 53–75.

Brewis, J. (1999) 'How does it feel? Women managers, embodiment and changing public sector cultures', in S. Whitehead and R. Moodley (eds), *Transforming Managers: Gendering Change in the Public Sector.* London: Taylor and Francis. pp. 84–106.

Brewis, J. (2000) 'Sex, work and sex at work: using Foucault to understand organizational relations', in J. Barry, J. Chandler, H. Clark, R. Johnston and D. Needle (eds), *Organization and Management: A Critical Text.* London: International Thompson. pp. 70–96.

Brewis, J. (2001) 'Foucault, politics and organizations: (re)-constructing sexual harassment', forthcoming in *Gender, Work and Organization,* 8 (1).

Brewis, J. and Linstead, S. (2000) *Sex, Work and Sex Work: Eroticizing Organization.* London: Routledge.

Brewis, J. and Sinclair, J. (2000) 'Exploring embodiment: women, biology and work', in J. Hassard, R. Holliday and H. Willmott (eds), *Body and Organization.* London: Sage. pp. 192–214.

Brewis, J., Hampton, M.P. and Linstead, S. (1997) 'Unpacking Priscilla: subjectivity and identity in the organization of gendered appearance', *Human Relations,* 50 (10): 1275–304.

Butler, J. (1990) *Gender Trouble: Feminism and the Subversion of Identity.* New York: Routledge, Chapman and Hall.

Butler, J. (1993) *Bodies that Matter: On the Discursive Limits of 'Sex'.* London: Routledge.

Cain, M. (1993) 'Foucault, feminism and feeling: what Foucault can and cannot contribute to feminist epistemology', in C. Ramazanoğlu (ed.), *Up Against Foucault: Explorations of Some Tensions Between Foucault and Feminism.* London: Routledge. pp. 73–96.

Cixous, H (1988) 'Sorties', in D. Lodge (ed.), Modern Criticism and Theory. London: Longman. pp. 286–93.

Daly, M. (1984) *Gyn/Ecology: The Metaethics of Radical Feminism.* London: The Women's Press.

Eisenstein, Z.R. (1993) *The Radical Future of Liberal Feminism.* Boston: Northeastern University Press.

Ellis, S., Barak, A. and Pinto, A. (1991) 'Moderating effects of personal cognitions on experience and perceived sexual harassment of women at the workplace', *Journal of Applied Social Psychology,* 21 (6): 1320–37.

Ferguson, K. (1984) *The Feminist Case Against Bureaucracy.* Philadelphia: Temple University Press.

Foucault, M. (1967) *Madness and Civilization: A History of Insanity in the Age of Reason.* London: Tavistock Publications.

Foucault, M. (1973) *The Birth of the Clinic: An Archaeology of Medical Perception.* London: Tavistock Publications.

Foucault, M. (1977) *Discipline and Punish: The Birth of the Prison.* London: Allen Lane.

Foucault, M. (1979) *The History of Sexuality.* Vol. 1, *An Introduction,* trans. R. Hurley. London: Allen Lane.

Foucault, M. (1980) *Power/Knowledge: Selected Interviews and Other Writings 1972–1977,* ed. C. Gordon. Brighton, Sussex: Harvester Press.

Foucault, M. (1982) 'The subject and power', in H.L. Dreyfus and P. Rabinow (eds), *Michel Foucault: Beyond Structuralism and Hermeneutics.* Brighton, Sussex: Harvester. pp. 202–26.

Foucault, M. (1985) 'Truth, power and sexuality', in V. Beechey and J. Donald (eds), *Subjectivity and Social Relations.* Milton Keynes: Open University Press. pp. 89–96.

Foucault, M. (1986) *The Foucault Reader,* ed. P. Rabinow. Harmondsworth: Penguin.

Foucault, M. (1988) *Michel Foucault, Politics, Philosophy, Culture: Interviews and Other Writings 1977-1984,* ed. L.D. Kritzman. New York: Routledge.

Fraser, N. and Nicholson, L.J. (1990) 'Social criticism without philosophy: an encounter between feminism and postmodernism', in L.J. Nicholson (ed.), *Feminism/ Postmodernism*. New York: Routledge. pp. 20–35.

Gandal, K. (1986) 'Michel Foucault: intellectual work and politics', *Telos*, 67: 121–35.

Gherardi, S. (1995) *Gender, Symbolism and Organizational Culture*. London: Sage.

Grey, C. (1995) 'Review article: gender as a grid of intelligibility', *Gender, Work and Organization*, 2 (1): 46–50.

Harlow, J. (1999) 'Men give 15 minutes a day to children', *The Sunday Times*, 23 May: 5.

Hartmann, H. (1981) 'The unhappy marriage of Marxism and feminism: towards a more progressive union', in L. Sargent (ed.), *The Unhappy Marriage of Marxism and Feminism: A Debate on Class and Patriarchy*. London: Pluto. pp. 1–41.

Hearn, J. (1993) 'Emotive subjects: organizational men, organizational masculinities and the (de)construction of "emotions" ', in S. Fineman (ed.), *Emotion in Organizations*. London: Sage. pp. 142–66.

Hines, R. (1992) 'Accounting: filling the negative space', *Accounting, Organizations and Society*, 17 (3): 314–41.

Hoffman, F. (1986) 'Sexual harassment in academia: feminist theory and institutional practice', *Harvard Educational Review*, 56 (2): 105–21.

Hutcheon, L. (1988) *A Poetics of Postmodernism: History, Theory, Fiction*. London: Routledge.

IDS Brief (1999) 'Focus on maternity and parental leave: the new rules on maternity and parental leave', 650, December: 11–17.

Jaggar, A.M. (1983) *Feminist Politics and Human Nature*. Brighton, Sussex: Harvester Press.

Kanter, R.M. (1977) *Men and Women of the Corporation*. New York: Basic Books.

Kerfoot, D. and Knights, D. (1993) 'Management, masculinity and manipulation: from paternalism to corporate strategy in financial services', *Journal of Management Studies*, 30 (4): 659–77.

Kerfoot, D. and Knights, D. (1996) ' "The best is yet to come?": the quest for embodiment in managerial work', in D.L. Collinson and J. Hearn (eds), *Men as Managers, Managers as Men: Critical Perspectives on Men, Masculinities and Managements*. London: Sage. pp. 78–98.

Kivimäki, R. (1998) 'How work is structured by the family: the impacts of parenthood on the work community'. Conference paper presented to the Gender, Work and Organization Conference, UMIST, Manchester, UK, 9–10 January.

Kleinman, S. (1996) *Opposing Ambitions: Gender and Identity in an Alternative Organization*. Chicago and London: University of Chicago Press.

Knights, D. and Vurdubakis, T. (1994) 'Foucault, power, resistance and all that', in J.M. Jermier, D. Knights and W.R. Nord (eds), *Resistance and Power in Organizations*. London: Routledge. pp. 167–98.

Lloyd, M. (1993) 'The (f)utility of a feminist turn to Foucault', *Economy and Society*, 22 (4): 437–60.

McDowell, L. and Court, G. (1994) 'Performing work: bodily representations in merchant banks', *Environment and Planning D: Society and Space*, 12: 727–50.

McNay, L. (1992) *Foucault and Feminism: Power, Gender and the Self*. Cambridge: Polity Press.

Martin, E. (1989) *The Woman in the Body: A Cultural Analysis of Reproduction*. Milton Keynes: Open University Press.

Maypole, D.E. and Skaine, R. (1983) 'Sexual harassment in the workplace', *Social Work*, 28 (5): 385–90.

Merton, R.K. (1957) *Social Theory and Social Structure.* New York: Free Press.

Mills, A.J. and Tancred, P. (1992a) 'Introduction', in A.J. Mills and P. Tancred (eds), *Gendering Organizational Analysis.* Newbury Park, CA: Sage. pp. 1–8.

Mills, A.J. and Tancred, P. (1992b) 'Organizational analysis: a critique', in A.J. Mills and P. Tancred (eds), *Gendering Organizational Analysis.* Newbury Park, CA: Sage. pp. 9–13.

Mitchell, J. (1971) *Woman's Estate.* Harmondsworth: Penguin.

Moore, S. (1988) 'Getting a bit of the other: the pimps of postmodernism', in R. Chapman and J. Rutherford (eds), *Male Order: Unwrapping Masculinity.* London: Lawrence and Wishart. pp. 165–92.

O'Donovan, K. (1985) *Sexual Divisions in Law.* London: Weidenfeld and Nicholson.

Parkin, W. (1993) 'The public and the private: gender, sexuality and emotion', in S. Fineman (ed.), *Emotion in Organizations.* London: Sage. pp. 167–89.

Pook, S. (2000) 'Two-year delay as parent leave case goes to Euro court', *Electronic Telegraph*, 24 May, issue 1825. Online. Available at http://www.telegraph.co.uk (accessed 14 June 2000).

Reed, M. (1985) *Redirections in Organizational Analysis.* London: Tavistock.

Ross, C.S. and England, R.E. (1987) 'State governments' sexual harassment policy initiatives', *Public Administration Review*, 47 (43): 259–62.

Rouse, J. (1994) 'Power/knowledge', in G. Gutting (ed.), *The Cambridge Companion to Foucault.* Cambridge: Cambridge University Press. pp. 92–114.

Sheppard, D.L. (1989) 'Organizations, power and sexuality: the image and self-image of women managers', in J. Hearn, D.L. Sheppard, P. Tancred-Sheriff and G. Burrell (eds), *The Sexuality of Organization.* London: Sage. pp. 139–57.

Sheridan, M. (1980) *Michel Foucault: The Will to Truth.* London: Tavistock.

Simons, J. (1995) *Foucault and the Political.* London: Routledge.

Smart, B. (1986) 'The politics of truth and the problem of hegemony', in D.C. Hoy (ed.), *Foucault: A Critical Reader.* Oxford: Blackwell. pp. 157–73.

Smyth, C. (1995) 'What makes a man?' *Attitude*, January: 32–6.

Taubman, S. (1986) 'Beyond the bravado: sex roles and the exploitative male', *Social Work*, 31 (1): 12–17.

Thompson, P. and McHugh, D. (1995) *Work Organisations: A Critical Introduction.* 2nd edn. Basingstoke: Macmillan Business.

Turner, B.S. (1992) *Max Weber: From History to Modernity.* London: Routledge.

Walton, P. (1998) 'Paid work and family life: changing the balance for men'. Conference paper presented to the Gender, Work and Organization Conference, UMIST, Manchester, UK, 9–10 January.

Weber, M. (1968) *Economy and Society: An Outline of Interpretive Sociology.* New York: Bedminster Press.

Weber, M. (1970) 'Bureaucracy', in H.H. Gerth and C. Wright-Mills (eds), *From Max Weber.* London: Routledge and Kegan Paul. pp. 197–244.

Weber, M. (1994) 'Bureaucracy', in H. Clark, J. Chandler and J. Barry (eds), *Organisation and Identities: Text and Readings in Organisational Behaviour.* London: Chapman and Hall. pp. 225–31.

PART 5

WRITING, THEORY AND BEYOND

13

The Language of Organization Theory

Robert Chia and Ian King

Language is the flower of the mouth.
In language the earth blossoms towards the bloom of the sky
Martin Heidegger (1971)
On the Way to Language

Where words break off
No thing may be

Stefan George
The Word
In M. Heidegger's (1971) *On the Way to Language*

Words convey ideas.
When ideas have been absorbed words cease...
Only those who can take the fish and forget the net are worthy to seek *Tao*
Kao Seng Chuan
Biographies of Eminent Monks
In C.-Y. Chang's (1963) *Creativity and Taoism*

Introduction

The academic study of organization is in transition. Some organizational writers
have recently begun to emphasize the importance of language in organizational

communication and sense-making (Czarniawska-Joerges, 1995; Deetz, 1992; Putnam et al., 1996; Watson, 1995; Weick, 1979, 1985), whilst others (see for instance, Gergen, 1992; Loseke, 1989; Mangham, 1986; Morgan, 1986; Sandelands and Drazin, 1989; Skölberg, 1992) have directed our attention to the effects of language on the process and product of organizational theorizing itself. This 'turn' to language in organization studies can be traced to a heightened awareness of the way linguistic expressions, rules, conventions and practices, shape or affect organizational practices, and more importantly for our consideration here, the formulation of organization theories and hence the plausibility or otherwise of their substantive claims. In other words, they reveal an increasing appreciation (albeit limited) that the *organization of language* and the *language of organization* themselves have significantly influenced the developmental direction of organization theory as an academic discipline.

Of the organizational writers we have mentioned above, however, only Sandelands and Drazin (1989), Gergen (1992) and Skölberg (1992) specifically deal with the linguistic form that theories of organization take, and allude to the necessary grammatical make-up of such theories of organization. By so doing, they redirect our attention away from the social study of 'organizations' and their inner 'workings' to the more general problem of *representation* in organizational theorizing. However, whilst Sandelands and Drazin continue to pursue the scientific ideals of rigor, clarity, consistency and parsimony in representing organizational reality, for Gergen and Skölberg, as it is for other social organization theorists such as Cooper (1992, 1993) and Kallinikos (1995), the act of representation is itself a technology of abstraction and organization. Symbolic representations, such as theories of organizational functioning, must not be understood as attempts to accurately mirror reality, but must instead be understood as 'standing for' the intractable and obdurate experiences of our organizational lifeworlds.

Representation is the quintessential organizing mode through which our social world is revealed and presented to us in its multifaceted manifestations. Language as a system of symbolic representation now becomes understood as an organizational template for ordering what would otherwise be an inchoate and undifferentiated mass of vague sensational experiences. What is generated, however, cannot be claimed to be an accurate picture-image of reality. As the mathematician and popular science writer John Casti (1995) points out:

> ... the nature of the relationship between what we see and our linguistic description of that observation – is exactly what Wittgenstein says we cannot express in language. And this conclusion holds regardless of the language used to compose the description, including the scientific languages of mathematics and computer programs ... it forms the basis for the unbridgeable gap between the real world and our models of that world. (Casti, 1995: 8)

Casti goes on to maintain that it is precisely the limits of language which serve as the fundamental reason for the constant emergence of *surprise* in our engagement with reality. What this brings us to is the realization that language is at once our most basic and arbitrary form of ordering and organization.

It is this organizational capacity of *language* to structure our thought-worlds and hence our social worlds through ongoing material acts of punctuating, ordering and classification, which provides an alternative theoretical focus for the 'turn' to language in organizational analysis. The study of organization now becomes the study of the organizational *method* through which language actively constructs social reality. The persistent refusal, amongst organizational theorists, to acknowledge the necessarily ontological character of language is what this contribution seeks to overturn. According to the position taken here, language must be understood as a representational *technology* that actively organizes, constructs and sustains social reality by systematically insinuating its operating logic into the very textual core of discursive expressions. These then come to form the instinctively shared calibration points for defining local reality. As the cultural linguist Benjamin Lee Whorf (1957) reminds us, all observers are not necessarily led by the same physical evidence to the same picture of the universe unless their linguistic backgrounds can be in some way calibrated and compared. Instead, 'We cut nature up, *organize* it into concepts, and ascribe significance as we do, largely because we are parties to an agreement to *organize* it in this way' (p. 213, emphasis added). Indeed, oftentimes we are very much at the mercy of that particular form of language which has become the common medium of expression for our own collectivity, so much so that the language habits of our community unconsciously predispose us to certain preferred choices of interpretation.

In this way, the structure of the socially organized world, that we find so immediately familiar and necessary, actively mirrors the dominant linguistic structures of our own particular community. Therefore, the act of languaging is the act of organizationally constructing and bringing forth a particular ordered and coherent version of the world to the necessary exclusion of other possible worlds. The multiplicity of languages to be found in diverse communities is thus instrumental in producing the correspondingly multiple organized worlds (Chia, 1998b; Goodman, 1984) within which we live. It is this broader understanding of the *language of organization*, and its effects on our comprehension of social reality, which will be developed in the pages that follow.

The linguistic 'turn' in organization studies

The recent turn to language in organizational studies has led to a spate of emergent concerns revolving around the issues of communication and sense-making *in* organizations and, more importantly for our concern here, to the broader metaphysical problems of the role of language in theory-building. In particular, Morgan (1986), Sandelands and Drazin (1989), Drazin and Sandelands (1992), Van Maanen (1989), Skölberg (1992) and Gergen (1992), have, amongst others, directed our attention to the problems of language in organizational analysis. For Sandelands and Drazin, '... the problems of organization theory are essentially problems in the use of words' (1989: 474) whilst Van Maanen points to the shameful truth that although we inadvertently traffic in communication by means of the written word, we have been blissfully inattentive to the rhetorical manner in which language works to stabilize meanings that we then uncritically mobilize in our attempts to persuade others to our point of view. Similarly, Gergen reminds us that '... our theories of organization are, first and foremost, forms of language. They are guided by existing rules of grammar, and constructed out of the pool of nouns and verbs, the metaphors, the narrative plots and the like found within the linguistic context' (1992: 207). These recent admonitions for our inattention to the role of language in organizational theorizing imply that we owe it to ourselves to effect a critical re-examination of how language organizes our understanding of organization and the theories thereby generated.

Perhaps a useful starting point for our discussion here is Sandelands and Drazin's (1989) important critique of our inattention to the role of language in organizational analysis. For them, the validity of theories of organization are substantially 'undermined by words that refer to unauthentic processes operating between uncompanionable objects. These words portray an unreal world where organizing appears to be explained, but is not' (p. 472). What is therefore needed, according to them, is the rigorous adherence to the proper use of words such that although these words need not directly refer to something observed, 'they must at least, refer to something. Behind them must stand a definite object or event of some kind. Where this minimum criterion is not met, words denote non-existent objects or events, which by virtue of not being observed, cannot easily be disputed. These are words for science to avoid' (Sandelands and Drazin, 1989: 458). For Sandelands and Drazin, therefore, the source of weakness in organizational theorizing does not lie in the essentially ephemeral nature of the social phenomenon being investigated, but in the lack of *rigor* and *discipline* on the part of researchers in formulating theories of organization. So, despite their reservations about the dominant tendency in organizational theorizing to formulate organizational activities and actions in achievement terms (see pp. 459–60), Sandelands and Drazin remain, on the whole, confident about the representational capabilities of language as a medium for accurately capturing the dynamic and complex character of organizational processes.

This interesting theoretical position, however, contrasts with Morgan's (1980, 1983a, 1983b, 1986) and Van Maanen's (1989) recent advocacy of the need for a more imaginative use of linguistic tropes in thinking about organization and in writing organizational research, as well as Skölberg's (1992) tightly argued response to Sandelands and Drazin's (1989) insistence on the need for a more judicious use of words in theory-building. For these organizational writers, there can be no simple, literal meaning assigned to words used in the theory-building process since meaning is inherently fluid, metaphorical and contextually circumscribed. Nor can we naively assume that the entire repository of human experiences can be systematically reduced to strict verbalized expressions. According to them, therefore, the proposal made by Sandelands and Drazin (1989) and their sympathizers is fundamentally unattainable. Such an alternative view explicitly acknowledges the limits of precise, literal language to convey the subtle nuances and immanent goings-on in organizational life. Yet, despite these important contributions, language remains, for the most part, thought of by organization theorists as a *medium* of communication and representation. It continues to be viewed as an obstacle to the provision of accurate accounts and thus constitutes an inextricable feature of the methodological 'problem' in organizational research. In this regard, organizational writers, in the main, remain, at core, committed to a representationalist view of the world.

Representationalism, as a dominant Western metaphysical attitude, takes reality, both material and social to comprise discrete, stable and self-identical things and events as well as causal mechanisms which are assumed to be simply located in space-time. Our language, correspondingly, is thought to comprise a complex, taxonomic repository of concepts, categories, terminologies, and symbols, each of which singly, or imaginatively combined with others, can be adequate to the multifarious task of accurately describing and representing organizational phenomena at their experienced level of complexity. Such a view underpins not just the dominant approaches to organizational theorizing but even some of the recent more appealing forms of organizational ethnography that have emerged as a response to the social constructionist critique of mainstream organization theory. However, an even more radical reconceptualizing of the study of organization is currently being pursued by a number of social theorists (see, for instance, Chia, 1998a, 1998b; Cooper, 1983, 1986, 1987, 1998; Gergen, 1992; Kallinikos, 1995; Law, 1994; Willmott, 1998) who see social and organization theory, not as a study of organizational functioning, but as a study of our *method* for dealing with the reality. Language is quintessentially our organizational *method* for constructing our relatively stabilized organizational world to the exclusion of other possible worlds. Willmott (1998), for instance, expresses much sympathy with this cause when he identifies and takes up a recurrent theme in the work of Robert Cooper (1983, 1986, 1987, 1989) and explores the question of social science, not as the producer of accurate accounts of social (organizational) reality, but as the study of our existential *method* for engaging with reality. Social science as Cooper reminds us 'is not the study of social action per se, but the study of *method*; i.e., method is our language for engaging reality ... the central problem of the social sciences (is) that their subject matter has the same form as that of those who study it' (Cooper, 1983: 218, emphasis original). Unlike those organizational writers previously mentioned who focus on acquiring greater sensitivity to organizational workings by attending to the ways in which talk, dialogue, stories, myths and conversation play a critical role in organizational sense-making, social theorists such as Cooper (1983, 1986, 1987, 1989), Kallinikos (1995) and Gergen (1992), in particular, see language itself as *the* quintessential method of organization.

This alternative social theoretical perspective on the *language of organization* leads us to recognize that it is the grammatical aspects of language that effectively shapes our discourse on organization through its ability to specify, differentiate and simply locate as well as legitimize objects of analyses. Human organizing takes place through language and comprises a complex, interlocking network of ontological acts of division, differentiation and reconstitution. The object of such organizational activities is, therefore, never simply to produce a utilitarian product or service. Instead, it is the 'preparation of objects by means of which the (observing) system can (then) distinguish itself from its primary subject and, therefore, be certain of itself' (Cooper, 1987: 408). In other words, linguistic organization works to construct legitimate objects of knowledge for a knowing subject. Through such ontological acts of organization, objects of knowledge acquire distinctive identities that allow them to be treated as existing independently of our perceptions. Once this has been achieved we are almost imperceptibly led more and more towards an object-oriented mode of theorizing. It, therefore, behoves us to undertake a more thorough analysis of how language, through its objectifying tendency, affects and organizes our material and social ways of life.

The organization of language

> By the meaningless sign linked to the meaningless sound we have built the shape and meaning of Western man. (M. McLuhan, *The Gutenberg Galaxy*, 1962: 50)

Language, writing and the organization of reality

Our knowledge of the world is inextricably shaped and conditioned by the language we use. Language actively organizes societal outlooks, priorities and aspirations. This is the point that McArthur (1986) makes when he identifies language in general and writing in particular with the basic impulse to order, classify and organize our lifeworlds. McArthur calls this the 'taxonomic urge' and maintains that it is this urge which has made modern civilization possible. Like McArthur, Goody (1987) observes that it is generally accepted amongst most anthropologists that 'man = language' (p. 261). By this he means that what defines humans is our capacity for language and that modern man, as we understand 'him' is very much a constructed 'effect' of the basic language instinct which acts as the primary civilizing force underpinning the emergence of modern societies. More specifically, it is 'writing', defined in its most basic sense as any act of material inscription or incision punctuating the otherwise undifferentiated flux and flow of our lifeworlds, which works to create an ordered, liveable world. ' ...it is writing that is linked with "civilization", with the culture of cities, with complex social formations' (Goody, 1987: 3). Writing, understood in this fundamental sense is, therefore, a technology of organization and representation which actively aided the rapid progress of modern civilizations. In so doing, it produces dramatic and wide-ranging consequences for the organization of society.

Ong (1986), for instance, maintains that language, and especially writing is a technology which structures thought in a fundamental way. According to him:

> Functionally literate persons, those who regularly assimilate discourse such as this, are not simply thinking and speaking human beings but chirographically thinking and speaking human beings (latterly conditioned also by print and by electronics). (Ong, 1986: 24)

The fact that we are not aware of the influence of language on our thought processes shows that we have in fact interiorized the technology of writing so deeply that we are often unable to recognize its presence and its pervasive influence on the process and product of our thinking. Ong notes that the invention of language in general and writing in particular was an intrusion (albeit an invaluable intrusion) into the early human lifeworld. However, writing or script is different from speech in that while the latter is inevitably learned by virtually all cultures, this is not necessarily the case for writing since only the 'tiniest fraction of languages have ever been written or ever will be' (Ong, 1986: 26). Nonetheless, the breakthrough into new worlds of knowledge was achieved when a coded system of visible marks was invented whereby:

> ... a writer could determine, in effect, without limit, the exact words and sequence of words that a reader would generate from a given text. ... a true writing system will reduce ambiguities to a negligible minimum and make those that occur readily clarifiable. (Ong, 1986: 34)

Once established, writing interacts extensively with all sorts of social structures and practices in a bewildering variety of ways. Ong cites Stock's (1983) analysis of the effects of literacy in Western Europe in the eleventh and twelfth centuries to show that:

> Sooner or later, and often very quickly, literacy affects marketing and manufacturing, agriculture and stock-raising activities, religious life and thought, family structures, social mobility, modes of transportation (a literate communication system laid the straight Roman roads and made the ancient Roman Empire, as Innis long ago pointed out), and so on ad infinitum. (Ong, 1986: 36)

Writing creates a number of generalizable effects the most crucial of which Ong identifies as 'separation'. Writing is 'diaeretic' in that it divides and distances in all sorts of ways. It separates the knower from the known. In particular, the alphabetic system does so most of all since it most thoroughly dissolves sounds into spatial equivalents. Moreover, whereas oral cultures make no distinction between interpretation and data, literate cultures separate these two aspects of knowledge. Writing also 'distances the word from sound, reducing oral-aural evanescence to the seeming quiescence of visual space' (Ong, 1986: 39). Through writing, experiences are spatially arrested and *de-temporalized*. Moreover, writing is abstractive and de-contextualizing. It distances the writer from the reader, both in time and space and removes the words from the context within which they are uttered. Once abstracted, they are reinserted into an entirely different set of circumstances and made to relate to other words, so much so that the immediate context of written words is, simply, other words. Meaning, therefore, emerges, not from the source of utterance, but from the web-like network of signifiers of which it now forms a part. However, because of this inherent loss, which is intuitively experienced, the attempt to recover it results in an artificially enforced verbal precision that is not otherwise experienced in primarily oral cultures. In the latter, context always includes much more than verbal output, so that less of the meaning conveyed by words rest in the words themselves. In literate cultures, on the other hand, written texts are made to bear more weight, to 'develop more and more precisely "defined" – that is "bordered" or contrastive meanings' (Ong, 1986: 40). Writing also leads to further and finer divisions and differentiations producing the plethora of taxonomies, hierarchies, bureaucracies, documentational practices and specializations which we find so familiar and necessary in the more literate societies of the West. Such administrative and organizational sophistry is relatively unknown in strictly oral cultures.

Another crucial separation that resulted from the advent of writing is that it irreversibly separated modern logic from rhetoric, and academic learning from wisdom. According to Ong the invention of logic is inextricably tied to the 'completely vocalic phonetic alphabet and the intensive analytic activity which such an alphabet demands of its inventors' (Ong, 1986: 41). However, because it makes possible the conveyance of highly organized and abstracted thought structures it becomes increasingly attractive to commit wise sayings to texts. By doing so, however, these sayings are 'denatured' and are unable to function the way they used to do in oral cultures. Finally, the most crucial and momentous of separation effected by writing is the separation of being from time. Being is de-temporalized and made to appear as fully available and immediately present to us in our encounters and reflections so much so that a false sense of comprehension and mastery of our circumstances is reinforced.

Ong's discussion of the effects of language and writing on thought and social structures and practices, reinforces the belief that the organization of language has had a pervasive influence on the organization of civilizations, cultures and societies and consequently on the knowledge bases and understandings they have generated. This has obvious consequences for our understanding of contemporary organized worlds and for the constructive role played by the 'hidden' meta-language of organization.

Meaning, logocentrism and the metaphysics of presence

Within the phonetically driven alphabetic system, the meaning of any term emerges not from any singular one-on-one relationship with an external referent but from the web-like network of signifiers of which it forms a part. This is the claim that the structural linguist Ferdinand de Saussure (see Saussure, 1974) made at the turn of this century and which has been endorsed by a number of structuralist and post-structuralist writers including especially the social anthropologist Claude Levi Strauss and the philosopher Jacques Derrida. For these writers, as for Saussure, far from providing a 'window' on reality, language brings with it a whole intricate network of significations which actively shape and reinforce a particular version of reality. Language is fundamentally a self-differentiating web-like network of meaning stabilizations that work differentially to generate and sustain the meaning of any singular term within itself. Contrary to the common representationalist view of language, structural linguists and their sympathisers maintain that there is no self-evident one-to-one link between the symbolic signifier and the referent signified. For instance, the word 'tree' in the alphabetic system bears little resemblance to the physical tree that it refers to yet because of extended conventionalized usage, the utterance of the word 'tree' almost immediately evokes the image of a tree. Thus, the word as spoken or written is said to be 'arbitrarily' but conventionally, linked to the concept it serves to evoke. Signs and symbols are defined, not by essential properties which link them to their referents, but by the differences which distinguish them from other signs. Therefore, they are not 'positive entities', but the negative effect of differences. The meaning of a sign is, therefore, never fully present in the term itself but is instead the outcome of a 'rebound' from other terms. Meaning lies somewhere else *between* terms rather than *in* them. In this sense terms never attain the fullness of meaning required for them to convey the exact sense they are intended.

Saussure's insistence that there are no positive terms in the linguistic system has been used by the French writer Jacques Derrida (1976) to launch a critique on what he (Derrida) calls *logocentrism*: the orientation of much of modern Western thought towards 'an order of meaning – thought, truth, reason, logic, the Word – conceived as existing in itself, as foundation' (Culler, 1983: 92). Logocentrism as *the* defining mode of Western thought rests on a *Metaphysics of Presence*, a relatively unexamined set of philosophical assumptions underpinning much of the natural and social sciences, in which it is implicitly believed that things and events are unproblematically given to us as fully present and self-identical in the immediacy of our experiences. These are deemed to be 'simple, intact, normal, pure, standard, (and) self-identical' (Derrida, 1977: 236). As Cooper emphasizes: 'logocentric presence is thus a form of covertly willed prior knowledge ... by claiming to be a kind of "perfect" foundation or origin' (Cooper, 1989: 490) for validating the status of conventional knowledge. It provides the necessary origination centre through which meanings and hence social reality can be stabilized and legitimized. This *Metaphysics of Presence* promotes a widely held belief that it is possible for an observing consciousness to achieve the fullness of the meaning of things through detached observation and reasoning and to unproblematically locate the originary sources of such meanings in space-time.

Such a 'logocentric' bias is inextricably linked to what Whitehead (1926/85: 61) called the mistaken assumption of 'simple location' whereby matter and hence causal mechanisms are assumed to be simply locatable at specific co-ordinate points in space-time. This conception of 'an *ideally isolated system*' (Whitehead, 1926/85: 58), in which the universe comes to be construed in atomistic terms, was what provided modern science with the badly needed foundational concept around which our current forms of knowledge could be built. This assumed *entitative* character of reality, in turn, provides the underlying rationale for the entire epistemology of *representationalism* to prevail since it serves as the foundational basis for centring our phenomenal experiences and for thereby 'anchoring' thought in rational analyses. For, if phenomenon can be simply located and identified, they immediately lend themselves to systematic classification and causal analysis. As Cooper (1998) puts it so succinctly, 'Simple location reconstitutes a world of finished subjects and objects from the flux and flow of unfinished, heteromorphic processes' (Cooper, 1998: 131).

Thus, academic descriptions and analyses of material and social processes presuppose this entitative conception of reality in which clear-cut, definite things are deemed to occupy clear-cut, definite places in space and time. Physical matter, social phenomena and events as well as causal mechanisms are all assumed to be simply locatable and hence identifiable at specific co-ordinate points in space-time. It is this fundamental ontological assumption which underpins logocentrism and which perpetuates the illusion that a pure self-authenticating form of knowledge is attainable through the ability to be fully present to objects of apprehension and to oneself in the act of knowing. Meaning, for the logocentric theorist, resides in the consciousness of the perceiver in the immediate act of apprehending an externality. It is not deemed to arise from the socio-cultural and historical contexts circumscribing the event of comprehension. As such, it ideally lends itself to static, taxonomic classification.

The language of modern organizing

> Books must be kept ... Chronological entries will be made daily, methodological entries – products, population tables, stock inventories, health records, moral conduct records, requests ... (J.-A. Miller, 'Jeremy Bentham's panoptic device', *October*, 41: 19)

Rationality, modernity and the organization of thought

One of the perennial key issues of any scientific inquiry is the problem of 'essences' – of how to adequately account for the nature and status of types of species, things, situations and other similar modes of differentiation within a general scheme of things. The classical Platonic view of such essences is that they constitute a fixed and unchanging realm of reality, which can be faithfully located, classified and represented through adequate systems of ordering. This 'taxonomic' orientation, first inspired by Aristotle and subsequently pursued by Linneaus and Darwin amongst others, has become the definitive feature of modern Western thought. Through this method of ordering, the world is presented to us as naturally differentiated and hence isolatable and locatable into pre-existing systems of classification. As greater and greater varieties of experiences are encountered, they are inserted into this 'master' taxonomic register for the purpose of future recall and conceptual synthesis. The creation of classificatory categories and taxonomies as systems of differentiations is, therefore, always also accompanied by such integrative attempts to relate the various elements together. From this preoccupation, organizational complexity is said to be high when the number of 'combinatorial' relationships rise (often exponentially) with an ever-increasing number of elements inserted in a system of classification since each new addition must now be in some way made to relate to the pre-existing ones. Thus a proliferation of possible combinations marks the path from the simple to the complex in this static ordering of things.

Taxonomic complexity thus is intrinsically related to the initial program of differentiation associated with the creation of stabilized self-identities, and the subsequent attempt to reassemble these previously differentiated elements back into a coherent conceptual system. Understood thus, the complexity of our modern organized world arose from what we now understand as the deliberate and even obsessive preoccupation with the systematic, rational ordering and classification of society in all its myriad forms; 'professionalization', 'disciplines', 'division of labour', 'administration', 'bureaucracy', etc. This widespread rationalization of virtually every aspect of modern life in (particularly) Western societies, has exercised the minds of a range of leading twentieth-century thinkers, including especially the social philosopher Max Weber.

For Weber, despite the rise and fall of modern institutions and the changing fortunes of their political ideologies and affiliations, the general drift of secular rationalization is indelibly marked in the sequence of socio-historical events which took place in Europe during and after the Enlightenment. The extent and direction of this process of systematic rationalization was, for Weber, measured by the degree to which the progressive 'disenchantment of the world' had been accomplished. Weber observed that the pervasiveness of this relentless purging of the world of 'magical' elements is best exemplified by the insistent application of the principles of instrumental rationality on even such an apparently subjective area of experience as that of music: 'The fixation of clang patterns, by a more concise notation and the establishment of the well-tempered scale; 'harmonious' tonal music and the standardization of the quartet of wood winds and string instruments as the core of the symphony orchestra' (Gerth and Mills, 1948: 51) were all seen by Weber as telling instances of the seemingly inexorable process of organization and rationalization occurring all around him and in every sphere of human activity. It was this observed all-pervasive influence of the language of rationality on everyday life which led Weber to devote his academic career to a better understanding of its effects on modern social life.

This widespread application of the axioms of rationality on virtually every aspect of (especially) nineteenth-century life in Western societies, which Weber observed during his own lifetime, were anticipated by the strict regimes of behavioural probity that were systematically imposed during the Victorian era. As Richard Schoenwald, in a fascinating unravelling of the great social reforms which took place in Victorian England, reveals the task of the nineteenth century was to teach men that they had to change their personal habits fundamentally in order to become more acceptable to the new rationalized norms of urban life. Thus:

> Learning that some smells are good, and that others are bad, re-enacts the great scene in man's developmental history when he began to walk erect. He could not maintain erect posture and still yield to the array of tempting aromas at ground level which drew his less highly developed animal forebears ... Stand up straight and act like a human being! You have to learn to live with other people, with lots of them in big cities, and you have to learn that they can't find your smells as beguiling as you do, or everyone will be down on all fours and riot and

rampage will run in the streets! Turn your nose away from the smell of lower parts, turn your eyes and your mind to higher things! (Schoenwald, 1973: 672)

To maintain itself, modern society must proclaim that things have their rightful and wrongful places whether within the biological organism or in the social field. The concept of the orderly body in an orderly society gradually became a fundamental but largely unconscious presupposition of an increasingly instrumentally organized world.

Nowhere is this ordering of the body more evident than in the process of excretory regulation that a child has to undergo in learning to grow up. In its first efforts towards learning to control bodily outputs – how pressing the need, how suitable the time and place – the child also gains basic conceptions of the disciplinary norms of work. Thus, even the rationalization of excretory behaviour was a crucial aspect of the systematic modernization of society. Society must arrange both for disciplined retention and scheduled letting-go in conformity with the axioms of orderliness. Hence, 'the water-closet and the sewer as bringers of order ... underscore and reinforce the restraints and controls necessary to keep an industrialized society producing and consuming' (Schoenwald, 1973: 683). Pragmatically, because of the scale of social changes required, the Victorian sanitary movement provided the most manipulable means for inculcating habits of orderliness on a mass basis.

In a similar analysis of the development of modernity, the French social philosopher Michel Foucault has charted the extent of this progressive rationalization of Western societies through a detailed examination of the 'discursive regimes' which were invented to enable the organization and control of the masses that converged on the cities, particularly during the period of the industrial revolution. Foucault (1979) noted that before the eighteenth century, the system of governance was based upon the model of the family and administrators adopted a paternalistic view in which the common welfare of the social collectivity was a paramount consideration. With the population increases and the concentration of the masses in the cities, the system of governance radically altered. Administrators struggled to manage a large amorphous mass whose sheer magnitude could only be understood in terms of statistical representation. Statistics, the 'science of the state' became, therefore, the dominant means for 'understanding' and thus managing the unruly masses. New terms such as 'population densities', 'death rate', 'birth rate', 'cycles of scarcity', provided the formal organizational language through which the masses could be brought under administrative control. Knowledge-at-a-glance was what administrators sought as a way of coping with the increasing problems that the masses created for urban management. It was this overriding concern with taming the urban masses which led Jeremy Bentham (1748–1832) to recommend his approach of 'methodization' as the organizing *meta-language* for the regulation and control of society.

'Methodization' entailed the spatial and temporal division of all categories of individuals; workers at their bench, pupils at school, prisoners in their cells, and so on. It enabled classification and counting, the rudiments of rational representation, to become a key practice in the administration of society. Thus: 'Books must be kept ... Chronological entries will be made daily, methodological entries – products, population tables, stock inventories, health records, moral conduct records, requests ...' (Miller, 1987: 19) were all to be entered for the purpose of proper social administration. By this process of 'methodization' (or rationalization), large numbers of people, distributed over a significant area, could be 'captured' in the small space of a book and made available 'at first glance' (Miller, 1987: 265). Like Schoenwald's (1973) earlier analysis of the effects of the Victorian era and Foucault's (1979) detailed study of the rise of discursive regimes for the control of society, Miller noted that these dramatic transformations in the administration of Western societies paved the way for the rise of modernity and the contemporary recognition that we live in an 'organizational society'.

It is this generic understanding of the language of organization as a generalized technology of simple location, representation and control, and its subsequent effects on our modern consciousness, which provides the alternative theoretical focus for organizational analysis. In a stimulating paper that explores this almost inexorable 'technologizing' of the world, Cooper (1998) similarly notes that a pervasive feature of the modern world is its ' "program" of *differentiation*' in which the world is first *broken up* into clear-cut, definite things occupying clear-cut, definite places in space and time and in so doing creating a freely available pool of infinitely usable resources which can be combined and recombined in an infinitude of ways. These differentiated elements can then be reconstituted as temporary 'assemblage' to meet immediate functional needs. For Cooper, this is the basic driving force behind the idea of *mass-production* and the automobile is one good example of such a reassembled object involving the creation of a whole complex of new relationship configurations. However, it is the paradigm of the alphabet which best exemplifies the possibilities and potentialities, as well as infinite complexities, created by this initial process of linear differentiation. Rescher (1996) observes that even if the number of constituents of a system were small, 'the ways in which they can be combined to yield products in space-time might yet be infinite' (p. 79). In the case of the alphabetic system, we are able to produce, from the initial twenty-six characters, impressive combinations of syllables, words, sentences, paragraphs, books, genres and so on. The seemingly inexhaustible libraries of books produced in the last few centuries are a testimony to the potency of the alphabetic system as a form of human expression. Indeed the whole sinew of Western thought is built up upon the ever-increasingly complex variations rendered possible by it.

The prestige, privilege and instrumentalized value given to taxonomically complex forms of knowledge is, thus, closely linked to its capacity to economically compress and reduce a vague, tacit and unwieldy form of understanding into a compacted frame of presentation in order to facilitate ease of comprehension, transferability and appropriate deployment. Strategies of simple locating and placing, are, as Cooper (1998: 131) reminds us, to *index* and to *placate* our need for fixing the flux and flow of our lifeworlds by ensuring that everything and everyone had their place and every place had a defined utilitarian function. They are 'ways of forcing the mute to speak, of disciplining the wildness of mutability' (Cooper, 1998: 131).

It is, in reality, another way of understanding how the still-dominant priorities and method of modern rationality continue to dictate our contemporary modes of thought including especially the analysis of organization. Indeed, it might be argued that the language of rationality has metamorphosed into a range of different forms, not least the scientific principle of *operationalism* which is still alive and thriving in organizational studies.

Operationalism, as an imperative in the knowledge-building process involves the deliberate and exhaustive translation of concepts and ideas into explicit measurable forms in order to render them more amenable to cognitive manipulation. Thus, as the physicist P.W. Bridgeman claimed in *The Logic of Modern Physics,* from the point of view of operationalism, any concept is nothing more than the set of operations which define it. Thus, the concept is synonymous with its corresponding set of operations. He writes:

> To adopt the operational point of view involves much more than a mere restriction of the sense in which we understand 'concept', but means a far-reaching change in all our habits of thought, in that we shall no longer permit ourselves to use as tools in our thinking concepts of which we cannot give an adequate account in terms of operations. (Bridgeman, 1928: 31)

Bridgeman's injunction implies that there cannot be any surplus or excess of meaning to any of the operationalized concepts. Any intimations of a field of knowing beyond that which is explicable are rendered illegitimate by the logic of scientific operationalism. In effect this rejection of an inarticulate or inarticulatable form of knowing which does not easily lend itself to economic expression means that science in general and organizational science in particular is authorized to deal with phenomena *only if they are expressible within the principles of operationalism.* Phenomena, or aspects of phenomena, which do not lend themselves to operationalization must be deemed to be non-existent or irrelevant. It is this widespread attitude which is clearly detectable in contemporary mainstream organizational theorizing.

The meta-language of organizational science

Organizational analysis as traditionally understood assumes 'organizations' to be the legitimate object of its focus. Such a view is traceable to the logocentrism associated with the Metaphysics of Presence previously discussed. It draws its inspiration from this widespread tendency to simply locate social phenomena and to reify them into object-like entities. Such a metaphysical orientation, buttresses the kind of instrumental rationality and operationalism underpinning contemporary organization studies and precipitates an in-built intolerance for phenomenal experiences which do not readily lend themselves to simple location and identification as well as economic expression. Thus, the scientific principles of literal precision, logical coherence, consistency and parsimony are upheld to be the exemplars for theory-building within organizational science.

It was this motivation to produce a respectably rigorous 'science' of organization which led Warriner et al. (1981) to invite organizational researchers to contribute to formulating 'a standardized list of *operationalized*, observable variables for describing organizations' (p. 173, our emphasis). Likewise, Pinder and Bourgeois (1982) and Bourgeois and Pinder (1983), in a spirited exchange with Morgan (1980, 1983a, 1983b) recommended the 'development of an analytical *taxonomy* of organizations' (Pinder and Bourgeois, 1982: 643). It, therefore, can be clearly seen that this 'taxonomic urge' is inextricably linked to the rise of instrumental rationality within the developed West. Like Bentham's advocacy of 'methodization', initiatives such as these form part of the almost inexorable urge to order and organize our fluid and fluxing phenomenal experiences into the static language of rational analysis.

It is this meta-language which continues to dictate the terms under which theories of organization are rendered acceptable or otherwise. Are they recognizable in terms of the *accept* conventions of the discipline? Can they be taxonomically located? Do they conform to the rigors of operationalism? Do they make a contribution which enhances the social status of the discipline? These are the questions which determine acceptance or otherwise of any contribution to scholarly journals. Even Sandelands and Drazin (1989), as we have seen, despite their criticism of contemporary approaches to organizational theorizing, remain insistent that the language used to describe organizational processes must be more rigorously deployed in order that a consensual body of knowledge about organizational functioning can be expediently attained. It thus transpires that it is the overriding obsession with *control* over the knowledge-production process which really motivates the desire to impose strict rules on the usage of organizational terminology. The goal of research, as it turns out for these organizational researchers, is not new insights or understanding into the human condition in late modernity, but predictability, recognizability and conformity of output.

This academic agenda is made even more transparent by Pfeffer's (1992) provocative argument when he called for the urgent establishment of a tight consensus regarding the fundamental questions organizational science ought to address and the set of methodological standards which needed to be consistently maintained (Pfeffer, 1992: 614) in order that better scientific progress could be made in the discipline. He maintains that for organizational science to compete with other social sciences such as economics for increasingly scarce resources, there are trade-offs which need to be made in the interest of securing the status of the discipline. Citing research which showed that the consensual level of a scientific field or academic department's paradigm development is directly related to a number of consequent effects such as departmental autonomy, job security, journal acceptance rates and review timeframes, Pfeffer urges us to work towards enforcing 'both theoretical and methodological conformity' by 'reserving the most desirable places only for those who conform to the disciplinary orthodoxy' (Pfeffer, 1992: 614). For Pfeffer, therefore, disciplinary identity and status are of the greatest importance since these are inextricably tied up with the pragmatics of individual careers and academic autonomy. The idealistic pursuit of knowledge, regardless of disciplinary conventions and boundaries can and must be sacrificed on the altar of pragmatism if needs be. Yet paradoxically, the results of academic outputs, thus compromised, are presented as idealistically inspired truth-claims precisely because they have been attained in adherence to the orthodox language and method of science.

What this brief discussion reveals is that it is the language and logic of simple location, instrumental rationality and scientific operationalism that controls the process of knowledge creation in our study of organization. This is again reinforced by what is allowed to pass through the key instruments of knowledge-legitimation, i.e. the academic journals. An examination of the stated aims and objectives of the more well-regarded journals in the field of study reveals how the language of organizational science is legitimized, perpetuated and reinforced. Strict conformity is sought from aspiring contributors. We are told that:

> If manuscripts contains no theory, their value is suspect. Ungrounded theory, however, is no more helpful than are atheoretical data … We are not receptive to a complete avoidance of grounding. (*Administrative Science Quarterly*, notice to contributors)

Clearly, there are a whole host of contentious issues one could raise with these instructions to contributors. For instance, it could be argued that no manuscript is totally devoid of some form of theory albeit implicit rather than explicit. It could also be argued that no theory (not even fiction) is entirely 'ungrounded' in some empirical observation. But what these counter-arguments *do* do, valid though they might be, is to distract us from the real reason behind introducing these instructional guides together with other rules and guidelines for style of presentation required. For, implicitly underlying this paraphernalia of instructions is the desire for control over the knowledge-creation process and hence for furthering the scientific status of the discipline. Organizational science, it turns out, is just a vehicle for legitimizing and controlling academic mindsets and orienting them towards utilitarian concerns so that predictability and conformity of views are assured and uncertainty eliminated. This is the *meta-language* which is learnt and oftentimes uncritically internalized by young unsuspecting organizational theorists.

Even the seemingly innocuous guides for presentation of manuscripts (four pages of instructions in the case of the *Academy of Management Review*) direct our attention to protocols of acknowledgement, footnotes, method of headings, method of referencing, appendixes and even instructions on the avoidance of sexist and other biased languages. It is not our purpose here to comment on questions of ethics or morality. Indeed, we are not even saying that this *disciplining* of the mind is necessarily bad at all. What we are concerned to show in this chapter is that these elaborate procedures and protocols constitute a realm of organization (or even better 'meta-organizing') not normally attended to in the analysis of organization. Yet, as we have tried to show, they have been developed as a legacy of the very processes of rationalization and modernization which Weber was trying to understand. It is this 'invisible' meta-language of organization which we have tried to draw attention to. To construe organization as a 'thing-like' entity with a circumscribed boundary and identity is already to overlook the meta-language of organization which deals with the ontologically prior processes of fixing, forming, framing and bounding rather than with the content or outcome of such processes. It is this meta-language of organization which operates to aggregatively carve out our all-too-familiar modern world from what would otherwise be an unliveable, fluxing and undifferentiated reality.

Conclusion

The generic language of organization is a language of forms, frames, listings, hierarchies of arrangement, sectioning, spacing and contrasts. These are universal factors common to all technologies of organization and representation. They are the organizational techniques which lie behind the human capacity to create a socially constructed reality. The basic impulse behind this meta-language of organization resides in our primordial need to fix and simply locate the otherwise inexorable flux and flow of our lifeworlds in order to placate our insatiable need for order, certainty, predictability and control. In contrast to the current emphasis on developing sensitivity to the ways in which linguistic expressions, rules, conventions and traditions shape social processes *in* organizations, this chapter has attempted to develop a wider appreciation of the more fundamental role of language as an instrument of organization. It is this ontological capacity of language to structure our thought-worlds, and hence our social worlds, which provides an alternative theoretical focus for an expanded realm of organizational analysis.

References

Bourgeois, V.W. and Pinder, C.C. (1983) 'Contrasting philosophical perspectives in administrative science', *Administrative Science Quarterly*, 28 (4): 608–13.

Bridgeman, P.W. (1928) *The Logic of Modern Physics*. New York: Macmillan.

Casti, J. (1995) *Complexification*. London: Abacus.

Chang, C.-Y. (1963) *Creativity and Taoism: A Study of Chinese Philosophy, Art and Poetry*. New York: Harper and Row.

Chia, R. (ed.) (1998a) *In the Realm of Organization: Essays for Robert Cooper*. London: Routledge.

Chia, R. (ed.) (1998b) *Organized Worlds: Explorations in Technology and Organization with Robert Cooper*. London: Routledge.

Cooper, R. (1983) 'The other: a model of human structuring', in G. Morgan (ed.), *Beyond Method: Strategies for Social Research*. London: Sage. pp. 202–18.

Cooper, R. (1986) 'Organisation/disorganisation', *Social Science Information*, 25 (2): 299–335.

Cooper, R. (1987) 'Information, communication and organization: a post-structural revision', *The Journal of Mind and Behavior*, 8 (3): 395–416.

Cooper, R. (1989) 'Modernism, postmodernism and organizational analysis 3: The contribution of Jacques Derrida', *Organization Studies*, 10 (4): 479–502.

Cooper, R. (1992) 'Formal organization as representation: remote control, displacement and abbreviation', in M. Reed and M. Hughes (eds), *Rethinking Organization: New Directions in Organization Theory and Analysis*. London: Sage. pp. 254–72.

Cooper, R. (1993) 'Technologies of representation', in P. Ahonen (ed.), *Tracing the Semiotic Boundaries of Politics*. Berlin: Mouton de Gruyter. pp. 279–312.

Cooper, R. (1998) 'Assemblage notes', in R. Chia (ed.), *Organized Worlds: Explorations in Technology and Organization with Robert Cooper*. London: Routledge. pp. 131–54.

Czarniawska-Joerges, B. (1995) 'Narration or science? Collapsing the division in organization studies', *Organization*, 2 (1): 11–33.

Culler, J. (1983) *On Deconstruction: Theory and Criticism After Structuralism*. London: Routledge and Kegan Paul.

Deetz, S. (1992) 'Disciplinary power in the modern corporation', in M. Alvesson and H. Willmott (eds), *Critical Management Studies*. Newbury Park, CA: Sage. pp. 21–45.

Derrida, J. (1976) *Of Grammatology*. Baltimore: Johns Hopkins University Press.

Derrida, J. (1977) 'Limited Inc.', in S. Weber and H. Susman (eds), *Glyph 2*. Baltimore: Johns Hopkins University Press.

Drazin, R. and Sandelands, L. (1992) 'Autogenesis: a perspective on the process of organizing', *Organization Science*, 3 (2): 230–49.

Foucault, M. (1979) *Discipline and Punish*. London: Penguin.

Gergen, K.J. (1992) 'Organization theory in the postmodern era', in M. Reed and M. Hughes (eds), *Rethinking Organization*. London: Sage.

Gerth, H.H. and Mills, C.W. (1948) *From Max Weber*. London: Routledge.

Goodman. N. (1984) *Of Mind and Other Matters*. Cambridge, MA: Harvard University Press.

Goody, J. (1987) *The Interface Between the Written and the Oral*. Cambridge: Cambridge University Press.

Heidegger, M. (1971) *On the Way to Language*. New York: Harper and Row.

Kallinikos, J. (1995) 'The archi-tecture of the invisible: technology is representation', *Organization*, 2 (1): 117–40.

Law, J. (1994) *Organizing Modernity*. London: Routledge.

Loseke, D.R. (1989) 'Creating clients: social problems work in a shelter for battered women', *Perspectives on Social Problems*, 1: 173–93.

McArthur, T. (1986) *Worlds of Reference*. Cambridge: Cambridge University Press.

McLuhan, M. (1962) *The Gutenberg Galaxy: The Making of Typographic Man*. London: Routledge and Kegan Paul.

Mangham, I. (1986) *Organizational Analysis and Development: A Social Construction of Organizational Behaviour*. Chichester: John Wiley.

Miller, J.-A. (1987) 'Jeremy Bentham's panoptic device', *October*, 41: 3–29.

Morgan, G. (1980) 'Paradigms, metaphors and puzzle solving in organization theory', *Administrative Science Quarterly*, 25 (4): 605–22.

Morgan, G. (1983a) 'More on metaphors: why we cannot control tropes in administrative science', *Administrative Science Quarterly*, 28 (4): 601–7.

Morgan, G. (1983b) *Beyond Method: Strategies for Social Research*. Newbury Park, CA: Sage.

Morgan, G. (1986) *Images of Organization*. Newbury Park, CA: Sage.

Ong, W.J. (1986) 'Writing is a technology that restructures thought', in G. Baumann (ed.), *The Written Word: Literacy in Transition*. Oxford: Clarendon Press.

Pfeffer, J. (1992) 'Barriers to the advance of organizational science: paradigm development as a dependent variable', *Academy of Management Review*, 18 (4): 599–620.

Pinder, C.C. and Bourgeois, V.W. (1982) 'Controlling trope in administrative science', *Administrative Science Quarterly*, 27 (4): 641–52.

Putnam, L., Phillips, N. and Chapman, P. (1996) 'Metaphors of communication and organization', in S. Clegg, C. Hardy and W. Nord (eds), *Handbook of Organization Studies*. London: Sage. pp. 375–408.

Rescher, N. (1996) *Process Metaphysics: An Introduction to Process Philosophy*. New York: State University of New York Press.

Sandelands, L. and Drazin, R. (1989) 'On the language of organization theory', *Organization Studies*, 10 (4): 457–78.

Saussure, F. de (1974) *Course in General Linguistics*. London: Fontana/Collins.

Schoenwald, R. (1973) 'Training urban man', in H. Dyos and M. Wolff (eds), *The Victorian City: Images and Realities*, Vol. 2. London: Routledge and Kegan Paul.

Skölberg, K. (1992) 'Through a glass, darkly. A critique of Sandelands and Drazin', *Organization Studies*, 13 (2): 245–59.

Stock, B. (1983) *The Implications of Literacy: Written Language and Models of Interpretation in the Eleventh and Twelfth Centuries*. Princeton, NJ: Princeton University Press.

Van Maanen, J. (1989) 'Some notes on the importance of writing in organization studies', in *Harvard Business School Research Colloquium*. Boston, MA: Harvard Business School.

Warriner, C.K., Hall, R.H. and McKelvey, B. (1981) 'The comparative description of organizations: a research note and invitation', *Organization Studies*, 2 (2): 173–80.

Watson, T. (1995), 'Rhetoric, discourse and argument in organization sense-making: a reflexive tale', *Organization Studies*, 16 (5): 805–21.

Weick, K.E. (1979) *The Social Psychology of Organizing*, 2nd edn. Reading, MA: Addison-Wesley.

Weick, K.E. (1985) 'Sources of order in underorganized systems: themes in recent organization theory', in Y. Lincoln (ed.), *Organization Theory and Inquiry: the Paradigm Revolution*. Beverley Hills: Sage. pp. 106–36.

Whitehead, A.N. (1926/85) *Science and the Modern World*. London: Free Association Books.

Whorf, B.J. (1957) 'Science and linguistics', in *Language, Thought, and Reality, Selected Readings of Benjamin Lee Whorf*. Boston, MIT: The Technological Press of MIT. pp. 207–20.

Willmott, H. (1998) 'Re-cognizing the other: reflections on a "new sensibility" in social and organization studies', in R. Chia (ed.), *In the Realm of Organization: Essays for Robert Cooper*. London: Routledge.

14

Meaning Beyond Language: Monstrous Openings

Stephen Linstead and Robert Westwood

Monsters cannot be announced.
One cannot say: 'here are our monsters',
without immediately turning the monsters into pets.

(Derrida, 1990: 80)

... the text produces a language of its own, in itself, which, while continuing to work through translation, emerges at a given moment as a monster, a monstrous mutation without tradition or normative precedent. (Derrida, 1984: 123)

A future that would not be monstrous would not be a future; it would already be a predictable, calculable, and programmable tomorrow. All experience open to the future is prepared or prepares itself to welcome the monstrous ... Texts and discourses that provoke at the outset reactions of rejection, that are denounced precisely as anomalies or monstrosities are often texts that, before being in turn appropriated, assimilated, acculturated, transform the nature of the field of reception, transform the nature of social and cultural experience, historical experience. All of history has shown that each time an event has been produced, for example in philosophy or in poetry, it took the form of the unacceptable, or even of the intolerable, of the incomprehensible, that is, of a certain monstrosity ... (Derrida, 1995: 386–7)

At the ~~end~~ of this book, ~~it~~ becomes necessary for us to say ~~something~~....

Well, we imagine you'll be relieved to know that we don't intend to continue in the style of the previous sentence. The sentence, with its use of Derrida's technique of placing words 'under erasure' is enough to make the point that the book, as an open reading, is never at an end and will be rewritten every time it is read. So it is not an 'end', but a (monstrous) beginning. Placing 'it' under erasure draws attention to the peculiarity of a linguistic convention that turns a state of being, indeed of becoming, into a thing-like object. We thus problematize the idea that the book is a thing and introduce the idea that it is a process – a being or a doing. We also want to put in question the sense of a stable meaning to that 'something' which is said. This book may be 'something', but what it is, is undecidable. Whoops – we did it again. The book doesn't stop at being, nor at the objective of what it seems to be doing, but is always changing, always becoming another reading, however nuanced and subtle the change may be. But if we go on like this it won't be a very easy ride for you, the reader, even if we are in the home straight, and by now you must be tiring a little if you've read all of it – unless you're one of those hermeneuticists who has to start at the back of the book to get a sense of where it's going before you begin. In either case, we don't want to risk irritating you with our stylistics, as we think we have other important points to make, and language doesn't make it easy for us to make them.

What we primarily want to address are the limits of language – specifically in articulating (about) organization, but also in a more general sense – and some means of moving beyond mere language in the exploration of meaning. So let us reflect for a moment on the difficulties of getting language to express its own limitations.

Musings on the limits of language

The appearance of theory and the silence of disorganization

We have argued that language is organization and organization is language. However, whilst we hold to that, it is incomplete, or rather it introduces an incompleteness and a limitation that we want to open up in this closing. The caveat might be that language is not only organization and that organization is not only language. Making the relationship necessary and sufficient forecloses on other possibilities. It also implies that there is only one type of language – and indeed one general category of phenomena that we can label organization. Before we consider some new ways to open up or extend the relationship, let us briefly consider some further points at which silences occur in the language of organization – as constituted in organization theory as writing.

Theories of organization, or indeed theories of anything, are preachings that proclaim to offer a true model of reality. They pretend to tell it like it is, to persuade and to convince that what is proffered is legitimate and true. But they do so by being blind to their own practice. Theory is an appearance not a representation. It is a manufactured construction that participates in its own language game. Theories are appearances constructed silently by a practice of language use and discourse that is not attended to, that is not revealed, and that is elided in its presentation. Oddly, theories, including theories of organization, are themselves 'organization' (Linstead and Grafton-Small, 1990). That is they have participated in those practices and processes by which an order is inscribed out of a disorder. They deploy language in highly structured ways: indeed, they are essentially structurings of language. They differentiate, integrate, engage in hierarchy, engender an inclusion-exclusion practice, construct a boundary. A theory of organization is then an organization of theory. Indeed, we might suggest that theory is the ultimate attempt at organizing, since it seeks to order, layout and make understandable phenomena that are somehow considered opaque, disordered and incomprehensible prior to the application of theory. It seeks to organize for us what is assumed to be an inchoate world. However, what speaks is the theory. What is visible is the theory. What the theory pretends to represent is lost, invisible, speechless. One cannot represent that to which the theory refers by terms or language outside of the theory. If one were to do so one would either reconstruct a different theory or speak in a different linguistic mode altogether. In either case the original phenomenon is lost from view.

In a similar vein, we cannot speak about that which precedes organization – the disorganized, since once we speak (or write) we have constructed (an) organization. In this sense organization is a trace of the disorganized. It is not a sign of the disorganized since that would mean that an order has been introduced. The signification 'disorganization' constitutes an organization in which disorganization is effaced.[1] What, if anything, can be discerned about disorganization in this trace? It can be nothing explicit (since again we run into formulations that organize). It is our view that we can 'sense' this disorganization, that we can have a kind of tacit apprehension of it. Perhaps this is why we speak – to insinuate organization so as to sublimate and repress this incipient chaos. Is this the motivation to organization?

Following this view, language can be seen as a controlling function, one which subjugates the flux and mutability of the world, which identifies abstract principles which allow us to classify and group phenomena and accordingly to do things with them, conceptually and materially. Leibniz, for example, viewed his calculus as a universal logical language (Eco, 1997: 269–92). Here the problem is in isolating and determining the proper principles, the true laws which should guide us, through language. But this idea of the perfectibility of language, or at least, the languages we have in use today, is perhaps the most ancient idea we have, running back to the creation myths found all over the world. Many civilizations have a myth that once there was a perfect language, perhaps a language of inner illumination rather than words (Eco, 1997) which perfectly expressed the essence of things, which were instantly understood in their fullness at the moment of expression. Philosophers and theologians have searched for indications of what such a perfect language might have been like, and have sought to move language towards such a model – but the number of attempts to do so, as Eco notes (1997: 1–2) has produced a proliferation of schemes rather than progress toward a common language. Yet the myth of perfect communication, perfect understanding between human beings, is a powerful one. On the one hand, we might see this as possible through polyglossia, the mastery by everyone of all available languages, of perfection through diversity, but this cuts across the notion of a universal standard of perfection, because if no language perfectly expresses its object, a combination of such languages, though having greater range, would have no greater ontological penetration, no better grasp of the essence of things. So the attempt to constrain movement within language, to identify and fix meaning, to exclude and discard waste, to deny the importance of the intuitive and implicit, to expunge the essential ambiguity of experience, continues a product of ontological insecurity.

Language used in this way sits in the shadow of logic, and appears to be a tool of logic, moving towards greater universality, rigour and clarity of expression. However, language is also a practical tool which enables us to act on the world at a distance, to get things done. Through speech, we can command, influence, control, persuade, entertain, seduce, move, instruct, warn, cajole – and all without the need for our presence in time or space. Language then is an extension of our physical bodies, allowing them to act remotely, a form of remote control, a prosthesis. From this perspective, rather than being an abstract construction in the ultimate service of universal principles, it is grounded in our bodily desires for action and creation. It is not so much grammatical as material, as Derrida constantly reminds us. Ironically, it is a product of our need to engage with the unsayable, and rather than surpassing the implicit, always rests alongside it and brings it silently into focus as an absent presence, and a present absence, through language's normal working processes. Those unspoken moods which language seeks to suppress, the very 'waste' which Nietzsche, Bataille and Baudrillard see language creating, are the source of language, its motivation, its desiring-force. Formal language, of which organization theory is our exemplar, does not, as it would appear, proceed *incrementally* by adding new concepts and formulations, incorporating them into its canonical lexicon; rather it proceeds *excrementally* by squeezing out ever more efficiently those elements that are resistant to easy incorporation, and that might threaten the canon itself. But because language, even in its theoretical form, is rooted in bodily experience and our need to extend ourselves, it remains, paradoxically, a prosthetic for action rather than a logic of action.

This excremental suppression of disorganization is one silence in the language of organization. As we shall discuss further below, emotion is silenced, the vernacular is ruled out, the body is forgotten. Indeed, in the absence of so many things which are signs of life, language seems to be not so much a prison-house as a tomb.

Language, death and desire

Language, as we have noted, is an intervention into the flow of experience which arrests it, seeks to fix it semantically, centres, marginalizes and organizes it, cuts into it and cuts part of it out, extracts from it and indeed interposes itself between living bodies. But it doesn't do this very well – the postmodern sceptic's suspicion of language recognizes that language betrays, undershoots, is overdetermined, misleads, and cannot do justice to its object, always leaving something important unsaid, some necessary unspoken remainder that is essential for understanding that which is articulated. In organization studies, which tends to be dominated by studies of language which are basically post-Wittgensteinian, where ontological assumptions are made they tend to be on the lines of 'the limits of my language are the limits of my world'. As these limits are accepted, the remainder is left as exactly that – what remains outside language.

This, as Wittgenstein was also aware, only holds true for ordinary language – 'normal' usage – and does not take account of other special uses of language (e.g. poetry) which seek to test language to its limits, or of bodily experience. Whilst speech is privileged in most accounts of organization (in phonocentrism) writing is the main focus as the operative ontology is one of the eye not the ear, or any of the other sense organs – smell or touch for example (which are actually an important part of the experience of organizational life). The body is largely excluded from language, and where it is acknowledged it is subordinated. This is an issue which Gendlin, discussed below, makes central to his philosophy – one of de-differentiating the senses and re-centring the holistic sense of the body and experience. Language takes its place as part of bodily experience, rather than the body being inserted into language. The body which is found in the language of organization theory is a lifeless body, a cadaver.

This should not be surprising to us, as we have seen that language is a way of arresting change – an illusory way of abstracting reality, of carving the living, breathing, reproducing world up into categories and boundaries and structures and decisions. Reality is in flux, a flow. Change and mutability – which are ontic conditions – are a central problem for most human philosophical systems – change which includes decay and death as well as growth (Dollimore, 1998). Change is ontic and inevitable, but language based approaches to organizational change tend to take the language game approach derived from Wittgenstein or one of its variants and suggest that if we change the Game (the language) we change the world (organization). But all we do, as Wittgenstein was aware, is intervene between and within language games here, the relation between language and 'form-of-life' being problematic and by no means isomorphic.

In this sense, language kills flow, restricts process – as Chia and King have noted, in English in particular we don't have much of a language for talking about these things and expressing change. Language kills change. Language deadens experience. Language is deathly. It requires the movement of the remainder, the negativity of the spaces between and beneath the words, to breathe life back into it, a move which runs counter to the emphasis on reason, clarity and rigour which characterizes approaches based on post-Enlightenment analytic philosophy, and which underpin the functionalism of mainstream organizational analysis.

But language is not entirely inert, as it is also a structure of desire. The meaning which language promises, and which is always deferred, is what motivates it. This search for meaning is rooted, Freud argues, in the desire for the other, the desire to know that which is not ourselves, to reintegrate and become whole. Hegel recognizes that the desire to know becomes the desire to control, and thus give the appearance of knowing, and Freud is of course following Hegel, and on a slightly different turn, Nietzsche, in recognizing language as the place where subjectivity is formed by reflection and return, in an asymmetrical but nevertheless reciprocal, or dialectical, relationship. Desire here is a lack of something that we seek to redress – language then is a lack of meaning that language promises to restore, which is what makes it a structure of desire. But this understanding of desire can be inverted – desire can also be seen as flow, exuberance, energy, lack of limits, a rhizomatic surge which naturally emerges and is not created by lack, but attaches itself to certain objects as it is territorialized and reterritorialized (as in Deleuze and Guattari, and Bataille). For Foucault, language, through discourse, creates desire; for Bataille and Deleuze, language merely channels desire.

But in either approach, and however paradoxically, language works as *the desire for the death of desire* – through fulfilment. Language *also desires its own death*, as the perfect language would be the absence of language and an instantaneous, intuited knowledge of the other. Absolute knowledge, as Hegel was aware, can only be absolute if it contains knowledge of its own death. But language does not actively seek its own annihilation, and has a tendency rather to proliferate. As much as it always fails, and always falls short of and betrays its object (and thus) betrays itself, so it sets up surrogates for fulfilment within language – things that language can appear to achieve to give the appearance of satisfying desire. Emotionally this is the easy and spurious satisfactions of kitsch; socially and teleologically, the progressive attainments of quantified objectives in work.

In setting up these surrogates for desire, language, and particularly organizational language, also then marginalizes those passions which cannot be contained within them, creating them as an abject category. But the abject by its very nature is that which is suppressed but cannot go away, and constantly resurfaces as a reminder of the extent to which we lack self-control, a reminder of our own mortality.

For Bataille, this returns us to the question of what it is to be human, but more specifically what we must do to be human, to differentiate ourselves from other forms of life. Humans are unique, for Bataille, because they actually forethink and desire their own death. They establish their sense of collectivity through communication, but not through the functional communication required for satisfying basic life needs, but from the *excessive* communication required to create the non-productive expenditure of poetry, art, humour, dancing, festivals, sport and the aleatory in general. Homogeneous society works through a restricted economy – an economy of work measures and rational objectives, which relegates this symbolic or general economy, this creative excess, to the margins of society. This productivity of the same, centring on work, rather than the heterogeneous celebration of the different and characteristically human, in dismissing 'poetry' to the margins (and replacing it with a much more anodyne 'poetics') is inherently dehumanizing. In other words, work is death in life, and by extension, the language of organizations which talks solely about work becomes a language in the service of death – a mausoleum.

When Bataille talks of the hatred of poetry, he is talking of, on the one hand, his antipathy to the comforting prettiness of all kinds of language which tidies away the disturbing from our view. On the other hand, he argues that the attention of the poet to language and precision is driven by a passionate frustration with it and a need to break its bounds – a need to kill language, to push beyond. Of course, as every creative artist knows, those who seek to extend their consciousness beyond the limits of expression risk madness and death. We cannot know what the sacrifice will be, what cost such excursions will extract, but Bataille infers that the cost of staying within our comfort zone is itself death, the living death of being dehumanized by language that will not risk itself. One response to this, in organization studies, and insofar as it can itself avoid becoming kitsch, a Derridean monster-turned-pet, might be the expletive organization theory which we discuss below.

Fighting the paralysis of language

The postmodern purview has recognized the restrictions of language, the pharmakon which enables communication yet at the same time restricts and distorts what is communicated. It could be argued that postmodernists have obsessed and harried the problem of language, not to elevate it as an essential analytic, but to full-frontally address the problems and difficulties constituted by language and our reliance upon it. This project has repeatedly thrown up a central paradox (or impasse if you prefer) – that it becomes impossible to reason, impossible to think logically, given what language is and does, but that language is the only tool we have to think, reason and express ourselves with. It is tempting to suggest that language is deeply flawed and inadequate, but that would be another attempt to get beyond language, to suggest that there is something outside of language that is flawless and perfectly adequate. Where would such perfection be located, and how would it find expression if there is no perfect language? The truth is that all we have is an endless circularity as language opens, not onto the world itself, but onto other significations, other streams and webs of linguistic relationships. It would seem that all we can know is language, which for the radical relativist or super-sceptic is as good as knowing nothing. Even the blanket refutation of the paradox – simply put if you claim that you know nothing because nothing is knowable, then you are in fact making a knowledge claim, since you cannot know that you know nothing without knowing something – really doesn't work, as it tries to take a strong and deterministic line to meaning where the original statement was more an example of weak thought. Not being certain that you know nothing still doesn't mean that you know anything specific. Neither does it mean that you can't act. And it certainly doesn't explain intuition.

Despite their differences in approach to its consequences, postmodern thinkers have not been paralysed by the problematics of language, indeed, for many that has been the very lifeblood of their productivity. Both Derrida and Foucault, for example, have made clear that their analytics do not provide a resolution and do not offer an escape from the 'prison house of language'. However, there are some who recognize the existence of the unsayable, the inexpressible, the unthinkable, the sublime, the movement of negativity and the efforts of art and literature to engage with and open onto it (Linstead, 2000). But is it possible to *go on from* such a position? Literally to *think with the unthinkable*? Once we open up language to reveal its own monsters, that which cannot be articulated, is it possible, not just to continue to speak (or write) in the light of such knowledge, but to use the anti-foundational as a foundation, to speak with the unspeakable? Can we make meaning beyond language, and can we make language work in non-linguistic ways?

Escape routes: experiments in going beyond language

Implicitness and the priority of experience

Now this, of course, cannot mean that we merely make the implicit explicit. There is *always* an implicit dimension to language, and our efforts to contain it merely make it edge away further. This is one of the problems with current initiatives in knowledge management which seek to 'capture' tacit knowledge, as though it is just waiting to be articulated and will give itself up to careful scrutiny and a touch of expressive ingenuity. Which isn't to say that seeking to manage knowledge more effectively in organizations doesn't have practical utility – we could no more manage without a concept of practical knowledge than we could without a concept of culture – but that the activity is misrepresented. To take the view, as many in the knowledge management field do, that if it can't be articulated it isn't knowledge, closes the door and walks away at the very point at which we believe we should be trying to push through. Of course, this view of knowledge derives directly from the still dominant assumptions in many areas of management studies that it is behaviours not meanings that count, and if it can't be measured it is not worth attention. A good deal of the field, frustrated by the obvious limitations of this view, now expends its energies in trying to measure that which can't be measured, creating and celebrating chimerae like emotional intelligence tests in the process. The concept of organizational culture was once a monster, and some of its wildness and subversive abundance is still celebrated by such bodies as SCOS (the Standing Conference on Organizational Symbolism) whose symbol is the dragon tearing down the organization chart. But in the mainstream of organization studies publishing, represented for example by the *Handbook of Organizational Culture and Climate* (Ashkanasy et al., 2000), the beast is thoroughly domesticated.

Just because the implicit is implicit doesn't mean that it isn't significant, or that it isn't ordered. One of the difficulties with postmodernism is that it still bears many of the hallmarks of structuralism, even as it rejects it, in that *people*, as linguistic subjects, can only experience *through* pre-existing structures. Those structures may, for thinkers like Deleuze and the process philosophy that draws variously upon Bergson, James, and subsequently Whitehead, flow and change. Whether they are seen as structures which are in a degree of process, or processes that occasionally assume structural forms, they are processes/structures which work through individuals, and the impact of individuals on those flows is often minimized and frequently ignored. Re-engaging with Bergson and his view of creativity has much to offer in reappropriating the postmodern subject and their role in change for organizational analysis without reverting to a humanistic re-centring of the self.

As Gendlin (1997: 34–5) argues, whilst it is a mistake to assume that social change must always move from the social or collective to the individual, individual development does not usually change social structure. But those rare conditions where 'social change moves *from* the articulation of experience *to* structural change' merit, Gendlin argues, something like a postmodern, yet experiential phenomenology. This may constitute a 'whole new branch of social science' which opens up when we begin to speak from and work with those implicit, situated, interactional aspects of experience that cause language to crack and creak under the strain rather than in terms with which we are already familiar, despite the occasional neologism. To indicate that which extends beyond the articulable, Gendlin uses the expression '......' [or occasionally (....)] as a gesture in the direction of the infinite, yet nevertheless a welcoming gesture. So where he considers it important to remember that a particular term significantly extends its sense beyond its obvious referent, Gendlin will remind us of it by adding '......'.

Gendlin makes two points in particular that we want to draw on here. The first is that the implicit has far more functionality than simply being the remainder of language (Lecercle, 1990). To summarize his discussion, we are already familiar with the working of the implicit in everyday speech and memory, but we overlook the obvious. Something implicit lets us *know* .... that we forgot something, and it also lets us know .... when we have remembered. It lets us know when a new step of thought is implied, and it functions to reject otherwise good proposals if they leave the .... hanging there, still implying something more precise, a reading between the lines. He also argues that something implicit *knows* our situation directly, and so what we want to say about something forms implicitly, and words *come*. In fact, something new can implicitly rearrange the language, so that quite new phrases form, and come, and as we improvise with them the implicit lets us know when 'the right' phrases have come. Similarly, if we feel we need to rephrase something that we said, we go on from the implicit sense of it, and a new word or neologism also makes sense implicitly before we learn to use it in other contexts. It also follows that taking a word or sentence in various ways is made possible by the implicit – differences in interpretation do not lie in the sentence itself but in 'how we think on from having taken the sentence in this way, rather than that way'. It is triggering the *thinking on* that is perhaps the most important creative function of the implicit. And as we do think on, the cumulative effect of a chain of thought is itself also implicit, which allows things not obviously connected, or even fragments, to form such chains; indeed *understanding itself is an implicit function* – or why else would we feel we have to say ' I *see* what you mean' (Gendlin, 1997: 21–2)?

Body/language

This makes emphatically clear how central the implicit is to the processes of sensemaking, both in ordinary understanding and in logical reasoning (Gendlin, 1962, 1965). Secondly, he emphasizes the importance of the body in the processes of knowing; indeed he wishes to displace the notion of perception as being prior to experience without re-centring the logos, or placing the body *before* language. Rather, he wants to locate body *with* language. Our bodies *know and feel our situations directly*, he argues (Gendlin, 1997: 26; 1992a, b, c, d) – whilst we say that 'we' know a situation and our bodies only react to what we know, this is not all they do. Bodies, for example, remember things that we have forgotten, and respond to evocation, reacting in ways that initially may puzzle us (Sperber, 1975). These situational bodies are not separate from their knowing – with five separate senses spread out before the body. Indeed, Gendlin (1992c) argues that we are embedded in and reacting to our situations in the same ways as plants, with undifferentiated senses, but our 'plant-bodies' are reflexive and *sense the ongoing interaction that they are*. Additionally, recognizing the extent to which bodies are self-organizing processes, it can be said that they *imply* their next bit of life process. That is to say, a body 'projects, *entwirft*, structures, organizes, enacts, expects, is ready to go into, implies ... its own next step' (Gendlin, 1997: 27). Following from this, speaking is a special case of bodily interaction, a response to something that we *want* to say (even though we may not know exactly what, or exactly how to say it). Animal bodies elaborate the nutritional and reproductive imperatives of plant bodies, and human bodies interpose more bodily and symbolic consummations than simple food searches for example, which speech helps to expedite. Yet the more these speech formations elaborate, they still do not leave our bodies behind, indeed:

> ... sophisticated linguistic and philosophical details can make *our bodies* uncomfortable. From such a discomfort the body can project (imply...) finely shaped new steps to deal with such a situation [this is similar to the idea that learning begins in bodily discomfort occasioned by cognitive dissonance arising from new ideas and experience – LW]. Such a .... Can exceed and rearrange the common phrases until we can speak from it. The body is not just an inferred precondition ... Rather our bodies shape the next thing we say, and perform many other implicit functions essential to language. With linguistic and cultural elaborations our bodies can imply *what we want to say*, which can be typical or something very new. It can surprise us. *Our bodies imply the next words and actions to carry our situations forward.* (Gendlin, 1997: 28)

So we see a carrying forward of the situation of this book as being into the implicit, trying to think and write with the implicit, and into a full recognition of the body's responses as part of the use of language. This has to lead to a recognition then of writing, the writing that Derrida sees as organization, as being the spaces as well as the inscriptions, the spaces being active and creative sites rather than gaps and lacks, and of being an organic, situated, embedded .... *bodily* activity. The body then does not *displace* linguistic analysis in organization theory – language is not in this sense dead – rather it intervenes to keep it alive, the body being the living element of language, which language in its more necrotic forms (positivist social science, analytic philosophy ....) sometimes forgets and becomes its own mausoleum. There is obviously a challenge here for the ways in which we try to write organization theory, as well as how organizations themselves may be written. In terms of the former, we have both made our respective attempts to engage with the fragmentary nature of experience, to reflect this situatedness in doing theory.

The stylistics

Stephen Linstead (1998) produced a piece which incorporated poetry, fiction, fact, theory and fragmentary logic and which was described as

> an extended example of the blending of fact and fiction .... a meditation on academic discourse, autobiography, writing, friendship and personal place ... a rich pastiche of themes and arguments, descriptions of persons and objects, exotic skylines and cultural icons. The nonlinear form and disjunctive relations are written with a nostalgic tone that give his story a decidedly postmodern feel [as it] deals with some of the problems of postmodern expression. (Banks and Banks, 1998: 22)

In one sense the piece was a conscious attempt to mix genres, yet the circumstances of its production were much more accidental. The first piece to be written dated back to the 1980s, a reflection on language initiated by an encounter with a hot-dog seller after a management strategy conference. Other pieces were written at different times and in different styles; some individual pieces were an amalgam of several different experiences, others were more literal and ethnographic. Prose poetry and a poem fragmented between sections of the argument were the other elements of the piece. None of this had been envisaged when any of the pieces were written, and indeed the piece only happened when he was asked if he had any creative pieces he could contribute to the book. Looking at the short fragments in notebooks and bits of paper in old carrier-bags, the force of the implicit seemed to emerge – a chain of thought and feeling, operating by a sort of fragmentary logic working on both mind and body seemed discernible, if not articulable. Somehow, the pieces seemed to be *organizing themselves* without formality. The challenge, and the risk, was to put these things together and let them be, rather than to fall prey to the temptation to tidy them up, to link them together with a logical thread and emergent themes, and over-organize them. In terms of organization theory and even ethnographic writing, it deployed a violently transgressive aesthetic, yet without the text having other violent qualities. Though much of the writing was emotionally charged, it nevertheless played with its own ideas, and so at least paid lip-service to academic ideas of 'originality'; it remained textual in terms of its primary impact. Robert Westwood (1999), however, though not working emotionally with language, produced a piece which challenged conventional assumptions about academic writing by being composed of short clips of others' work laid out to have dramatic visual impact through which to convey its arguments. Westwood (1999) showed a similar sensitivity to the fractal, in a 'paper' that sought directly to express the fragmentary and undecidable nature of organization/language by deploying the notion of samples. The whole piece is comprised of samples, that is selected pieces of already existing 'sayings', bits of text, that apparently had some bearing on the issue of organization–

language relationships and power relations inherent in that. These fragments were 'organized' into a single piece the coherence or otherwise of which was intentionally drawn attention to through and in this practice so as to magnify and make visible the processes of organization in writing. The fragmentation was amplified by the use of non-standard textual presentational forms – the use of boxes, inserts, wrap-arounds, unusual spacings and juxtapositions, and so on. The purpose and the effect was to play with the possibilities of organization and disorganization within a textual space. The question posed (or one of the questions posed) was at what point does the violation of standard textual forms of organization start to come undone and slip into incoherence and disorganization? The self conscious artifice of constructing and organizing the text in such a deliberate and visually obvious manner was intended to draw attention to that very process by which organization is constituted in writing and to point to where the limits begin to appear. It was happily following Cooper in a deliberate encounter of the boundary of organization–disorganization. In short, it was an attempt to write not about organization but to actually write organization.

Westwood's (1999) piece was also a parody and critique of the conventions of academic writing. It did this most obviously through its violation of the sacred standards of originality, authorship, acknowledgement and citation. There was nothing original in the text – except in the organization of the fragments. The use of fragments of Westwood's own earlier work was not an attempt to preserve notions of originality, but only to further parody the conventions of referentiality. Deliberately failing to honour the principles and standards of academic writing and practice was not merely to be playful and bloody-minded (although it was that too); more serious points about authorship, originality and textuality were being made. However, it did also seek to raise the issue of style – in writing. We take the view that style is not an add-on, is not a mere matter of aesthetics, or convention. Style cannot be separated from form, content and function in this manner. The stylistics of organization studies writing are distinctive, uniform, restricted and restrictive. Such a form of writing is more than just a convention of style, it imposes significant limitations on the meanings that are invested in and retrieved from the text. There is a straitjacket which is not only aesthetically stultifying, but which limits and demeans meaning potential. It is a form of writing that is historically, politically, geographically and institutionally localized and particularizsed. Hence, Linstead (2000) and others recourse to other stylistics – in forms and genres such as poetry and literature. This is not only an attempt to say things in another way – although that has value – but more radically and importantly to actually say things which cannot be expressed in the conventional form of academic language.

Expletive discourse

One obvious characteristic of the language of academic theory is its niceness. That is, it is a refined, genteel, non-caustic, clean, moral, non-offensive language. Which in a way is to suggest that it is the argot of a particular section of society – the language of bourgeois society. It is also usually the language of white, middle class, male society – but that is a whole set of other issues which we don't choose to address here. What is silenced in this convention is the course, the colloquial, the profane, the taboo, the rustic, the confrontational, the vitriolic and other possibilities of language. This, again, is not just a matter of language codes – although it might be instructive to analyse the academic form as a restricted code – but of meaning potentialities. Strict adherence to this one form, this one rather restricted code, erases and silences other ways of expression and thus other modes of meaning and understanding. As just one aspect of opening up these possibilities without having recourse to the perhaps equally bourgeois options of poetry and literature – which often prettify language to the extent that Bataille argued for the hatred of poetry – is to deploy what we want to call an expletive discourse. Of course that discourse would not call itself that – more likely we would have to call it a 'fucking different way of speaking'. What would happen to a discussion of organization theory if we dropped the nice language of academic convention and spoke in a course vernacular, in an expletive mode? One aspect of that would be that organization theory could be written in a language closer to those who actually constitute organizations through their talk and conversations. But we are not talking about an ethnographic practice here in which organization members account for and theorize their own organizations, we are talking about a style of writing, and therefore a style of reading and a mode of organization, born out of a coarse lingua franca. One thing that would happen is that we wouldn't have to piss around being polite to other academics whose work we thought was poxy and whom we thought, as people, were tossers.

Indeed, we might suggest (now there's a fucking prissy form of address for you) that vernacular poetry – such as the work of reggae poets or rappers – is already fulfilling a similar function in literature and is already making comments about organization if we care to listen. Bataille, as we noted earlier considers that the 'hatred of poetry' has two dimensions – on the one hand his hatred of the prettifying aesthetic of much poetry which turned away from the fear and horror which was equally part of our experience of the world, and equally present to our apprehension of beauty in reality; on the other, poetry itself must hate the limitations which language places on it and must always strive to transgress these, to break them down, to glimpse whatever may lie beyond language (Linstead, 2000). Why then should we not take this poetic turn, to refuse to accept the limitations which theorizing places upon itself, to write with a hatred of theory, a hatred of organization?

A current chart-topping expletive rap hit is 'The Real Slim Shady' by white-rapper Eminem (Marshall Mathers) who rhetorically inquires 'Will the real Slim Shady please stand up?' The rapper's 'character' offers a role model for subversion whilst simultaneously attacking his imitators, but makes the point that his iconoclasm is not just his and that you never know where the 'real' Slim Shadies are to be found. They might just be out there now in Burger King, writing their own body poetry by 'spitting on your onion rings', finding their own ways to break out of the stifling anonymity of shithouse organization, fucking mindless work, and the sort of conformist pressure that would at best turn them into what Norman Mailer called 'medium assholes' (Mailer, 1970). There's organization theory throughout the song, if you care to find it – bollocks, it's right in your fucking face. This kind of discursive theorizing moves us away from the incremental language of theory we noted earlier, and leaves us wallowing in the excrement, uttering expletives, giving the mainstream arseholes the finger and loving it. Fucking A.

Text and emotion

We have even scared ourselves a little with that preceding paragraph, but it does draw attention to another silence in academic theory language: the silence of emotion. Emotion is absent both in the mode of expression and as an intended response in the reader. Other forms of writing do incorporate emotion into the writing–reading practice. They do so because it opens up different possibilities for experience, meaning and understanding. It is particularly fruitful for drawing the reader into a self-awareness of their interaction with the substance of what they read. Nietzsche was very clear that his philosophical writing required a conceptual analysis and comprehension, but also that it would and should evoke a range of emotional dispositions in the reader, and both he and Heidegger experimented with poetic expression (see Deleuze, 1986; Heidegger, 1971; Nietzsche, 1974). Emotion is equally silenced in organization theory writing, and we should be encouraged to open up this space with writing practices that are emotionally alive and that find ways to engender emotional responses in the reader. This is not a matter of writing about issues that are presumed to have emotional connotations (such as suicides in the organization for example), but to find a style and mode of writing that compels an emotional engagement as well as a cognitive one. We think that Gibson Burrell (1997) tried to do this when he wrote *Pandemonium*, to create a place where time and place, pleasure and pain, power and passion, story and theory can be engaged with on equal terms, and as we noted earlier, we have made and continue to make, our own attempts to reforge the genre.

Another attempt to engage with emotion in the actual writing of organization theory appears in Frost et al. (2000) in which the authors present selections from accounts of compassion shown in everyday working situations. They choose to conclude by using the technique of the 'found poem' drawn from the work of Annie Dillard, in which the words of a respondent are turned into a poetic form – words being added occasionally but never taken away. The idea is that there is poetry in everyday life, if we care to express it.

There is an irony here, however, in that the authors in their own writing style constantly keep emotion *out there* – it is others' compassion to which they bear witness. Yet at least one of the authors has suffered from a potentially terminal illness, and their experiences with this must have been an important motivator for this research. Whilst talking *about* emotion, complaining about a field full of 'deadened accounts of work feeling' (Frost et al., 2000: 28) which is 'emotionally anorexic' (Fineman, 1993: 9 cited in Frost et al., 2000: 28) and conveying others' stories of it, they do so in a style which is itself emotionless, in which there is no visible personal emotion, no passion. It is almost as though they could only talk about their own emotional experiences through the experiences of others – indeed, this is perhaps an element in all research. Their self-styled 'insights' – 'that people often act compassionately in the face of pain without knowing what is appropriate or how compassion should be conveyed', and 'organizations create an emotional ecology where care and human connection are enabled or disabled' are hardly insights – indeed for the emotionally literate they would be considered commonplaces, Emotion 101 stuff. Do the authors ever go to the movies? Surely they must have seen *Saving Private Ryan* and realized, despite the sentimentality of the ending, that it wasn't just about war?

When it comes to writing about and with emotion, organization theorists have a lot to learn from other more emotionally mature disciplines. Just because organization theorists have never remarked upon an emotional phenomenon before, because of the constraints of 'scientific objectivity' and the emotional aridity of the genres in which they are most often constrained to write, and the field appears not to know much about it, is not sufficient to make any comment at all upon it insightful. It marks our entry as a field into an area in which we are novices, but is not a contribution in itself. Such a moment is often characterized by romanticism – a tendency to emphasize the brighter and more attractive aspects of the topic in focus at a general level; political naivety – a tendency to neglect the effects of power on experience; and an overly altruistic approach to a subjectivity which is often viewed as autonomous and dyadic, person-to-person, with culture operating primarily as context. Frost et al. (2000: 38–9) do draw attention to some aspects of the shortcomings in their account from these perspectives, but they fail to see that this is partly a product of the immaturity of emotional discourse in this field of human social inquiry, with its continuing pretences to scientificity, right down to the fact that they feel compelled to describe what they found as an *ecology*.

We should add as well that simply having a go at writing differently will not automatically produce outputs of value. Just because poetry may be found in everyday life does not mean that it amounts to good poetry, because poetry tends in the opposite direction to everyday language, and indeed may be said to start at exactly the point where everyday language becomes inadequate. 'Found' poetry, just because it appears to be naturally occurring, is no more authentic than those products created with more conscious and obvious artifice; and it is no less likely to exhibit the features of kitsch. As Benjamin notes, even the subconscious is filled with second-hand images and ideas; Fineman (2000: 6) observes that 'what we think is really "me" is always borrowed from elsewhere' and cites Wetherell (1996: 134) on love ... 'the words instead are second-hand, already in circulation, already in there, waiting for the moment of appropriation'. It is this sense which prompted Bataille's 'hatred' of poetry – or at least the language which turned its back on the need to struggle with its own limits.

It isn't easy to write well, or originally, whether in poetry or fiction, and we should not expect our data to do the job for us. We should not be deterred by this, but we must remain mindful that when we seek to introduce an emotional dimension into our writing on organization, we are entering upon an enterprise which is exceptionally difficult, which needs to be nurtured, and from which we perhaps should not expect too much, too soon. It is never sufficient simply to embark on an enterprise in a creative spirit. We must re-learn our craft.

Coda

> Our language, even if we are pleased to speak it, has already substituted too many articulations for too many accents, it has lost life and warmth, it is already eaten by writing. Its accentuated features have been gnawed through by the consonants. (Derrida, 1976: 226)

We have nothing left to work with then, other than a tired language. Language that is a *pharmakon*, that enables so much and yet which subverts, often violently, our purposes within its own constraints, that never says what we mean, and yet when it becomes writing disseminates into a plurality of meanings over which we have little or no control. Yet language also can take us to its own limits, can give us a ground from which to push on beyond it, and a place to which to return. A place to engage some of our monsters without taming them. A place where even our tired and overworked language might gain some renewed vigour.

So despite our awareness of its limitations and shortcomings, and the necessity to attempt to articulate what remains outside language, we continue to work with theoretical language in one corner of the problematic, building and dismantling our conceptual edifices, and try to push language this way and that in another part. There is a dispersed quality to our work as a result, but we don't feel constrained by the need to be consistent in any conventional sense, feeling that an aleatory process will reveal its own logic, its own continuity, in time, if there is any. This will be our way forward as we continue to try to think with the implicit, to recognize in our writing the integration of body and language amidst the fragmentary nature of thought and situation. What forms of organizing might this open onto? How will the practice of organizing change to respond to our changing linguistic practices? We think it's too early to tell, as we haven't yet gone far enough with language, have not explored organization in theory and practice with a sufficient range of linguistic strategies, mutating genres and word-plays. But language and bodies are not disconnected, and language change can and does change the way we experience the world – if we can create a language of organization that is more subtle, more alive and less brutal than the forms we currently work within, perhaps we will be better able to deal with the violence of organizational experience. But the first challenge is to find a language that can let the body back in more fully to organization theory (Hassard et al., 2000). Well, that at least is where we think our bodies are telling us we're moving forward to, the subject perhaps for the next book – but it won't be normal science, that's for sure, even in an uncertain world.

Note

1   This is akin to some theological arguments which suggest that God cannot be apprehended through signs, but only through traces. Any absolute singularity cannot survive its origin since a secondary representation is not the original singularity, but something else. A repetition is a copy, or simulacrum and as such is only a trace of the original singularity and cannot be a sign of that singularity.

References

Ashkanasy, N., Wilderom, C. and Peterson, M. (eds) (2000) *The Handbook of Organizational Culture and Climate*. Thousand Oaks, CA: Sage.

Banks, S.P. and Banks, A. (1998) 'The struggle between fact and fiction', in A. Banks and S.P. Banks, *Fiction and Social Research: By Ice or Fire*. Walnut Creek, CA: AltaMira. pp. 11–29.

Burrell, G. (1997) *Pandemonium: Towards a Retro-Organization Theory*. London: Sage.

Deleuze, G. (1986) *Nietzsche and Philosophy*, trans. H. Tomlinson. London: Athlone Press.

Derrida, J. (1976) *Of Grammatology*, trans. G.C. Spivak. Baltimore, OH: Johns Hopkins Press.

Derrida, J. (1984) 'Deconstruction and the Other', in R. Kearney (ed.), *Dialogues with Contemporary Continental Thinkers*. Manchester: Manchester University Press.

Derrida, J. (1990) 'Some statements, etc.', in D. Carroll (ed.), *The States of Theory*. Stanford, CA: Stanford University Press.

Derrida, J. (1995) 'Passages – from traumatism to promise', in E. Weber (ed.), *Points-Interviews 1974-1994*. Stanford, CA: Stanford University Press.

Dollimore, J. (1998) *Death, Desire and Loss in Western Culture*. London: Allen Lane.

Eco, U. (1997) *The Search for a Perfect Language*. London: Fontana.

Fineman, S. (1993) *Emotion in Organizations*. London: Sage.

Fineman, S. (2000) 'Introduction: emotional arenas revisited', in S. Fineman (ed.), *Emotion in Organizations*. 2nd edn. London: Sage. pp. 1–24.

Frost, P., Dutton, J.E., Worline, M.C. and Wilson, A. (2000) 'Narratives of compassion in organizations', in S. Fineman (ed.), *Emotion in Organizations*. 2nd edn. London: Sage. pp. 25–45.

Gendlin, E. (1962) *Experience and the Creation of Meaning*. New York: Free Press.

Gendlin, E. (1965) 'What are the grounds of explication statements? A problem in linguistic analysis and phenomenology', *The Monist*, 49 (1) reprinted in H.A. Durfee (ed.) (1976) *Analytic Philosophy and Phenomenology*. The Hague: Martinus Nijhoff.

Gendlin, E. (1992a) 'Thinking beyond patterns: body, language and situations', in B. den Ouden and M. Moen (eds), *The Presence of Feeling in Thought*. New York: Peter Lang.

Gendlin, E. (1992b) 'The primacy of the body, not the primacy of perception', *Man and World*, 25, Nos. 3–4.

Gendlin, E. (1992c) 'Meaning prior to the separation of the five senses', in M. Stamenow (ed.), *Current Issues in Linguistic Theory: Current Advances in Semantic Theory*. Philadelphia, PA: Benjamin Publishing.

Gendlin, E. (1992d) 'The wider role of bodily sense in thought and language', in M. Sheets-Johnstone (ed.), *Giving the Body its Due*. Albany, NY: SUNY Press.

Gendlin, E. (1997) 'How philosophy cannot appeal to experience, and how it can', in D.M. Levin (ed.), *Language beyond Postmodernism: Saying and Thinking in Gendlin's Philosophy*. Chicago: Northwestern University Press. pp. 3–41.

Hassard, J.S., Holliday, R. and Willmott, H. (eds) (2000) *Body and Organization*. London: Sage.

Heidegger, M. (1971) *Poetry, Language, Thought*, trans. A. Hofstadter. New York: Harper Collins.

Lecercle, J. (1990) *The Violence of Language*. London: Routledge.

Linstead, S.A. (1998) 'The dishcloth of Minerva: absence, presence and metatheory in the everyday practice of research', in A. Banks and S.P. Banks, *Fiction and Social Research: By Ice or Fire*. Walnut Creek, CA: AltaMira. pp. 235–53.

Linstead, S.A. (2000) 'Ashes and madness: the play of negativity and the poetics of organization', in S.A. Linstead and H. Höpfl (eds), *The Aesthetics of Organization*. London: Sage. pp. 61–92.

Linstead, S.A. and Grafton Small, R. (1990) 'Theory as artefact: artefact as theory', in P. Gagliardi (ed.), *Symbols and Artefacts: Views of the Corporate Landscape*. Berlin and New York: Walter de Gruyter. pp. 387–419.

Mailer, N. (1970) *Why are we in Vietnam?* London: Panther.

Nietzsche, F. (1974) *The Gay Science: with a Prelude in Rhymes and an Appendix of Songs*. London: Vintage Books.

Sperber, D. (1975) *Rethinking Symbolism*. Cambridge: Cambridge University Press.

Westwood, R.I. (1999) 'A "sampled" account of organization: being a de-authored, reflexive parody of organization/writing', *Studies in Cultures, Organizations and Societies*, 5 (1): 195–233.

Wetherell, M. (1996) 'Romantic discourse and feminist analysis: interrogating investment, power and desire', in S. Wilkinson and C. Kitzinger (eds), *Feminism and Discourse: Psychological Perspectives*. London: Sage.

Name Index

Subject Index

Lightning Source UK Ltd.
Milton Keynes UK
UKOW04f1141200514

231987UK00001B/10/P